PROGRAM LOGIC

M000302377

Second Edition

MARJORIE M. LEESON

GLENCOE

Macmillan/McGraw-Hill

Lake Forest, Illinois
Columbus, Ohio
Mission Hills, California
Peoria, Illinois

Acquisition Editor   Michael J. Carrigg
Development Editor   Molly Gardiner
Cover and Text Designer   Paul Adams
Cover Photo   Charles Messina
Compositor/Illustrator   The Clarinda Company

Library of Congress Cataloging-in-Publication Data

Leeson, Marjorie.
  Programming logic.

  Includes index.
  1. Electronic digital computers—Programming.
I. Title.
QA76.6.L39   1988   005.1   87-32399
ISBN 0-574-18700-6

Imprint 1990
Copyright © 1989 by the Glencoe Division of Macmillan/
McGraw-Hill Publishing Company. Copyright © 1988
by Science Research Associates, Inc. All rights reserved.
Printed in the United States of America. No part of this
publication may be reproduced, stored in a retrieval
system, or transmitted, in any form or by any means,
electronic, mechanical, photocopying, recording, or
otherwise, without the prior written permission of the
publisher.
Send all inquiries to: Glencoe Division, Macmillan/
McGraw-Hill, 936 Eastwind Drive, Westerville, Ohio
43081.

MUR
2 3 4 5 6 7 8 9 10 11 12 13 14 15 — 00 99 98 97 96 95 94 93 92 91 90

PROGRAMMING LOGIC

Second Edition

MARJORIE M. LEESON

GLENCOE
Macmillan/McGraw-Hill

Lake Forest, Illinois
Columbus, Ohio
Mission Hills, California
Peoria, Illinois

CONTENTS

PREFACE   ix

CHAPTER 1   1   Introduction to Structured Design and Program Development

                    2   What Does a Programmer Do?
                    5   The Development of Programming Standards
                    7   Structured Design and Programming Standards Emerge
                   12   Criteria Used to Evaluate Structured Programs
                   14   Steps in Designing and Completing a Program
                   24   Did You Answer the Question Correctly?
                   24   Summary
                   25   Discussion Questions
                   26   Key Words
                   27   Exercises
                   29   Problem
                   29   Interactive Exercises
                   35   Self-Evaluation Test

CHAPTER 2   41   Tools Used by Analysts and Programmers

                   42   HIPO Charts
                   43   Characteristics of an Acceptable Method for Developing a Logic Plan
                   43   Methods Covered
                   44   Program Specifications
                   44   Pseudocode
                   51   Structured Flowcharts
                   59   Nassi-Shneiderman Charts
                   60   Warnier-Orr Diagrams
                   68   Summary
                   69   Discussion Questions
                   70   Key Words
                   71   Exercise
                   73   Problem
                   75   Interactive Exercise
                   79   Self-Evaluation Test

CHAPTER 3   83   Selection: A Powerful Programming Tool

                   84   Selection Logic
                   87   Simple IF Statements
                   94   Nested IF/THEN/ELSE

102   Case Entry
103   Creating an Order Entry Program
111   Stub Testing
112   Summary
113   Discussion Questions
114   Key Words
115   Exercises
117   Problem
117   Interactive Exercise
121   Self-Evaluation Test

CHAPTER 4   127   **Creating Loops**

128   Conditional Loops
134   Count-Controlled Loops
146   Summary
147   Discussion Questions
148   Key Words
149   Exercise
149   Problem
150   Interactive Exercises
153   Self-Evaluation Test

CHAPTER 5   157   **Effective Use of Tables**

160   Types of Tables
166   Survey Program
174   Summary
175   Discussion Questions
175   Key Words
176   Exercises
177   Problem
178   Interactive Exercises
183   Self-Evaluation Test

CHAPTER 6   187   **Printing Reports**

188   Types of Reports
190   Designing Reports
190   Print Layout Forms
194   Detailed Logic Plan for the Inventory Exception Report
201   Multilevel Reports
211   External Reports
216   Extraction Programs
218   Other Types of Reports
219   Summary
220   Discussion Questions
221   Key Words
222   Exercises
223   Problem
223   Interactive Exercises
227   Self-Evaluation Test

© SRA 1988, 1983

CHAPTER 7   231   **File Processing**

232   Record Storage
234   File Organization
238   File Specification Form
245   Record Layout
247   Creating the Payroll Master File
254   Adding New Fields to an Existing Master File
256   Adding the Stock Deduction Data to the Payroll Master File
262   Summary
264   Discussion Questions
266   Key Words
267   Exercises
267   Problem
267   Interactive Exercises
273   Self-Evaluation Test

CHAPTER 8   277   **File Maintenance**

278   Maintenance Programs for the Payroll System
279   CHANGE Program
287   Providing Delays for Reading Screens
294   Correcting the Payroll Master File Records
300   Adding New Employees to the Payroll Master File
302   Master File Update Program
306   Backing Up and Recreating the Payroll Master File
308   Summary
309   Discussion Questions
310   Key Words
311   Exercise
311   Problem
311   Interactive Exercises
315   Self-Evaluation Test

CHAPTER 9   319   **Editing Data**

320   Editing in an Interactive Environment
330   Editing in a Batch Environment
330   Creating a Transaction File
333   Producing the Sales Invoices
338   Creating an Edit Module and Error Report
349   Summary
350   Discussion Questions
351   Key Words
352   Exercises
352   Problem
353   Interactive Exercise
357   Self-Evaluation Test

CHAPTER 10   361   **Menus and Variable Length Records**

362   Creating a Menu Program
371   Variable Length Records
380   Summary

381 Discussion Questions
382 Key Words
383 Exercise
383 Problem
384 Interactive Exercise
387 Self-Evaluation Test

CHAPTER 11   391 Documentation for the Payroll Register Program

392 How Documentation Is Used
395 Discussion Questions

APPENDIX I   413 HIPO Charts

APPENDIX II   419 Decision Tables

APPENDIX III   423 Answers to Checkpoint Questions

GLOSSARY/INDEX   439

© SRA 1988, 1983

PREFACE

This text was written to facilitate the development and implementation of a programming logic course and to serve as a guide for developing structured programs and systems. The text is based on the principle of teaching new concepts correctly. In the very beginning students develop correct, and lasting, techniques that become a foundation upon which to build. Students learn why well-structured programs that are easy to understand and maintain should be developed. A simple, well-structured program is then developed to illustrate how the guidelines should be applied.

In the past decade there has been a marked improvement in the quality and quantity of software designed, coded, tested, and documented. The development and use of design and programming standards are primarily responsible for the improvements. If this trend is to continue, it is imperative for individuals who wish to design and implement computer applications to develop a foundation based on state-of-the-art guidelines and practices that provides for future growth.

Educational institutions that have implemented programming logic courses have found a marked improvement in the quality of the programs written by students in COBOL, BASIC, FORTRAN, Assembler, PASCAL, C, and other high-level languages. Students need less assistance from instructors and spend less time debugging programs. Better designed and documented programs usually decrease the amount of time students need to enter, edit, and test source code.

The emphasis throughout this text is on current state-of-the-art practices. Students learn how to develop interactive programs used in transaction processing; use a menu approach to develop *help screens* and internal documentation; create and maintain files; utilize files and tables; and develop a menu that provides access to the programs within a system. While sequential processing and online batch processing are covered, card processing has been, by design, omitted.

ORGANIZATION OF THE TEXT

The text is learner-oriented and friendly. The concepts introduced early in the course are those that students can most easily understand and visualize. As new topics are gradually introduced, the concepts introduced earlier in the text are reviewed and reinforced. Each chapter contains the following features:

LEARNER-ORIENTED PERFORMANCE OBJECTIVES   On the opening page of each chapter is a list of learning objectives. Reading the objectives provides the student with a quick overview of the chapter. After the chapter is studied, the objectives can be converted to questions to determine whether the material within the chapter has been mastered.

AN INTRODUCTION   The introduction is designed to provide a transition from the previous to the current chapter and to present an overview of the material to be included.

CHECKPOINT QUESTIONS   After a section of text material is presented, questions designed to reinforce the concepts and to test the student's understanding of the material are provided. Students should answer the questions and then check their answers with those provided in Appendix III.

SUMMARY   The major topics presented in the text are summarized in one or two sentences. The summary reinforces the concepts covered in the chapter and can also be used as a reference.

KEY WORDS   Terms that must be mastered in order to understand the concepts are listed. Each of the words or phrases listed is defined in the glossary/index.

DISCUSSION QUESTIONS   These questions are designed to encourage class discussion and to show specific applications of the concepts presented in the chapter.

EXERCISES   The exercises require students to use the new concepts presented in the chapter. For example, the exercises following the chapter on creating loops ask students to develop selected modules that use WHILE, UNTIL, and count-controlled loops.

PROBLEMS   Given the program specifications, the logic for a complete program must be developed. However, until reports and files are covered, *stubs* are used for reading files and printing reports. By using this approach, stub testing is illustrated, problems are shortened, and students develop only the modules that apply concepts already illustrated.

INTERACTIVE EXERCISES   The programs used as illustrations in the text are coded in BASIC. Students can execute the code and see what happens as the program is executed using valid and invalid data. Sometimes students are asked to list a section of the program, make certain changes, and answer questions about the results obtained. Students who are interested can list the source code and see how the logic plan is implemented.

SELF-EVALUATION TESTS   Objective tests that contain completion, multiple choice, and true/false questions are provided. So that the student may obtain immediate feedback, the answers are provided on the same diskette as the interactive exercises. For each false question, a *brief* explanation of why the question is false is provided. Using the software provides immediate feedback, saves class time, and gives students a correct study guide from which to review.

FEATURES INCLUDED IN THE LEARNING SYSTEM

A learning system must include more than a textbook. The needs of the faculty and learner must be considered in developing the system. The following goals were established for the learning system:

- *To be relevant to today's business environment.* Throughout the book, examples, illustrations, problems, and cases exemplify the real world of business.

- *To emphasize interactive transaction-processing.* Punched-card logic is replaced with interactive computing and job execution.

© SRA 1988, 1983

- *To incorporate state-of-the-art techniques such as the design and use of menus, interactive processing, and the retrieval and display of information.*

- *To present the current tools and techniques used in developing logic plans.* However, the selection of the method to be emphasized and used in completing exercises and problems is determined by each faculty member.

- *To teach basic techniques used in designing programs.* The material is generic and is not tied to any one language. Pseudocode is used to illustrate logic and good formatting techniques.

- *To present structured design concepts from the very beginning.* Students should not be required to learn new techniques that replace those presented early in the course.

- *To use a ''building block'' approach for learning how to utilize state-of-the-art techniques in designing, coding, testing, and documenting programs.* Concepts are introduced gradually, applied in programs and projects, and reinforced through review in subsequent chapters and problems.

- *To emphasize testing and documentation.* In the interactive exercises and problems illustrated in the text, students are frequently asked if the test data adequately tests both the normal and error-processing procedures.

- *To be comprehensive.* The book is intended to be both a text and a helpful reference. Techniques used in interactive processing, creating help screens, the retrieval and display of information, creating and maintaining files, as well as batch processing using transaction and master files, are explained and illustrated.

- *To be learner-oriented.* The text is organized and designed to facilitate the learning process. Each chapter begins with student-oriented objectives. Checkpoint questions are interspersed throughout each chapter to permit student self-assessment. Each chapter concludes with a summary, a list of key words, and projects that apply the concepts presented in the chapter in a meaningful way.

- *To assist instructors.* An extensive Instructor's Guide is part of the learning system and includes lecture outlines, representative answers and solutions for solving exercises and problems, and suggestions regarding the presentation of the material. Both a computerized and printed test bank are included. When the computerized test generator is used, questions can be added, deleted, or changed.

EVALUATION OF THE LEARNING SYSTEM

Although the goals listed were established at the beginning of the project and have been incorporated into the design of the learning system, how well this has been done can be determined initially by studying the table of contents, reading the material presented in each chapter, and evaluating the learning aids, projects, self-evaluation tests, and software. However, the final evaluation of the effectiveness of this material will be made as students progress through other courses, such as programming and systems analysis and design, and become productive members of the work force.

ACKNOWLEDGMENTS

A learning system that meets the needs of students, faculty, and industry is similar to a successful computer system. Ideas based on past experience, including problems that occurred and had to be solved, the current state-of-the-art, and anticipation of what will occur in the future are all incorporated into its design. Just as users are consulted when an analyst designs a new computer system, input used in the development of this learning system was received from faculty, students, and representatives from industry. It is with sincere appreciation that I thank the many individuals who provided ideas and suggestions.

The original outline was reviewed and many of the suggestions of the following individuals were incorporated into the design of the text: Dennis McNeal (Delta College), Chi Chen (St. Louis Community College at Meramec), Susumu Kasai (St. Louis Community College at Meramec), Gayla B. Stewart (St. Louis Community College at Meramec), Thomas K. Tate (Lehigh County Community College), and W. Mark Woods (Dundalk Community College).

The manuscript was revised and greatly improved through the suggestions of the following reviewers: Marjorie Feroe (Delaware County Community College), Dennis Guster (St. Louis Community College at Meramec), Y. Dolly Hwang (Guilford Technical Community College), and Allen W. Schmidt (Madison Area Technical College).

Allen Schmidt not only contributed suggestions that made the text more relevant but also reviewed the software and the Instructor's Guide. Because of his assistance, many improvements were incorporated into both the text and the Instructor's Guide.

Harris Lemberg and Tom Fleming, students at Madison Area Technical College, helped by giving the software a final check to make sure it is user-friendly.

Turning the manuscript into an exciting textbook involved the work and talent of many individuals. The editing and many of the details involved in the production of the text were coordinated by Molly Gardiner. Molly's creativity and attention to detail helped to transform the manuscript into a learner-oriented text.

To all of the individuals listed and to many other individuals who worked behind the scenes, a very special thank-you is given.

Marjorie M. Leeson

© SRA 1988, 1983

INTRODUCTION TO STRUCTURED DESIGN AND PROGRAM DEVELOPMENT

1

After reading the chapter and completing the learning activities, you will be able to:

- Describe the responsibilities assigned to programmers.

- Explain why programmers in the late sixties and early seventies were unproductive and why this led to the development of structured design and programming concepts.

- Explain the characteristics identifying a well-written, structured program.

- Identify the advantages of designing and developing structured programs rather than writing unstructured programs.

- List and explain the steps required to design and complete a program.

- Identify the guidelines used in developing a hierarchy chart.

- Identify the characteristics of a well-developed, detailed logic plan.

- Explain why team walkthroughs may reduce the time required to test and debug programs.

- Explain why complete, up-to-date internal and external documentation should be available for all programs.

- Define and use the terms listed in the Key Word section of this chapter.

If you were asked to write a simple program that would compute the first five months' interest on a loan, what would you do? In answering the question, assume you know how to use a personal computer, have access to one, and know how to program in a language such as BASIC. Also, assume that a friend of yours having little experience working with computers has asked you to write the program. You might answer that you would do one of the following:

- Load the **BASICA interpreter** into the memory of the computer and key in the program. The BASICA interpreter is a program that will translate each statement written in the BASIC programming language into machine language commands that the computer can understand and execute. As your program is interpreted, clerical and **syntactical errors** will be detected and displayed on the **VDT (visual display terminal)**. Syntactical errors are violations of the rules that apply to the language being used. VDTs are also referred to as CRTs (cathode ray tubes).

- Write the **source code** on a coding form and then key it into the memory of the computer. Source code is your program written in a language such as BASIC, COBOL, or PASCAL.

- Question your friend regarding what input is needed to produce the required results. After determining what input is needed, you will write and enter the source code.

If you were the manager of a software company or a computer information services department, would you feel any of the answers are acceptable? To most data processing professionals interested in the development of error-free programs, none of the three answers is acceptable. As you learn what is expected of today's programmers and learn why programming standards were developed, you will see why all these answers are unacceptable.

WHAT DOES A PROGRAMMER DO?

Because the sales manager of a well-established organization has decided that the present computerized sales system is inadequate, he has made a formal request to Computer Information Services to have a **transaction-processing system** developed. When the new sales system is developed, sales data will be entered for processing when and where transactions occur. If the request is approved, a systems **analyst** will work with the sales department in order to determine the characteristics of the system. Questions—such as "What output is required?", "When is the information needed?", and "How should data be entered?"—must all be answered. Working with the sales department, the analyst will develop the objectives and general specifications for the transaction-processing system. More detailed objectives and specifications will be developed for each program that makes up the transaction-processing system.

Although usually the specifications for the system and the individual programs are given to the programmer, nonetheless the design and development of successful systems are a team effort. Users, analysts, and programmers work together, and there should be continuous communication between the individuals assigned to the project. Once the objectives and specifications are developed, programmers are primarily responsible for the tasks listed in Figure 1–1.

© SRA 1988, 1983

Figure 1–1 Major tasks assigned to programmers.

RESPONSIBILITIES ASSIGNED TO PROGRAMMERS

- Develop a detailed logic plan for each program showing how the input will be processed in order to obtain valid output.

- Write and enter the source code.

- Create test data that will test the routines that check for errors, process valid data, and output the required information.

- Test the program to determine the validity of the output.

- Document each program.

Developing detailed logic plans

If you were going to build a house, would you start by going to the lumberyard to obtain a hammer, nails, and lumber and then return to your building site to start building your house? Although not a builder, you would probably answer "Of course not." Most professional builders will develop specifications to meet the building codes, and procure a blueprint to show exactly how to construct the house. A detailed logic plan might be compared to the detailed blueprints used in construction.

If you were going to drive from San Diego to New York for the first time, would you pack your car, fill your tank with gas, and start out for New York? More likely, you would determine the best route to follow, obtain the necessary road maps, and then develop a plan. A detailed logic plan is as essential to a programmer as road maps are to travelers driving on a new route or in a strange city.

There are different ways to develop detailed logic plans. While some programmers may prefer to use a detailed **flowchart**, others might elect to use **pseudocode** or some other method. Pseudocode is an English-like nonprocessible language used to describe how data will be entered into the computer and processed. Flowcharts are developed using standard symbols to denote functions such as entering data, making a decision regarding which steps to follow, or outputting data. The techniques used in developing pseudocode and flowcharts, as well as other types of logic plans, will be discussed in detail later.

Gerald Weinberg, a well-known teacher, author, and consultant, is often quoted in discussions about designing, coding, and implementing programs. One of his now-famous statements is "Resist the urge to code." Although some programmers may still start to develop a program by writing source code, it has been proven that the time spent in developing a well-defined logic plan pays off. When a detailed logic plan is developed and tested prior to writing source code, less total time is needed to produce an error-free operational program. Although programmers who are skilled at developing good logic plans may spend more time in the design stage, they need far less time to code and to debug the program than when they do not develop a logic plan before coding.

**Writing and entering
source code**

Once a logic plan is developed, it must be converted to source code. Usually within an organization all application programs are developed using the same language. Alternatively, at least one language, such as COBOL (COmmon Business Oriented Language), is used for business applications and a second language, such as PASCAL or FORTRAN, is used for scientific applications. It is unwise to let each programmer within an organization determine what language to use because the cost of developing and maintaining programs in several languages is much higher than when only one language is used. Also, if a programmer writes source code in a seldom-used language, and then leaves an organization, it might be difficult and time-consuming for the remaining programmers to maintain such programs.

Because terminals or personal computers are usually used for entering source code, many programmers key in their own source statements. Although a professional keyboarder may be able to key in the statements faster, the programmer usually checks the code as it is being entered and makes the necessary corrections.

Testing programs

An important part of a programmer's job is to test the programs he or she designs and develops. Usually a program is tested first by using valid data and checking the accuracy of the output.

Next the program is tested using invalid data. For example, a company has 100 sales representatives who are assigned the numbers 1–100. An **error routine** must be *written and tested* to provide an error message if a sales representative's number is less than 1 or greater than 100. Error routines are one or more source-code statements designed to detect errors.

After each error routine is tested using invalid data, the program is tested without using any data. What will happen when an error occurs and the file being processed doesn't contain any records? A diagnostic routine must be available to detect the fact that the file is empty, and an appropriate message must be displayed. The test data used must test all commands used to process the input and to output the required information.

Today's programmers test programs to prove that valid results are produced and that invalid data is detected. If a programmer develops a well-defined logic plan, tests the plan, and tests all parts of the program, the program should not **abort**. A job aborts when an error routine is not provided to handle a critical error. Only when the computer has not been instructed on how to handle the error will the job cancel or abort.

Today management, users, and consumers depend on having data processed as transactions occur. From remote locations, terminals gain access to programs that retrieve, process, and format data into meaningful information. It is imperative that programs not abort and that the computer be available to process data and retrieve up-to-date information.

Documenting programs

Programs should be internally and externally documented. Internal documentation is placed within programs to explain what occurs when each section of a program is executed. These statements will not be displayed unless the

© SRA 1988, 1983

source code is listed. The statements are put within programs for the benefit of maintenance programmers and other persons within the organization, such as auditors, who need to know how input is checked for accuracy and processed.

Another type of internal documentation provides what are called *help screens*. At the request of the terminal operator, instructions for entering data or information explaining the options available are displayed. When the program is designed, the programmer or analyst should make certain that help screens are available to provide directions and explain the options available.

External documentation includes the program specifications, **record layouts**, **print layouts**, the detailed logic plans, and directions for running the program and determining the validity of the output. Record layouts show how the input and output records are formatted. The programmer can determine the location of each field within a record, the size of each field, and the type of data stored within each field. The print layout illustrates the information to be printed on a report and where it will be printed. This type of documentation is created during the design phase of the development of a program and put in final form before the program is considered operational.

It is estimated that programmers spend 10 to 15 percent of their time documenting programs. The ease with which a program can be understood and maintained is directly related to the quality of its internal and external documentation.

THE DEVELOPMENT OF PROGRAMMING STANDARDS

In the very beginning

Are programmers still writing programs in the same way that they did when **ENIAC,** the first programmable computer, was developed in 1946? At that time there were only a few highly skilled mathematicians who wrote programs in the machine language executed by the computer. Since **standards** for developing and writing programs were not available, programming was not considered a profession. The person writing the program had to provide instructions for each machine-language command needed to input the data, process the data, and output the required information. Many instructions were needed to develop a program that would read a few numbers from a punched card, perform a series of simple calculations, and print a simple report.

Standards for designing, developing, and evaluating programs did not exist and no programming tools were available to assist programmers in developing and testing programs. If a program canceled or if the computer failed, a programmer often spent hours determining the cause of the problem. Input had to be read in from cards, and output was either punched into cards or printed. The size of the computer's memory and the I/O devices had a direct impact on the type of programs that could be developed.

During this period (from 1946 to 1966) very little time was spent in the design phase of programming. In fact, seldom was the term *design phase* used. Each programmer developed his or her own programming techniques. Since computer memories and online file storage were limited in size, little internal documentation was included in programs. Since systems and programs were usually behind schedule, complete external documentation was seldom available when the system became **operational**. A system is considered operational when its programs are used on a regular basis to process input and produce output.

The impact of operating systems

In 1966, twenty years after ENIAC was accepted as being the first programmable computer, computers were much larger, faster, and more sophisticated. **Operating systems** became part of most computer systems. A computer system is composed of **hardware**, software, people, data, and **procedures.** Hardware consists of the computer and the input/output devices. Software consists of the operating system and **application programs**. People who work with computers include analysts, programmers, operators, and support personnel. Data is unprocessed facts; information is the result of processing data. Procedures are formalized methods for accomplishing tasks and should be well documented.

Operating systems are composed of many complex programs that control the execution of application programs and manage the resources of the computer system. Application programs process data, such as sales or payroll data, rather than controlling the resources of the computer system. Analysts worked with the individuals who requested software in order to define the problem and determine how the input should be processed to produce the desired output. Although users were consulted, they were seldom *directly* involved in determining how the data would be processed.

In 1966 computers were identified as being part of the "third generation" and their sophisticated operating systems made programming easier. No longer was the programmer required to program the computer to perform every task that needed to be done. For example, when data stored on magnetic tape was to be processed, commands that were part of the operating system software checked to see that the proper reel of tape was mounted and that the programmer had correctly identified how the data was stored on the tape. Software for doing frequently performed tasks, for diagnostic routines, and for error-handling was included as part of the operating system software.

Although improvements had been made in hardware and in control software, how programs were developed and documented had changed very little. Since standards and guidelines were seldom available, programming was not considered a science. Compared to today's programmers, most programmers of that era would be considered unproductive.

Management became concerned about the high cost of developing programs. One study made in 1965 indicated that an average COBOL programmer produced only 10 to 12 lines of **debugged** source code a day. Debugged code is free of clerical or syntactical errors and can be translated into the machine-language commands that are executed by the computer. Since a complex program may contain thousands of lines of source code, the concern of management was justified. It was estimated that each line of source code cost from six to eight dollars.

Lack of productivity

Who or what was responsible for this apparent lack of productivity? Many programmers were self-taught and spent most of their time and energy trying to keep pace with the rapidity of change. It seemed that as soon as an application was developed, debugged, and documented it had to be changed. Changes were required because new hardware or software was obtained; changes occurred within the organization or in laws that affected how its data had to be processed; or the user was dissatisfied with the results obtained. It was both time-consuming and expensive to make the required changes. Often the programmer who had developed the application software had left the company and someone else was assigned the task of modifying the source code.

© SRA 1988, 1983

As each year passed, a larger percentage of programming budgets was spent on changing old programs than on developing new ones. From 50 to 90 percent of programming staff time was spent in maintaining programs.

Too often management was not concerned with *how* the application software was developed. Their only concern seemed to be that applications were up-and-running as soon as possible. Each programmer was permitted to develop the software in his or her own unique way. Due to the lack of standards and well-defined procedures, most application software was over budget and behind schedule.

In summary, little time was spent in the design phase while much time was spent debugging programs. Both maintenance programmers and users complained about the poor quality of documentation. Because programs were poorly developed and not completely tested, jobs often aborted (or canceled) during execution. Management also became concerned about the cost of the reruns required due to job aborts or invalid output.

CHECKPOINT QUESTIONS

1. What tasks are normally assigned to programmers?
2. Before coding a program, why should a detailed logic plan be developed?
3. Why should programmers "resist the urge to code"?
4. Why is it unwise to let each programmer within the organization decide what language should be used for coding programs?
5. How should programs be tested?
6. Why are programs both internally and externally documented?
7. What might be considered the "driving forces" behind the development of design and programming standards?
8. Did the use of operating systems increase the productivity of programmers?
9. During the late sixties and early seventies, was management concerned about how programs were developed and programmed?

STRUCTURED DESIGN AND PROGRAMMING STANDARDS EMERGE

Even a well-designed program may need to be changed. Today many companies report that anywhere from 50 to 80 percent of their programming effort and budget is still used to maintain existing software. Poorly designed programs are difficult and more costly to maintain than ones that are well designed. Figure 1–2 summarizes the problems that still exist in some installations. In other installations, design and programming standards were developed and are being followed. Sometimes the concepts being used are part of what is referred to as **structured design** and **structured programming.**

Structured design

Although the development and utilization of structured design standards have not solved all problems, the productivity of programmers has increased, and the cost of developing and maintaining programs has decreased. Structured programs are easier to develop, code, test, and document than unstructured programs.

Figure 1–2   Problems that lead to the development of structured design and structured programming.

PROBLEMS THAT EXIST IN SOME INSTALLATIONS

- Lack of design and programming standards.
- Poorly designed systems and programs.
- Low level of programmer productivity.
- Excessive costs required to develop and maintain programs.
- Undetected errors cause programs to abort.
- Projects completed late and over the projected cost.
- Inadequate documentation made program maintenance difficult.

USING A TOP-DOWN APPROACH   When structured design concepts are used to design a program, a **top-down** approach is used to develop the logic. Programs are divided into **modules**. Each module contains code related to *one major function or task that must be accomplished*. In order that the modules are manageable, it is considered good practice to limit code to 50 or fewer lines. As illustrated in Figure 1–3 there is always one control module which calls, or invokes, the major modules. Each of the major modules, which are identified in the diagram as *initiation, process sales records,* and *termination,* may invoke one or more subordinate modules. When a top-down approach is used in designing and implementing programs, major modules are designed and developed before the supporting modules.

INVOKING MODULES   When a module such as initiation is invoked, control passes from the main control module (sales commission program) to the module being invoked. After the commands within the module are executed, control returns to the calling module. When a module is invoked or called, control passes to

Figure 1–3   In a structured program the main control module invokes the other major modules.

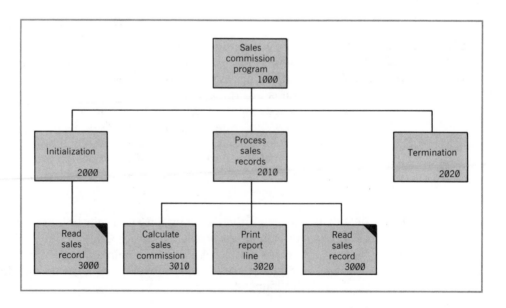

© SRA 1988, 1983

the module invoked and then returns to the statement following the one that passed control to the subordinate module.

CONVENTIONS ILLUSTRATED BY THE HIERARCHY CHART   When a program is designed, **conventions**, as well as guidelines and standards, are used. A convention is a practice that is routinely followed by a programmer or analyst. The **hierarchy chart** shown in Figure 1–3 illustrates the relationships that exist between modules. Figure 1–3 illustrates the following conventions:

- The main-control-module was given a meaningful name that indicates what the program will accomplish. Since the program will read sales data and calculate commissions, the name sales commission program was used.
- The main-control-module is assigned the number 1000. It will control the 2000 level modules.
- The modules invoked by the main-control-module will always be assigned the numbers 2000, 2010, 2020, and so forth.
- The modules invoked by the 2000 level modules will be assigned the numbers 3000, 3010, 3020, and so forth.
- When the upper right corner of the symbol is shaded, the module will be called by two or more modules. However, the code is only written one time.

The read-sale-record module is invoked the first time from the initialization module. This is done so that when the process-sale-records module is invoked there will be data to be processed. When the module is invoked from both the initialization and the process-sales-records modules, it enables the programmer to treat the first record read the same as any other record. Also once a module is entered, the statements within the module must be executed as each module must have a single entry, single exit point.

Single entry, single exit

When a top-down approach is used to develop the logic for a program, the logic is developed for the 1000 module, then for the 2000 level modules, the 3000 level modules, and so forth. When a program is structured, there is only one entry and one exit point for each module. This means that control cannot branch from one module into the middle of a second module. Figure 1–4 illustrates the concept of single entry, single exit. For each module shown on a hierarchy chart there will be a separate logic plan. A hierarchy chart can also be called a **VTOC (Visual Table Of Contents)**.

Indicators

Figure 1–4 also illustrates the use of an **indicator.** Indicators are special data fields used by the programmer to control the logic of the program. The programmer would have set the contents of the END-OF-FILE field to N. As long as END-OF-FILE contains N, records will continue to be processed. When the end of file is detected, Y is stored in the END-OF-FILE field. Although indicators can also be referred to as *switches* or *flags*, in this text the term *indicator* will be used. The rationale for this term is that the contents of the field *indicates* what will occur.

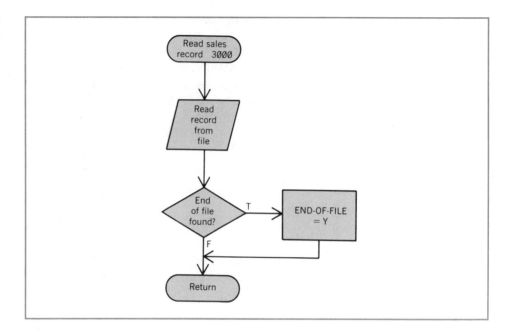

Figure 1–4 The concept of single entry, single exit is illustrated for the read-sales-record module.

Another convention that will be used throughout the text is to use Y for *yes* and N for *no*. When responses are entered by an operator, using a single letter rather than YES or NO decreases the possibility of making an error and saves time.

Control structures used in developing structured programs

The work of many individuals contributed to present-day guidelines for designing and developing *structured programs*. A structured program is one that is developed and executed from the top down and according to guidelines such as a single entry and exit point for any given section (or module) of source code. Corrado Böhm and Giuseppe Jacopini who first introduced the concept of structured programming pointed out that any program could be written by using the three control structures illustrated in Figure 1–5.

Figure 1–5 Control structures used in developing structured programs.

CONTROL STRUCTURES

- **Sequence**   The computer will execute commands in the sequence in which they are stored within the computer.

- **Iteration**   Another term for iteration is looping. A section of program will continue to execute as long as a given condition is true or until a specified condition is met.

- **Selection**   One of two courses of action will occur depending upon whether a condition is true or false.

© SRA 1988, 1983

Since many programmers want to develop structured programs according to the accepted standards, most program languages make it possible to write programs using sequence, iteration, and selection control structures to execute the logic of a program. The programming statements that provide for looping (iteration) and selection are usually considered to be the most useful and powerful statements available within the language's subset.

ITERATION OR LOOPING   In BASIC a loop might have been created as follows:

```
10   REM   THIS IS AN EXAMPLE OF A LOOP        (REM is a remark)
20   LET RECORDS = 'Y'                         (Indicator is set to Y)
30   WHILE RECORDS = 'Y'                       (Start of the loop)
40      PRINT 'AN ENDLESS LOOP IS CREATED'     (Prints statement specified)
50   WEND                                      (End of loop)
60   END                                       (End of program)
```

In the example, the statement within the WHILE/WEND loop will be executed as long as the condition specified (RECORDS = "Y") exists. WHILE indicates the beginning of the loop and WEND denotes the end of the loop. Since the value stored in the field called RECORDS was initially set to Y and never changed, an **infinite loop** was created. An infinite loop is one that will continue until the operator causes the program to abort by pressing a key such as break, the computer is turned off, or there is a power failure.

Programmers do not want to create infinite loops. If a programmer creates an infinite loop, it will be detected and corrected during the testing phase of the program. The RECORDS field used in the WHILE/WEND loop is another example of an indicator.

SELECTION   Regardless of the language used, selection usually involves the use of an IF statement. For example:

```
100  IF HOURS > 40 THEN OVERTIME = (HOURS − 40) * RATE * 1.5
        ELSE OVERTIME = 0
```

In the example, the HOURS field contains the total number of hours that an employee worked during a given week. If the employee works more than 40 hours, the hours over 40 are to be compensated at 1.5 times his or her regular hourly wage. As you progress through the text, you will see that most of the computer's logic is derived from selection and based on true or false questions that can be either simple (as the one illustrated) or extremely complex.

USE OF GO TO STATEMENTS   Edsger W. Dijkstra of the University of Eidenhoven, The Netherlands, further advanced the concept of structured programming. In 1965 he suggested that GO TO statements be eliminated from programs. He believed that programs without GO TO statements were better designed and more structured than those that contained GO TO statements. Most programming languages support the use of GO TO statements, which cause the control of the program to pass to the location specified in the statement. The following GO TO statement causes control of the program to branch to the instruction located at the source statement identified as line 5000.

```
120   GO TO 5000
130   . . . .        (any number of programming statements may be coded
                     before statement 5000)
5000  PRINT 'CONTROL PASSED TO LINE 5000'
```

Once control passes to statement 5000, there is no way of returning to the statement that follows 120 unless another GO TO statement is used. When GO TOs are used, the person reading the source code and attempting to follow its logic will have to skip down to line 5000 to see what occurs. In contrast, when a module is invoked, control passes to the first statement of the module, the code within the module is executed, and then control returns to the statement that follows the one that invoked the module.

In some cases a well-thought-out GO TO that transfers control to a *point within a module or to the exit point for the module* may be acceptable. Also some languages, such as the very early versions of BASIC, make it necessary to use GO TO statements because statements such as the IF/ELSE statement illustrated are not available.

CRITERIA USED TO EVALUATE STRUCTURED PROGRAMS

The work of Böhm, Jacopini, Dijkstra, and others led to the development of criteria that could be used to evaluate programs. Many individuals now agree that a well-designed and well-written program must meet the standards listed in Figure 1–6.

For several years, *structured design and programming* was much talked about. In the late 1970s, many conferences and seminars were devoted to the topic. When these concepts were tested, they resulted in programs with fewer logical errors produced in less time than when structured design and programming methods were not used.

For example, a project leader who works for a major automotive company attended a structured design and programming seminar. Although not entirely convinced the concepts would produce the promised results, he conducted workshops for his programming staff. When the concepts were used to develop a new system, the entire project was completed in half the estimated time and was also under budget.

Because there is a misconception that all shops and programmers now use structured design and programming concepts to develop systems, less is heard about the topic today. Much evidence now indicates that structured programs

- are developed in less time and at lower cost than unstructured programs.
- have fewer bugs than unstructured programs after being put into production.
- are easier to test. Since the programs are developed from the top down, testing can begin as soon as the major modules are completed.
- are easier to maintain. Some shops have experienced as much as a 50 percent reduction in the cost of maintaining programs.
- are easier to understand.

Once design and programming standards are developed for a given installation, it is much easier to evaluate the productivity of analysts and programmers.

© SRA 1988, 1983

CHARACTERISTICS OF A WELL-WRITTEN PROGRAM

1. *Modular.* A module contains code for one function and the tasks closely related to that function. Usually modules contain 50 or fewer lines of code. Most programs contain basic modules that can be thought of as *building blocks.*

2. *Well-designed.* The logic should be developed from the top down and each module should have one entry point and one exit point. The major modules containing the control logic will be developed first. Then the supporting modules that contain more detailed instructions will be developed. If each module has a single entry point and a single exit point, the reader will always know where the control of the program goes and, after the commands within the module are executed, where control returns.

3. *Easy to follow.* The readability of a program becomes important when a maintenance programmer is assigned the job of changing a program or when an auditor must determine how data is processed.

4. *Well-formatted.* Although many languages permit code to be written in a free format rather than requiring that certain positions within the statement must be used for given functions, the conventions established for the installation must be followed. In the following example, the reader can easily see what occurs when the specified condition is true and when it is false.

```
1020    REM   CALCULATE OVERTIME PAY
1020    IF  OVERTIME-HOURS > 0 THEN
            OVERTIME-PAY = OVERTIME-HOURS * RATE * 2.0
        ELSE
            OVERTIME-PAY = 0
```

In the example, the SELECTION control structure is used and the convention illustrated requires the IF and ELSE portions of the statement to be coded on separate lines. Indenting the action portion of the statement also increases the readability of the program.

5. *Constructed using meaningful names.* In the previous example, the reader or maintenance programmer can see that if overtime hours are greater than zero, overtime pay will be calculated by multiplying the hours times twice the normal rate. In many programming languages an * is used to denote multiplication.

6. *Simplistic.* Whenever possible a straightforward, easy-to-follow approach should be used. Today each major job or procedure has a separate program; each major function has a separate module.

7. *Designed so that the logic will be executed by using the SEQUENCE, ITERATION, and SELECTION control structures.*

8. *Written without, or with very limited use of, GO TOs.* Sometimes the use of a GO TO within a module can prevent the complex nesting of IF/ELSE statements.

9. *Internally documented and externally documented.* Internal documentation consists of comments describing the function of the program and those of each module. The comments relating to a module's functions should be placed at the beginning of the module. The careful use of meaningful module, file, and date names decreases the amount of internal documentation needed to make the program easy to follow.

10. *In compliance with the installation's design and programming standards.*

Figure 1–6   Structured design and programming standards.

CHECKPOINT QUESTIONS

10. What problems regarding the design and development of programs still exist in some organizations?

11. What is a hierarchy chart?

12. What is an indicator?

13. What three control structures are used to develop a structured program?

14. What criteria should be used to evaluate a structured program?

STEPS IN DESIGNING AND COMPLETING A PROGRAM

Figure 1–7 identifies the steps required to design, code, test, and document a program. To demonstrate the steps listed more meaningfully, a simple example illustrates the completion of each step. As you study the example you may think, "All this just to write that simple little program." True! However, just as an infant must creep before it walks, you must learn to apply basic techniques to simple problems before attempting to design complex programs.

The modules presented in the illustration are the *building blocks* for all future programs. Complex programs can be developed easily if designed from the top down and one module at a time. The problem described earlier in the text will be developed.

Figure 1–7 Steps required to design, code, test, and document a program.

STEPS REQUIRED TO ANALYZE A PROBLEM AND DESIGN
AND IMPLEMENT A PROGRAM

1. Define the problem.
2. Determine the Output/Input needs and formats.
3. List the major tasks that must be accomplished and determine the modules that will be needed.
4. Determine if another program, similar to the one being developed, has modules that can be used in the program being designed.
5. Develop a rough draft of the hierarchy chart that identifies the modules and the relationships that exist between the modules.
6. Develop a detailed logic plan for each module. This may require that modification be made to the original hierarchy chart.
7. Test the design. Testing the design is often called a walkthrough and is used to detect flaws in the logic of a program.
8. If necessary, revise the hierarchy chart and logic plan.
9. Code the program in the language used in the installation and by following the established coding standards.
10. Enter the code and correct the syntactical and clerical errors.
11. Walk through the code. The programmer plays computer in an effort to detect syntactical errors, logical errors, and omissions.
12. Test the program.
13. Complete the documentation.
14. Evaluate the program. Were the stated objectives met?

© SRA 1988, 1983

Defining the problem

Your friend Robert Peters has asked you to write a program that will calculate the interest he must pay on the unpaid balance of his loan. Since his first payment is due in August, he is interested in determining how much interest he will have to pay during the remainder of the current year. Robert's loan is for $50,000, the interest rate is 9.75 percent, and his payments are $500 per month.

When a problem is being defined, it is important to determine the objectives for the program, the **specifications** regarding the type of output required, the source of the data to be entered as input, and the type of **controls** that are needed. Controls are techniques used to determine the validity of the input and output.

A programmer cannot design or code a program unless the specifications are clearly defined. Some of the specifications involve routine items such as what information is to be printed on the report, whether the report is to be single- or double-spaced, and what totals are required. In other cases, major decisions may need to be made. For example, is an **online system** that utilizes remotely located terminals being designed, or is the procedure being designed part of a **batch application.** In online systems, transactions are entered from terminals when and where they occur. Terminals can also be used to retrieve information from online files. In a batch system, units of data are accumulated and then processed all at once. For instance, all sales or payroll data for a given period of time is accumulated and then processed at one time.

O/I needs and formats

OUTPUT The output requirements are determined before deciding what input is needed or what calculations are required. In our example, the output is to be displayed on the VDT (CRT or screen). Robert has requested that the payment number, old balance, amount of interest, and new balance be displayed. He would also like to have displayed the total amount of interest paid from August through December.

In other programs, output might be written into a file stored on magnetic tape, magnetic disk, or on a laser-optical medium. In terms of the type of output created, programs are often classified as a file create, update, or maintenance program. Other programs may be classified as either detailed or **exception report** programs. An exception report lists only the deviations from normal, such as customers who have not used their accounts within the past two years or employees who have overtime exceeding 20 hours.

When files are to be created or reports printed, the user and analyst work together to determine the data to be stored or printed, the size of each of the fields, and the type of data that will be stored within each field.

INPUT After the output is determined, it is necessary to decide what input is needed to produce the desired results. In the example, the data required for the calculations will be included as constants in the initiation module.

In other programs, data to be outputted must have been obtained in one of the following ways:

1. Read from a **master** or from a **transaction file**. Master files contain updated data and data that is considered permanent. Usually the data stored in a master file is used in a number of different application

programs and over a long period of time. Records stored in transaction files contain current data that will be used for a limited number of applications and for a limited period of time.

2. Entered from a terminal or the operator's console.

3. Established within the program as a constant.

4. Calculated by the program.

5. Obtained from a table contained within the memory of the computer.

In our example, the information displayed will be calculated using constants established in the initialization module.

Once the programmer has determined what **variable data** is required, it is necessary to determine what medium should be used for entering the data into the system. Variable data changes from job to job or from processing cycle to processing cycle. The programmer must determine how the data should be entered and what type of controls should be built into the system to establish its validity.

In many application programs, the majority of the data to be processed or outputted is obtained from files. For example, in calculating the payroll most of the required data is entered from the payroll master file and a limited amount of data is entered from the payroll transaction file. In development of a system such as payroll, it is important that the analyst and programmer determine what should be retained in the master file so that the desired reports can be produced and, when needed, information can be retrieved and displayed.

Major tasks and modules needed

Although it is necessary to determine what major tasks are to be completed and what modules are required, experienced programmers may complete this step only in their thought process. Programmers with less experience will find it beneficial to make a list of the major tasks required and then determine what modules are needed.

In our example, you as the programmer would determine that there will be the main control module (this is a must for all structured programs). In addition there will be the initialization, process-loan-data, and termination modules. Since we wish to calculate the interest for each of five months, the process-loan-data module must be executed five times and will invoke the two supporting modules. The first module invoked will perform the necessary calculations and the second will display the results of the calculations. Control will remain within process loan-data for five cycles—until the data for August through December is processed. Keep in mind that the calculations and displaying of the output could be done within the process-loan-data module. However, these are distinct functions—calculate output and display the output—and are therefore separate modules. Since the display module contains only one statement, another programmer might have included the display statement within the process-loan-data module.

Although guidelines exist for the development of structured programs, common sense must also be used. For example, if only one or two calculations are required, it may be unnecessary to create a separate module to accomplish the required task.

© SRA 1988, 1983

Figure 1–8   Hierarchy chart for the loan program.

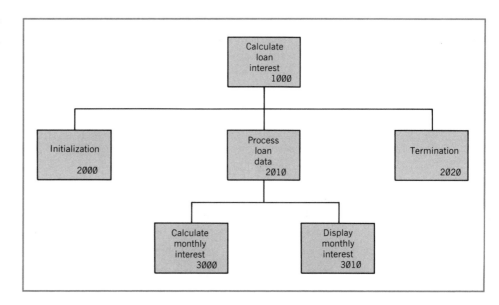

Have you written another similar program?

In our example, the answer to "Have you written another similar program?" is probably "No." However, in many cases you will find that a program falls into one of the categories mentioned earlier, and you may have developed one very similar to the one you must now design. In that case, you should study the program similar to the one you wish to develop, to determine similarities and differences. Many modules developed for an early program may appropriately be incorporated into the design of subsequent programs.

Developing a hierarchy chart

Figure 1–8 illustrates the hierarchy chart that would be needed for the loan program being developed. Since this problem is simple, our first draft will also be the one included in the final documentation. However, in developing more complex programs it may be necessary to revise the original hierarchy chart. The original chart cannot be developed until the scope of the problem and the tasks needed to accomplish the objectives are determined. A hierarchy chart (or VTOC) is a visual table of contents for a program; relatively few guidelines pertain to its development. The guidelines that do apply are:

1. There will never be more than one main control module that governs the execution of its subordinates.
2. The names and/or numbers used on the chart will also be used in the individual logic plan that supports each module and in the internal documentation for the program.
3. A hierarchy chart usually has from three to five levels. It is seldom necessary to have modules above the 5000 level. Before placing a subordinate module under the module it is invoked by, ask the questions, "Must the commands within the subordinate module be executed in order for the calling module to accomplish its assigned tasks?" Unless the answer is yes, the module should not be listed under the one identified as the calling module.

4. The span of control for a single module is usually limited to seven or fewer modules. In Figure 1–7 you can see that the main module controls three modules and the process-loan-data module controls two.

Some shops that totally support structured design and programming have software that will create the final hierarchy chart from the application program. For a complex program the chart may contain a large number of modules. However, if a top-down approach is used for programming and testing, the entire program is no more complex than the development and testing of a single module.

USING MEANINGFUL NAMES   Using meaningful names for data, files, and modules reduces the amount of internal documentation that is required. Module names should usually consist of an action verb, an adjective, and a noun. The following are good examples of well-constructed module names:

VERB	ADJECTIVE	NOUN
READ	CUSTOMER	RECORD
DISPLAY	CUSTOMER	RECORD
PRINT	DETAIL	LINE
PRINT	REPORT	HEADINGS
READ	SALES	RECORD

In constructing names it is sometimes helpful to ask, "What major task will be completed when the commands within the module are executed?" If the major task completed within the module is to read a sales record, the name READ SALES RECORD will add to the reader's understanding of what the module will accomplish.

THE 2000 LEVEL MODULES   The majority of the programs that will be described within the text have three 2000-level modules. Although it may seem to contradict the discussion regarding the construction of meaningful names, within this text the 2000-level module will always be referred to as *initialization* and the 2020-level module will be referred to as *termination*. The rationale for this decision is:

1. The INITIALIZATION module contains the code needed to get the program started. The tasks within the module will only be executed one time—at the beginning of the program. Also, the module performs more than one major function and the tasks closely related to that particular function. Another name that might have been used is LET'S GET STARTED or GETTING READY TO PROCESS DATA.

2. The code needed to wrapup or terminate a job is included in, or invoked by, the TERMINATION module. Commands within the module might invoke the routine that prints the report totals, displays a statement such as "All data has been processed," and closes the files.

© SRA 1988, 1983

The 2010 module usually contains commands that will be executed as long as there is data to be processed. The 2010 module usually invokes several support modules and controls the processing of the input and the displaying or writing of the output. As long as there is data to be processed, the commands within the 2010 loop will be executed.

Developing a detailed logic plan for each module

Figure 1–9 illustrates a structured flowchart that is one type of detailed logic plan. A detailed logic plan should be:

1. Related to the hierarchy by using the same module names and numbers.
2. As generic as possible and not tied to a given programming language.
3. Developed using meaningful names that help the reader understand what will occur during the execution of the program.
4. Nontechnical. Technical terms and jargon should be avoided and clear, concise language used in the development of the logic plan.
5. Developed by following the rules and guidelines pertaining to the technique being used.
6. Complete. It is very important that all details be included in the plan.

As you review Figure 1–9, determine if the basic guidelines listed for the development of a logic plan have been followed. However, do not be concerned about the rules that were followed (Item 5 on the list) in the development of the flowchart. These rules will be covered in the next chapter along with a more complete explanation of the symbols used in constructing a flowchart.

A *rectangle with a line across the top* is called the *predetermined process symbol* and is used to indicate that the module specified will have its own detailed flowchart. The hexagon is called the *preparation symbol* and is used for activities that are sometimes referred to as "housekeeping." In the illustration, the preparation symbol is used to establish the value of the constants and work fields. A *diamond* is used to represent a *decision point* in the program where one of two possible paths will be followed.

Once the detailed logic plan is created for a module, the hierarchy chart should be reviewed and may have to be modified. If a module contains several major tasks, the module should probably be further divided into individual modules that each perform one major function and the tasks closely related to the function.

If a complete, accurate logic plan is available, a maintenance programmer can quickly determine how the data is being processed and make any changes that are required. Also, auditors and others not skilled in the development of computerized systems and programs can determine what is occurring. Since the logic for each module is developed individually, when a program is modified it is usually only necessary to revise the documentation for one or two modules.

Within well-run computer information service departments, one policy usually enforced states, "When a program is modified, the new version cannot be put into production (considered operational) until the documentation has been updated and the new version of the program completely tested."

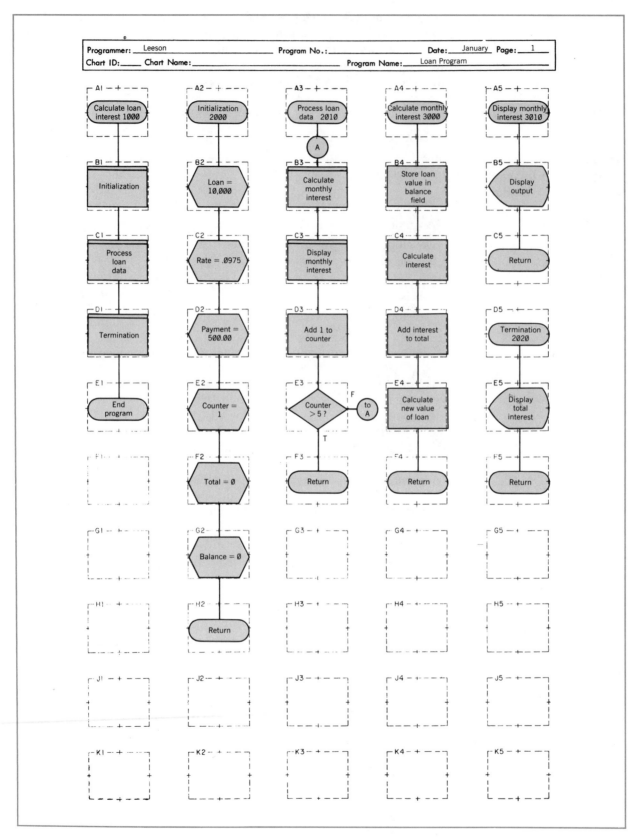

Figure 1-9   Structured flowchart for the loan program

Test the design

After the logic plan has been developed, the plan must be tested. A **walk-through** should be conducted to determine whether the plan will work or whether there are omissions or logical errors. In a walkthrough, the programmer plays computer. In our example the program is mentally executed as if the original values were established in the initialization module, the calculations made in the calculations module, and the output displayed for each month. You should also determine that the process-loan-data module is executed the correct number of times and that the total amount of interest paid will be displayed.

If the programmer carefully walks through the logic, errors and omissions can be detected. In installations where team programming is supported, one or more other programmers will participate in the walkthrough. The programmer who developed the logic plan supplies each team member with the objectives, specifications, file layouts, report layouts, hierarchy chart, and detailed logic plan. The team members are to look for omissions, logical errors, or ways in which the program can be simplified.

The suggestions made should be *constructive* and considered as such by the programmer. The members of the project team should not be in positions that require them to evaluate the programmer making the presentation. A team walkthrough *is not an evaluation of the programmer* but a technique used to detect errors and improve the quality of the program. Errors detected at this point are easy and inexpensive to correct. Errors detected later are far more costly and time-consuming to correct.

In walking through the logic, the team members start with the assumption they will find errors. When presenting the logic verbally, the programmer may detect his or her own errors. The other members of the team are more likely to find the errors since they can study the logic plan more objectively and do not have preconceived ideas about how the program will execute. The programmer or project leader should evaluate each suggestion to determine whether it should be incorporated into the design.

Code the program

The logic plan is now translated into the programming language to be used. While the source statements written for most programming languages can be entered in a free format, guidelines exist in most successful computer service departments that pertain to how source code is to be written. The purpose of the guidelines is to achieve uniformity and to make the code easier to write, understand, and maintain.

Well-formatted code

```
100  IF HOURS > 40  THEN
          OVERTIME = (HOURS - 40) * RATE * 1.5
     ELSE
          OVERTIME = 0
```

Unformatted Code

```
100  IF HOURS > 40  THEN OVERTIME=(HOURS - 40) * 1.5 ELSE
          OVERTIME = 0
```

Although both of the statements illustrated will produce valid results, the first example is easier to read and comprehend than the second. In more complex examples, unless code is formatted it can be difficult to read and understand. Often guidelines indicate that the statements to be executed when a condition is true should be separated from those to be executed when the condition is false.

Walk through the code

Usually a terminal is used to enter the source code recorded on a coding form into the computer. Once a clean listing—one without clerical and syntactical errors—is obtained, a walkthrough should be conducted. Most **compilers** or interpreters catch clerical errors such as the incorrect spelling of a field or file name. However, a compiler or interpreter cannot detect logical errors such as setting an indicator to the wrong value or the omission of source code.

In a code walkthrough, the programmer or review team evaluates the code to determine the answers to the following questions:

1. Does the source code follow the logic plan?
2. Is all the required code present?
3. Are there any unnecessary statements?
4. Are indicators, totals, and constants initially set to the correct value?
5. Do the reports and output files contain all the required information?
6. Is all the data required for the calculation statements available?
7. Is the program's internal documentation clearly stated, and is enough detail provided?
8. If the program is interactive, are additional "help screens" needed?

Test the program

Before a program can be tested, test data that effectively tests all routines must be developed. Since the data for our loan illustration was preset in the initialization module and the output displayed on the VDT, the only way to test the program is to make the same calculations as will be executed by the computer. The results of your calculations will then be compared to the output displayed on the VDT.

Documentation

Programs should be both internally and externally documented. Internal documentation includes a brief overview of the program and a brief explanation of the purpose of each module. External documentation includes a history of the project, a definition of the program, program specifications, file and report layouts, hierarchy chart, the logic plan, source listings, detailed information on how the program was tested, directions for executing the program, and an evaluation of the program.

Management, auditors, users, programmers, and operations personnel each use documentation in different ways. Management and auditors need to know what occurs when various programs are executed. Clients need to know what occurs when data is entered into the system, what error messages might be generated, and what will occur when an input error is detected. Programmers

© SRA 1988, 1983

assigned to maintaining a program must understand the logic plan and how data is entered, processed, and outputted.

For batch jobs initiated by operations personnel instructions for loading the program, readying the I/O devices, entering the data, responding to error messages, and determining if the job executed correctly must be provided. When jobs are initiated from terminals by users, help screens must be incorporated into the design of the programs. Until the terminal operator becomes familiar with the program, the help screens will provide the necessary instructions for the execution of the program.

In the loan illustration, the majority of the documentation was completed during the step-by-step development of the problem. Some types of documentation, such as file and print layouts, are not required in our example and are therefore not illustrated.

Evaluate the program

The final step in the development of an application program is to determine if the objectives specified for the program are achieved. In our example, did Robert get the information he needed?

When an entire system, such as payroll or sales, is designed and implemented, an initial evaluation will be made as soon as each program is operational. Many analysts or project leaders will ask for an additional evaluation after the program has been operational for five or six months. Sometimes users will request that additional features be incorporated into the system or into an individual program. Or program modifications are needed due to changes in an organization's policies or in laws that have a direct impact on how an organization's data must be processed.

If well-designed, modular programs were developed, modifications are easy to design, code, test, and document.

CHECKPOINT QUESTIONS

15. Why should the user be directly involved in defining the problem?
16. Why are the output needs and formats determined prior to deciding what input is needed?
17. How does a programmer determine what modules will be needed?
18. Why can a hierarchy chart also be referred to as a VTOC?
19. How is the hierarchy chart related to the detailed logic plan and to the source code?
20. Why should nontechnical language be used in developing a detailed logic plan?
21. If a team walkthrough is conducted, should the programmer consider the program being reviewed as his or her own creation?
22. Why have guidelines been developed regarding how code should be formatted?
23. In the loan example, how is the program tested?
24. If a program is documented internally, why is it necessary to also provide external documentation?
25. Would operations personnel and programmers require the same type of documentation?

DID YOU ANSWER THE QUESTION CORRECTLY?

Remember in the beginning of the chapter you were asked what you would do if your friend requested you to write a program. You should have answered you would have worked with your friend to determine the objectives and specifications for the program. Next you would determine the precise output needed, the data to be entered as input, and the major tasks required to provide valid output. After determining what modules are needed, you would develop a hierarchy chart. For each module a detailed logic plan will be developed. After the logic plan is checked for validity, source code will be written and entered into the computer. After the program is tested, the documentation will be put into final form and the program will be evaluated to determine if its objectives were achieved.

SUMMARY

- Designing and developing good software is a team effort that involves users, analysts, and programmers.

- Although programmers communicate and work with the analysts and users during the development of a system or program, programmers are responsible for:

    Developing the hierarchy chart.

    Developing detailed logic plans.

    Writing and entering the source code.

    Testing programs.

    Documenting programs.

- Programs are usually tested using:

    Only good data.

    Invalid data.

    No data.

- Programs should be internally and externally documented. Some internal documentation will only be displayed when the program is listed, although other internal documentation provides help screens for the terminal operator.

- Due to the rapid changes in hardware, software, and the times and places data is entered, programming standards and guidelines were not developed until management became concerned about several factors:

    1. the quality of the software.

    2. the lack of programmer productivity.

    3. the high cost of modifying programs.

- In some installations, the following problems still exist:

    Design and programming standards aren't available.

    The cost of developing and maintaining programs is excessive.

    Systems and programs are poorly designed.

    The productivity of programmers is too low.

    Projects are late and over budget.

    Programs placed into production still contain errors.

© SRA 1988, 1983

- Structured programs are designed and developed using guidelines that emphasize:

     Each organization should develop its own detailed standards for designing, coding, testing, and documenting programs. The standards and procedures must be followed by its analysts and programmers.

     Top-down design, programming, and testing.

     Modularity: each major function should have its own module.

     Single entry, single exit to or from any module.

     Use of the sequence, selection, and iteration control structures.

     The use of internal indicators.

     Limited and careful use of GO TO statements.

     The development of complete objectives and specifications before developing the hierarchy chart or detailed logic plan.

     Simplicity of design and readability of both the logic plans and source code.

     Complete testing, documentation, and evaluation of systems and programs.

- Design and code walkthroughs should be conducted in order to detect errors or omissions and to improve the quality of the program. In a team review, additional ideas are brought into the project. The constructive suggestions of the team members should be evaluated by the programmer to determine if the design and code should be changed to include the changes.

- There should be ongoing evaluation of systems and programs to determine what modifications are needed.

DISCUSSION QUESTIONS

1. What are the differences between a transaction-processing and a batch program?

2. Although the design and development of programs are a team effort, what tasks are specifically assigned to a programmer?

3. When and why were design and programming standards developed?

4. Were structured design and programming standards or guidelines developed by any one individual? Do all organizations follow the same standards?

5. Why is it considered productive to use a top-down approach to developing and writing programs?

6. Why should there be single entry and single exit for each module?

7. If invoking a module causes control to go to a given module and then return to the statement following the one that invoked (or called) the module, why is this approach better than using GO TO statements?

8. What is an indicator?

9. If you were given a source listing of a program, what criteria should you use to evaluate the program?

10. What evidence is there to support the concepts incorporated into the guidelines and standards used for developing structured programs?

11. What steps should be followed in designing and implementing a program?
12. Why is it important that the developing and implementing of systems and programs be considered a team effort?

KEY WORDS

abort
analyst
application program
BASICA
batch application
compiler
controls
conventions
debugged
ENIAC
error routine
exception report
flowchart
hardware
hierarchy chart
indicator
infinite loop
interpreter
master file
module
online system

operating systems
operational
print layout
procedure
pseudocode
record layout
source code
specification
standard
structured design
structured programming
syntactical errors
top-down programming
transaction file
transaction-processing system
variable data
Visual Display Terminal (VDT)
Visual Table Of Contents (VTOC)
walkthrough

PROJECTS

Usually three types of projects are included at the end of each chapter.

1. Exercises. New concepts presented in the current chapter will be used in completing exercises that do not require the development of a complete logic plan.
2. Problems. From the specifications provided, a hierarchy chart and a logic plan will be developed. In some cases, a program developed in a previous chapter will be modified.
3. Interactive exercises. Programs are provided that let you see what occurs when the examples and concepts used as illustration are programmed. These exercises will help you to visualize what actually occurs.

EXERCISE 1–1

A friend of yours runs a store that gives a discount of either 15, 18, or 22 percent, depending on the customer's classification code. The digits 1, 2, and 3 are used to represent the classification codes. Customers with a 1 classification code pay sales taxes whereas customers in the other two classifications do not. Your friend wants the VDT to display the following information pertaining to each sale:

Price of the Product	XXX.XX
Discount	XXX.XX
Discounted price	XXX.XX
Sales tax	XXX.XX
Total price	XXX.XX

In the example Xs are used to indicate the field size. Two digits will be displayed to the right of the decimal point.

Although all sales are cash sales, each customer has a plastic identification card to indicate his or her discount classification. The price of the product and the customer's discount code are keyed in by the sales person. A personal computer is dedicated to running this one program. At the end of the day totals are to be displayed for gross sales, discounts given, net sales, sales tax, and cash collected.

After the above objectives and specifications were determined, the tasks that must be completed were determined and then grouped into modules. The hierarchy chart illustrated in Figure 1–10 was then developed. You will note that the enter-sales-data module is executed first by the initialization module and later by process sales records. This is done so that the first time control passes to the process-sales-record module, the input required to make the calculations is available. In Chapter 3 the advantage of using this technique for obtaining the first record of data will be explained in more detail.

Directions:

Based on the description of the task or the characteristic described, indicate what module contains the code to accomplish the task described. Place the module's number, as shown on the hierarchy chart in Figure 1–10, in the space provided. In a few cases, more than one number is required.

_____ 1. Totals are displayed after all daily sales are entered and processed.

_____ 2. The module invoked by two different modules.

_____ 3. The final total fields are established and set to 0.

_____ 4. The module that uses selection in order to determine which commands will be executed.

_____ 5. The major module that consists of a loop. Control remains within the loop as long as there is more data to be entered.

_____ 6. The major module that controls the execution of initialization, process sales records, and termination.

_____ 7. The discount is determined.

Figure 1–10 Hierarchy chart for the cash sales program.

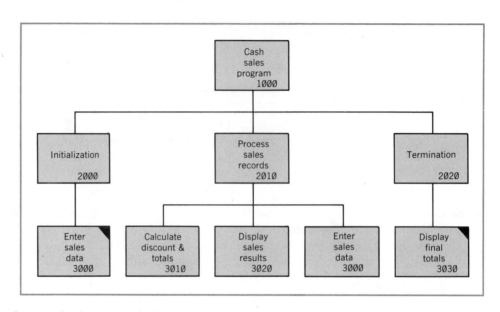

8. The module that might have invoked a help screen module that would describe what the program does, what data is to be entered, and how the data is to be entered.

9. An indicator used to control the process-sales-records module is given the value of Y. In which module is the indicator given the value of Y?

10. The modules that have as their span of control three modules.

11. The module where the control of the program returns after the commands within the initialization module are executed.

12. The individual amounts are added to the final totals.

13. The code within which modules is only executed once each time the program is run.

14. The module that contains more than one selection statement.

15. The module containing the code needed to wrap up the job.

EXERCISE 1–2

Using the information provided in Exercise 1–1, complete the following statements pertaining to the execution of the program:

1. The program is loaded into the memory of the computer for execution and the operator enters the command RUN. Control will enter the _____ module and then be transferred to the _____ module. From there the enter-sales-data module is invoked and the code executed. Control returns from enter sales data to initialization. After all code within initialization is executed control returns to the _____ module.

2. The next major module to be invoked is _____. Execution of the program is controlled by that module until _____. When the indicator (END-OF-FILE) used to control the loop has a value other than N, control of the program returns to the _____ module.

3. The last major module to be executed is _____. The last command executed in that module might be to display a statement such as PROGRAM COMPLETED SUCCESSFULLY or JOB FINISHED.

© SRA 1988, 1983

PROBLEM 1–1

You wish to design a program that will determine how many months it will take you to repay your car loan. You have borrowed $6,000 at an annual rate of 8 percent. Each month you make a $250 car payment which includes the amount to apply on the principal along with the interest. The only output that you want is the number of months required to repay the loan. However, you will need to calculate the amount of interest and the new balance for each month. As long as the new balance is greater than zero you will stay in the process-loan-records module.

In this program the amount of the loan, payments, and annual interest rate are established in the initialization module. Therefore, it is unnecessary to read records or enter input from a terminal.

1. List the tasks that will need to be performed by the computer in order to produce the required results. In determining what tasks need to be executed, pretend you are a computer and execute the calculations and decisions that are required in order to obtain the solution.
2. Figure 1–11 contains the hierarchy chart for determine-loan-months program. Below each module list the tasks that will be accomplished within the module.

INTERACTIVE EXERCISE 1–1

In the first exercise you will learn to use the menu program. Your instructor will give you instructions for loading the operating system and BASIC. However, before you load the menu program you should become familiar with the PC keyboard. Figure 1–12 illustrates the function keys, typewriter keyboard, and the numeric keypad that are found on IBM personal computer keyboards and IBM-look-alike keyboards.

To the left of the typewriter keyboard are the function keys. When the BASIC interpreter is being used, you may press one of the function keys rather than keying in a command. For example, pressing F2 will cause the program to be executed and is easier than keying in the RUN command.

F1   LIST displays the line of a program on the screen.

F2   RUN causes the program in memory to be executed.

F3   LOAD finds your program stored on a disk or diskette and stores it in the memory of the computer.

F4   SAVE stores the program currently in memory on a disk or diskette.

Figure 1–11 Hierarchy chart for the determine-loan-months program.

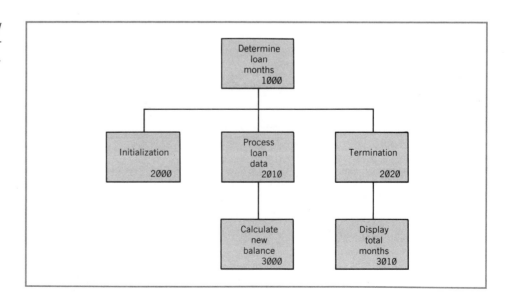

The Keyboard

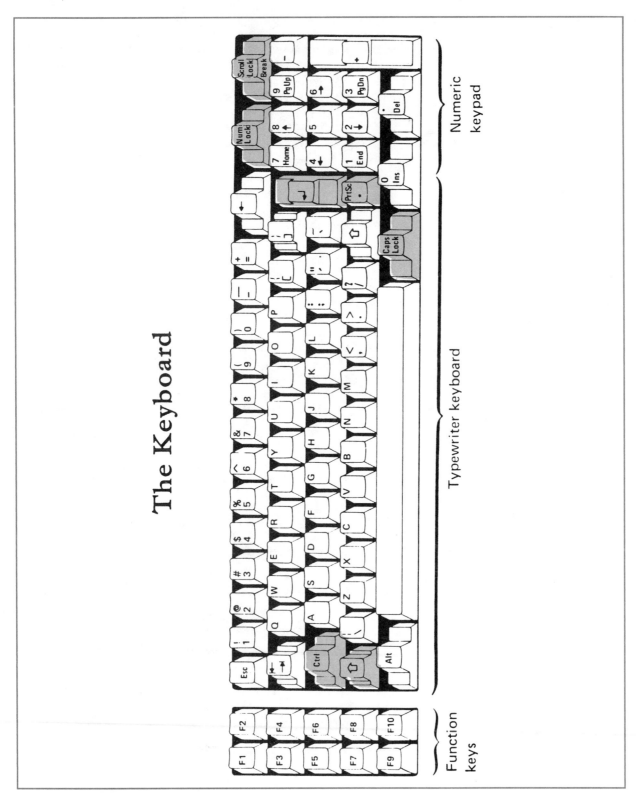

Numeric keypad

Typewriter keyboard

Function keys

Figure 1–12 IBM PC keyboard

© SRA 1988, 1983

The keys to the right and left of the alphabetic keyboard are used to perform a number of useful functions:

Ctrl   The CONTROL key is used with another key to perform a command or function. When CTRL and another key are to be pressed and held at the same time, it will be designated by a statement such as CTRL/BREAK.

SHIFT changes lowercase letters to capitals.

ENTER is used to transmit the data keyed into a buffer into the computer for processing. Until the ENTER key is depressed, you may correct the data keyed in by moving the cursor to the point of error and keying in the correct data.

Caps
Lock   When the key is pressed, letters will be entered in uppercase. Pressing the key again will return to the lowercase mode.

Num
Lock   When pressed the numeric keypad can be used to enter the digits from 0–9. When pressed again, the cursor control keys and PgUp (page up) and PgDn (page down) keys are activated.

PrtSc   When pressed with the shift key the data displayed on the screen will be printed. If pressed without the shift key, PRINT SCREEN will cause an * to be displayed or printed.

When CTRL is used with the following keys, the following functions will be executed:

CTRL/SCROLL LOCK/BREAK   This causes an interrupt to occur and the program being executed will stop running. The line number where the interrupt occurs is identified. When the program seems to be a loop and you wish to exit from the program, the CTRL and SCROLL LOCK/BREAK keys should be pressed and held at the same time.

CTRL/NUM LOCK   A pause occurs and the program being executed stops running. When any key is pressed, the program will continue to be executed.

More information regarding how other keys are used can be found in the system's Guide to Operations manual.

Directions:

1. After your computer has been booted and A> appears on your screen, key in **BASIC** (or **BASICA**) and then press **ENTER**.
2. Place the diskette that contains the menu program, application programs, and test data on Drive A.
3. In response to OK, press **F3** (the **LOAD** key). LOAD" will appear on your screen. Key in **MENU** and press the **ENTER** key.
4. In response to OK, either key in **RUN** and press **ENTER** or press **F2**. The main menu will be displayed.
5. In response to the message ENTER NUMBER OF DESIRED OPTION key in **5** and press **ENTER**. The help menu will be displayed. Use the numbers located on the top row of your keyboard.

6. In response to ENTER NUMBER OF DESIRED OPTION key in **1** and press **ENTER.**

7. When the information is displayed regarding the menu program, use the **shift** key (⇧) and the **PrtSc** key. The information displayed on the screen will be printed on your printer. When you answer the questions pertaining to the menu program you may need to refer to the printout. Press **ENTER** and return to the Help menu.

8. Key in **2,** press **ENTER,** and print the information displayed on the screen. Return to the **help menu** and display the information available by responding with a **3, 4,** and **5.** After all five screens have been printed, return to the main menu by keying in **6** and pressing the **ENTER** key.

Answer the following questions regarding the menu program.

1. What two menus are displayed?

   _____

2. What keys were pressed, and held, in order to print the data displayed on the screen?

   _____

3. When you indicate that you wish to run a program you will select one of the first four menus and then select the program you wish to run. When the program you wish to run is loaded into memory, is the menu program still in memory?

   _____

4. When will you reply with a Y to the question RETURN TO MAIN MENU?

   _____

5. When writing a BASIC program, for what purpose is REM used?

   _____

6. What is the difference between LIST and LLIST?

   _____

7. How do you end BASIC and return control of the computer to the operating system?

   _____

8. What must the operator do if a ? mark is displayed or a flashing cursor appears on the screen?

   _____

   _____

INTERACTIVE EXERCISE 1–2

In Exercise 1–2 the source code developed for the logic plan illustrated in Figure 1–9 will be executed. In order that you may see the control passing from one module to another, additional display statements (PRINT or INPUT statements in BASIC) have been added to the program.

Directions:

1. Load the operating system and then enter **BASIC** (or **BASICA**) in response to A>.
2. **Press F3.** When LOAD" is displayed key in **MENU** and press the **ENTER** key. Press **F2** to run the program.
3. When the main menu is displayed, select option 1. Key in **1** and then press the **ENTER** key.
4. When the menu for Chapters 1–4 is displayed, select option **1.** Key in **1** and then press the **ENTER** key.

© SRA 1988, 1983

5. Read the information displayed on your VDT. You will be asked to press the **ENTER** key so that the next command in sequence can be executed.

6. By observing the information displayed on your VDT, record the following information:

August interest	=	_____
September interest	=	_____
October interest	=	_____
November interest	=	_____
December interest	=	_____
Total interest for August–December	=	_____

7. How many times were the commands in the loop created within the process-loan-data module executed? _____

INTERACTIVE EXERCISE 1–3

The additional print and input statements have been removed from the program illustrated in Figure 1–9. The program stored on the program diskette as C1–2 now conforms to the specifications developed by working with Robert. Without the statements that show how the control of the program passes back and forth between the various modules, it executes much faster and only the output specified is displayed.

Directions:

1. While the main menu is displayed, select option **1**.
2. When menu 1 is displayed, select option **2**. Key in **2** and press **ENTER.**
3. After the program is executed DO NOT return to the main menu. You will modify the program and then run the modified version. Respond **N** to RETURN TO MAIN MENU?

Assume that you would like to modify the program so that the interest for the entire year would be calculated and printed on the printer rather than being displayed on the VDT. The field that controls the loop contained in process loan data is COUNTER. Answer the following questions and perform the tasks specified.

1. Study the flowchart on page 20 and determine what changes must be made in order to execute the program 12 times. Changes will be required in what two modules?

_____

_____

2. Make the necessary changes in the program by doing the following:
   a. Use the **LIST** command and display the contents of line 370. To do this enter:

   LIST 370 <ENTER>

   Usually when you are to press the **ENTER** key, instead of saying **"press ENTER"** the <ENTER> format is used.
   b. Move the cursor to the location of the data that must be changed and replace **6** with **13**.
   c. Key in the required change and use the <**ENTER**> key.

d. List statement 560 and change **PRINT** to **LPRINT.** If your computer has an insert key (lower right with INS printed on the key), move the cursor to the **P** in print, **press insert,** and key in an **L** followed by the use of the <**ENTER**> key. You have now changed the PRINT statement to LPRINT which causes the information to be printed rather than displayed.

e. Run the program. Either press **F2** or key in **RUN** and press **ENTER.**

f. If you do not obtain valid results, **LIST statements 370 and 560** to make certain the required changes were made.

3. If you were an analyst or programmer and were asked to make recommendations as to how the program could be improved, what suggestions would you make? The changes you will probably recommend can be done very easily, but it seemed wise to keep the illustration as simple as possible.

_____

_____

_____

_____

4. Return to the Main menu and Select option **6** which will return control of your computer to the operating system.

5. Remove the program diskette from the computer and return it to its proper storage location.

© SRA 1988, 1983

SELF-EVALUATION TEST 1

Name _____

Section Number: _____

I. Record the key term being defined in the space provided. When a small blank appears within the statement, it indicates where the term is needed.

_____ 1. A hierarchy chart which shows the relationship of the modules can also be called a _____.

_____ 2. A section of code or part of a program dedicated to one function. It usually contains 50 or fewer lines of code.

_____ 3. A person who works with users to develop systems, objectives, and specifications for programs and procedures.

_____ 4. A program consisting of modules, or building blocks, that was developed from the top down using the three basic control structures.

_____ 5. A user-defined nonprocessible language used to describe how data will be entered into the computer and processed.

_____ 6. A file consisting of records that contain current data. The file is used for a limited number of applications during a given fiscal period.

_____ 7. Routines built into a program to determine that the data and resulting output are valid.

_____ 8. A field used in controlling the logic of the program. Usually the programmer controls the contents of the field.

_____ 9. A term used to denote the review of either the design or the coding of a program.

_____ 10. A technique used to develop a program which permits the major modules to be tested before their supporting modules are fully developed.

_____ 11. Software that controls the execution of computer programs and manages the resources used by the computer. Routines are also included to verify that the correct disk or tape file is being used.

_____ 12. If a program is not completely tested and _____, during the execution of a production run it may abort.

_____ 13. Before a hierarchy chart or the logic of a program can be developed, the objectives and detailed _____ for the program must be developed.

_____ 14. Data that changes from job to job or from processing cycle to processing cycle. An example is the hours that an employee worked during a specified pay period.

_____ 15. One of the most frequently used sources of data, which contains updated and permanent records that may be used in many different programs.

II. Multiple Choice. Record the letter of the *best* answer in the space provided.

_____ 1. A syntactical error is a
   a. clerical error.
   b. mechanical error.
   c. one that violates a rule of the language being used.
   d. logical error.

_____ 2. After a detailed logic plan is developed,
   a. the source code is written.
   b. a walkthrough should be conducted to see if the plan is complete and if valid output will be produced.

    c. a walkthrough should be conducted to evaluate the programmer.

    d. the first draft of the hierarchy chart is constructed.

3. In testing most programs, the program is tested
   a. using only valid data.
   b. using only invalid data.
   c. using first valid data, then invalid data, and then using no data.
   d. by the user after the program is considered operational.

4. Documentation, such as record and print layouts, is
   a. developed after the program is operational.
   b. developed during the design phase.
   c. developed during the design phase and put into final form before the program is considered operational.
   d. used primarily by the users.

5. When programs were developed for the early computers, such as ENIAC,
   a. the person programming the computer had to provide far more detailed statements than are now required.
   b. standards regarding design and programming were not available.
   c. the term "design phase" was seldom, if ever, used.
   d. All of the above statements are true.
   e. None of the above statements is true.

6. A computer system consists of five elements including
   a. hardware, an operating system, application programs, data, and personnel.
   b. hardware, software, data, personnel, and procedures.
   c. the computer, I/O devices, an operating system, data, and procedures.
   d. hardware, software, data, personnel, and documentation.

7. In reference to a hierarchy chart, the main control module
   a. invokes supporting modules such as the read-records module.
   b. only invokes the first major module to be executed (initialization).
   c. has multiple entry and exit points.
   d. invokes each of the major modules such as initialization, process records, and termination.

8. When the upper right corner of a hierarchy chart symbol is shaded it means that
   a. a detailed logic plan is not provided for the module.
   b. the module will be invoked by more than one module.
   c. control will return from that module to a different module than the one by which it was invoked.
   d. the source code for the module has not been developed.

9. The date for the report is to be entered from a terminal and will remain constant during the entire program. The logic will be detailed in the
   a. initialization module.
   b. main-control module.
   c. process-records module.
   d. termination module.

10. The module that usually consists of a large loop that will continue until all the data is processed is often referred to as the
    a. main-control module.
    b. termination module.
    c. process-records module.
    d. initialization module.

11. A module
    a. has multiple entry and exit points.

© SRA 1988, 1983

    b. usually has more than 50 lines of code.

    c. performs several major tasks.

    d. All of the above answers are true.

    √ e. None of the above answers is true.

_____ 12. A field called END-OF-FILE was given a value of Y in the initialization module and will control the loop created in the process-records module. This field is often called

    a. an indicator.

    b. a switch.

    c. a flag.

    √ d. an indicator, a switch, or a flag. However, in this text *indicator* is the preferred term.

_____ 13. Logic of a program is executed using three control structures which are

    a. GO TO, sequence, and iteration.

    √ b. sequence, iteration, and selection.

    c. sequence, iteration, and GO TO.

    d. selection, GO TO, and IF statements.

_____ 14. Today there are fewer seminars and workshops conducted on structured design and programming than there were in the middle and late seventies because

    a. all installations now have guidelines and standards for developing structured programs.

    b. there is little proof that structured programs are easier to maintain than unstructured programs.

    √ c. there is a misconception that all programmers develop well-structured programs.

    d. today less time is spent in the design phase than was spent during during the sixties and early seventies.

_____ 15. The output requirements are determined

    a. after the input requirements.

    b. after the decisions regarding what files are to be used are made.

    √ c. before decisions regarding how and where input will be entered are made.

    d. after decisions about which calculations and controls are required are made.

_____ 16. In determining what tasks must be completed and which modules will be needed for a new payroll program, a programmer

    a. should not consider the other programs that have been developed as part of the payroll system, as this will influence his or her creativity.

    b. should refer to the hierarchy chart for the program.

    √ c. should refer to similar programs developed for the payroll system to determine if some of the modules may be used in the program being developed.

    d. should work independently and not consult with the analyst who developed the specifications or the user.

_____ 17. A detailed logic plan should be

    a. related to its hierarchy chart.

    b. generic.

    c. developed following the rules and guidelines established for the method being used.

    √ d. all of the above statements apply.

    e. none of the statements applies to the development of detailed logic plans for structured programs.

_____ 18. In walking through the logic, the team members

    √ a. start with the assumption they will find errors.

    b. evaluate both the program and the programmer.

    c. make recommendations that will always be included in the design.

    d. should keep in mind that the program is the creative work of the programmer and should not be concerned if the program is more complex than necessary.

_____ 19. In regard to structured design and programming, which statement is false?
    a. Structured programs are less expensive to maintain than unstructured programs.
    b. Structured programs are usually more readable and easier to follow than unstructured programs.
    c. Since more time is spent in the design phase, structured programs are more costly to develop and implement than unstructured programs.
    d. The guidelines for structured design and programming pertain to designing, coding, testing, and documenting of programs.

_____ 20. When programmers design and develop programs, they should consider
    a. the program as their own creation, as it is unique.
    b. the program as part of a team effort and rely on other team members for the detection of errors or omissions.
    c. the program as part of a team effort and make certain it complies with established standards, meets its stated objectives, produces valid output, and is well documented.
    d. the program successful as long as its objectives were met and valid output was produced.

III.   True or False. Record a T or F in the blank provided. For each false statement, indicate why the statement is false or make the changes needed to correct the statement.

_____ 1. An interpreter is a program that translates a BASIC statement into one or more commands that can be executed by the computer.

_____ 2. Programmers generally develop the program objectives and specifications and then take them to the user for approval.

_____ 3. Programmers are usually only responsible for developing the detailed logic, coding the program, and testing the program.

_____ 4. Less total time will usually be required to develop and implement a program if a detailed logic plan is developed prior to writing the source code.

_____ 5. In most of today's computer information services departments, each programmer is free to use any of the languages available on the department's computer for developing a computerized information retrieval system for management. This policy increases the overall productivity of the department.

_____ 6. If programmers develop and test their logic plan, they should still expect to find _bugs_ (or logical errors) in their programs.

_____ 7. Help screens are considered a form of internal documentation.

_____ 8. Programmers often spent 10 to 15 percent of their time completing internal and external documentation.

_____ 9. Programming could not be considered a profession until standards for the design and development of programs were established.

_____ 10. Because users are often anxious to use their new programs, a program should be considered operational as soon as the output appears to be valid.

_____ 11. When third-generation computers became available, their operating systems performed many of the tasks required to execute application programs that had previously been coded by a programmer.

_____ 12. Studies made in 1965 indicated that programmers were very productive and most programmers produced over 100 lines of debugged code a day.

_____ 13. Prior to the development of structured design and programming standards, more time was spent in designing than in coding programs.

_____ 14. All of the concepts incorporated into structured design and programming were introduced by Corrado Böhm and Giuseppe Jacopini.

© SRA 1988, 1983

_____ 15. Iteration (the creation of loops) and selection are considered extremely powerful programming control structures.

_____ 16. A GO TO statement should never be used unless it transfers control of the program outside the module in which the statement is used.

_____ 17. Within the program being coded, programmers can use any names they wish. For example, a statement such as PAY = HOURS * Z + O * Z * 2 would be considered good code.

_____ 18. In many applications the majority of the data entered and processed is stored in master files.

_____ 19. Since each module has its own logic plan and source code, it is difficult to relate the logic plan and the code to the hierarchy chart.

_____ 20. A detailed logic plan should be developed using the technical terms related to the language that will be used to code the program.

TOOLS USED BY ANALYSTS AND PROGRAMMERS

2

After reading the chapter and completing the learning activities, you will be able to:

- Identify the major characteristics of HIPO diagrams.

- Identify the characteristics of an acceptable method of developing and illustrating a detailed logic plan.

- List the decisions that should be made before developing a hierarchy chart.

- Identify the meaning of the key words used in writing pseudocode.

- Explain the purpose of each of the ANSI flowcharting symbols.

- Identify the four symbols used to develop a Nassi-Shneiderman chart.

- Explain how universals, executables, and decisions are used in developing a Warnier-Orr diagram.

- When given specifications for a program similar to the cash sales example, follow the guidelines provided and develop logic plans using pseudocode, structured flowcharts, Nassi-Shneiderman charts, and Warnier-Orr diagrams.

Analysts and programmers who work with users to develop systems and programs must be familiar with the hardware and software used for developing and running application programs. When dealing with a new computer, the computer information services staff usually receives inservice training to learn its capabilities. Its memory capability, operating system, peripheral equipment supported and obtained, the online information storage capacity, and the number of online terminals supported all must be considered when designing systems and programs.

Since many of the capabilities of the computer are derived from its operating system, the operating system or systems used determine the type of applications that can be developed. The operating system software controls the execution of application programs and allocates the system's resources. Although only a small portion of a typical operating system resides within the real memory of the computer, complete programs and routines are stored online and can be retrieved, stored in memory, and executed.

Operating systems were originally designed to increase the productivity of the computer, to improve communication between operators and the computer, and to decrease the amount of detailed instructions needed to enter and process data and to output information. When managers and other users became directly involved with microcomputers, the need for *user friendly* operating systems and application software became obvious.

When standards became available for designing and writing structured programs, many programming languages that had been developed in the late fifties and early sixties (such as FORTRAN and BASIC) were changed so that programs could be written using only sequence, iteration, and selection. More statements became available for creating loops and selection statements were made more powerful.

As improvements were made in hardware, software, design standards, and programming standards, many organizations and individuals attempted to develop new methods for illustrating the flow of data and the logic used in executing individual programs. When a new method was developed, seminars and workshops followed to explain how it could be used to develop detailed logic plans. The supporters of a new technique described its advantages; programmers and analysts who did not support the new method described its disadvantages.

HIPO CHARTS

At one time many individuals felt that **HIPO (Hierarchy plus Input-Processing-Output)** diagrams developed by International Business Machines Corporation (IBM), would become the standard for the industry. Appendix I on pages 414–416 has an illustration of a HIPO template, a worksheet, and a HIPO diagram.

Both the file requirements and the fields needed for input and output must be determined before a HIPO can be constructed. This requirement, to analyze completely the input and output needed, is considered one of the major advantages of using HIPO diagrams to illustrate the logic of a program. Also, since each module has its own HIPO diagram, the diagrams are easy to maintain. Because HIPO diagrams do not graphically show the logic of a program or module, many people believe there are better ways to develop a logic plan. Therefore, HIPOs have not become the accepted standard for developing and maintaining detailed logic plans.

© SRA 1988, 1983

CHARACTERISTICS OF AN ACCEPTABLE METHOD FOR DEVELOPING A LOGIC PLAN

Although many different methods are used to develop logic plans, any acceptable method for constructing diagrams or charts must:

- be standardized.
- make the construction of a plan as easy as possible.
- make it easy for persons other than the plan's author to understand the logic of the program.
- provide a way of maintaining the plan's integrity.
- permit the development of the logic plan in a top-down manner. It must be possible to code and test the higher-level modules before the modules containing routine detail are completed.
- provide a means of including documentation that increases the reader's understanding of the program.
- provide for referencing the individual modules to the hierarchy chart and to the source code.

Unless the symbols and key words used in formulating a logic plan are standardized, persons other than the author may misunderstand what will occur when data is being processed. While flowcharting symbols have been standardized by **ANSI (American National Standards Institute),** other methods use key words and symbols that have become the accepted standard because of continued use.

If ANSI standards are not available for the method being used by a given department, a standards manual should be established to describe the development of logic plans. Key words and symbols used should be explained. If everyone within the department complies with these standards, logic plans will be easier to develop, understand, and maintain.

When a top-down approach is used, the major modules can be designed, coded, and tested before creating the modules which require routine details. For example, if the process-sales-records module invokes a print-detail-line module, a *stub* can be placed in the program in the location where the invoked module will be located. The stub might cause a statement such as "CONTROL HAS PASSED TO THE PRINT-DETAIL-LINE MODULE." to be printed. When the process-sales-records module is tested, the programmer can determine that all supporting modules will be executed in the correct sequence and under the right conditions. This technique of testing the major modules before completing the more detailed modules is referred to as **stub testing.** Later the stubs are replaced, one by one, with the detailed logic.

METHODS COVERED

In this chapter you will be introduced to the guidelines used to develop detailed logic plans using pseudocode, structured flowcharts, **Nassi-Shneiderman (N-S) charts,** and **Warnier/Orr diagrams.** The same example will be used as an illustration for each of the four methods presented. This will enable you to decide which method is the easiest for you to construct, understand, and maintain. You might also wish to consider which method provides the best graphic presentation of how the data will be processed.

As each method is discussed, the tools that can be used in constructing the diagram or chart will also be covered.

PROGRAM SPECIFICATIONS

The program to be used in the illustration is the cash sales program presented in Exercise 1–1 on pages 27–28. Before constructing a logic plan, the analyst and user would have made the following decisions:

OUTPUT: Displayed will be the price of the product, the discount, the discounted price, the sales tax, and the total amount to be paid by the customer. After all data is processed, final totals will be displayed.

INPUT: The sales representative will key in the price of the product and the customer's discount classification code.

CALCULATIONS: The discount allowed, discounted price of the product, sales tax, and total to be paid by the customer must be calculated. Final totals for each of the fields must also be computed. The following discount code is used in calculating the sales discount:

Code	Discount
1	15 percent
2	18 percent
3	22 percent

Customers with a 1 discount code pay 6 percent sales tax while customers with a 2 or 3 discount code do not pay sales tax.

VALIDATION: The sales representative must visually verify the input. If the input was keyed in incorrectly, it must be possible to rekey the data.

The modules illustrated in the hierarchy chart shown in Figure 2–1 will be used.

PSEUDOCODE

Pseudocode, also called structured English, is a user-defined, noncompilable shorthand used to express logic. Programmers can use pseudocode to express their thoughts in natural English. Their thought processes are not hindered by trying to comply with syntactical rules or trying to draw some type of chart.

Guidelines for writing pseudocode

For years, programmers have been using some form of pseudocode. Like other techniques for developing logic, pseudocode can be structured or unstructured. The following guidelines should be followed when pseudocode is used to develop structured logic plans.

1. A standardized form to identify the program, programmer, and module should be used. The form should also make it easy to format the pseudocode. Vertical lines are sometimes drawn on the form so that the statements will be indented properly.

2. Each operation and function should be on a separate line.

3. The functions may be expresed in English-language statements or by using formulas.

4. When IF/THEN/ELSE is used:
   a. An END IF is used for each IF. END IF may be written as ENDIF.
   b. If statements are not required for the ELSE portion of an IF/THEN/

© SRA 1988, 1983

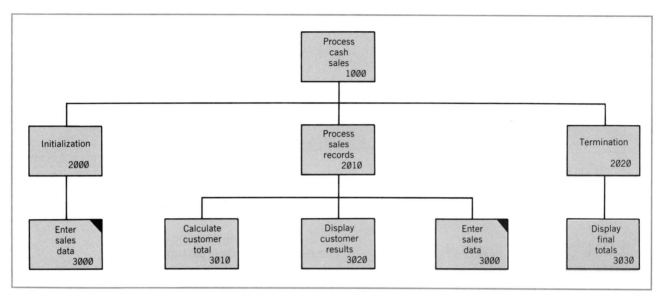

Figure 2–1   Hierarchy chart for the program used in the illustrations.

ELSE, NULL should be used to indicate there is no omission in the logic.

c. IF, ELSE, and ENDIF should all start in the same vertical column.

d. Use proper indentation to improve readability and clarity. The following illustration shows how a simple IF/THEN/ELSE statement should be written. Additional illustrations will be provided when more complex versions of IF statements are presented.

```
IF hours > 40 THEN
    over-time-pay = (hours - 40) * rate * 2.0
ELSE
    over-time-pay = 0
ENDIF
```

5. **Key words,** such as those defined in Figure 2–2, should be written in capital letters. The key words illustrated are used by most individuals who write pseudocode or develop other types of logic plans such as HIPO charts.

6. Follow the basic guidelines developed for writing structured programs:
   a. Single entry, single exit for each module or program.
   b. Top-down control.
   c. Develop logic by using:
       (1) Iteration—expressed in pseudocode by using DO WHILE, DO UNTIL, or PERFORM/UNTIL.
       (2) Selection—expressed by using versions of IF/THEN/ELSE.
       (3) Sequence—top-to-bottom flow of control.
   d. A GO TO should only transfer control of the program to a point within the module in which it is used. If at all possible, GO TO statements should be avoided.
   e. Division of the program should be in functional modules. Each module performs only one major function and the tasks closely related to the function.
   f. Provide enough documentation so that the reader understands what will occur in each module. In the illustration provided in Figure 2–3

KEY WORDS USED IN WRITING PSEUDOCODE

Key Word and Example	**Explanation**
ACCEPT ACCEPT date-in	Data is entered from the console or a terminal.
CALL CALL fedtax	A **subroutine** is retrieved from an online library.
DISPLAY DISPLAY 'normal job ending'	A message or information is to be displayed on a VDT.
DO DO 3000-Enter-data	An internal subroutine, or module, is executed and control returns to the statement following the DO.

DO
    DO (counter = 1 to 100)
        any required code
    END DO
	A count-controlled loop is established. The statements within the loop will be executed 100 times.

DO-UNTIL
    DO-UNTIL (end-of-file = Y)
        any required code
    END DO
	A loop is created that will be executed until the condition specified is met.

DO-WHILE
    DO-WHILE (end-of-file = N)
        any required code
    END DO
	A loop is created that will be executed as long as the condition specified is true.

IF/THEN/ELSE
    IF hours > 0 THEN
        pay = hours * rate
    ELSE
        pay = 0
    ENDIF
	If the condition(s) expressed is true, the statements under the IF portion of the code will be executed. IF the statement is false, the statements under ELSE will be executed.

PERFORM PERFORM 2020-termination	Control branches to the point specified and then returns to the statement following perform.

PERFORM/UNTIL
    PERFORM 2010-process-records
        UNTIL
            end-of-data = Y
	Control branches to the module specified. A loop is created and the statements within the module will be executed until the condition specified is met.

PRINT PRINT detail line	Print is used to specify the printing of a heading, detail, or total line.
READ READ disk-file	A record is read from a file.
REWRITE REWRITE student master record	An updated record is written into a file. The record is read, updated, and is then rewritten into the same location from which it was read.
WRITE WRITE student record	A record is written into a file. The file may be stored on hard disk, a diskette, or on tape.

Figure 2–2   Key words used in writing pseudocode.

© SRA 1988, 1983

Program Name: <u>Process cash sales</u> Module Name and Number: 1000-Main control 2000-Initialization <u>2010-Process sales records</u>

Programmer: <u>Leeson</u> Date Developed: <u>January</u> Revised: _____ Page <u>1</u> Of <u>3</u>

```
*1000-Process-cash-sales module. Main control module.
PERFORM 2000-Initialization
PERFORM 2020-Process-sales-records
    UNTIL
        end-of-data  = Y
PERFORM 2030-Termination
END 1000-Cash sales


*2000-Initialization.   Establish indicators and fields used for input and
                        calculation.
end-of-data = N
valid-input = N
discount code, price, discount, net-price, sales-tax, total-due, tprice,
tdiscount, tnet-price, tsales-tax, ttotal-due = 0
PERFORM 3000-Enter-data
    UNTIL
        valid-input = Y
END 2000-Initialization



*2020 Process-sales-records module.   Code within the loop is executed until the
      end-of-data field contains Y.
PERFORM 3010-Calculations
PERFORM 3020-Display-results
valid-input = N
DISPLAY 'End of data?'
INPUT end-of-data
IF end-of-data = N or end-of-data = n
    PERFORM 3000-Enter-data
        UNTIL
            valid-input = Y
ELSE
    NULL
ENDIF
END 2020-Process-sales-records module
```

Figure 2–3 Part 1 Pseudocode for the main control, initialization, and process-sales-records modules.

Program Name: <u>Process cash sales</u> Module Name and Number: <u>3010-Calculate customer total</u>

2000-Termination
3000-Enter sales data

Programmer: <u>Leeson</u> Date Developed: <u>January</u> Revised: _____ Page <u>2</u> Of <u>3</u>

```
*2030 Termination.          The display total module is invoked.
PERFORM 3030-Display-final-totals.
END 2030-Termination


*3000-Enter-sales-data.  Data is entered and visually verified.  Control
      remains within the  module until Y is entered in the valid-input field.
DISPLAY 'enter amount of sale and discount code'
INPUT price, discount-code
DISPLAY 'if data is correct, enter a Y'
INPUT valid-input
END 3000-Enter-sales-data


*3010-Calculate-customer-total.  The discount, net-price, sales-tax, total-
                                 due, and final totals are calculated.
IF discount-code = 1 THEN
    discount = price * .15
ELSE
    IF discount-code = 2 THEN
        discount = price * .18
    ELSE
        discount = price * .22
ENDIF
net-price = price - discount
IF discount-code = 1 THEN
    sales-tax = net-price * .06
ELSE
    sales-tax = 0
ENDIF
amount-due = net-price + sales-tax
total-price = total-price + price
total-discount = total-discount + discount
total-net-price = total-net-price + net-price
total-sales-tax = total-sales-tax + sales-tax
total-due = total-due + amount-due
END 3010-Calculate-customer-total module
```

Figure 2–3 Part 2   *Pseudocode for the termination, enter-sales-data, and calculate-customer-total modules.*

© SRA 1988, 1983

Program Name: ___Process cash sales___ Module Name and Number: 3020-Display customer results / 3020-Display final totals

Programmer: ___Leeson___ Date Developed: ___January___ Revised: _____Page __3__ Of __3__

*3020-Display-customers-results module.   The results of the calculations are displayed in a well-formatted screen.

clear screen

DISPLAY captions and price, discount, net-price, sales-tax, and amount-due

END 3020-Display-customer-results.

*3030-Display-final-totals module.   The screen is cleared and the captions and final totals are displayed.

clear screen

DISPLAY captions and final totals.

END 3030-Display-final-totals module

Figure 2–3 Part 3   Pseudocode for the display-customer-results and display-final-totals modules.

an * is used to denote the documentation at the beginning of each module.

g. Mark the end of each module by using END followed by the number and name of the module.

Advantages and disadvantages of pseudocode

Developing logic using pseudocode is faster than any other method. The guidelines are easy to remember and apply. If the standard key words and the accepted guidelines are followed, the logic of the program being illustrated is easy to understand. If word processing is used to develop the pseudocode, additions, deletions, and modifications to the existing code are easy to make. However, programmers often write psuedocode hurriedly, using poor (if any) format. Then the pseudocode is difficult to follow and is unacceptable as documentation.

Pseudocode for the cash sales program

Figure 2–3 illustrates the pseudocode for the cash sales program. As you study the pseudocode you will note that two indicators are used. In the initialization module, the end-of-data indicator is given a value of N. At the end of each pass through process-sales-records module the sales representative will be asked, "End of data?" If the operator responds with an N, control remains within the process-sales-records module. Any other response will cause the control of the program to return to the main-control module. The 2030-termination module will be executed and the program will be ended.

The second indicator, valid-input, is used to control the execution of the 3000-enter-data module. Before the module is invoked, N is placed in the valid-input field. As long as valid-input contains an N, the commands within 3000-enter-sales-data will continue to be executed.

You will also observe that the pseudocode contains statements such as "DISPLAY captions and final totals." When the source code is written for the module, each line to be displayed will require a statement that provides the constant (such as PRICE OF THE PRODUCT) and the name of the field that contains the variable to be displayed (such as price). Since the programmer designed the screens before developing the pseudocode, it is not necessary to show each line that will be displayed.

In the illustration, the pseudocode for several modules is coded on one form. For ease of maintenance, each module should be coded on a separate sheet. If this suggestion is followed, updating the pseudocode included as part of the documentation for a program is much easier. Only the modules that must be changed will be rewritten.

CHECKPOINT QUESTIONS

1. What is a HIPO chart?

2. Are templates and special forms used in developing HIPO charts?

3. In looking over the illustration found in Appendix I, what similarities exist between the HIPO chart example and the pseudocode illustrated in Figure 2–3?

4. In evaluating a method or technique used to illustrate the logic of a program, what factors should be considered?

© SRA 1988, 1983

5. What is pseudocode?

6. What advantages and disadvantages are associated with using pseudocode?

7. Why are key words used in writing pseudocode?

8. In reference to the key words used in writing pseudocode, what is the difference between the following sets of words?
   a. ACCEPT and READ
   b. DO-WHILE and DO-UNTIL
   c. DO 3000-Enter-data and PERFORM 3000-enter-data
   d. WRITE and PRINT

9. What is a NULL else?

10. Why should a form be developed and used for writing pseudocode?

STRUCTURED FLOWCHARTS

Flowcharting is probably the oldest means of developing detailed logic plans. Since flowcharts are easier to construct if proper tools are used, programmers should use a **template,** such as the one illustrated in Figure 2–4, and flowcharting forms. An IBM **flowcharting worksheet** is illustrated in Figure 2–5. The actual forms are more than twice the size of the one illustrated.

Using a flowcharting worksheet helps ensure that proper identification will be recorded on each page. Note that the programmer completes the top of the form by providing his or her name, the program number, date, page number, chart ID, and program name.

Letters and numbers are used to identify the various boxes on the form. Horizontally, numbers are used; vertically, letters are used. When using the form, connectors can be eliminated by referring to the box number.

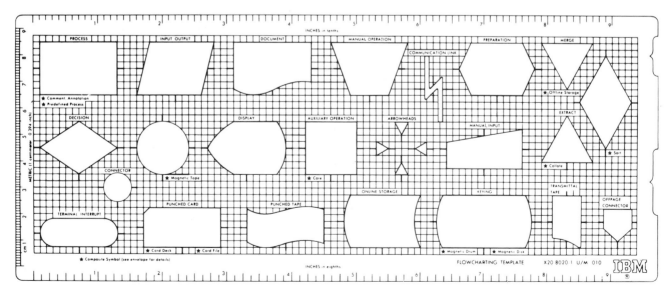

Figure 2–4   *IBM flowcharting template. (Courtesy of International Business Machines Corporation)*

Advantages and disadvantages of flowcharting

Flowcharting provides the best graphic representation of what occurs when data is processed. Well-constructed flowcharts can be understood by auditors, managers, users, analysts, and programmers. Since each module is usually developed on a separate flowchart worksheet, little maintenance is required to keep the charts up-to-date. Usually any modification in a program will influence only one or two modules. Although the logic plan for those modules should be changed, the remainder of the flowcharts need not be altered.

Some programmers and analysts think flowcharting is less efficient and more time-consuming than other types of logic development. Frequently when students take a language class, they may select whichever method they wish to develop a detailed logic plan. Often they elect flowcharts, which are especially useful for students first learning how to develop structured programs. However, as students become familiar with programming design, pseudocode becomes easier and programs are developed faster than when flowcharts are developed.

Guidelines for developing flowcharts

A flowchart should not be constructed until after the specifications for the program are determined. In addition, the following guidelines should be followed:

1. Before starting, make sure you:
   a. identify the required output.
   b. identify what data must be entered as input and what data is available in existing files.
   c. list any facts, formulas, and data relationships that apply to the procedures being flowcharted.
   d. list all information that must be calculated either as an intermediate result or as part of the output.
   e. list the procedures that must be used to validate the input and output.
   f. determine what modules will be needed and construct the first draft of the hierarchy chart.

2. Use a template and flowcharting worksheets. If other than a processing step is required, draw the appropriate symbol inside the box. Align the symbols by using the vertical and horizontal lines on the template. Although templates with different size symbols are available, use the same size symbols for the entire flowchart.

3. Always use the correct symbols to identify the tasks being performed. Figure 2–6 illustrates the standard ANSI symbols that should be used.

4. Within the symbols, keep the explanation clear and simple. Technical terms should be avoided. If the explanation is not clear, a comment annotation symbol can be used to provide additional information.

5. Formulas or a statement such as CALCULATE GROSS can be included within the processing symbol.

6. Flowlines should be drawn from one symbol to another.

7. Flowcharts are usually constructed from top to bottom and from left to right. An arrowhead on the flowline shows the flow direction that the logic will take.

© SRA 1988, 1983

8. Only one flowline should enter a symbol. However, more than one flowline may leave a symbol.

9. Use an **offpage connector** to show continuation to another page.

10. Label all branches and decision points by using either a connector or referring to a box number.

11. Develop the mainline logic first and then develop each supporting module.

12. Test your flowchart. Walk through it by using sample data. Make sure the data will be processed correctly. In selecting sample data, make certain all pathways of the flowchart are tested.

13. If in conducting a walkthrough a logic error or omission is detected, correct your flowchart and retest.

14. After the program is written, the coding can be cross-referenced with the flowcharting symbols by writing the line number or source statement number of the source code on the flowchart. For example, the line number for the calculation for gross pay might be 2050. The number, 2050, can be placed next to the block containing the statement CALCULATE GROSS PAY.

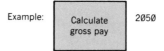

Example: Calculate gross pay   2050

Flowcharting the cash sales program

As you study the structured flowchart illustrated in Figure 2–7 for the cash sales program, note that the main-control module is identical to the ones developed for the illustrations used in Chapter 1. The annotation symbol is used to list the indicators, input and work fields, and the total fields that must be set to zero. Because screen layouts will be developed to display the information for each sale and the final totals, the display modules did not indicate the number of statements that would be required to format the screen and display the required information.

Unless there is a deviation from the normal top-to-bottom flow, arrow points may be omitted from the data flowlines. You might also note that letters or numbers are not used within connectors unless there are two of the same letter or number. For example, the enter-sales-data module on page 57 has a connector with an "A" at the top and a connector with "To A" at the bottom of the module. The second connector with an A indicates that a branch occurs that returns control to the commands located at the beginning of the module.

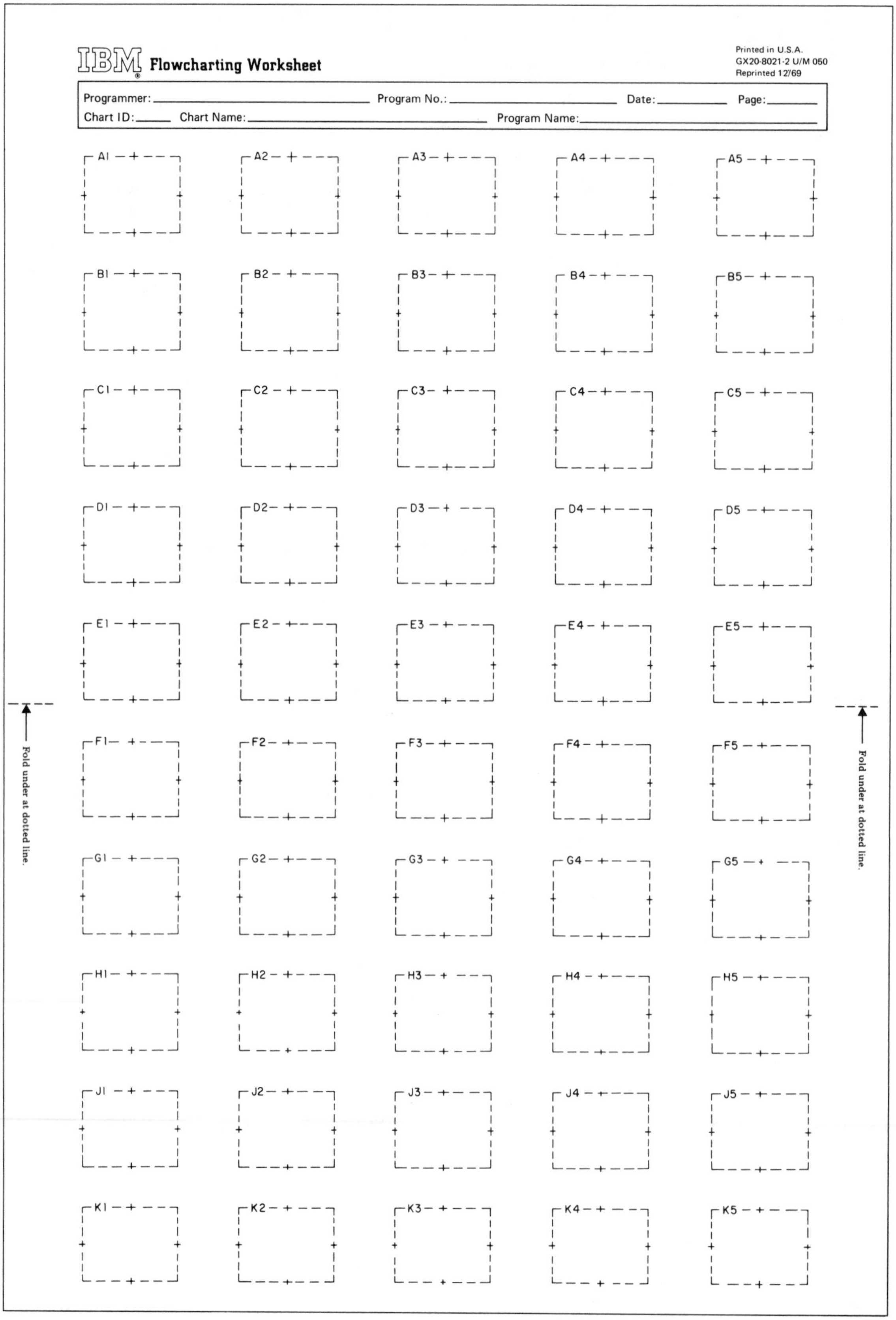

IBM Flowcharting Worksheet

Printed in U.S.A.
GX20-8021-2 U/M 050
Reprinted 12/69

Programmer: ______ Program No.: ______ Date: ______ Page: ______
Chart ID: ______ Chart Name: ______ Program Name: ______

A1 A2 A3 A4 A5
B1 B2 B3 B4 B5
C1 C2 C3 C4 C5
D1 D2 D3 D4 D5
E1 E2 E3 E4 E5
F1 F2 F3 F4 F5
G1 G2 G3 G4 G5
H1 H2 H3 H4 H5
J1 J2 J3 J4 J5
K1 K2 K3 K4 K5

Fold under at dotted line.

Fold under at dotted line.

Figure 2–5 *IBM flowcharting worksheet. (Courtesy of International Business Machines Corporation)*

© SRA 1988, 1983

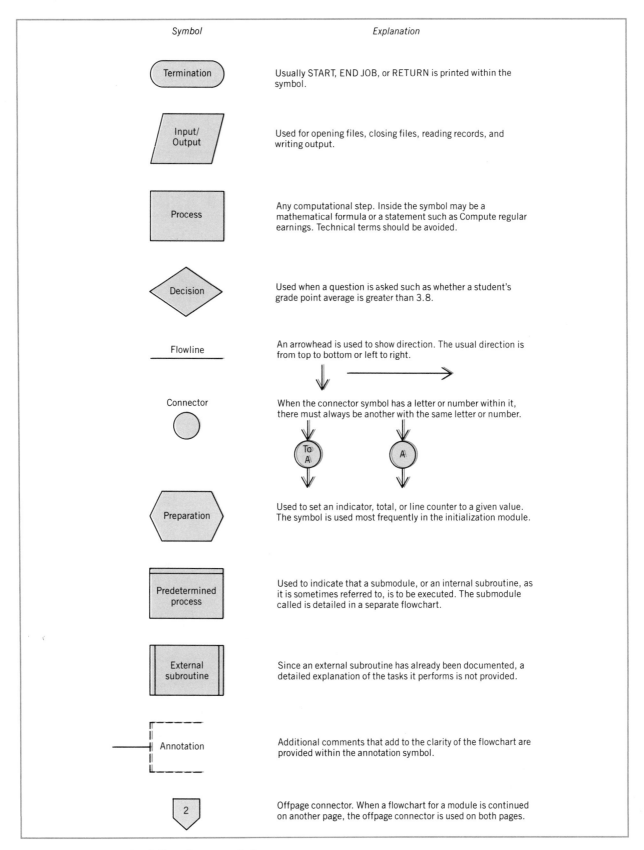

Figure 2–6 **Standard flowchart symbols.**

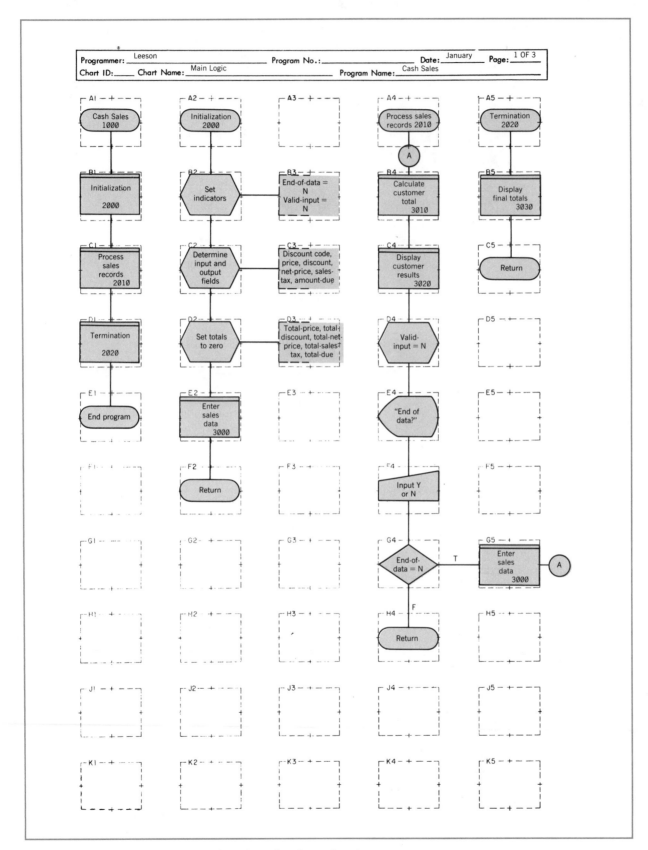

Figure 2–7 Part 1 *Structured flowchart for the cash sales program.*

© SRA 1988, 1983

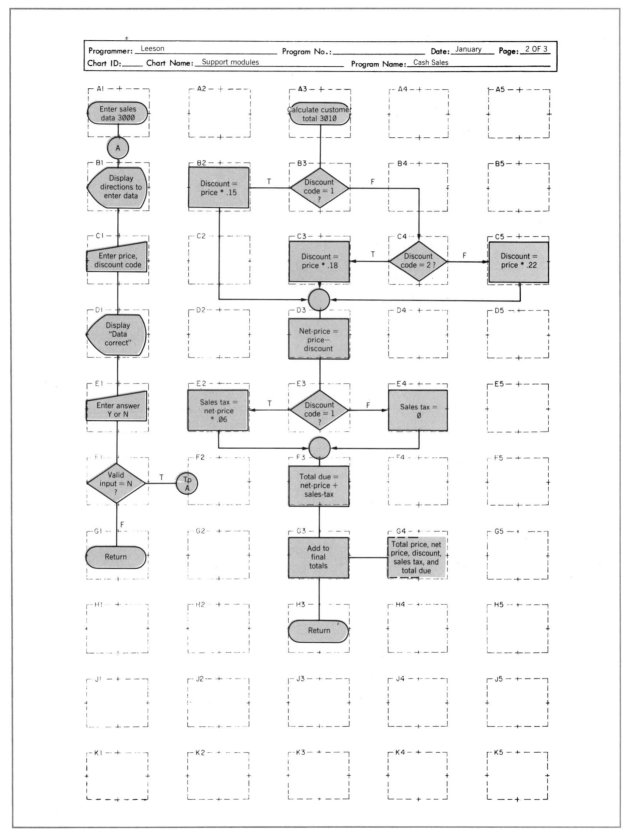

Figure 2–7 Part 2 Structured flowchart for the cash sales program.

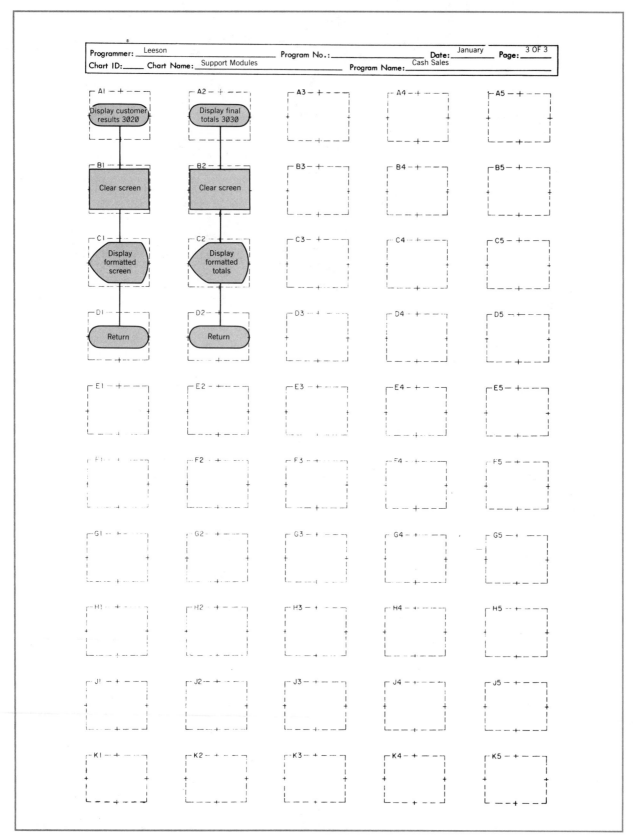

Figure 2–7 Part 3 Structured flowchart for the cash sales program.

© SRA 1988, 1983

11. Is the use of structured flowcharts to illustrate the logic of a program one of the newer or older methods used?

12. Why should ANSI symbols be used in developing structured flowcharts?

13. How are flowcharts developed?

14. What can be written inside of the processing symbols?

15. Under what circumstances will the annotation symbol be used?

16. In developing a structured flowchart, what tools will the programmer use?

17. When is an offpage connector used?

18. Is it always necessary to use arrowheads to show direction?

19. Will a module have only one connector that contains a letter such as A or B?

20. When an external subroutine symbol is used, why isn't a detailed logic plan developed for the external subroutine?

NASSI-SHNEIDERMAN CHARTS

In 1973, I. Nassi and Ben Shneiderman developed a charting technique compatible with structured programming. Symbols were provided for process, decisions, DO WHILE, and **case entry.** Case entry is a concept that is used when a response or condition might be one of several. In the cash sales program, the case entry structure may be used when checking the status of the discount-code field. The following discount codes are valid:

- 1 = discount rate of 15 percent
- 2 = discount rate of 18 percent
- 3 = discount rate of 22 percent

Using case entry, if a value other than a 1, 2, or 3 is stored in the discount-code field, an error routine can be invoked and the operator given an opportunity to make the necessary correction. In our example, an error routine was not included. Although the operator did visually confirm the input, the logic should have included an error routine that would be invoked if the discount code field contains a digit other than a 1, 2, or 3.

If only the four basic symbols are used, it is impossible to develop a logic plan that is not structured. Figure 2–8 illustrates the four basic symbols used in constructing Nassi-Shneiderman (N-S) charts. Connecting lines and arrows are not needed. Basic symbols are combined into a structure that usually fits on an 8½″ × 11″ form.

Within the basic symbols, formulas or statements like everyday English are used, employing key words. Depending on the size of the symbols used, it is usually possible to include as much explanation as is necessary. Since the logic for a module normally fits on a page, offpage connectors are not required.

Note that in the loop created in part 2 of Figure 2–8 the key words, such as WHILE and PERFORM, are in capital letters. Also, the statements within the loop are indented. The END DO WHILE statement aligns with the DO WHILE. When a PERFORM is used, both the name and number of the module to be executed are provided.

Advantages and disadvantages of using Nassi-Shneiderman charts

Unless a module has a great many nested IF statements, the N-S chart is easy to construct. Because of the way the IF/THEN/ELSE symbols are used, it is easy to determine what will occur when the condition is either true or false. The scope of DO WHILEs and IF/THEN/ELSE is well defined. If only the four symbols are used to construct the chart, then the single entry, single exit rule must be followed.

If key words and meaningful names are used within the symbols, then documentation is provided and the logic of the program is easy to follow. Perhaps the only disadvantage of using Nassi-Shneiderman (N-S) charts occurs when IF/THEN/ELSEs are nested to such extent that space for the description within the symbol becomes inadequate.

The Nassi-Shneiderman chart for the cash sales program

Although standardized forms are not available for N-S charts, an organization should develop a form that meets their needs. The one used in Figure 2–9 has a ruled heading with space to record the name of the author, name of the program, date, hierarchy ID, module name, and module function. For ease of maintenance, each module should be documented on a separate sheet.

Note that many key words used in pseudocode, such as DO WHILE, END DO WHILE, PERFORM, DISPLAY, and ACCEPT, are used in developing N-S charts. Although the data names used on the chart are meaningful, in writing the source code the names might be spelled a little differently. For example, not all languages permit a data name to be written "end-of-data." Some languages may require that it be written "ENDOFDATA."

CHECKPOINT QUESTIONS

21. What four symbols or structures are used to develop a Nassi-Shneiderman N-S chart?
22. How are decisions shown on a N-S chart?
23. How is a loop shown on a N-S chart?
24. Give an illustration of when the case entry control structure could be used.
25. Why should a standard form be developed, and used, for constructing an N-S chart?
26. What type of information is contained with the process symbol?

WARNIER-ORR DIAGRAMS

The basic concept for the use of diagrams in program design was developed by Jean-Dominique Warnier. Later Ken Orr extended the basic concept to include system design. The diagrams have been widely used for some time in France and are gaining acceptance in the United States. The diagrams have been described as a hierarchy chart turned on its side or as structured pseudocode. The structure is developed using a series of brackets.

Warnier-Orr diagrams can be used to represent sequence, iteration, selection, and case entry. These diagrams tend to emphasize the hierarchy and modularity of a program while structured flowcharts tend to emphasize sequence and modularity. Warnier-Orr diagrams are read from left to right rather than from top to bottom.

© SRA 1988, 1983

NASSI-SHNEIDERMAN SYMBOLS

gross pay = (regular-hours * rate) + (overtime-hours * rate * 2)
PERFORM   Display-customer-results   3020

Process: A rectangle is used for calculations, calling external subroutines, invoking internal subroutines, establishing fields, and setting indicators to their proper value. The size and shape of the symbols vary depending on the space available and amount of data to be recorded. In the illustration, gross pay is calculated and the print module is invoked.

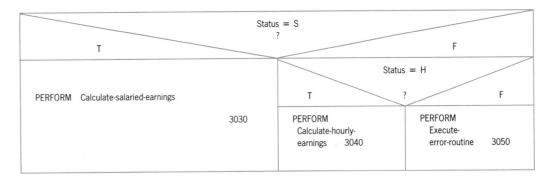

Decisions: A rectangle, divided into three triangles, is used to show a decision. In the example, a code is used to indicate if an employee is hourly or salaried. Either an H or an S should be stored in the status field. If any other character is stored in the field, an error routine should be executed.

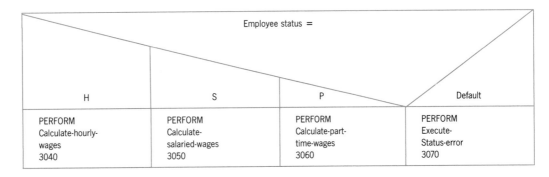

Case Entry: Case entry is used when a response or condition can be one of several. In the illustration, our company has three types of employees represented by the following codes:

S = Salaried
H = Hourly
P = Part-time

Separate modules are used to calculate the gross pay for each type of employee. If a character other than an S, H, or P is stored in the field, an error routine should be invoked.

Figure 2–8 Part 1   Nassi-Shneiderman symbols used for process, decision, and case entry.

NASSI-SHNEIDERMAN SYMBOLS

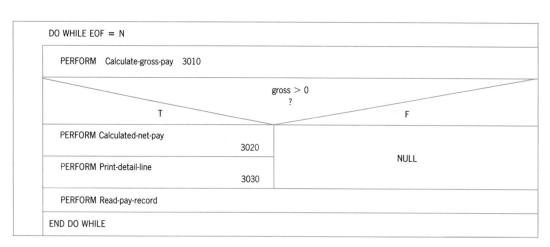

Iteration: A loop is shown by using an inverted L. As long as the condition specified is true, control remains within the loop. Note that the loop begins with DO WHILE and ends with END DO WHILE.

In the illustration, the commands within Process records will be executed as long as the value stored in EOF (end of file) is equal to NO. Three modules are invoked (Calculate gross, Calculate net, and Read record) and one decision is made. If the condition is true, two statements are required. If the condition is false, Null is used to indicate no action will be required.

Figure 2–8 Part 2   Nassi-Shneiderman iteration symbol.

© SRA 1988, 1983

Figure 2–9 (Part 1)
Nassi-Schneiderman charts for process-cash-sales, initialization, and enter sales data.

AUTHOR: Leeson	SYSTEM/PROGRAM: Cash sales DATE: January PAGE 1 OF 8
HIERARCHY ID: 1000	MODULE NAME: Process cash sales

FUNCTION: Control execution of the cash sales program

PERFORM Initialization 2000

PERFORM Process-sales-records 2010

PERFORM Termination 2020

END program

AUTHOR: Leeson	SYSTEM/PROGRAM: Cash sales DATE: January PAGE 2 OF 8
HIERARCHY ID: 2000	MODULE NAME: Initialization

FUNCTION: Set values in indicators and calculation fields; get first record

End-of-data = N

Valid-input = N

Discount-code, price, discount, net-price, sales-tax, and amount due = 0

Total-price, total-discount, total-net-price; total-sales-tax, and total-due = 0

PERFORM Enter-sales-data 3000

RETURN to 1000

AUTHOR: Leeson	SYSTEM/PROGRAM: Cash sales DATE: January PAGE 3 OF 8
HIERARCHY ID: 3000	MODULE NAME: Enter sales data 3000

FUNCTION: Display directions and input data

DO WHILE Valid-input = N

DISPLAY Directions to operator

INPUT Discount-code, price

DISPLAY "Data correct?"

INPUT Valid-input

END DO WHILE

RETURN

Figure 2–9 Part 2
Nassi-Shneiderman chart
for process sales records,
termination, and display
final totals.

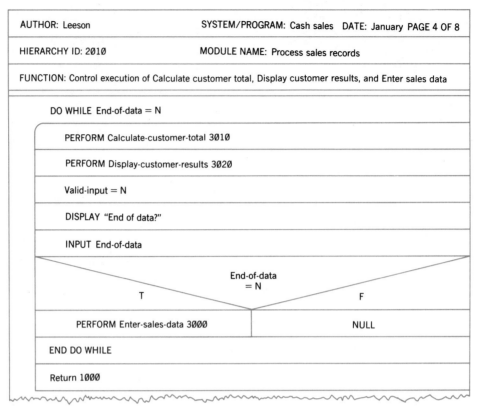

AUTHOR: Leeson	SYSTEM/PROGRAM: Cash sales DATE: January PAGE 4 OF 8
HIERARCHY ID: 2010	MODULE NAME: Process sales records
FUNCTION: Control execution of Calculate customer total, Display customer results, and Enter sales data	

DO WHILE End-of-data = N

PERFORM Calculate-customer-total 3010

PERFORM Display-customer-results 3020

Valid-input = N

DISPLAY "End of data?"

INPUT End-of-data

End-of-data = N

T	F
PERFORM Enter-sales-data 3000	NULL

END DO WHILE

Return 1000

AUTHOR: Leeson	SYSTEM/PROGRAM: Cash sales DATE: January PAGE 5 OF 8
HIERARCHY ID: 2020	MODULE NAME: Termination
FUNCTION: Cause Display totals to be executed	

PERFORM Display-final-totals 3030

Return 1000

AUTHOR: Leeson	SYSTEM/PROGRAM: Cash sales DATE: January PAGE 8 OF 8
HIERARCHY ID: 3030	MODULE NAME: Display final totals 3030
FUNCTION: Display final totals	

Clear screen

DISPLAY Formatted screen showing final totals

Return 2020

© SRA 1988, 1983

*Figure 2–9 Part 3
Nassi-Shneiderman chart
for the calculate customer
total and display customer
results.*

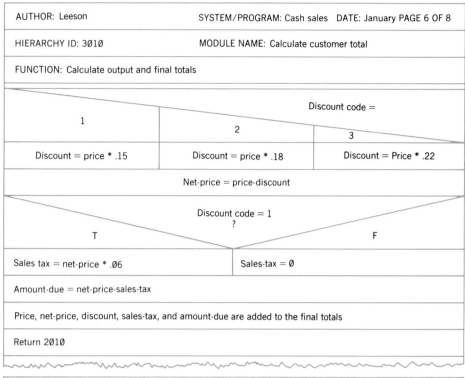

Warnier-Orr diagrams consist of the following elements:

1. **Universals** Included as universals are the names of modules and external subroutines. When the program is coded, the universals usually appear as part of the internal documentation. In the illustrations, the universals are in capital letters. The number of the module is also included as part of the universal.

2. **Executables** Included as executables are statements such as CALCULATE GROSS PAY, EOF = 'YES', and PERFORM enter-sales-data. When the source code is written, each executable will be coded as one or more source statements.

3. **Decisions** IF/THEN/ELSE statements are represented by placing the $\oplus$ symbol between two elements each of which is followed by a brace. The $\oplus$ symbol indicates that the statements included in *only one* set of braces will be executed. A NULL condition is shown by using the term SKIP. Case entry is shown by using more than one $\oplus$ symbol.

Rules used to develop Warnier-Orr diagrams

Perhaps one of the major advantages in using Warnier-Orr diagrams is that there are very few rules. However, these guidelines should be followed:

1. A separate brace is used for each module.
2. If sufficient space is available, the executable elements of a module should be listed on the same chart as its universal element (the name of the module).
3. IF/THEN/ELSE logic is illustrated by using the ⊕ symbol. Braces are needed for both the IF and ELSE portion of the statement. If no action is required when the statement is true or false, SKIP is used to illustrate a NULL condition. The false portion of the IF/THEN/ELSE statement has a bar over the condition which indicates the statement specified is *not* true.
4. Case entry is illustrated by using additional ⊕ symbols. A brace must be used for each alternative.
5. Loops are constructed by using either WHILE or UNTIL. The WHILE or UNTIL, along with the loop exit condition, is enclosed in parentheses.
6. The module names and numbers used on the hierarchy chart should be included as universal elements.
7. Counters and accumulators are initialized outside the loop in which the counting or accumulating is accomplished.
8. Each chart should include as identification the name of the programmer, name of the system or program, date, page number, hierarchy identification, and names of the modules included on the chart.
9. Key words should be written in capital letters.

In order to make the diagram as clear as possible and to limit the explanation to as few words as possible, key words such as DO, WHILE, UNTIL, DISPLAY, and ACCEPT are used. One diagram may contain one or several modules. When necessary, details of the module referenced by the universal element can be included on a separate sheet.

Advantages and disadvantages

Warnier-Orr diagrams take less time to construct than do HIPO charts, structured flowcharts, or N-S diagrams. Of the methods discussed, only pseudocode requires less time to develop a detailed logic plan.

Although there appear to be no major disadvantages, a recent survey indicated that only about 10 percent of the responding organizations endorsed Warnier-Orr diagrams as standard for developing detailed logic plans. However, some organizations and academic institutions have used them exclusively for several years.

The Warnier-Orr diagram for the cash sales program

In reviewing Figure 2–10, you can see that most of the modules fit on Part 1 of the illustration. Since the cash sales program requires few decisions and processing steps, all but the calculations module fits on the one page. Because no standardized form is available, a form was designed to include the infor-

© SRA 1988, 1983

mation needed to identify the diagram. A large outside brace was also included on the form. Most templates have braces of various sizes that can be used in constructing the inner braces.

In the illustration, capital letters are used for the universals and for the key words. The module names and numbers are the same ones that were used on the hierarchy chart.

When Warnier-Orr diagrams are used, a rough draft is made before the walkthrough. The modifications are incorporated into the diagrams and the source code is written and tested. If errors or omissions are detected, the chart is corrected. After all the modifications and corrections are made, the chart will be put in final form and included as part of the documentation for the program.

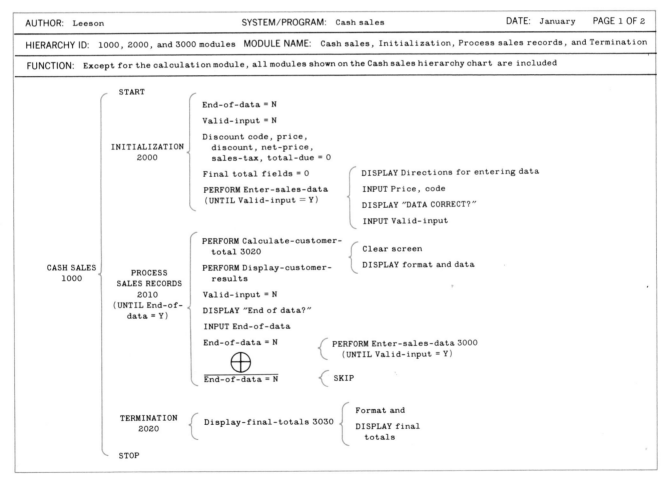

Figure 2–10 Part 1   *Warnier-Orr diagram for the main control and major modules of the cash sales*

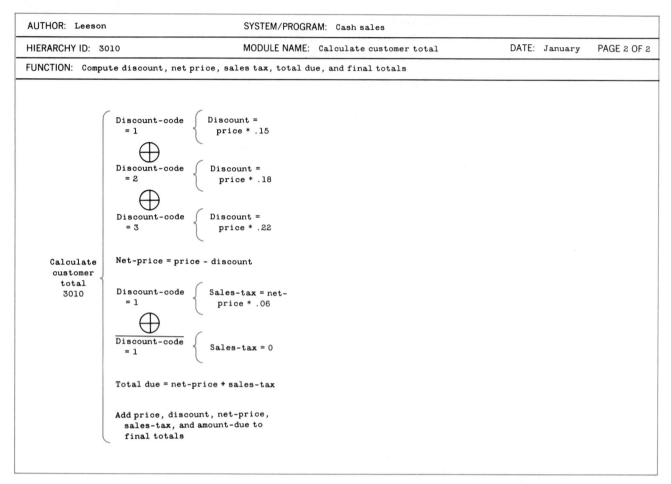

AUTHOR: Leeson	SYSTEM/PROGRAM: Cash sales		
HIERARCHY ID: 3010	MODULE NAME: Calculate customer total	DATE: January	PAGE 2 OF 2
FUNCTION: Compute discount, net price, sales tax, total due, and final totals			

Figure 2–10 Part 2   *Warnier-Orr diagram for the calculations module of the cash sales program.*

CHECKPOINT QUESTIONS

27. What is the difference between a universal and an executable?
28. How might a Warnier-Orr diagram be described?
29. What rules apply to constructing a decision point on a Warnier-Orr diagram?
30. How is a loop constructed?
31. When contrasted to Nassi-Shneiderman charts or structured flowcharts, what are the major advantages in using Warnier-Orr diagrams?
32. What information should be provided on the form used to develop Warnier-Orr diagrams?

SUMMARY

- The hardware, operating system, and programming language all impact the way a program can be designed and implemented.

- Because of the impact of microcomputers on computer technology, operating systems are becoming more user friendly. Applications programs must also be user friendly.

© SRA 1988, 1983

- An acceptable method for construction of a logic plan must:

  Be standardized.

  Make it easy to develop the plan.

  Result in a plan that is easy to understand.

  Permit top-down development.

  Provide for ease of maintenance.

  Provide a means of documenting the plan.

  Provide a means of relating the plan to the hierarchy chart and source code.

- HIPO (Hierarchy plus Input-Process-Output), developed by IBM, requires the input, processing steps, and output for each module to be listed. In developing the processing steps, pseudocode is used.

- Program specifications must be completed before a logic plan can be developed.

- When writing pseudocode, programmers should follow established guidelines. Key words, such as PERFORM, DISPLAY, and INPUT, must be used and the code should be formatted.

- In constructing structured flowcharts programmers should be sure that each module has its own chart, ANSI symbols are used, they use templates and flowcharting worksheets. By using the annotation symbol, additional documentation may be added to the chart.

- Nassi-Shneiderman (N-S) charts are developed using four basic symbols which are *process, decision, DO WHILE,* and *case entry.* If only the basic symbols are used, the resulting charts will be structured.

- A Warnier-Orr diagram can be described either as structured pseudocode or as a hierarchy chart turned on its side. The elements that make up a Warnier-Orr diagram are universals, executables, and decisions. Loops are constructed by using WHILE or UNTIL, along with the condition, outside of the brace.

- Advantages and disadvantages can be listed for each of the four methods covered in the chapter. Within a single organization, one method should be selected, supported by all analysts and programs, and guidelines for its use developed.

DISCUSSION QUESTIONS

1. Refer to the guidelines listed for developing a logic plan using pseudocode and explain why each should be followed.

2. Why are key words used in writing pseudocode?

3. In the guidelines for generating a flowchart, what tasks must be completed before starting to develop the flowchart? Must these same tasks be completed before developing any type of detailed logic plan?

4. Why should the standard ANSI flowcharting symbols be used to develop a structured flowchart? Why is it advantageous to use standard flowchart worksheets?

5. Describe the four symbols used to develop Nassi-Shneiderman charts.

6. Why isn't a template for drawing standard symbols used in developing a N-S chart?

7. Describe a Warnier-Orr diagram and the guidelines used in drawing such a diagram.

8. Contrast the use of pseudocode and structured flowcharts and identify the major advantages and disadvantages associated with each method.

9. Contrast the use of N-S charts and Warnier-Orr diagrams and identify the major advantages and disadvantages associated with each method.

10. Assume that the CIS manager asks you which of the four methods should be used be all CIS programmers. Which method would you support? Give the rationale for your decision.

KEY WORDS

American National Standards Institute (ANSI)

case entry

decisions

executables

flowcharting worksheet

Hierarchy plus Input-Processing-Output (HIPO)

key words

Nassi-Shneiderman (N-S) chart

offpage connector

stub testing

pseudocode

subroutines

template

universals

Warnier-Orr diagram

© SRA 1988, 1983

PROJECTS

Your company has an online sales order system. While sales representatives are in their customers' offices, they use terminals to gain access to a centrally located host computer. After a sales representative enters his or her account number and password, the customer's number is entered. The computer will determine if the customer's credit limit has been exceeded. If not, the following occurs:

A. The item number is entered and the required inventory master record is retrieved. The sales representative also enters the quantity ordered.

B. The inventory master record contains the following fields of data that will be used in making the necessary calculations:

> MF-item-number
> MF-product-description
> MF-cost-price
> MF-markup-code
> MF-quantity-on-hand
> MF-reorder-point

In constructing data names, MF will be used to denote fields stored within a master file.

C. Although each sales order may include several items, each customer places only one order. Within a large organization, the sales representative might call on another customer and obtain a second order. However, this would be treated as a separate customer and order.

The programmer in charge of the project has determined that the modules illustrated in Figure 2–11 will be used. You have been asked to develop the detailed logic plan for the process-sales-orders module and were given the following specifications:

Input into the module:
> These items are part of the inventory master file record.
> > MF-item-number
> > MF-product-description
> > MF-cost-price
> > MF-markup-code
> > MF-quantity-on-hand

The following data was entered by the operator:
> Customer-number
> Item-number
> Quantity-ordered

Processing required in 2010-process-sales-data
> Determine if there is sufficient quantity of the product to process the order and to invoke module 3040. If not, invoke a backorder routine and bypass the rest of the processing.
>
> Cause a detail line to be printed.
>
> See if the customer wants to order another item.

Calculations required in 3040-calculate-sales-data
> Determine the new quantity on hand.
>
> If the new quantity on hand is below the reorder point, invoke the 4000-reorder-inventory-item module.
>
> Calculate the selling price. If the markup code is 1, the markup is 80% of the cost price. If the markup code is 2, the markup is 65% of the selling price. If the code is 3, the markup is 50% of the cost price.
>
> Determine the extension—selling price times quantity.
>
> Add the extension to the order-total field.

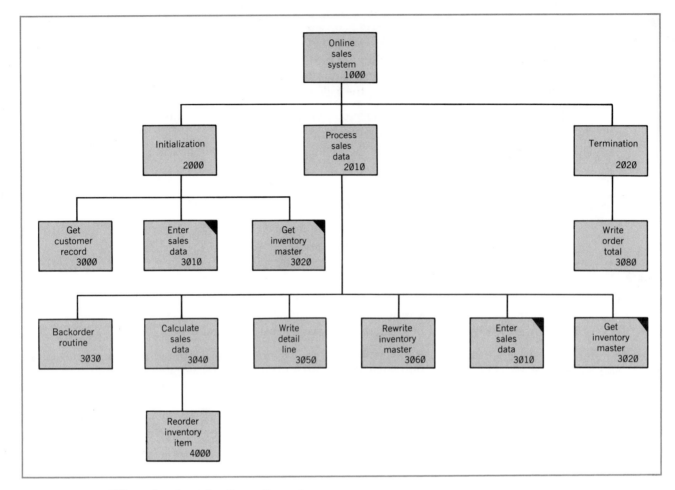

Figure 2–11   *Hierarchy chart for the online sales program.*

Output:
 Data for the detail line
 Data for the backorder record
 Data for the reorder record

Directions

Do not be concerned about details such as how the master records are read or what might be included in some of the modules for which you will not develop detailed logic plans.

 1. Answer the following questions:

 A. Since each order may include orders for several different items, the process-sales-data module may need to be executed several times. What indicator will you use to control the execution of the loop?

 _____

 B. In what module will you set the indicator to a value that will permit the commands within the process-sales-data module to be executed until all of the items requested have been entered?

 _____

© SRA 1988, 1983

C. How, and in what module, will you change the value of the indicator so control will return to the main-control module?

2. Develop the detailed logic for the process-sales-data module (2010) and the calculate-sales-data (3040) module by using each of the following methods: pseudocode, flowchart, Nassi-Shneiderman chart, and a Warnier-Orr diagram.

3. Assuming that the online sales system, initialization, get-customer-master, enter-sales-data, get-inventory-master, and termination modules have been designed, the logic checked, and the code written and tested, how can you test your process-sales-data module if the back-order-routine, reorder-inventory-items, write-detail-line, rewrite-inventory-record, and the write-order-total modules have not been developed?

4. You would like to write the source code and test the process-sales-data and calculate-sales-data modules. Test data has already been developed and is stored in the customer master and inventory master files. In order to test the process-sales-data module, what will you need to do?

PROBLEM 2–1

You work for a contractor and have the task of estimating the cost of a job. A sales representative submits a form to you that has the customer's name, address, and phone number, the item number quantity of the material required, and the estimated time needed to complete the job. Sales representatives work on commission, and it is part of their job to follow up on estimates.

Each time the program is executed, only one cost estimate is printed. The job is terminated by printing the section of the bill that contains the total cost of materials, the sales tax, the estimated labor cost, and the total cost for the job.

Labor costs are determined as follows: If the cost of the materials is less than $10,000, the labor cost is 1.5 times the cost of materials. If the cost of materials is $10,000 or more, labor is estimated at 1.45 times the cost of materials.

The following specifications were developed for the job:

Output:

Printed report	Each customer's cost estimate will be on a separate page and will include his or her name and address; itemized list of materials that includes the item number, description, cost per item, and total cost for each item; the total cost for materials; sales tax; estimated cost for labor; and estimated total.

Input:

Data from the inventory master	Item number, description, cost price, and markup. The actual percentage that the item is to be marked up is stored in the markup field.
Data entered by operator	Customer's name, address, tax code, and estimated time to complete the job. This information is entered in the enter-customer-name module invoked by the initialization module. The tax code is also entered. If a T is entered, tax code will be computed at .06. Any other response indicates that it is a tax-exempt customer.
	As part of the get-inventory-data module, the operator keys in the item number. After it is determined that the correct record is retrieved, the quantity required is entered.

Processing required: Enter name, address, and tax code.
Print the report heading.
Enter item number.
Retrieve the first inventory record.
Enter the quantity needed.
Calculate the cost for the item entered.
Add to the material cost total.
Print the item line on the report.
See if another item is required.
Calculate the sales tax.
Estimate the labor cost.
Determine the total cost estimated.
Print the remainder of the estimate.

Although the following modules are invoked from modules you will complete, you need *not* do a detailed logic plan for the following modules:

Enter customer name
Print report headings
Get inventory master— In this module the item number is entered, the record retrieved, and confirmation made that the correct record was obtained.
Calculate job data
Print detail line
Print total lines

In determining the logic for the program you can assume that there is enough material on hand to complete the job. The report is to be printed in the following format:

```
ESTIMATED  COST  OF  MATERIALS  FOR        John Blake
                                           1518 Center Drive
                                           Canton, Ohio 47345


MATERIALS  REQUIRED
    Item          Description          Quantity      Cost      Total Cost
    1234     XXXXXXXXXXXXXXXXXXXXXXXX      10      X,XXX.XX    XXX,XXX.XX
    1289     XXXXXXXXXXXXXXXXXXXXXXXX      12      X,XXX.XX    XXX,XXX.XX
             TOTAL  COST  OF  MATERIALS                                   XXX,XXX.XX
             SALES  TAX                                                   XXX,XXX.XX
             ESTIMATED  COST  FOR  LABOR                                  XXX,XXX.XX
             TOTAL  ESTIMATE                                              XXX,·XXX.XX
```

Directions

1. Develop a complete hierarchy chart that includes the six modules listed as well as the three major control modules.

2. Once you have a rough draft of your hierarchy chart, list the tasks that will be executed in each of the modules.

3. Test the logic. Go through the logic as if you are the computer to determine if all the output is calculated and if tasks are performed in the correct sequence. If, for example, you have the print-report-heading module invoked by the termination module, your report would be printed incorrectly.

4. Develop the detailed logic plans for the modules you have selected to use. In the initialization module, include a step that states, "Open inventory master." In the termination module, include

© SRA 1988, 1983

a step that states, "Close inventory master." (Reasons for these steps will be discussed later.) You need not develop a logic plan for the six modules that were listed.

Your instructor will tell you which method to use to develop the detailed logic for your modules.

5. Test your plan using the following data:

John Smith, 1278 Lakewood Drive, Canton, Ohio 47345
Sales tax code: T
Estimated time: 10 hours
Item 1234, quantity of 10
Item 4976, quantity of 100
Item 7832, quantity of 80

Play computer and make certain you would have the data available to print the desired report.

6. Assume that the program is operational. It has been in use for several months. You contact the manager who is responsible for supervising the development of estimates and ask him to evaluate the program. What changes, or additions, do you think he might want made? In nontechnical terms describe the changes you believe should be recommended and indicate which modules you think need to be changed. One example of a suggested change is provided.

Module(s)	Describe Change
Enter name, Print heading	Enter and print the customer's phone number

_____

_____

_____

_____

INTERACTIVE EXERCISE 2–1

The source code for the cash sales program is provided so that you can determine what will occur when the program is executed. You will first run the program and input the data specified and mathematically prove that valid results are achieved.

Directions

1. Boot the system by loading the operating system. When A⟩ appears on the screen, key in **BASIC** (or **BASICA**) and press **ENTER**.
2. Place the program diskette on drive A, press **F3**, and key in **menu**. Press **ENTER**. Press **F2** (RUN).
3. From the main menu, select option **1**. Key in **1** and press **ENTER**.
4. From menu **1**, select option **3**. Key in **3** and press **ENTER**.
5. Since you will need to execute the program several times, do not return to the main menu. In response to "Return to Main Menu?" enter an N. You may execute the program again by pressing F2.
6. Enter the data specified below. Each time data is entered, visually check to see that you have keyed in the data correctly. If you detect an error *before* you press the ENTER key, move your cursor to the incorrect data and enter the correct data. In the price, the decimal must be entered. However, a sum such as 500.00 may be entered as 500 or as 500. rather than 500.00.

   If you have a printer, use **Shift/PrtSc** (print Screen) and make a printed copy of each screen. You will need the printed copy to do part 7. B. of the exercise.

   lst sale   Price   100.00
                     Discount code   1
                     End of Data?   N

2nd sale	Price	200.00
	Discount code	2
	End of Data?	N
3rd sale	Price	197.58
	Discount code	3
	End of Data?	Y

7. Assume that the program is still in the test mode and you must prove that the output is valid.

   A. Explain why you feel the test data used is sufficient (or not) to test the program.

_____

_____

_____

   B. On a separate sheet of paper, do the calculations necessary to prove that the output is valid.

   C. If you were to list the program you would observe that the WHILE statement was written as:

     WHILE V$ = "N" OR V$ = "n"

     Why was the statement written in that manner rather than as WHILE V$ = "N"?

_____

_____

     Programming tip: If your computer can store both upper and lower case letters, always check for either condition. Also, use single letter responses rather than YES or NO; TRUE or FALSE.

8. What will occur under the following circumstances?

   A. In the initialization module, E$ was set to N. E$ is used to represent END-OF-DATA.

     1) List line 210 and change it to read:

       210 E$ = "Y"

       After changing statement 210, make certain you use the ENTER key so that the revised source code will be executed.

     2) Run the program. Enter the data listed for the first sale. _Do not return to the main menu._

     3) Refer to the logic plans presented on pages 56–58 of the text, and explain exactly what occurred when the program was run. Which modules were executed?

_____

_____

_____

_____

_____

     4) Change line 230 to:
       230 V$ = "Y"

       Run the program and then _return to the main menu._ When you return to the main menu and select menu 1 option 3, the original version of the cash sales program will be loaded into memory for execution.

       Refer back to the logic plans presented in the text, and explain what occurred when the program was run. When V$ was equal to "y", which modules were executed?

© SRA 1988, 1983

_____

_____

_____

9. Reload the program by selecting option 1 from the main menu. From menu 1, select option 3. After completing A, do not return to the main menu.

    A. Run the program using the input provided below:

Sales 1	Price	100.00
	Discount code	1
	End of data?	N
Sales 2	Price	200.00
	Discount code	4
	End of data?	Y

        1) When the second set of data entered, why was the discount $15?

_____

_____

_____

        2) How should the logic plan be changed so that an invalid discount code will be detected by the program?

_____

_____

_____

        Programming tips: When case entry is used, always provide a default option that will detect an invalid value.

        It is the programmer's responsibility to know what is stored within fields. In many cases it may be necessary to reset fields to zero between each cycle of a program.

    B. Run the program again by pressing F2; enter the following data:

Sales 1	Price	200.00
	Discount code	B
	End of data?	Y

    Return to the main menu.

        1) What occurred when the B was entered?

_____

_____

_____

        2) What might have occurred if the message "Non-numeric data in input field" was not displayed and the operator provided another chance to enter the data?

_____

_____

        Programming tip: Although visual verification of data is provided when data is entered from a terminal, other methods should also be used to validate input.

© SRA 1988, 1983

SELF-EVALUATION TEST 2

Name _____

Section Number _____

I. Record the key term being defined in the space provided. When a small blank appears within the statement, it indicates where the term is needed.

_____ 1. A statement on a Warnier-Orr diagram that does not result in executable code; it is often the name and number of a module.

_____ 2. A logic structure that describes multitest conditional branching.

_____ 3. A diagram described as either a hierarchy chart on its side or as structured pseudocode.

_____ 4. A user-defined noncompilable shorthand used to describe the required input, process, and output. Key words are used to identify basic functions such as PRINT or WRITE.

_____ 5. A device used to draw the ANSI symbols used in developing a structured flowchart.

_____ 6. Used to show the continuation of a flowchart onto a new page.

_____ 7. When constructing a Nassi-Shneiderman chart, an inverted L is used to define a _____.

_____ 8. Words such as PERFORM, WHILE, and UNTIL used in writing pseudocode or in developing N-S charts or Warnier-Orr diagrams are called _____.

_____ 9. A _____ chart has three major sections. Separate sections are used for input, processing, and output.

_____ 10. The _____ develops standards for products, programming languages, flowcharting symbols, and so forth.

II. Multiple Choice. Record the letter of the best answer in the space provided. The choices for the following questions are:

A = Nassi-Shneiderman chart
B = pseudocode
C = structured flowchart
D = Warnier-Orr diagram
E = HIPO (Hierarchy plus Input-Process-Output)
F = all of the above

_____ 1. Although guidelines must be followed regarding the way that statements are formatted, the logic of a program can be illustrated faster by this means than by any of the other four methods.

_____ 2. May be described as a hierarchy chart placed on its side.

_____ 3. Symbols are used for the four basic constructs involved in developing the logic plan. The symbols used are for process, decision, case entry, and creating a loop.

_____ 4. May require using an offpage connector.

_____ 5. The method was developed and supported by IBM.

_____ 6. Of the methods listed, which one is the oldest used for developing a detailed logic plan?

_____ 7. Is sometimes described as being structured pseudocode.

_____ 8. A decision is shown by dividing a rectangle into three triangles.

_____ 9. The program specifications must be developed prior to its use.

_____ 10. Requires the use of ENDIF. IF, ELSE, and ENDIF should all be aligned.

_____ 11. Provides the best graphic presentation of a program.

_____ 12. Although it is easy and fast to construct good logic plans using this particular method, a survey indicated that programmers in only 10 percent of the organizations surveyed used it to develop detailed logic plans.

_____ 13. When used, the method provides a means of relating the logic plan to the hierarchy chart and to the source code.

_____ 14. Which two methods use standardized worksheets and templates?

_____ 15. A separate brace is used for each module. When IF/THEN/ELSE logic is shown, both the IF and the ELSE require a separate brace.

III. Multiple choice. Record letter of the best answer in the space provided. All of the questions in this section refer to the use of key words.

_____ 1. Used to indicate a detail line is to be written on a report.
    a. REWRITE   b. PRINT   c. WRITE   d. LIST

_____ 2. Used to indicate that an external subroutine is to be retrieved from an online library and executed as part of the program being developed.
    a. PERFORM   b. DO   c. CALL   d. DO-UNTIL

_____ 3. Information is to be written into a file stored on tape or disk.
    a. PRINT   b. DISPLAY   c. WRITE   d. REWRITE

_____ 4. Data is to be entered from the operator's console.
    a. ACCEPT   b. INPUT   c. READ   d. PRINT

_____ 5. An updated version of a record is to be written back into an existing file.
    a. WRITE   b. PRINT   c. REWRITE   d. DISPLAY

_____ 6. Directions are to be exhibited on the operator's VDT.
    a. PRINT   b. DISPLAY   c. WRITE   d. INPUT

_____ 7. Used to construct a loop that will be executed as long as the condition specified is true.
    a. DO-UNTIL   b. DO   c. DO-WHILE   d. PERFORM

_____ 8. Used to branch to a module and execute the commands within the module as long as the condition specified is NOT true.
    a. DO-UNTIL   b. PERFORM/UNTIL   c. DO-WHILE   d. DO

IV. True or False. Record a T or F in the blank provided. For each false statement, indicate why the statement is false or make the changes needed to correct the statement.

_____ 1. When designing a program, the programmer need not be concerned about the characteristics of the hardware, software, or programming language being used.

_____ 2. Today's operating systems must be designed to improve communication between the computer and the operator and must also be user friendly.

_____ 3. Hierarchy plus Input-Processing-Output (HIPO) charts were developed by Digital Equipment Corporation (DEC).

_____ 4. A major advantage of HIPO charts is that the input and output requirements must be determined in detail before a chart can be constructed.

_____ 5. When writing pseudocode, programmers can express their thoughts in natural English and are not hindered by trying to draw symbols or a chart.

_____ 6. In writing pseudocode, key words are written in capital letters.

_____ 7. Since it is faster to write, pseudocode should be unformatted.

© SRA 1988, 1983

8. Iteration can be expressed by using DO WHILE, DO UNTIL, or PERFORM/UNTIL.

9. GO TO statements should be used to transfer control outside of a module.

10. In the cash sales example, two indicators are used. One controls the execution of process sales records and the other the execution of the enter data module.

11. Indicators are usually given their initial value in the module they control. For example, end-of-data is initially set to N within the process records module.

12. NULL is used to indicate that no further action is required and the program will be terminated.

13. Many programmers feel that constructing flowcharts is more efficient than writing pseudocode.

14. Each programmer decides what symbols should be used to represent the basic tasks to be performed.

15. If a letter, such as an A, appears within a connector, there must be a second connector that also contains an A.

16. If only the four basic control structures are used to construct a Nassi-Shneiderman chart, it is difficult to develop a structured logic plan.

17. Warnier-Orr diagrams emphasize the hierarchy and modularity of a program.

18. The statement "calculate gross" is an example of a universal.

19. In developing a Warnier-Orr diagram, a separate brace is used for each module.

20. Warnier-Orr diagrams take less time to develop than do structured flowcharts or Nassi-Shneiderman charts.

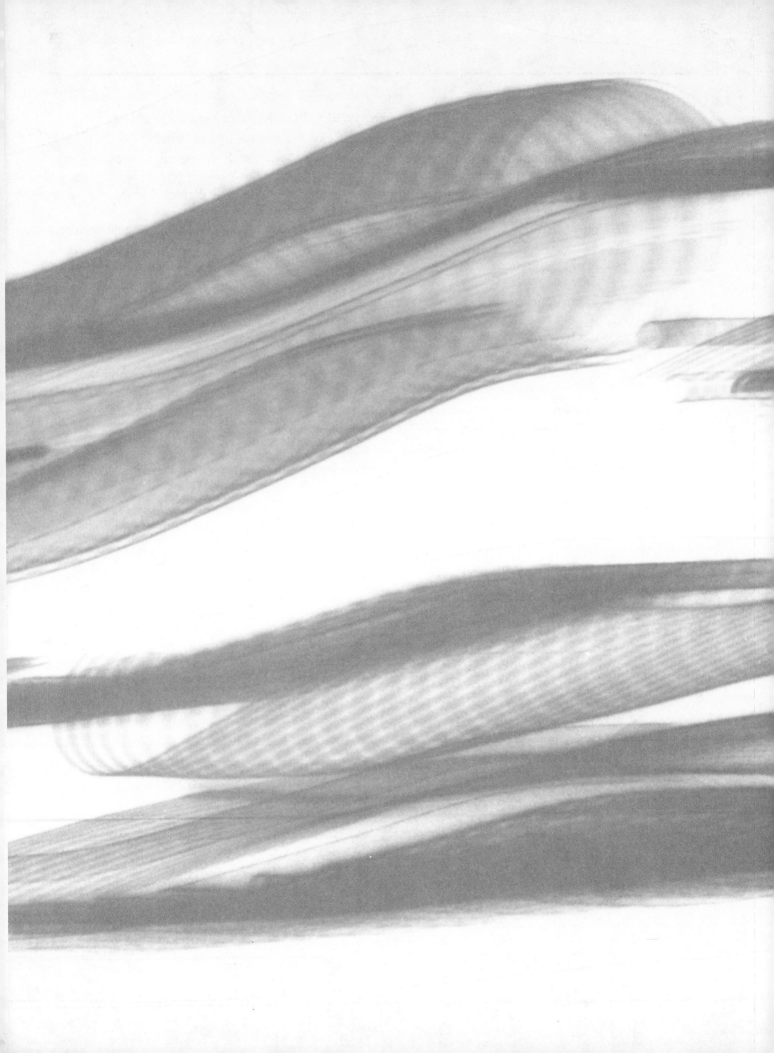

SELECTION: A POWERFUL PROGRAMMING TOOL

3

After reading the chapter and completing the learning activities, you will be able to:

- Have a better understanding of the logical ability of computers.

- Be able to develop logic plans using simple IF statements, case entry, and nested IF/THEN/ELSE statements.

- Identify and use relational and logical operators.

- Develop a truth table for multicondition statements using AND or OR.

- Identify the functions typically performed in the initialization module.

- Use case entry to develop a help menu.

- Explain how stub testing can be used to test selected modules before a program is completely designed and coded.

- When given the program specifications and detailed design of selected modules, determine what data is needed to test both the normal and abnormal conditions that may occur.

In the previous two chapters, selection was introduced and two versions of IF statements were presented: a simple IF statement and case entry. This chapter is designed to provide a better understanding of what occurs within a program when a **branching command** is executed. A branching command causes the control of the program to leave the normal pattern of executing the next command in sequence. Instead control branches to a point in the program where a subroutine, or module, will be executed. Consider the following pseudocode:

```
IF   status = 'S' THEN
     PERFORM 3040-salaried-employee-routine
ELSE
     IF status = 'H' THEN
         PERFORM 3050-hourly-employee-routine
     ELSE
         PERFORM 3060-invalid-status-routine
ENDIF
```

Although it is not necessary to include the module number as part of the module name, many COBOL programmers use the module number as the first part of the module name. This convention will be followed throughout the text.

Regardless of the programming language used, an IF statement will be written in source code. The PERFORM indicates that the compiler or interpreter must generate a branching command. After the module specified is executed, control returns to the statement following the IF statement. The **address** of where the module is stored within the program is generated from the 3040-salaried-employee-routine portion of the statement. An address is a location within memory where either data or a command is stored. Also before the branching command is executed, the address of the next command in sequence is saved so control returns to the proper location.

If BASIC is used to code the program, the statement would be coded as follows:

```
100 IF STATUS$ = 'S' THEN GOSUB 3000
    ELSE IF STATUS$ = 'H' THEN GOSUB 3200
         ELSE GOSUB 3400
```

GOSUB is a statement that causes a module to be executed and control to return to the statement following the GOSUB. The line number which follows GOSUB will be translated into the address where the module is stored. Which routine is executed depends on whether an S, H, or some other value is stored in the STATUS$ field.

This chapter is designed to illustrate what occurs within the computer when selection occurs and what type of selection statements may be used. More attention will also be given to creating a "user-friendly" program. User-friendly programs provide prompts for entering data, help screens which explain how data is entered, and sufficient internal documentation to explain how the data is processed.

SELECTION LOGIC

What power does the computer really have in the decision-making process? Because of powerful operating systems, programming languages, and **database languages** available, complex statements can be created using expressions with

© SRA 1988, 1983

syntax similar to standard English that will generate many machine-language commands. A database is a collection of data stored together to serve one or more applications. Database languages are user-oriented and permit nondata processing personnel to extract information from databases by answering questions and using statements very much like standard English.

You have read many times that the computer has the ability to answer true/false or yes/no questions. Today, however, you can give verbal instructions to the computer that seem far more complex than when simple Yes/No questions are asked. For example, you might verbally state:

FIND MARY HENDERSON'S RECORD IN THE ACCOUNTS RECEIVABLE DATABASE AND DETERMINE IF HER BALANCE IS GREATER THAN HER CREDIT-LIMIT.

The database program which accepts the statement recognizes certain key words and is programmed to perform the following tasks. First, MARY HENDERSON'S record is retrieved from the database specified. The computer recognizes the names of two fields, BALANCE and CREDIT-LIMIT, and compares their contents. A great many decisions are made as the database software is executed. However, it finally comes down to the computer's true decision-making ability: two values are compared and a determination is made to see if the first is higher than, lower than, or equal to the second.

Comparisons can be made on **alphanumeric data** (sometimes called **string data**) or numeric data. An alphanumeric field can contain special symbols, letters of the alphabet, or digits. However, when comparisons are made, alphanumeric data is compared to another alphanumeric field or constant. An alphanumeric constant is usually enclosed in single or double quotation marks. For example, if a search is being made for Mary Green's record, the required IF statement would appear as follows:

```
IF MF-employee-name = 'Mary Green' THEN
    PERFORM 3050-display-employee-record
ELSE
    NULL
ENDIF
```

In the illustration the contents of the field called MF-employee-name is compared to an alphanumeric constant.

A field defined as numeric would be compared to another numeric field or to a numeric constant. For example,

```
IF MF-account-balance  > 10000 THEN
    PERFORM 3050-execute-audit-routine
ELSE
    NULL
ENDIF
```

When the program specifications are developed *before designing the program,* the size of each field and type of data stored within each field are determined.

Another request into a database using a database program might be written as follows:

Please LIST STUDENTS from STUDENT-MASTER with a GPA >= 3.8 who live in the CITY of Midland and who are FEMALE.

Many people find the computer's ability to retrieve information using such a statement awesome and mysterious. However, the analyst and programmer who wrote the complex software that can recognize the key words, ignore the extra words (such as *please*), and translate the request into machine-language commands had to start by learning the power of IF statements.

Early IF statements

FORTRAN (FORmula TRANslation), the first high-level compiler language used by programmers, permitted a three-way branch to occur. This was based upon the computer's ability to compare two values. The FORTRAN statement to compare balance and credit-limit would have been written as follows:

```
              Neg   Zero  Pos
IF (JBAL - JLIMIT) 100,  110,  120
```

The computer subtracted credit limit (JLIMIT) from balance (JBAL) and if the results were negative, control branched to statement 100. If the results were zero, control branched to statement 110, and if the results were positive, control branched to statement 120. The three numbers—100, 110, and 120—are line numbers. Each line number is translated by the computer into an address. An address is a location within memory where either data or a command is stored.

By today's standards, this type of statement leaves much to be desired. The branching command created is a GOTO and control does not return to the statement following the IF. The versions of FORTRAN used today make it possible to write structured programs. However, the IF statement illustrated was the first of many ways to write powerful IF statements.

IF statements today

IF statements can range from the simplest IF/THEN, based on one decision, to extremely complex statements that pose many true/false type of questions. The statements can also be nested. In a **nested IF statement**, a second IF statement can be within the first; within the second, a third IF statement can be nested. The following example illustrates the format that would be used:

```
IF . . .
    IF . . .
        IF . . .
        ELSE . . .
    ELSE . . .
ELSE . . .
ENDIF
```

The level of nesting permitted depends on the compiler or interpreter being used. To add to the complexity, both the IF and the ELSE portion of an IF statement may contain nested IF/THEN/ELSE statements. However, keep in mind the structured guideline which states, "avoid undue complexity." If too many levels of nesting occur, undue complexity may result. Often additional modules can be added to lessen the complexity of nested IF statements.

The simplest form of an IF statement will be reviewed and then more complex versions of the IF statement will be covered.

© SRA 1988, 1983

SIMPLE IF STATEMENTS

The simplest form of an IF statement can be written in one of three ways:

- with true actions only
- with false actions only
- with both true and false actions.

Each of the three situations will be illustrated. Assume that a customer's master file record is retrieved and that his or her record contains a balance field with the amount the customer owes. The MF-credit-limit field contains the amount of credit extended to the customer.

With true actions only

The credit manager would like to create a file that contains the name, address, and sales representative of all customers who have a zero balance. The records in the file will be sorted by sales representative. Each sales representative will receive a listing of the persons who have a zero balance and will call on each customer to determine why their account has not been used. The pseudocode statement would be written as follows:

```
IF MF-account-balance = 0 THEN
    PERFORM 3030-write-transaction-file
ELSE
    NULL
ENDIF
```

With false action only

The credit manager has asked you to write a program that will list all customers who have exceeded their credit limits. In pseudocode the statement will be written:

```
IF MF-account-balance is less than or equal to
MF-credit-limit THEN
    NULL
ELSE
    PERFORM 3020-write-over-limit-report
ENDIF
```

The statement could have been written differently so that the true action would have been executed. Simple IF statements should be coded so they are easy to read and meaningful to the programmer.

With both true and false actions

An online sales order entry system is being developed. The customer's master file record is retrieved. Before the order can be processed, the sales representative must determine the status of the customer's account. If the customer has exceeded his or her credit limit, a screen showing the customer's account activity will be displayed and the order will not be processed. The pseudocode statement will be written:

```
IF MF-credit-limit is greater than MF-customer-balance THEN
    PERFORM 3020-process-sales-order
ELSE
    PERFORM 3030-review-customer-credit
ENDIF
```

Figure 3–1
Flowcharting simple IF
statement.

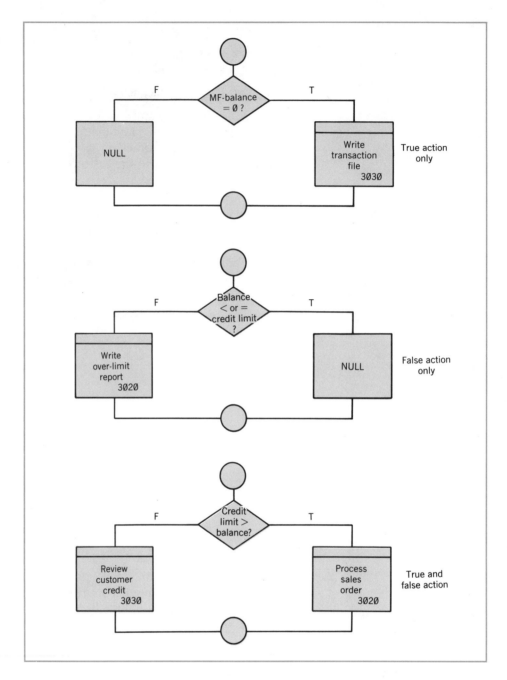

Figure 3–1 illustrates how each of the conditions would be flowcharted.

Relational operators

In formulating IF statements, **relational operators** may be used. Many programming languages permit the use of the relational operators shown in Figure 3–2. They can also be used to conserve space on flowcharts and, since programmers understand their meaning, in writing pseudocode. However, if the pseudocode is written using word processing on a microcomputer or terminal, the programmer should make certain the printer has all of the required symbols. If not, the operators should be spelled out. Figure 3–2 illustrates the

© SRA 1988, 1983

Figure 3–2   Relational operators used in writing IF statements.

Relational Operators

Operator	Relation Tested	Example
=	Equal	`IF balance = credit-limit THEN`
< >	Not equal	`IF balance < > credit-limit THEN` `alt: IF balance NOT = credit-limit THEN`
<	Less than	`IF balance < credit-limit THEN`
>	Greater than	`IF balance > credit-limit THEN`

< =	Less than or equal	`IF balance <= credit-limit THEN`
		`alt: IF balance < credit-limit OR`
		`     balance = credit-limit THEN`

> =	Greater than or equal	`IF balance >= credit-limit THEN`
		`alt: IF balance > credit-limit OR`
		`     balance = credit-limit THEN`

operator, the relation tested, an example, and an alternative that may, when necessary, be used.

From the illustration you can see that tests can be made to see if one number is greater than, equal to, or less than another. In addition, many languages permit the symbols to be adjacent to one another so that a test can be made for "less than or equal to" as well as "greater than or equal to." Still more power may be given a simple IF statement when the **logical operators** AND, OR, and NOT are used.

Arithmetic operators

When using arithmetic operators within IF statements or other types of calculations, the order in which the expression will be executed should be considered. Figure 3–3 illustrates the order in which an arithmetic expression will be executed.

Although it is not a rule that parentheses be included in pseudocode, whenever formulas are used rather than a simple statement such as "compute

Figure 3–3   Hierarchy of arithmetic operations.

Arithmetic Operators

Symbol	Operation	Order of Execution
( )	Expressions are executed in innermost parentheses first.	1st
**	Exponentiation (raise to the power of)	2nd
* /	Multiplication and division	3rd
+ −	Addition and subtraction	4th

When operations of equal value are to be executed, the order of execution is from left to right.

gross pay" the expression should be written accurately. If not, the person writing the source code may not include the parentheses, and invalid results will be achieved. However, an omission such as this should be detected in the code walkthrough. If the error is not detected, an error in logic is created that may be difficult to detect.

Logical operators

USING AND　When AND is used, all of the conditions specified must be true or the ELSE portion of the statement will be executed. Assume that you want to print a report listing all *female students* who live in Midland and have grade-point-averages of 3.8 or higher. The fields containing the data are called Sex$, City, and GPA. The sex field will contain either an F or M; the city field a code (18 is for Midland); and the GPA field contains the student's grade point average.

The selection statement written in pseudocode would be:

```
IF MF-sex-code = 'F' AND MF-city-code = 18 AND MF-GPA >=
3.8 THEN
    PERFORM 3020-print-detail-line
ELSE
    NULL
ENDIF
```

PERFORM 3020-print-detail-line will be executed *only* if all three conditions are true. Does this make the database example used earlier a little more understandable?

Assume that you wish to print a report listing all salaried employees who are enrolled in the credit union and earn more than $20,000. In the master file the status field contains an S for salaried employees, the credit-union field contains the monthly deductions, and the salary field contains the employee's gross salary. The required statement in pseudocode would be:

```
IF MF-salary > 20000 AND MF-status = 'S' AND
MF-credit-union-ded > 0 THEN
    PERFORM 3020-print-detail-line
ELSE
    NULL
ENDIF
```

The section of the flowchart related to the compound question would appear as follows:

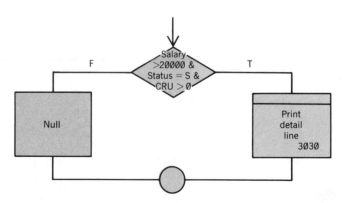

© SRA 1988, 1983

Since some form of action is required only when the conditions specified are true, the section of the flowchart could also have been constructed as follows:

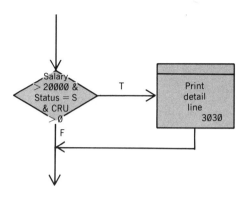

USING OR   When OR is used, *at least one* of the conditions specified must be true. If not, the ELSE portion of the statement will be executed. Assume that a report lists all customers who reside in the 48002, 48003, and 48004 zip code areas. The MF-zip-code field contains the customer's zip-code number. The pseudocode statement would be written as follows:

```
IF MF-zip-code = 48002 OR MF-zip-code = 48003 OR
MF-zip-code = 48004 THEN
    PERFORM 3020-print-detail-line
ELSE
    NULL
ENDIF
```

Assume that the inventory manager would like a report listing all items that are either out of stock, below the reorder point, or have items on backorder. The fields involved are MF-quantity-on-hand, MF-reorder-point, and MF-on-backorder. In some cases, all three conditions might be true. However, as soon as one condition is found to be true, the THEN portion of the statement will be executed. The pseudocode for the statement would be written as follows:

```
IF MF-quantity-on-hand = 0 OR MF-reorder-G point >
MF-quantity-on-hand OR MF-on-backorder > 0 THEN
    PERFORM 3030-print-detail-line
ELSE
    NULL
ENDIF
```

SUMMARY OF LOGICAL OPERATIONS AND AND OR   Figure 3–4 summarizes what occurs when a compound condition involving two evaluations is made using either AND or OR. The summary is also referred to as a truth table.

USING NOT   The logical operator NOT reverses the truth of a single operator. The argument is evaluated, and if it is found to be true, the results are reversed. For example, assume that an employee has an S stored in his or her status field. A report is to be printed listing all employees who are not classified as hourly or salaried. The pseudocode would be written:

```
IF MF-status NOT = 'S' AND MF-status NOT = 'H' THEN
    PERFORM 3020-print-detail-line
ELSE
    NULL
ENDIF
```

In evaluating the expression in which the status field considered does contain an S, the following evaluation process occurs:

1. MF-Status is equal to S so the condition is true. Using NOT reverses the results, so the condition is false.
2. MF-Status is not equal to an H so the condition is false. Using NOT reverses the results, so the condition is true.
3. When AND is used, both arguments must be true. Since only one condition is true, the ELSE portion of the statement will be executed.

If the MF-status field had contained a P for part-time or a T for temporary employee, both evaluations would be true and the THEN portion of the statement would be executed.

When only a single argument is used, there may be an easier way to write a statement than by using NOT. For example, suppose that all customers who have a zero balance are to be listed on a report. The statement could be written in either of the following ways and the same result would be achieved.

```
IF MF-balance NOT > 0 THEN
               or
IF MF-balance = 0 THEN
```

In using NOT, a programmer must be careful that valid results are achieved. Just as there is a hierarchy for evaluating arithmetic expressions, there is also one for logical operators. After the relational operators are evaluated, the logical operators are evaluated. In order of priority, from highest to lowest, NOT takes precedence, then AND, and finally OR.

A WORD OF CAUTION Since two of the goals of structured programming are "avoid undue complexity" and "ease of maintenance," the use of NOT should be avoided when possible. AND and OR should be avoided *if their use adds to the complexity of the program or makes program maintenance more difficult.*

Review of the simple IF

In what has been termed the "simple IF" there is a great deal of power. The statement may include one or many conditions that will be evaluated using the logical operators described in Figure 3–2. The use of the logical operator AND or OR permits compound evaluations to be made with the results indicated in Figure 3–4. The logical operator NOT reverses the true or false condition determined by using only the data and the relational operators. Therefore, when NOT is used in conjunction with either AND or OR, the results should be thoroughly tested.

© SRA 1988, 1983

Figure 3–4 Summary of multicondition statements using AND or OR.

Truth Table

Condition 1	Condition 2	Condition 1 AND Condition 2	Condition 1 OR Condition 2
True	True	True	True
True	False	False	True
False	True	False	True
False	False	False	False

CHECKPOINT QUESTIONS

1. In the previous chapters, what two types of IF statements were discussed?

2. What happens when a branching instruction is executed?

3. In a program a branching command is generated from a PERFORM or GOSUB statement. After the commands located within the module specified are executed, how does the computer know which command should be executed next?

4. In developing the logic of a program, can the contents of a field defined as alphanumeric be compared to the contents of a field defined as numeric?

5. In what three ways can a simple IF statement be written?

6. What are the relational operators?

7. When a statement with multiple evaluations is coded, how does the use of the logical operators AND and OR differ?

8. What occurs when the logical operator NOT is used in an evaluation?

9. Why do programmers sometimes avoid using NOT, AND, and OR?

10. When writing a formula used in pseudocode or on a Nassi-Shneiderman chart, why is it a good idea to include any necessary parentheses?

11. The following statement is written in pseudocode:

    ```
    Over-time-pay = (hours - 40) * rate * 2
    ```

    a. If hours equal 45 and the rate equals $12, what will be stored in the over-time-pay field after the calculations are completed? In what sequence were the arithmetic operations performed?

    b. Assuming the hours and rate are the same, what value would be stored in over-time-pay if the parentheses had been omitted?

12. If the parentheses are omitted from the source code:
    a. When *should* the error be detected?

    b. If the error is not detected until after the source code is entered into the computer, will the employees receive the correct amount of overtime pay?

NESTED IF/THEN/ELSE

Although some of the previous illustrations of IF statements had compound conditions using either AND or OR, only one statement was executed for either the true or false portion of the IF statement. Also, a NULL might have been used for either the true or false part of the statement. The illustration provided in this section requires more than one statement to be executed when the condition is either true or false. In addition, within the THEN (when the condition is true) and the ELSE (when the condition is false) portion of the IF statement there will be nested IF/THEN/ELSE statements. When the logic plan is translated into source code, programmers must make certain nested IF statements are coded correctly. When pseudocode is used, proper formatting helps to make sure that *every IF has its own ELSE and ENDIF.*

When source code is compiled or interpreted, the assumption is made that the ELSE closest to an IF is the one that should be used. If an ELSE is omitted, results can be disastrous.

An Example

Assume that the following fields of information are available either from a transaction file or from the payroll master file. The IF statements appear within the compute-gross-pay module. To keep the illustration as simple as possible, unless an employee has both a transaction record and a master file record the compute-gross-pay module will not be executed. The following data must be available when the compute-gross-pay module is executed:

MF-status	If an H is stored within the field, the employee is hourly. An S designates a salaried employee's record.
TR-nopay	If a salaried worker has an N in the nopay field, the employee is not to be paid a regular salary. However, the employee may still receive a portion of his or her bonus.
MF-salary	Only salaried employees have an amount is this field.
MF-pay-periods	Dividing pay periods into salary gives a salaried employee's weekly wage.
MF-rate	The field contains the rate hourly employees are paid.
TR-hours	The total hours an hourly employee worked per week. Our employees receive 1.5 their normal rate for all hours over 38.
MF-bonus	If the value stored in the bonus field is greater than zero, the amount stored in the bonus field is divided by the MF-bonus-payments field to determine how much is to be paid in this pay period.

While MF is used to indicate the data is stored in the master file, TR is used to designate the transaction file. The value to be calculated is the employee's total gross pay. However, separate amounts are to be calculated for regular, overtime, and bonus pay. Also before the nested IF statement is executed, a simple IF statement was used to determine that the value stored in the status field was either an S or an N.

Figure 3–5 illustrates how the pseudocode would be written. Braces have been added to the pseudocode to emphasize how the IF statements are nested. Also the small numbers to the right of the statements will be used when we

© SRA 1988, 1983

```
                        Nested IF/THEN/ELSE Statements

        IF MF-Status = 'S' THEN
            Overtime-pay = 0                                            1
            IF TR-Nopay NOT = 'N' THEN                                  2
                IF-MF-Pay-periods > 0 THEN                              3
                    Regular-pay = MF-Salary / MF-Pay-periods           4
                ELSE                                                    5
                    PERFORM 3080-Execute-error-routine                6
                    Regular-pay = 0                                   6A
                ENDIF
            ELSE
                Regular-pay = 0                                        7
            ENDIF
        ELSE
            IF TR-Hours <= 38 THEN                                     8
                Regular-pay = TR-Hours * MF-Rate                      9
                Overtime-pay = 0                                     10
            ELSE                                                      11
                Regular-pay = MF-Rate * 38                           12
                Overtime-pay = (TR-Hours - 38)  * MF-Rate * 1.5      13
            ENDIF
        ENDIF

        IF  MF-Bonus > 0 THEN                                         14
            IF MF-bonus-payments > 0 THEN                            15
                Bonus-pay = MF-Bonus / MF-bonus-payments            16
            ELSE
                PERFORM 3080-Execute-error-routine                  17
                Bonus-pay = 0                                       18
            ENDIF
        ELSE
            Bonus-pay = 0                                            19
        ENDIF

        Total-pay = Regular-pay + Overtime-pay + Bonus pay          20
```

Figure 3–5 *Nested IF statements.*

walk through the logic. Neither the braces nor the numbers would usually be included as part of the pseudocode. As you examine the code, note:

1. There are two nested IF statements. The first determines the calculations needed to compute regular and overtime pay. The second statement is used to calculate bonus pay. In order to avoid paying an excessive rate of income tax in one pay period, bonus payments are spread over several pay periods.

2. The THEN portion of the IF statement pertaining to salaried employees contains two additional levels of IF/THEN/ELSE. The ELSE portion pertaining to hourly employees has one nested IF.

3. In many cases both the THEN and ELSE portion of the IF statement have more than one statement.

4. When nesting occurs, the nested IF statements are indented and each has its own ELSE and ENDIF.

Testing the logic   The numbers to the right of the pseudocode were placed there to make it easier to walkthrough the code. In the walkthrough, the following data is used to determine if *valid* results will be produced.

EMPLOYEE	MARY	GEORGE	CARL	SUE	MANUEL
MF-status	S	H	H	S	S
MF-nopay	N				
MF-salary	52,000	0	0	26,000	39,000
MF-pay-periods	52	0	0	52	0
MF-rate	0	10.50	9.48	0	0
TR-hours	0	40	35	0	0
MF-bonus	0	0	1000	0	500
MF-bonus-payments	0	0	0	0	5

Based on the test data listed, the program will determine which statements within the module will be executed. Remember, the calculate-gross-pay module will only be executed if an employee has a status code of an S or an H. An employee must have both a transaction and master file record. Also, statement 20 is executed for all employees. Therefore, it is imperative that regular-pay, overtime-pay, and bonus-pay are either calculated or set to zero each time the module is executed.

THE WALKTHROUGH   *Mary*   Since MF-Status = "S" is true, statement 2 is executed and the test under 3 is false (the use of NOT reversed the results of the evaluation). Her TR-nopay is equal to an N, and so control goes to statement 7 and regular-pay is set to zero. Control then goes to statement 14. Because MF-bonus is equal to zero, control passes to statement 19. When statement 20 is executed, Mary's pay will be equal to zero.

George   Since the employee's status is not an S, control immediately passes to statement 8. Since the test hours <= 38 is false, control passes to 11 and the employee's regular and overtime earnings are calculated. Control passes to 14 and because the test is false, statement 19 is executed.

Carl   Since the employee's status is not an S, control passes to statement 8. The conditions tested in 8 are true; therefore, regular-pay is calculated and overtime is set to zero. The test in 14 is true and statement 15 is executed. Because the test is false, statements 17 and 18 are executed. Control branches to the error routine specified and then returns to the following statement (18).

Why is the test "IF MF-bonus-payments > 0" included? If an attempt is made to divide by a field that has the value of zero, the program will usually abort. If the job doesn't abort, an error condition is set. It is still up to the programmer to set an **error trap** and write the necessary code to recover from the error.

Sue   The employee's status is an S, so statement 1 and then 2 will be executed. Since the test in 2 is true, the test specified in 3 is executed and found to be true. After Sue's regular-pay is calculated, control passes to statement 14. That condition is false, and therefore the ELSE portion of the IF is executed and bonus-pay is set to 0.

Manuel   Because the employee's status is an S, statements 1 and 2 are executed. The test in 2 is true, and so control passes to statement 3. Since the test in 3 is false, the error routine specified in 5 is executed. After the error routine is executed, control returns to statement 6A and regular-pay is set to

© SRA 1988, 1983

0. Control then passes to 14 when the conditions in both 14 and 15 are true. Bonus is calculated by dividing 5 into 500. Statement 20 is then executed.

Were all conditions tested?

Consider the test data used:

MF-status	Data for both salaried and hourly employees was provided.
TR-nopay	The record for Mary tested the nopay code.
MF-salary	Sue's record tested to see that a salaried employee's pay would be calculated correctly.
MF-pay periods	Sue's record tested a valid condition; Manuel's record tested the error routine.
MF-rate	The mathematical calculations for George and Carl test the calculations for both regular pay and overtime pay.
MF-bonus	Both the valid condition and error condition are tested. Sue's bonus-pay will be zero and Manuel's will be $100.

In the calculate-gross-pay module, all conditions that might occur were tested. If the programs that created the transaction and master file programs are well-written and completely tested, the error routine should never be invoked since the test performed in statement 4 or statement 10 should never be true. When a salaried person is hired or receives a pay increase, their salary and number of installments over which it will be received is recorded in their master file record. Pay-periods should never be equal to zero. Also, if a person has a bonus, the number of installments to be received must be recorded in the MF-bonus-payments field. However, over the years programmers have learned to test for the "it can never happen" conditions. For example, when the master file record for a salaried employee was created, an error message indicated that the pay-period field was zero. However, the person responsible for correcting the error failed to make the necessary correction.

Key points to be remembered

Make certain a value from a previous cycle through a program is either recalculated or set to zero. George had two hours of overtime which resulted in overtime pay of $31.50. When Carl's pay is computed, it is on the basis of 35 hours. If overtime-pay is not set to 0, George's overtime pay could be added to Carl's total pay. Resetting numeric fields to zero between program cycles can be done in several different ways.

The "it can never happen" conditions must be tested! Programmers should remember Murphy's law: "If something can go wrong, it will." Today computers have large memories and a great deal of online storage space is available. There is no excuse for not testing for errors that *should not* but sometimes do occur.

Sometimes you hear a computer operator or programmer say, "That program has been operational for two years and never aborted. Why did it abort now?" In investigating the problem, the maintenance programmer will find that one of three things finally happened: an error-condition occurred that had not been tested; one of those "it can never happen" situations finally occured; or when the program was modified a logical error occurred which was not detected when the revised program was tested.

Alternate method

As with any program or module, there are alternate ways of achieving the same results. For example, prior to writing the IF statements, all of the fields used in the calculations should have been set to zero. The logic would show:

- Regular-pay = 0
- Over-time pay = 0
- Bonus-pay = 0
- Total-pay = 0

If this were done, some of the statements located within the nested IF/THEN/ELSE could either be eliminated or changed to NULL. This approach

Figure 3–6 Nassi-Shneiderman chart for the calculate-gross-pay module.

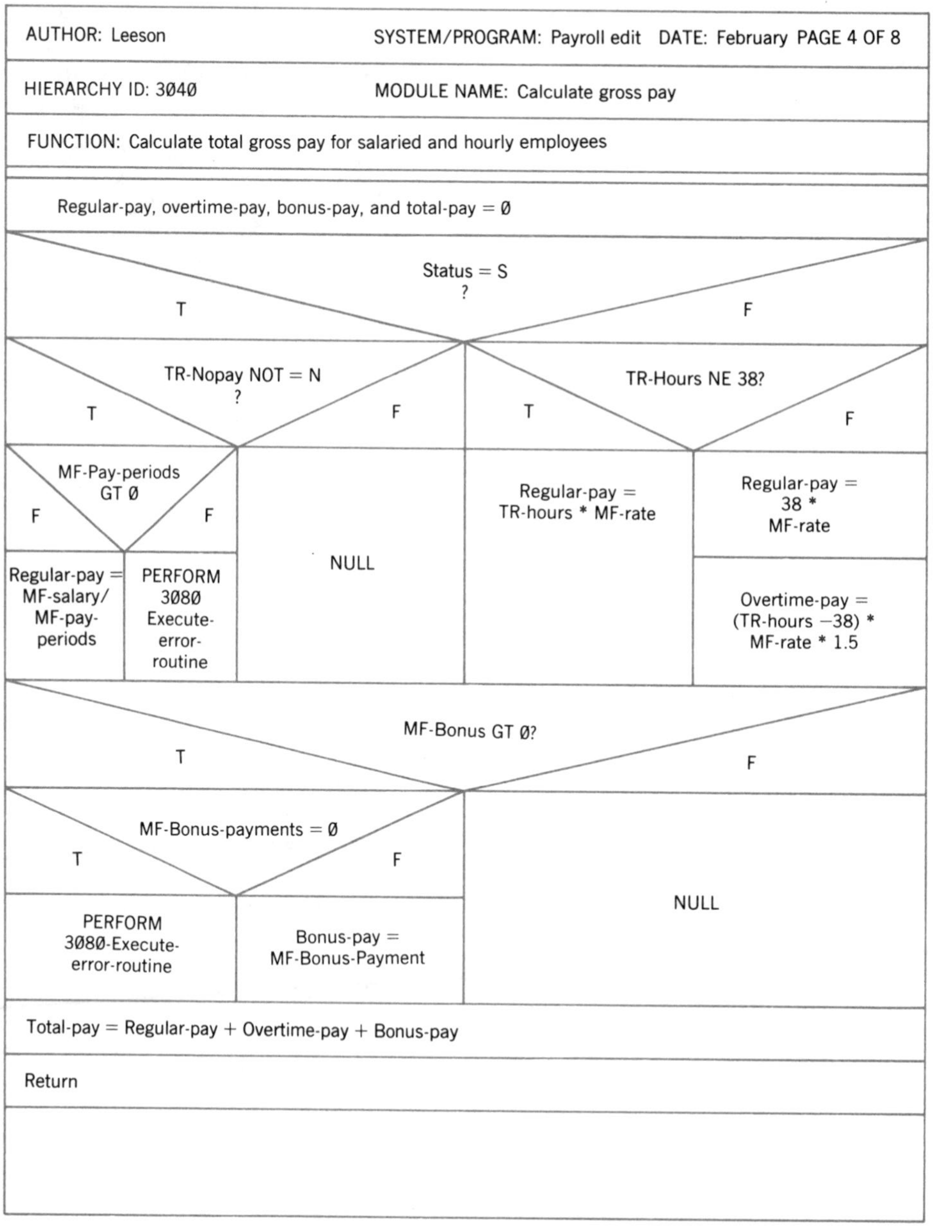

AUTHOR: Leeson	SYSTEM/PROGRAM: Payroll edit DATE: February PAGE 4 OF 8
HIERARCHY ID: 3040	MODULE NAME: Calculate gross pay

FUNCTION: Calculate total gross pay for salaried and hourly employees

Regular-pay, overtime-pay, bonus-pay, and total-pay = 0

Status = S ?
T — F

TR-Nopay NOT = N ?   TR-Hours NE 38?
T — F   T — F

MF-Pay-periods GT 0
F — F

Regular-pay = MF-salary/ MF-pay-periods

PERFORM 3080 Execute-error-routine

NULL

Regular-pay = TR-hours * MF-rate

Regular-pay = 38 * MF-rate

Overtime-pay = (TR-hours −38) * MF-rate * 1.5

MF-Bonus GT 0?
T — F

MF-Bonus-payments = 0
T — F

PERFORM 3080-Execute-error-routine

Bonus-pay = MF-Bonus-Payment

NULL

Total-pay = Regular-pay + Overtime-pay + Bonus-pay

Return

© SRA 1988, 1983

would save only one statement. Therefore, in terms of efficiency, both methods are essentially the same. The method that seems the clearest and easiest to maintain should be used. The Nassi-Shneiderman chart illustrated in Figure 3–6 illustrates the second method. In both the Nassi-Shneiderman chart and the Warnier-Orr diagram illustrated in Figure 3–7, GT is used for greater than (>), LT is used for less than (<), and LE is used for less or equal to (<=).

The structured flowchart for the compute-gross-pay module is constructed in the same way the pseudocode was written. In this example, the true conditions are to the right and the false conditions are to the left of the decision point. Because of lack of space, in two cases when the condition is true the process block is placed directly below the decision. Although there is no rule stating in which direction the true statements are to be placed, a programmer should be consistent. Therefore, in all future flowcharts, when the condition is true the required statements will be either to the right of the decision point and the required false statements will be to the left or directly underneath the decision point.

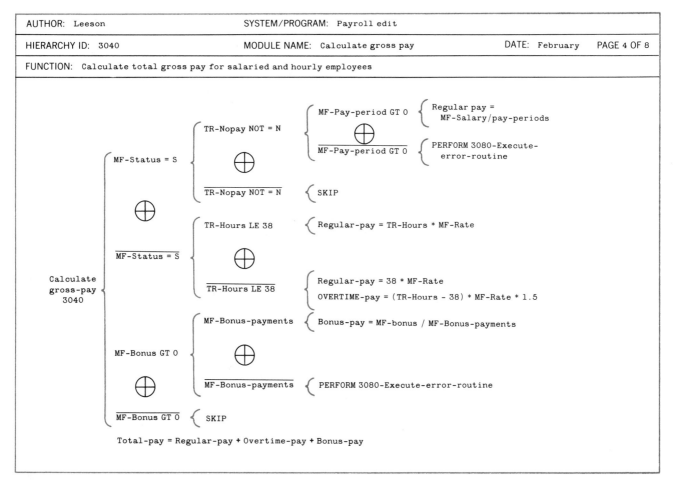

AUTHOR: Leeson	SYSTEM/PROGRAM: Payroll edit		
HIERARCHY ID: 3040	MODULE NAME: Calculate gross pay	DATE: February	PAGE 4 OF 8

FUNCTION: Calculate total gross pay for salaried and hourly employees

Figure 3–7 *Warnier-Orr diagram for calculate-gross-pay module.*

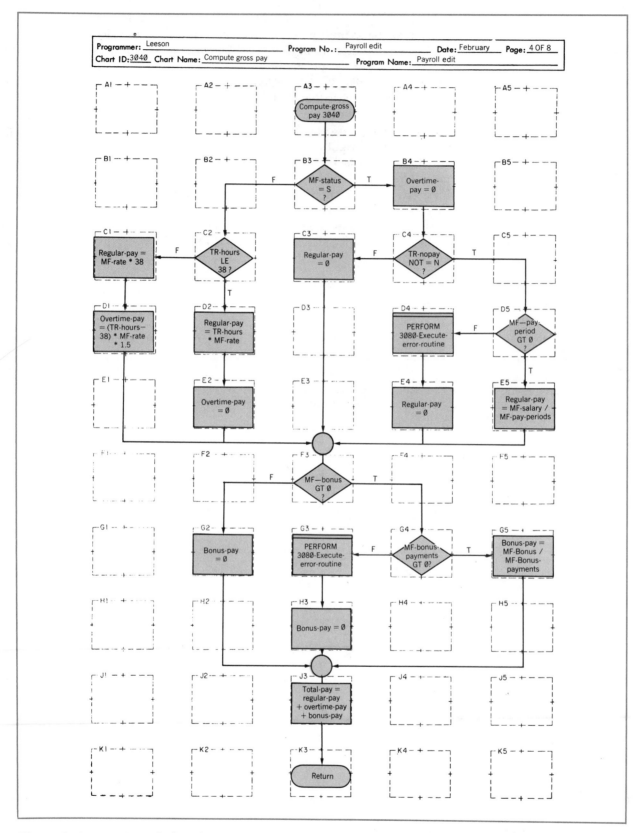

Figure 3–8 Structured flowchart for the calculate-gross-pay module.

© SRA 1988, 1983

13. When nested IF statements are coded in pseudocode, what two key words must be used for each IF statement?

14. In coding a nested IF statement, the programmer forgot to code one of the NULL ELSE statements. The IF statement was nested as follows:

```
IF condition-1
    IF condition-2
        IF condition-3
        ELSE condition-3
    ELSE condition-2
ELSE condition-1
```

What could occur if the innermost ELSE for condition-3 were omitted?

15. Why should nested IF statements be formatted in the manner illustrated in question 14?

16. Must an IF statement always have an ELSE?

17. Why should a test be made to see if a field equals zero before dividing the contents of that field into another field?

18. In Figure 3–4, why was statement 19 (MF-bonus-pay = 0) included rather than using a NULL ELSE?

19. In the calculate-gross-pay module, would it have been more efficient to set all of the values to zero at the beginning of the module rather than setting them as the IF/THEN/ELSE logic was being executed?

20. In writing pseudocode, how are the various levels of nesting shown?

21. In the Nassi-Shneiderman chart, how was it indicated that a predetermined process was to be executed?

22. In developing a Nassi-Shneiderman chart, what problem might exist if five levels of nesting were required? In Figure 3–5 only three levels of nesting were required.

23. In the Warnier-Orr diagram, what does the bar above a statement such as "MF-bonus GT 0" indicate?

24. How is nesting shown on a Warnier-Orr diagram?

25. Using the Warnier-Orr diagram shown in Figure 3–6, calculate the gross pay for each of the following cases:
    a. MF-status = S, MF-salary = 46,000, MF-nopay has a space stored in the field, MF-pay-periods = 0, MF-bonus = 1000, MF-bonus-payments = 5
    b. MF-status = H, MF-rate = 0, TR-hours = 40, MF-bonus = 0
    c. MF-status = H, MF-rate = 10, TR-hours = 44, MF-bonus = 800, MF-bonus-payments = 8

26. In the above example, there is obviously invalid data in a. Since the field of data (rate) came from the record retrieved from the master file, when should the error have been detected? Should a check such as "IF MF-rate <= 0" have been included in the calculate-gross-pay module?

27. Using pseudocode, how would you write the statements needed to display an appropriate error message? Assume the payroll clerk is keying in data for a new employee and the following "checks" are to be included in the program that adds the new employee records to the file:

a. When the MF-status-code is equal to an S, the salary field must have an amount greater than zero stored within the field and the MF-pay-periods must be greater than zero.

b. All hourly employees must have an hourly rate which is greater than zero.

c. When the bonus field is greater than zero, the times field must contain a number that is greater than zero.

CASE ENTRY   Case entry structures are used whenever similar multitest conditions occur. Rather than having nested IF statements or separate IF/THEN statements, the entire structure is considered one statement. Today most programming languages support the use of both nested IF statements and case entry structures. Case entry could be used in the following situations.

- An educational institution has employees classified as follows: administrative (A); faculty (F); maintenance (M); classified (C); secretarial (S); and part-time (P). Each group's pay is calculated differently and separate totals are maintained for each group.

- In a program six different types of error could occur. When an error occurs, a value of from 1 to 6 is placed in the error-type field. In error module, case entry is used to determine the error description that is to be displayed as part of the message. The message contains the number and name of the employee and the description of the error.

- The sex field should contain either an F or an M. If the field contains an F or M, one is added to either the female or male total. Any other value stored in the field will cause an error routine to be executed.

- The personnel department would like to know how many employees were born in each of the following years: 1928, 1929, 1930, 1931, and 1932. A separate total will be developed for each of the five years.

In the first example, if the MF-status-code is not an A, F, M, C, S, or P, a default routine should be invoked. In the second example, since the programmer determines what is stored in the error-type field, a default error routine is not provided. In the third example, if the value stored in the MF-sex field is not an F or M, an error routine should be executed. In the last example, only the birth years of 1928–1932 are to be included in the survey. Although the other years represent valid data, no action is required when the year is not one ranging from 1928–1932.

Case entry structures for the last example will be developed using a flowchart, Nassi-Shneiderman chart, Warnier-Orr diagram, and pseudocode. Note that in both the pseudocode and N-S chart NULL is used to indicate that the coding for a default condition has not been overlooked.

When case entry structures are used, if the conditions specified are true, then either a single statement, multiple statements, or a statement calling either an internal or external subroutine may be used.

When the source code is written, the entire structure is coded as one IF/THEN/ELSE statement. Also when the logic is developed and the code is written, the situation that will occur the most is coded first. As soon as a true condition occurs, the required statements are executed, and control passes to

© SRA 1988, 1983

the statement which follows the complete IF/THEN/ELSE statement. Using the case entry structure is more efficient than using separate IF/THEN statements.

CHECKPOINT QUESTIONS

28. Will a case entry structure always provide for a default routine?
29. In terms of program execution, why is using case entry more efficient than using a series of IF/THEN/ELSE statements?
30. In the example used to demonstrate nested IF/THEN/ELSE statements, under what circumstances could case entry be used?

CREATING AN ORDER ENTRY PROGRAM

When online, interactive programs are developed, every effort should be made to make them user friendly. An interactive program is one in which the operator had two-way communication with the computer. Often the operator is a user who is unfamiliar with both the computer and the software. Messages are displayed and the operator responds to questions. Because computers have larger memories and more online storage is available, the trend is to have more internal documentation displayed to provide background information. In addition, directions for entering data and executing the program may also be

Figure 3–9 Flowchart and Warnier-Orr diagram for case entry.

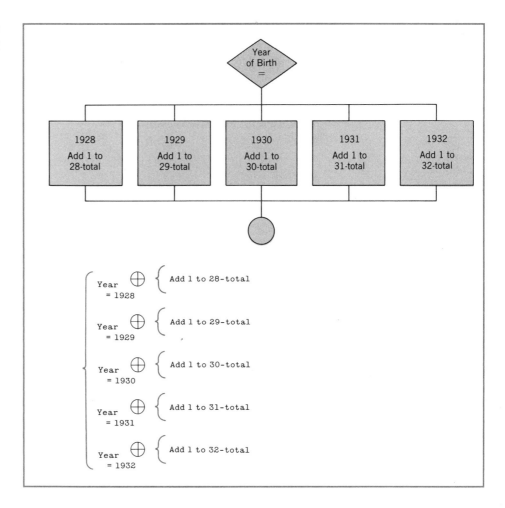

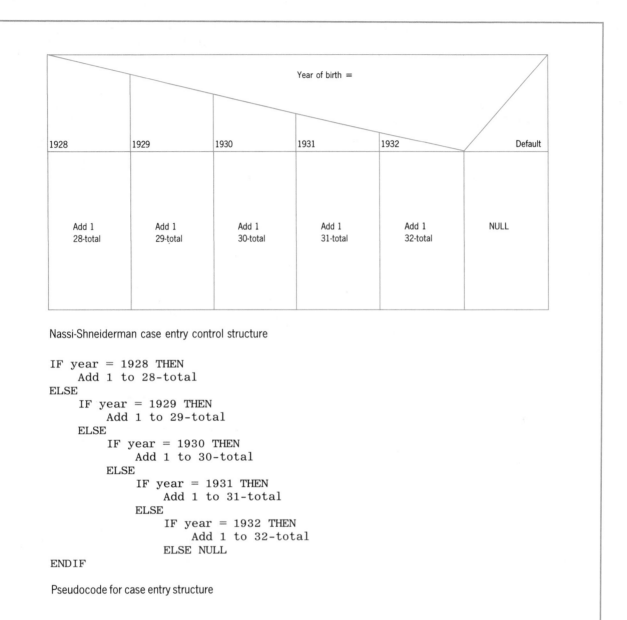

Figure 3–10   Nassi-Shneiderman and pseudocode for case entry structure.

provided. Often a help menu is provided to list the types of instructions that are available; this can be displayed on the VDT.

Since data entered into an interactive program is processed immediately, every effort must be made to make certain that:

- operators entering the data understand the correct procedure, what occurs if invalid data is entered, and what must be done to correct the error.
- every effort is made to ensure the validity of data entering the system.
- all directions are clearly stated in a consistent manner.
- prompts are provided that indicate what data is to be entered, the format used for entering the data, and in some cases the length of the field.

© SRA 1988, 1983

Providing prompts

The operator who enters the data should be able to determine if the help screen is to be displayed. Prompts such as PLEASE ENTER THE DATE AS MM-DD-YYYY should be provided each time the program is run. One screen should explain that in the MM-DD-YYYY format November 13, 1988 is entered as 11-13-1988.

Operators familiar with the program do not need help screens. New operators, who are unfamiliar with the program, need specific instructions.

Data to be entered

In the example provided in Figure 3–11, data is entered into an online order-entry system by an operator talking to a sales representative. The sales representative remains in contact with the terminal operator until the order is en-

---

Program Specifications for the Order-Entry Program

Input keyed by operator	Results
Beginning invoice number	Each time an order is entered, 1 is added to the number. The number entered is the last invoice number from the previous day's sales order processing.
Date	The date for all invoices will be the date keyed in by the operator.
Account number	Customer's master file record is retrieved and the customer's name and address are displayed. If the wrong name is displayed, or a record does not exist for the customer, a new number must be entered.
	When the right record is retrieved, the customer's credit is checked. If the customer has exceeded his limit, permission to place the order must be obtained from the credit manager. Processing of the account is suspended until the credit manager determines if the order can be processed.
Item number	The required inventory master file record is retrieved and the description of the product is displayed. If the description displayed does not match the one provided by the sales representative or if an invalid number is entered, the sales representative will be asked to check the item number.
Quantity ordered	The quantity ordered is checked with the quantity on hand. If there is not enough on hand to process the order, the items that can be substituted are displayed. The operator gives this information to the sales representative and one of three things can occur: the order for the item is cancelled, the customer orders the substitute items, or the item is placed on backorder.

Master file records
Customer master
Inventory master

Output
Printed sales invoice
Sales invoice file
Backorder file

Controls
Visual confirmation of customer's name and address
Visual confirmation of product description
Visual confirmation of quantity ordered
Edit quantity to determine that only numeric data is entered.

Figure 3–11   Program specifications for the order-entry program.

tered. A customer may order more than one item of merchandise. To simplify the problem further, assume that orders are sent out immediately. The data is entered, the **sales invoice** printed, and the order assembled and shipped immediately. All orders are "on account" and a discount is given for payments received within ten days.

Figure 3–11 provides the program specifications. Since we are concerned only about the detailed logic plan for the initialization and help modules, detailed information regarding the contents of the files is not provided.

Modules illustrated

The order-entry example is only concerned with the main control, initialization, and help modules plus the supporting modules controlled by the help module. Figure 3–12 illustrates the *beginning* of the hierarchy chart. Although the hierarachy chart should be fully developed, this shows only the major modules as well as the ones illustrated in Figure 3–13. Figure 3–13 provides the detailed logic for the online-order entry, initialization, and initiate-help-screens modules as well as the logic for the modules that may be invoked by initiate help screens. Those modules, along with stubs for the process-sales-data and the termination modules, will be coded and used as one of the interactive projects.

Note that the main control module still invokes the three major modules—initialization, process sales data, and termination.

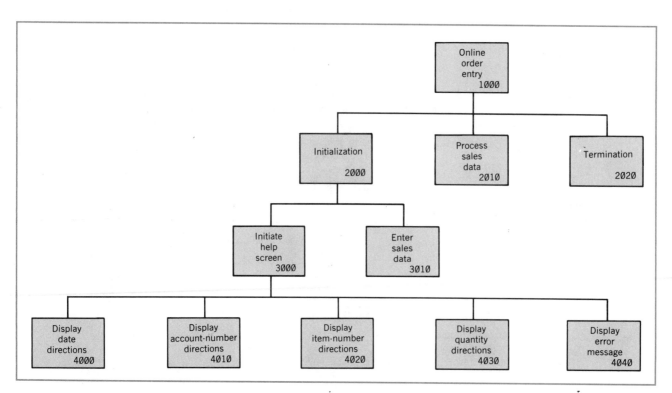

Figure 3–12   Incomplete hierarchy chart for the online sales order-entry system.

© SRA 1988, 1983

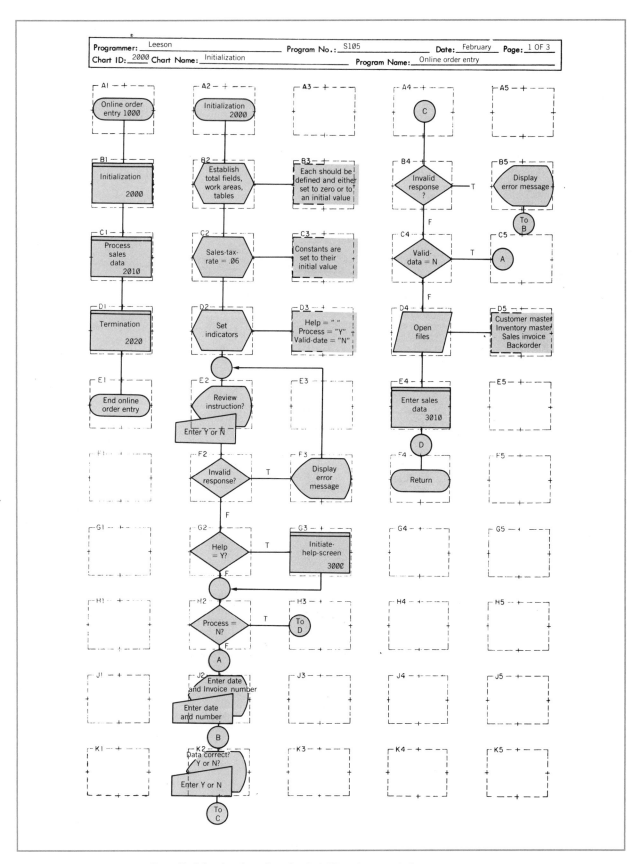

Figure 3–13 Part 1   Detailed logic plan for the initilization module.

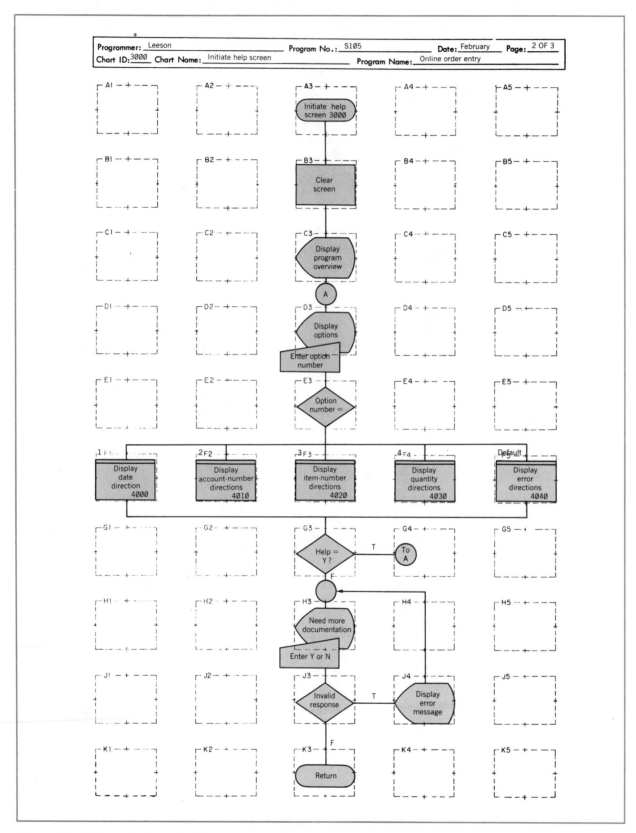

Figure 3–13 Part 2   Detailed logic plan for the initiate-help-screen module.

© SRA 1988, 1983

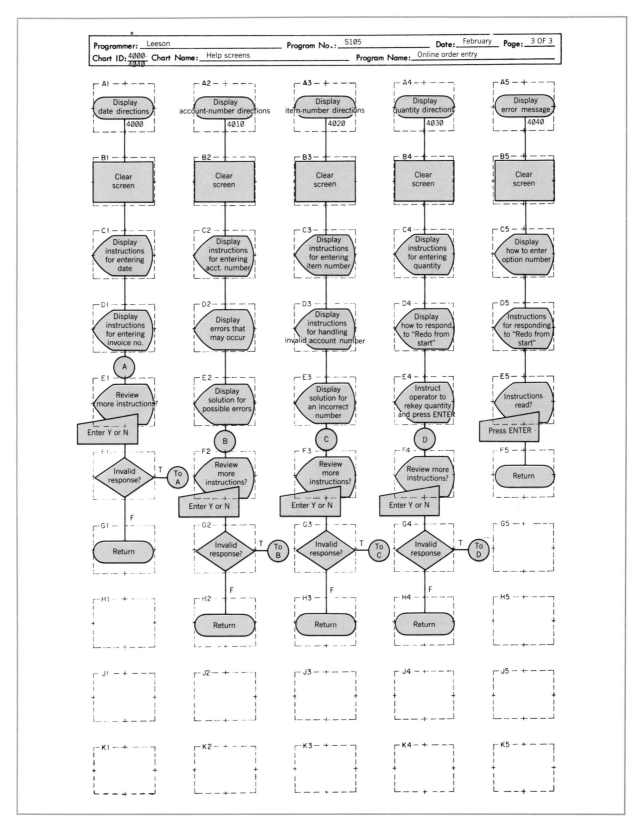

Figure 3–13 Part 3 Detailed logic plans for the help screens.

INITIALIZATION What belongs in the initialization module? This module might also be called the "let's gets started" or "housekeeping details" module. Since the individual fields that will be used to maintain totals and in developing intermediate answers have not been determined, the flowchart for the initialization module in some areas is generic rather than specific.

As you study the illustration provided in Figure 3–13, note that the following tasks are performed:

1. Total fields, work areas, and indicators are established. Usually each of these will be listed and set to their proper value.

2. Constants are established. When it is necessary to change a constant, the maintenance programmer knows exactly where to look. Also, although the constant may be used in several statements, it is only necessary to make one change. In the program, a constant is established for the rate used in calculating sales tax.

3. The operator is given an opportunity to review the information provided in the help screens. If the operator responds to the question "REVIEW INSTRUCTIONS? Y or N?" with a Y, the initiate-help-screens module will be invoked.

4. Constants such as the date are entered. The date and invoice number are entered once each time the program is run. Each time an order is processed for a new customer, one will be added to the invoice number. As long as an N is stored in valid-date, control remains in the loop and the operator can rekey the date and invoice number. The question DATE AND INVOICE NUMBER CORRECT? Y OR N? requires a response. Hopefully before responding to the message, the operator reviews the data keyed in. In this case the valid-date indicator is set to N just prior to the loop being executed.

5. Files are opened. Why files must be opened and what occurs when they are opened will be covered in Chapter 6, File Handling.

6. The enter-sales-data module is invoked. This permits the first record of data to be processed in the same fashion as the last record of data. The alternatives available when multiple input files are used will be covered in Chapter 6.

7. An indicator, called *process*, is used as a means of by-passing the **imperative statements** used to enter the date, open the files, and to invoke the Enter-sales-data module. Imperative statements are those that generate commands, or action, while **declarative statements** only establish fields and addresses. Also if this indicator is set to N, the statements in the Process-sales-data and Termination modules will be by-passed.

The sequence of these tasks may vary. However, each programmer should determine the sequence in which the required initialization tasks will be accomplished. Using a consistent pattern for performing the required tasks helps to eliminate omissions and errors.

HELP MODULES Although all of the instructions in the example could have been included in one module, a separate module is used for each type of instruction. This is consistent with the guidelines that state, "Keep the logic as simple as possible," and "Modules should not exceed 50 lines of code." If the operator elects to have the documentation displayed, the first screen of information pro-

© SRA 1988, 1983

vides an overview of the program. A help menu is then displayed which allows the operator to obtain directions for:

1. Entering the date and invoice number.
2. Entering the account number.
3. Entering the item number.
4. Entering the quantity.

Note that the initiate-help-screens module provides an excellent example of case entry. Control stays within the module until the operator indicates that additional instructions are not required. Programmers differ in the amount of detail they include in the help modules. In working with information to be displayed on screens, the capacity of the screen must be known. Further, a response is usually required before the next screen is displayed. Frequently the statement PRESS THE ENTER KEY TO CONTINUE is displayed; until the key is pressed, new data will not be displayed.

Another technique that may be used is to display a full screen of data (perhaps 12 double-spaced lines) then pause several seconds before displaying the next screen. Unless the programmer requires a response or causes a delay, **scrolling** results. When scrolling occurs new lines are displayed, the top lines move upward and eventually off the screen. However, when a full screen of data is displayed and the operator is required to respond before the next screen appears, scrolling does not occur. The first screen clears completely *before* the second screen is displayed.

Figure 3–13 Part 2 illustrates the logic used in developing the help module. The screen is cleared and the cursor returned to the first line of the screen. Although the logic plan only shows "display program overview," several lines of general information regarding the program are displayed.

The menu of options available is displayed and the operator selects the option desired by entering either a 1, 2, 3, or 4. After directions are displayed on the screen for the first option selected, the operator is asked MORE IN-STRUCTIONS? Y OR N? If the operator responds with a Y, control returns to the point in the program where the menu is displayed again. After all of the instructions are reviewed, the operator is asked TERMINATE PROGRAM TO STUDY DOCUMENTATION? Y OR N? If the operator responds with a Y, the job will be terminated without the remaining imperative statements being executed in the initialization module. In addition, the commands in the process-sales-data and termination modules will not be executed.

Figure 3–13 Part 3 illustrates the logic used in developing the modules which display the instructions. If an invalid number (one other than 1–4) is entered, the display-error-message module will be executed. All five modules are very similar. The screen is cleared, instructions displayed, and the statement PRESS ENTER TO CONTINUE is displayed at the bottom of the screen. After the ENTER key is pressed, the question MORE INSTRUCTIONS NEEDED? Y OR N? is asked.

STUB TESTING

Interactive exercise 3–1 permits you to test the online-order-entry, initialization, and the initiate-help-screen modules. Stubs are provided for process-sales-data and termination modules. While one programmer writes and tests those modules, a second programmer might be assigned to develop the logic, code, and test the remaining modules. However, the program specifications must be determined before this can occur. Because the intent of the illustration is to show how case entry can be used in creating a menu and how the initialization module is developed, complete specifications were not developed. In the initialization module, additional fields, such as the ones used to store invoice number and the date, should have been established.

31. If directions are provided, should prompts still tell the operator what fields are to be entered?

32. In general, what tasks are performed in the initialization module?

33. What options were displayed on the menu?

34. How can scrolling be prevented so that the operator can read one screen of data before additional information is displayed?

35. On the flowchart, what technique was used to show that instructions requiring a response are to be displayed on the screen?

SUMMARY

- Depending on the source language used to code the program, an IF/THEN/ELSE statement can require:

    Only true actions.

    Only false actions.

    True and false actions.

- IF/THEN/ELSE statements can have more than one true or false action.

- Relational tests can be made for:

=	Equal
< >	Not equal
<	Less than
>	Greater than
< =	Less than or equal to
> =	Greater than or equal to

- The following logical operations can be used:

AND	All conditions specified must be true in order for the IF portion of IF/THEN/ELSE to be executed.
OR	One or more of the conditions specified must be true in order for the IF portion of IF/THEN/ELSE to be executed.
NOT	NOT reverses the truth of a single argument.

- The order in which the commands created by an arithmetic expression are executed is:

( )	The innermost parentheses are cleared, then the outer parentheses are cleared from left to right.
**	Exponentiation occurs.
* /	Multiplication and division.
+ −	Addition and subtraction.

© SRA 1988, 1983

- When operations of equal value are executed, the order of execution is from left to right.

- IF/THEN/ELSE statements can be nested. In executing the statements, the ELSE closest to the IF will be paired with it. The inner statements must be completely enclosed by the outer IF statements. In order to avoid undue complexity, additional modules can be created to avoid complex nesting of IF/THEN/ELSE statements. Good formatting of pseudocode and source code makes it easier to determine how the statements will be executed.

- Case entry is used for multitest conditions. Usually some type of error routine is invoked by default if none of the conditions specified is true. Greater efficiency results if the condition which occurs most frequently is tested first, the condition which occurs next most often second, and so forth.

- In the initialization module illustrated in this chapter:

    Total areas, work areas, and tables are defined and set to their initial value.

    Constants are established.

    Indicators are established and set to their initial value.

    Variables, such as the date for a report or the beginning invoice number, are entered.

    Files are opened.

    The initial record (or records) may be read.

    A provision may be made for permitting the operator to review the directions for entering data.

    An option may be provided to permit orderly exit from the program. The reason the operator elects to cancel the program should be identified.

- In establishing menus that provide a series of options, case entry is usually used.

- Scrolling is prevented by requiring the operator to press a key, such as ENTER, before additional data is displayed.

- When only some of the modules are designed and coded, they may be tested by inserting stubs in place of the modules which are not yet designed and coded.

- In testing programs, test data must be provided to test both the normal occurrences and error conditions that may exist. The logic must also provide for the "it-can-never-happen" type of errors.

DISCUSSION QUESTIONS

1. Must action be specified for both the IF (true) and ELSE (false) portions of an IF statement?

2. What relational tests can be made when an IF statement is coded?

3. According to the summary of multicondition statements using AND or OR, what are the differences shown by using AND rather than OR?

4. What rules apply to the nesting of IF statements?

5. Give an illustration showing when case entry should be used. Why is using case entry more efficient than using a series of IF statements that provide action only when the condition specified is true? How should a case entry statement be coded?

6. What tasks are usually accomplished in the initialization module? What determines if the task will be in the initialization module or the process-sales-data module? Does it make any difference in what order the various tasks to be accomplished are shown on the logic plan and then coded?

7. Why is a menu of options pertaining to instructions regarding how data is entered by the operator included in the program rather than in some type of printed documentation?

8. The manager of the computer information services department made the statement "It is better to design, code, and then test the entire program than to use stub testing." Tell why you agree or disagree with his statement.

KEY WORDS

address	imperative statement
alphanumeric data	logical operator
branching command	nested IF statement
database language	relational operator
declarative statement	sales invoice
error trap	scrolling
FORTRAN	string data
GOSUB	

© SRA 1988, 1983

PROJECTS

Your instructor will indicate if pseudocode, structured flowcharts, Warnier-Orr or Nassi-Shneiderman charts are to be used in completing the exercises or problems.

The dean would like a program that computes each student's grade point average for the current semester. The grades are read from a file which has already been created. The following fields of data stored in the file will be used in the program:

> Student name, address, and school code
> Courses taken. For each course the following information is provided:
>> Course number
>> Credit hours
>> Grade received

The hierarchy chart for the program is illustrated in Figure 3–14. In computing the honor points, the following point values are given for the letter grade received. A = 4; B = 3; C = 2; D = 1; and E = 0. Honor points for a single course then equal the credit hours time the points given for the grade received. For example, a B in a 4 credit hour course would provide 12 honor points (3 × 4).

Directions

1. Develop the portion of the logic plan used to calculate the honor points for a single course.

2. The print-detail-line module is invoked when a student has a grade point average equal to or higher than 3.5. Do the portion of the logic plan that will cause the print-detail-line module to be executed if the condition specified is true.

3. After the program is designed, coded, tested, and documented, will it be executed in an interactive or batch mode?

_____

4. If the hierarchy is complete, why isn't some type of help module included?

_____

_____

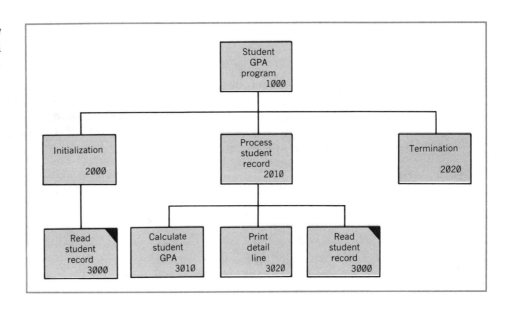

Figure 3–14 Hierarchy chart for the student GPA program.

EXERCISE 3–2

Sales discounts are given on the following basis:

Range	Percent
10,000 or under	1.0
10,001 to 20,000	1.5
20,001 to 30,000	2.0
30,001 to 50,000	2.5
over 50,000	3.0

The discount is computed by multiplying the amount of the sale times the percentage. Sales tax is computed only if the number stored in the sales-tax-rate field is greater than zero. If sales tax is to be calculated, the rate is stored in the sales-tax-rate field.

1. Develop the logic required to calculate the amount of the discount.
2. Develop the logic that must be used to calculate the amount of sales tax.

EXERCISE 3–3

A report is to be printed regarding the type of employees hired by our company. The master file contains the following fields of data that will be used in producing the report:

Field	Contents
MF-sex	M or F
MF-employment-class	H or S
MF-age	Exact age of the employee

The report must provide the following totals:

Age	Male Hourly	Male Salaried	Female Hourly	Female Salaried
25 or under	10	15	18	5
26–40	8	11	20	2
41–50	12	9	14	3
over 50	6	19	10	1

In the example, if an employee is male, salaried, and 51, 1 will be added to the over-50-male-salaried field.

1. Determine the names for the fields in which the totals are accumulated. Devise a scheme that is meaningful and easy to use. You will need 16 different fields. Assume that you must have the name of the field start with a letter of the alphabet and that dashes can be used within the field name. What technique will you use in developing the names of the total fields?

   _____

   _____

2. Why should the names of the fields be meaningful?

   _____

3. Use pseudocode and develop the logic required to calculate the required totals. In determining the solution, use nested IF/THEN/ELSE statements.

© SRA 1988, 1983

PROBLEM 3-1

Your instructor will tell you what type of logic plan is to be developed.

Refer to problem 2-1 on p. 73. The CIS manager would like to revise the program to include a help module that contains an overview of the program and specific instructions for entering the data. In developing the help module, you must:

a. Use a menu approach.
b. Provide directions for printing the information displayed on the VDT. You may assume that you have a PrtSc key on your keyboard. When the key is pressed along with the shift key, the information displayed on the screen will be printed.
c. Prevent scrolling and give your operator time to read the information.
d. Allow the operator to select only those instructions that are needed.

Directions:

1. Revise the initialization module created for Problem 2-1.
2. Develop a detailed logic plan for the Help module and the modules used to display directions to the operator.
3. Review the description of the problem provided on pages 73-75 and give the rationale for including a help module in this particular program.

INTERACTIVE EXERCISE 3-1

The source code is provided to show what occurs when stub testing is used to test the initialization and help modules developed in this chapter.

Directions

1. Review the on line logic of the order entry program that is detailed on pages 103-112.
2. Boot the system and load **BASIC**. Press **F3**, key in **MENU**, and press the **ENTER** key. Press **F2** (RUN) to execute the program. Select menu **1**, Option **4**.

   Do not return to the main menu after the program is executed. You will execute the program several times.

   a. The operator does not want to review the instructions and only valid data is entered. The prompts that will be displayed and the data you are to enter are listed:

Displayed	*Enter*
REVIEW INSTRUCTIONS? Y OR N?	**N**
ENTER DATE AS MM-DD-YYYY	**07-14-1988**
ENTER INVOICE NUMBER	**12345**
DATE AND INVOICE NUMBER CORRECT? Y OR N?	**Y**
RETURN TO MENU PROGRAM? Y OR N?	**N**

   b. The operator does not want to review the instructions. However, the operator enters the wrong date and invoice number.

   Depress **F2** or key in **RUN** <**ENTER**>.

   Note: **RUN** <**ENTER**> is the same as stating, "Key in **RUN** and press the **ENTER** key."

Displayed	Enter
REVIEW INSTRUCTIONS? Y OR N?	**N**
ENTER DATE AS MM-DD-YYYY	**07-18-1988**
ENTER INVOICE NUMBER	**12344**
DATA CORRECT? Y OR N?	**N**
Enter the date as 07-19-1988 and the invoice number as 12345.	
RETURN TO MENU PROGRAM? Y OR N?	**N**

3. The operator wants to review the instructions. Good data will then be entered first and then an invalid option number will be entered. Enter **RUN** <**ENTER**> or press **F2**.

Displayed	Enter
REVIEW INSTRUCTIONS? Y OR N?	**Y**
NUMBER OF HELP SCREEN TO BE DISPLAYED?	**1**
REVIEW MORE INSTRUCTIONS? Y OR N?	**Y**
NUMBER OF HELP SCREEN TO BE DISPLAYED?	**2**
REVIEW MORE INSTRUCTIONS? Y OR N?	**Y**
NUMBER OF HELP SCREEN TO BE DISPLAYED?	**3**
REVIEW MORE INSTRUCTIONS? Y OR N?	**Y**
NUMBER OF HELP SCREEN TO BE DISPLAYED?	**4**
REVIEW MORE INSTRUCTIONS? Y OR N?	**Y**
NUMBER OF HELP SCREEN TO BE DISPLAYED?	**7**
NUMBER OF HELP SCREEN TO BE DISPLAYED?	**B**
NUMBER OF HELP SCREEN TO BE DISPLAYED?	**4**
REVIEW MORE INSTRUCTIONS? Y OR N?	**N**
CONTINUE PROGRAM EXECUTION? Y OR N?	**Y**
ENTER DATE IN MONTH, DAY, YEAR FORMAT	**07-18-1988**
ENTER INVOICE NUMBER	**12345**
DATA CORRECT? Y OR N?	**Y**
RETURN TO MENU PROGRAM? Y OR N?	**T**
When RETURN TO MENU PROGRAM is displayed again	**N**

4. Make the following changes in the program:

LIST 330 <**ENTER**>

LET VALIDDATE$ = "N" will be displayed.

Change the **N** to a **Y**. Press **ENTER.**

RUN <ENTER> or press F2.

REVIEW INSTRUCTIONS? Y OR N? **N**

After you are sure you can answer the questions, RETURN TO MENU PROGRAM? Y OR N? **Y**

What occurred? To help answer the question you may wish to list statements 330–400. Key in **LIST** 330–400 <ENTER>.

_____

_____

What is VALIDDATE$ called?

_____

Why is a WHILE statement used that contains the code for entering the date and invoice number?

_____

_____

© SRA 1988, 1983

5. Select menu **1**, option **4**, and press **F2**. This reloads the unrevised version of the online-order-entry program. Execute the program again, responding to the questions in whatever way you wish.

6. Evaluate the data you entered. When you entered the data to complete the assignment, were all phases of the initialization module (as it is now coded) and the help modules tested? Explain your answer.

_____

_____

_____

Are there errors that an operator might make that will cancel the program?

_____

_____

Programming tips: Whenever possible, validate input and fields used in mathematical calculations. Check to see if the divisor is equal to zero.

If a Y OR N? response is required, provide code that checks to see if the response was either a Y, y, N, or n. If an invalid response was entered, display an error message, display the prompt again, and allow the operator to key in the correct response.

In creating user-friendly programs, provide prompts, help menus, and detailed instructions for entering data. Case entry should be used in creating menus.

© SRA 1988, 1983

SELF-EVALUATION TEST 3

Name _____

Section Number _____

I. Record the key term being defined in the space provided. A small blank within the statement indicates where the term is needed.

_____ 1. A language designed for the use of nondata processing personnel used primarily for the retrieval of information.

_____ 2. A compiler language, developed during the fifties, that was designed for scientific applications.

_____ 3. Data which can include numbers, alphabetic characters, and special characters. Record the answers in 3 and 4.

_____ 4.

_____ 5. Statements included in source code that generate machine-language commands.

_____ 6. _____ are used within IF statements to set up the conditions that must be met for the statement to be either true or false.

_____ 7. A _____ command causes an instruction other than the next one in sequence to be executed.

_____ 8. In a _____ the innermost statements must be completely enclosed within the outermost statements.

_____ 9. AND, OR, and NOT are called _____.

_____ 10. When invalid data, such as a zero in the field to be used as the divisor, occurs, an _____ can be set so that an error message is printed and the job will continue rather than being aborted.

II. Multiple Choice. Record the letter of the best answer in the space provided.

_____ 1. Both PERFORM and GOSUB cause
  a. the next command in sequence to be executed.
  b. a branch to occur to the address specified. The remainder of the commands within the module that contain the PERFORM or GOSUB will not be executed.
  c. the program to terminate.
  d. a branch to occur to the address specified. After the commands within the module are executed, control returns to the statement following the PERFORM or GOSUB statement.

_____ 2. High-level database languages are
  a. designed primarily for the use of professional programmers.
  b. mathematical in nature and require the use of complex formulas.
  c. user-oriented, permitting the user to utilize statements much like standard English.
  d. not available for microcomputers.

_____ 3. A simple IF statement can have
  a. only a true action.
  b. only a false action.
  c. either a true or false action.
  d. a true action, or a false action, or both a true and false action.

_____ 4. In a complex arithmetic statement such as:

    IF HOURS >= 40 THEN
        GROSS-PAY = ((HOURS - 40) * RATE * 1.5) + (40 * RATE)

  the first operation to be executed is:

a. 40 * RATE
b. HOURS − 40
c. RATE * 1.5
d. none of the above.

_____ 5. When nested IF/THEN/ELSE statements are used,
   a. an innermost statement must be completely enclosed in the statements in which it is nested.
   b. undue complexity caused by nesting several statements within the outermost IF can be avoided by invoking additional modules.
   c. indenting each so that the matching IF and ELSE are aligned makes it easier to understand what will occur when the statement is executed.
   d. all of the above.

_____ 6. When a company has four classes of employees, such as hourly, salaried, part-time, and classified, and the pay for each class is computed differently, then
   a. nested IF/THEN/ELSE statements should be used.
   b. a series of simple IF/THEN/ELSE statements should be used.
   c. case entry should be used.
   d. a separate module must be coded for each classification.

_____ 7. When developing flowcharts,
   a. the true action is always to the right.
   b. the true action is always to the left.
   c. the true action can be either to the left or right of the diamond in which the condition being tested is specified.
   d. good technique attempts consistently to have the true condition shown to the right of the diamond.

_____ 8. Before coding and testing any portion of a program,
   a. complete specifications should be developed.
   b. the entire logic plan should be developed.
   c. all of the master files must be created.
   d. none of the above.

_____ 9. The help module for the online-order-entry program
   a. only provided specific instructions for entering data.
   b. had to be executed each time the program was run.
   c. permitted the operator to cancel the program if further instructions were needed.
   d. only provided an overview of the program.

_____ 10. When online, interactive programs are developed,
   a. help modules containing directions and explanations tend to make the program more user-friendly than when only printed documentation is available.
   b. less internal documentation is included than when data is entered into a file and then processed in a batch.
   c. menus are seldom used.
   d. prompts are not used that display information regarding the data to be entered. Since this information is included in the directions for entering data, prompts are not required.

III. True or False. Record a T or F in the space provided. For each false statement, indicate why the statement is false or make the changes needed to correct the statement.

_____ 1. When a statement such as GOSUB 3000 is coded and compiled, the 3000 portion of the statement is a line number which ultimately becomes the address of where the machine-language commands within the module are stored.

_____ 2. An alphanumeric field can only contain the letters of the alphabet and numeric digits.

© SRA 1988, 1983

_____ 3. A computer's logic is restricted to the comparison of two values in order to determine if one number is larger than, smaller than, or equal to another. Using compiler languages, the programmer can write statements that generate a series of such comparisons.

_____ 4. An address is a location within real memory.

_____ 5. If only one action is specified for an IF statement, the action must occur when the condition is true.

_____ 6. In coding an IF statement, relational operators cannot be adjacent to one another.

_____ 7. When AND is used in an IF statement, only one of the conditions specified must be true for the true action to occur.

_____ 8. NOT reverses the truth of a single evaluation.

_____ 9. In a complex mathematical statement, exponentiation occurs before any other arithmetic functions such as multiplication or division.

_____ 10. In the statement X = A * B / C, the first step the computer will take to solve the expression is to divide C into B.

_____ 11. In the online order entry program, an error message was displayed if a response other than a Y or N was entered.

_____ 12. In the initiate-help-screen module, when the number of the help screen was entered a default option was not provided.

_____ 13. If the operator keyed a T in response to "REVIEW ADDITIONAL INSTRUCTION? Y OR N?," the program aborted.

_____ 14. Prompts usually indicate the date that is to be entered, the format of the data, and the length of the field.

_____ 15. In the online order entry program responding with a N to "CONTINUE PROGRAM EXECUTION? Y OR N?" caused the commands within the process-sales-data module not to be executed and the job to terminate.

_____ 16. Consider the following pseudocode:

```
IF  A = B  THEN
        C = X - Y
        IF  A > B  THEN
            C = X * Y
ELSE
        C = X - Y
```

In the example, the ELSE will be matched with the first IF statement.

_____ 17. In a nested IF statement, each condition specified will be evaluated whenever the statement is executed.

_____ 18. Most case entry statements do not provide a default option.

_____ 19. In a case entry statement as soon as a condition is true and the action specified is completed, control goes to the statement which follows the coding for the case entry.

_____ 20. In Nassi-Shneiderman charts, Warnier-Orr diagrams, and pseudocode, NULL is used to indicate that the default condition has not been overlooked.

_____ 21. When case entry is used, when a condition is true only one statement may be used.

_____ 22. In a Warnier-Orr diagram, the bar above a statement such as TIMES > 0 indicates that the action will occur if the statement is true.

_____ 23. When stub testing occurs, dummy, or stub, modules are inserted to see if the main control module passes control to the three major modules.

_____ 24. Case entry is often used when a menu of available options is displayed. However, since only digits, such as 1–4, are used to specify the available options, default statements are seldom used.

_____ 25. When documentation for entering data is included within a program, the operator must always review the instructions before any of the modules that enter or process data is executed.

© SRA 1988, 1983

CREATING LOOPS

4

After reading the chapter and completing the learning activities, you will be able to:

- Identify the two types of loops.

- Identify the difference, in regard to the exit decision, between WHILE, UNTIL, and PERFORM/UNTIL loops.

- Utilize WHILE, UNTIL, and PERFORM/VARYING in developing detailed logic plans.

- Identify the characteristics of a typical count-controlled loop.

- Utilize count-controlled loops in developing detailed logic plans.

- Use properly formatted pseudocode to illustrate the use of nested count-controlled loops.

- Determine when, and why, an early exit from a count-controlled loop may be necessary.

- Explain why using tables to store data decreases the amount of coding needed.

You are now well aware that the logic of a program can be developed by using three basic control structures: sequence, selection, and iteration. You also know that the computer executes commands according to the sequence in which they are stored within memory. An exception occurs whenever a branching command is encountered. However, when a PERFORM or GOSUB is executed, control returns to the command following the branching command.

Depending on the language being used, there are usually several versions of the IF statement that can be used to implement selection. Which command will be executed depends on whether the evaluation of the conditions specified within the IF statement are true or false.

The ability to create loops is very important. In most programs, the process-input-records module, and the modules it controls, must be executed until all of the data has been processed. Within the main processing module, some code may require execution either a specific number of times or until a stated condition becomes true.

Most languages support both **conditional loops** and **count-controlled loops.** In the programs illustrated to this point, only one type of conditional loop has been used. Many programs require the use of additional looping techniques.

This chapter illustrates the various types of loops that can be constructed and when each should be used. Although tables are introduced in this chapter, a detailed explanation of when and why they should be used will be given in Chapter 5.

CONDITIONAL LOOPS

The two types of conditional loops are DO WHILE and DO UNTIL. The difference between them was briefly covered in Figure 2–2 which illustrated some of the key words used in writing pseudocode. The DO portion of the statement is used in writing the pseudocode but some other key word such as PERFORM or FOR might be needed when the source code is written. In each programming language, a slightly different technique is used in writing the WHILE or UNTIL source statement.

Some programming languages support both DO WHILE and DO UNTIL conditional loops. Other languages may support only one of the two. For example, most versions of COBOL support both WHILE and UNTIL. Some versions of BASIC support only WHILE; early versions of BASIC supported neither WHILE nor UNTIL.

Changing the value of an indicator

The major difference between WHILE and UNTIL is *when* the decision to exit from the loop is made. When either type of conditional loop is used, an exit can occur because the value of the indicator used to control the loop has changed. The value may have been changed because of:

* the end of a file being detected. When the end of the transaction file is detected, the value of the indicator used to control process-input-records is changed.

© SRA 1988, 1983

- a calculation performed within the loop. Management wishes to send out letters to the first 500 customers who have an unpaid balance greater than $10,000. Each time the condition specified is met, the customer's name and address is placed in a file and 1 is added to the total. When the total equals 500, an exit will be made from the loop.
- the operator entering a value from a terminal or the console. The statements within the loop are to be executed UNTIL more-data is equal to N. If in response to the question "ALL DATA PROCESSED?" the operator enters an N, an exit will be made from the loop.
- reading a new value from a file. A loop is created that is to process records beginning with account number 10,000 through account number 20,000. Processing will continue UNTIL account-number equals 20,000 or WHILE account-number is less than 20,001.

Using logical operators

Compound conditions can be used in determining if the statements within the loop are to be executed. For example, an operator must enter a Y for processing to continue. The character entered is stored in a field called continue. The WHILE or UNTIL may be written in pseudocode as follows:

```
DO WHILE (continue = Y OR continue = y)
DO UNTIL (continue <>Y AND continue <>y)
                 or
DO UNTIL (continue NOT = Y and continue NOT = y)
```

A loop which controls the reading of records and the selection of those to be printed on the report is to continue until 1,000 names are printed on the list. Each time the conditions specified are met and a name is printed on the list, 1 is added to a field called count. However, it is possible that the end-of-file condition may occur prior to that time. When the end-of-file is detected, N is stored in a field called more-records. More-records was initialized to Y. The WHILE and UNTIL statements could be written in pseudocode as follows:

```
DO WHILE (count < 1001 AND more-records = Y)
DO UNTIL (count = 1000 OR more-records = N)
```

WHILE

In a DO WHILE loop the **exit decision** occurs before any of the statements within the loop are executed. If the condition specified is true, the statements within the loop are executed. Control then returns to the point at which the exit decision is made.

Control is to remain in the process-sales-records module WHILE a field called more-records contains a Y. Figure 4–1 illustrates how the DO WHILE loop would be constructed. The loop still conforms to the basic rule of "single entry, single exit." When N is stored in more-records, an exit will be made from the loop. Control will return to the main control loop and control will branch to the termination module.

Figure 4–1
Construction of a DO
WHILE loop.

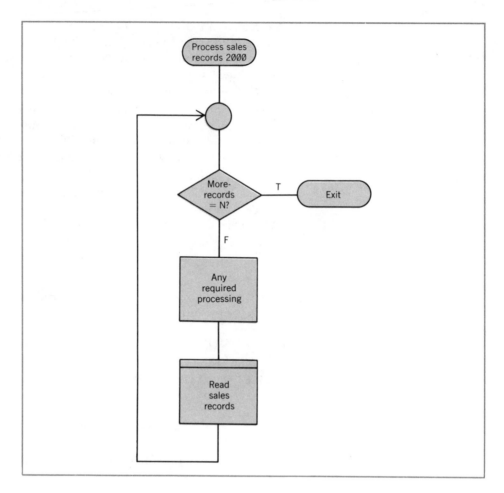

CODING WHILE LOOPS   In writing pseudocode, or actual code, it is not necessary to show the actual test. When a WHILE statement is used, the test is included as part of the WHILE. The example illustrated in Figure 4–1 would be written in pseudocode as follows:

```
DO WHILE (More-records = Y)
     Any required processing steps
     PERFORM 3000-read-sales-records
END DO
```

If BASIC is used to code the example, the following statements would be needed.

```
100        WHILE MORERECORDS$ = 'Y'
110            Any required processing steps
120            GOSUB 2500
130        WEND
```

Both the pseudocode and BASIC code illustrate that the test determining whether the loop should process records is generated from the WHILE statement. An IF statement need not be coded to test the condition specified when a WHILE loop is used.

© SRA 1988, 1983

HOW WHILE LOOPS ARE USED   Process records, the main processing loop of a structured program, may be controlled by a WHILE statement. If the indicator used, more-records, is initially set to Y, the loop is continued until the value of the indicator is changed. In many programs that you will design, code, and test, the normal processing is terminated when the end of a transaction file is reached. When this occurs, an N can be stored in more-records which will terminate processing. Usually when the end of a sequential file is reached, the programmer can specify what action will occur. In our example, an N would be moved into the more-records field. Control returns to the main control module after all the transaction records have been processed.

A WHILE loop can be created that permits the operator to determine when the exit from the loop will occur. For example, you want the operator to enter the date to be printed on the paychecks and the beginning check number. It is essential that the operator enter the data correctly. Therefore, you want the operator to review what was entered and to determine if the information must be rekeyed. The pseudocode would be written as follows:

```
Good-date = N
DO-WHILE  (Good-date = N or Good-date = n)
    DISPLAY 'enter date'
    ACCEPT date
    DISPLAY 'enter check number'
    ACCEPT check-number
    DISPLAY 'Date and check number correct? Y or N?'
    INPUT Good-date
END DO
```

By coding the statement good-date = N, followed by DO WHILE Good-date = N or Good-date = n, the programmer knows that the statements within the loop will be executed at least one time. If in response to "Date and check number correct? Y or N?" the operator enters an N (or an n), the statements within the loop will be executed at least one more time.

In using a WHILE statement, the programmer must make certain that the proper value is initially stored in the control field. In the enter-date example, if a Y had initially been stored in the good-date field, the statements within the loop would not have been executed.

UNTIL   In a DO UNTIL loop, the exit decision occurs after the statements within the loop are executed. Because the exit decision occurs last, the statements within the loop will be executed at least once.

Again assume that we wish to process records UNTIL more-records = N, Figure 4–2 shows how a DO UNTIL loop would be illustrated. The pseudocode for the DO UNTIL statement will be written as follows:

```
DO UNTIL (more-records = N)
    Any required processing statements
    PERFORM read-record-3000
END UNTIL
```

Note that the pseudocode for the DO WHILE and DO UNTIL is written in the same manner. When illustrating the logic for the DO UNTIL, pseudocode is

Figure 4–2
Construction of a DO
UNTIL loop.

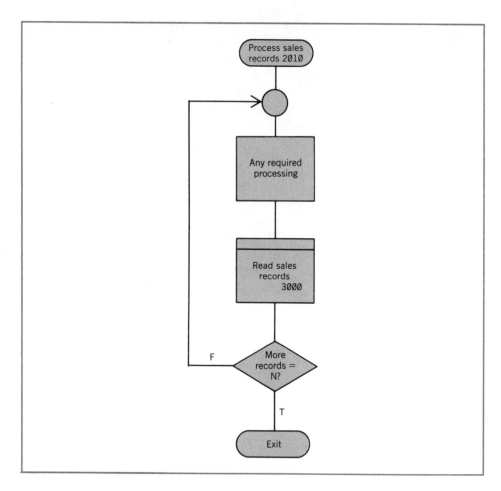

not provided for the required exit test. The only difference between the DO WHILE and DO UNTIL is:

- How the condition to be tested is stated.
- When the exit test is made.

WHEN NOT TO USE DO UNTIL   Although it may seem that two statements, WHILE and UNTIL, can be used interchangeably, when the test occurs may be of major importance. DO UNTIL should not be used when a situation might arise in which the statements within the loop *must not be executed—even once.*

Assume that "DO UNTIL (more-records = N)" is used to control the execution of the process-records module. What will occur if the transaction file does not contain any records? When the first attempt is made to read a transaction record, more-records is set to N. This occurs because of the way the programmer coded the READ statement used to read the transaction records. However, the statements within the process-records module must be executed once before the test is made. Unless an additional indicator is used that will cause the commands within the module to be bypassed, the job may abort or some very strange output may be generated. Obviously UNTIL should not have been used.

If UNTIL were used rather than WHILE, when should the error have been detected? In the design walkthrough, the question "What if the transaction file

© SRA 1988, 1983

is empty?" should have been asked and the design changed. If the error went undetected until the source code was written and the program was being tested, will the error be detected? If the programmer tests first with all valid data, then with invalid data that tests each error routine, and finally with no data, the error will be detected. When an empty transaction file is detected, an appropriate message should be printed and the statements within the process-records modules should not be executed.

WHEN EITHER WHILE OR UNTIL CAN BE USED   In the second example used in illustrating the use of DO WHILE, the programmer wanted the operator to be able to enter the date and check number *at least once.* In this case, since it is of little concern to the analyst or programmer when the exit test will be made, either WHILE or UNTIL can be used. However, the programmer still needs to make certain that the proper value is stored in the field that controls the WHILE or UNTIL.

Figure 4–3   The PERFORM/UNTIL in the main control module controls the execution of the process-sales-records module.

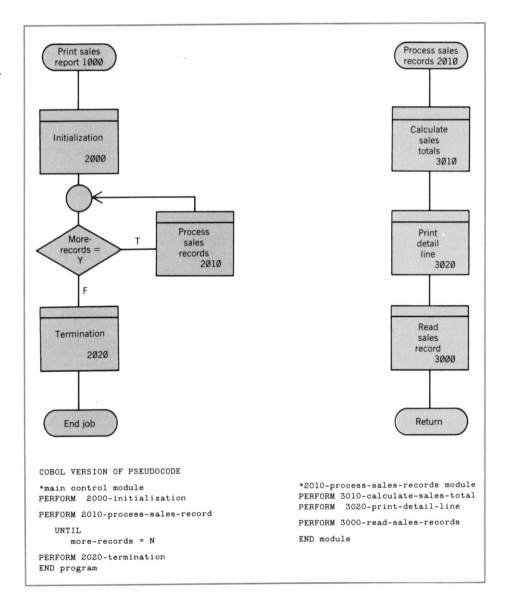

```
COBOL VERSION OF PSEUDOCODE

*main control module
PERFORM  2000-initialization

PERFORM 2010-process-sales-record

    UNTIL
        more-records = N

PERFORM 2020-termination
END program


*2010-process-sales-records module
PERFORM 3010-calculate-sales-total
PERFORM  3020-print-detail-line

PERFORM 3000-read-sales-records

END module
```

PERFORM/UNTIL

If COBOL is used to write the source code, PERFORM/UNTIL is used rather than DO WHILE or DO UNTIL. In a PERFORM/UNTIL the exit test is made *before* any of the commands within the module are executed. There is also another major difference. To determine if commands in the process-sales-records module should be executed, the test is made in the main control module rather than in the 2010-level module.

Figure 4–3 illustrates how the main control module controls the execution of the process-sales-record module. In the initialization module more-records is set to Y. When the programmer or analyst knows COBOL will be used to write the source code, the detailed logic plan will differ in *where* the decision regarding the exit from the process sales records loop is shown. Also note the format of the PERFORM/UNTIL pseudocode statement:

```
PERFORM 2010-process-sales-records
    UNTIL
        more-records = N
```

In order to keep the text generic and not to relate it specifically to one language, the DO UNTIL format for illustrating logic will be used rather than the rather unique COBOL PERFORM/UNTIL format. However the differences that exist when a count-controlled loop is coded in COBOL, rather than a language such as PL/I, FORTRAN, or BASIC, will also be illustrated.

CHECKPOINT
QUESTIONS

1. What are the two major types of loops used in constructing structured programs?
2. What is the major difference between a DO WHILE and DO UNTIL loop?
3. How does the structured flowchart for a WHILE differ from the one created for a UNTIL?
4. Is the pseudocode written for a DO WHILE different from the pseudocode written for a DO UNTIL?
5. When the source code is written from the flowchart or pseudocode, will the programmer need to write an IF statement to test the exit condition?
6. If PERFORM/UNTIL is used in coding the print-sales-report program, in what module is the test made to determine whether or not the commands within the 2000-process-sales-records module will be executed?
7. When PERFORM/UNTIL is used, is the test made before or after the commands within the module being controlled by the statement are executed?
8. In the statement DO-WHILE (End-of-file = N), why is the end-of-file field considered an indicator? Referring back to an earlier chapter, what other two terms might be used in referring to the end-of-file field?

COUNT-CONTROLLED
LOOPS

Count-controlled loops are executed a given number of times. When a count-controlled loop is coded, the following usually occurs.

1. A beginning value is set for the **counter.**
2. Each time the statements within the loop are executed, a given value is added to the counter.

© SRA 1988, 1983

3. A check is made to see if an exit should be made from the loop.

Assume that you wish to make a series of calculations and to print the results 100 times. Figure 4–4 illustrates two ways in which a count-controlled loop might be flowcharted. In the illustration the commands within process-loan-records are to be executed 100 times.

Flowcharting a count-controlled loop

In the example, the Process-loan-record module will be controlled by a count-controlled loop rather than by an indicator. Figure 4–4 illustrates how the flowchart would be constructed. The flowchart on the left more clearly depicts

Figure 4–4 Two ways of flowcharting a count-controled loop.

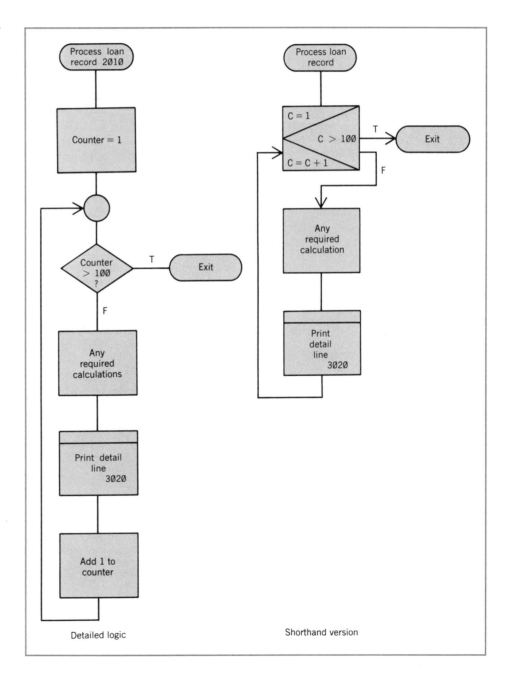

what will occur when the program is executed than the shorter version on the right. Before the commands within the loop are executed, the counter is set to 1. The first time the commands within the loop are executed, the counter is equal to 1. At the bottom of the loop 1 is added to counter. Therefore, when the test is made the second time to see if the counter value is greater than 100, it has a value of 2. However, the commands within the loop have only been executed once. When counter is equal to 100, the commands within the loop will be executed for the 100th time. At the bottom of the loop, 1 is added to counter and its value is now 101. When the test is made at the top of the loop, the condition is true and an exit is made from the loop.

In the illustration on the right a rectangle is divided into three triangles. The top triangle shows the initial value of the counter (C = 1). The middle triangle illustrates the condition that must be met in order to exit from the loop (C > 100). The lower triangle shows the value that will be added to the counter each time the statements within the loop are executed (C = C + 1).

The symbol used to illustrate the count-controlled loop is not one of the standardized ANSI symbols but it is understood by most programmers, widely used, and accepted by most individuals who construct structured flowcharts.

Using pseudocode to illustrate a count-controlled loop

The following illustration shows how pseudocode would be written to illustrate a count-controlled loop:

```
DO (counter = 1 to 100 BY 1)
    Any calculations required
    PERFORM print-report-3010
END DO
```

In the illustration, *by 1* should ideally be specified but may be omitted. If only (counter = 1 to 100) is used, it is understood that by default the counter will be incremented by 1 each time the statements within the loop are executed.

In some cases the counter must be increased by a value greater than one. The following pseudocode illustrates how the code would be written when the counter is to be incremented by 3 rather than 1.

```
DO (counter = 1 to 10 BY 3)
    Any calculations required
END DO
```

The statements would be executed until the value stored in the counter field is greater than 10. In the example, the loop would be executed 4 times: when counter is equal to 1, 4, 7, and 10. An exit from the loop occurs when the value stored in counter is greater than 10.

Programming a count-controlled loop in BASIC

Most programming languages support the use of count-controlled loops. In BASIC the module would be coded as follows:

```
1500    REM PROCESS-RECORDS MODULE    'INTERNAL  DOCUMENTATION
1510    FOR COUNTER = 1 TO 100
1520        Any calculations required
1530        GOSUB 3000                ' BRANCHING STATEMENT
1540    NEXT
1550    RETURN                        ' BACK TO MAIN-CONTROL
```

© SRA 1988, 1983

The FOR/NEXT loop is very similar to the pseudocode. The initial value of the counter is provided, the exit value is given, and the number used to increment the counter is shown. In writing BASIC, STEP need not be used unless the counter is to be incremented by a value other than 1. Also, when either BASIC or pseudocode is used, the end of the loop has to be indicated by using NEXT (in BASIC) or END (in writing pseudocode). When either pseudocode or actual code is written, the programmer does not need to increment the counter or use an IF statement to illustrate the exit decision.

Figure 4–5 Establishing a count-controled loop using PERFORM/VARYING.

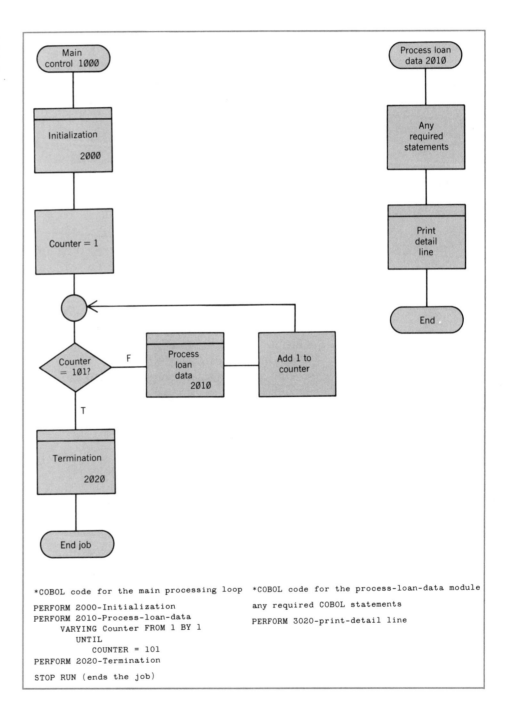

```
*COBOL code for the main processing loop
PERFORM 2000-Initialization
PERFORM 2010-Process-loan-data
      VARYING Counter FROM 1 BY 1
          UNTIL
              COUNTER = 101
PERFORM 2020-Termination

STOP RUN (ends the job)
```

```
*COBOL code for the process-loan-data module
any required COBOL statements

PERFORM 3020-print-detail line
```

A COBOL count-controlled loop

Just as DO UNTIL and PERFORM/UNTIL differ in regard to how and where the loop is controlled, COBOL's count-controlled loops differ from those created when other languages are used. Figure 4–5 illustrates how a count-controlled loop would be established in the main control loop that would control the execution of the process-loan-data loop. The commands within the process-loan-data loop are to be executed 100 times.

The code illustrated in Figure 4–5 shows that using a PERFORM/VARYING statement provides the three essential elements of a count-controlled loop:

1. The counter is set to its initial value (counter FROM 1 . . .)
2. After the statements within the controlled module (2010-process-loan-data) are executed, 1 is added to the counter (BY 1)
3. A check is made to see if the commands within the loop should be executed again (UNTIL counter = 101).

When COBOL is used to write the source code, the PERFORM/VARYING statement that establishes and controls the loop is in one module and the commands to be executed are in a second module. Since COBOL is unique in this respect, the illustrations showing the use of count-controlled loops assume that the statements controlling the loop and the commands to be executed are in the *same module.*

When count-controlled loops are used

Table handling, which will be covered in Chapter 5, often requires the use of a count-controlled loop. A **table** or **array** is an area defined within memory or on a storage device that consists of two or more elements (or areas). Each area of the table can be addressed individually. Tables can store data for either sequential or random retrieval. Using tables saves a great deal of coding.

A company with 20 sales representatives wishes to store their names in memory. Instead of defining 20 separate areas (one for each sales representative), a table can be defined that has 20 individual areas. The table can be defined in one statement rather than the 20 statements needed to define individual fields. For example, in BASIC the following statement establishes a table with 20 storage areas.

```
DIM SALESREPS (20)
```

When an individual area of a table is to be addressed, a **subscript** must be used. A subscript must be a whole, positive number that is not greater than the maximum number of elements in the table. The subscript tells the computer which area in the table is addressed. Think of the table as the street on which you live and each area in the table as the individual houses on your street. To find your house you use the STREET (house number). In regard to tables, count-controlled loops are used to:

1. clear a table to zero or spaces. In a table defined as containing numeric data, zeros will be placed in each area. In a table defined as containing alphanumeric data, spaces (or blanks) will be placed in each area.
2. store data sequentially in a table.
3. search a table for specific data.
4. retrieve data sequentially from a table.

© SRA 1988, 1983

Other uses for count-controlled loops include:

1. to perform calculations and to print the results a given number of times. A program might be needed to calculate the interest on a daily basis and print the amount of interest that is received for each month and for each year.
2. to execute a particular function a given number of times. You wish to print 12 name and address labels for each customer. You would like to read 1000 records, print 12 stickers for each customer, and then exit from the loop. The outer loop will be executed 1000 times; each time the outer loop is executed the inner loop will be executed 12 times.

Nested count-controlled loops

Nested within a count-controlled loop may be one or more loops that are either controlled by a counter or are WHILE or UNTIL loops. The level of nesting permitted for count-controlled loops depends on the language and compiler being used.

PROGRAM SPECIFICATIONS Figure 4–6 illustrates the hierarchy chart for the program designed to calculate interest for the month, year, and for a 10-year period. The specifications for the program are:

Output: Total amount of interest for the month
               Total amount of interest for the year
               Total amount of interest for 10 years

Processing: Compound the interest daily.
               Interest is to be calculated on the basis of a 30-day month.

Input: Amount of the investment
               Interest rate

The amount of the investment and rate of interest will entered by the operator. After the date is keyed in, the operator must be given a chance to check

Figure 4–6 Hierarchy chart for the calculate interest program.

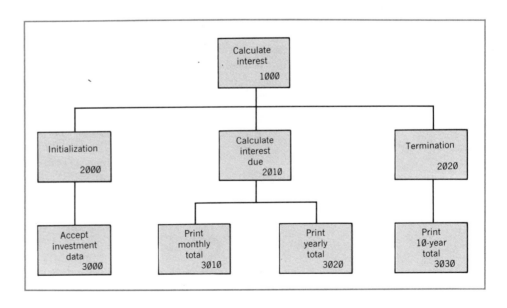

the data and, if necessary, rekey the data. The data is entered from the terminal rather than using hardcoded constants so that varying amounts can be used for the investment and/or interest rate. When a constant is hardcoded, a statement such as LET INVESTMENT-AMOUNT = 10000 will be coded.

Because all of the data other than the initial value of the investment and the interest rate is generated by the program, the hierarchy chart appears different than others presented. A read-detail-record module is not required. Although one print module could have been used, in order to comply with the concept that "each major function should have its own module," three separate modules are used. Since the major function and tasks closely associated with that function can be included in a module, within the print modules the totals will be rolled and the appropriate total cleared. While it would not be considered wrong to put the mathematical functions in separate modules, remember another guideline, "keep it simple and avoid undue complexity." If a program has too many one- and two-line modules, it becomes confusing and inefficient.

FLOWCHARTING NESTED COUNT-CONTROLLED LOOPS The calculate interest program provides an excellent illustration of the use of a UNTIL and nested count-control loops. In working with totals (monthly interest, yearly interest, and the ten-year total), three major factors must be considered.

1. Totals must accumulate one cycle before they are printed. The monthly total is accumulated during the daily loop; the yearly total during the monthly loop; and the ten-year total during the yearly loop.

2. It is more efficient to **"roll totals"** than to add to each of the three totals each time a calculation is made. When you roll totals the monthly total is added to the yearly total and the yearly total is added to the 10-year total.

3. Each time a total (such as monthly total) is added to the next level total (yearly total), the minor total field (month) must be reset to zero.

This program can be executed by running Interactive Exercise 4-1. You may also elect to list the source code to see how the program is written. Although the flowchart indicates the information is to be printed, the program displays the output on the VTD rather than using the printer. Therefore, some of the BASIC statements needed to format the output on the screen and to clear the screen are not included in the detailed logic plan.

As you study Figure 4-7 Part 2 you should be aware that three count-controlled loops are used. The outermost loop is executed 10 times. For each time the outermost loop is executed, the intermediate loop is executed 12 times. Each time the intermediate loop is executed, the innermost loop is executed 30 times. The following occurs:

Year = 1	Month = 1	Day loop executes 30 times; monthly total prints.
	2	Day reset to 1; loop executes 30 times; monthly total prints.
	. . .	
	12	Day reset to 1; loop executes 30 times; monthly total prints. Year total prints. Month reset to 1.
Year = 2	Month = 1	Day loop executes 30 times; monthly total prints.

© SRA 1988, 1983

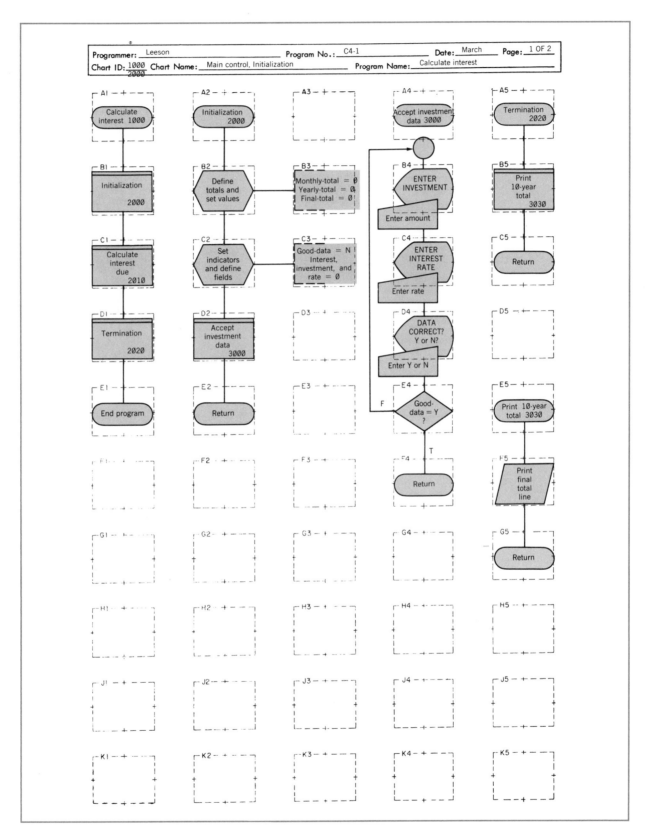

Figure 4–7 Part 1   Flowchart for the calculate interest program.

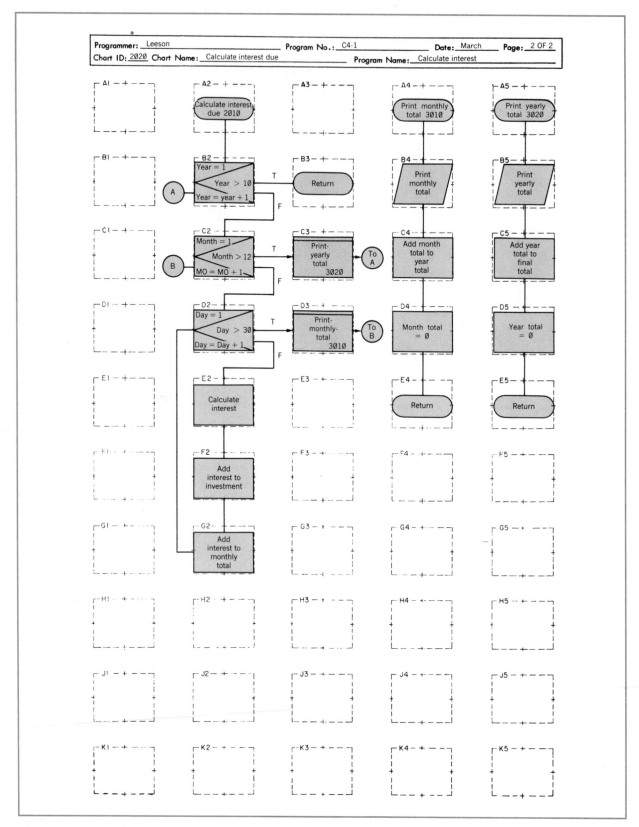

Figure 4–7 Part 2   Flowchart for the calculate interest program.

© SRA 1988, 1983

While year is equal to 1, how many day and month loops will be executed? The day loop executes 30 times for each month or for a total of 360 times. The month loop will be executed 12 times for each year. Each year the calculations within the day loop will be made 360 times. When the month changes, day is automatically reset to 1 and whenever the year changes, month is automatically reset to 1.

PSEUDOCODE FOR THE PROCESS-RECORDS MODULE In writing the pseudocode, it is important the DO is matched with its own END DO. Errors are less likely to occur if the pseudocode is formatted as illustrated:

```
*  Process-records module for the calculate-interest program
*  Three count-controlled loops must be used
   DO (year = 1 to 10)
       DO (month = 1 to 12)
           DO (day = 1 to 30)
               calculate interest
               add interest to investment
               add interest to monthly total
           END DAY
           PERFORM monthly-routine-3000
       END MONTH
       PERFORM yearly-routine-3010
   END YEAR
```

In the example, END DAY was used rather than END DO. Using the name of the counter rather than DO, helps to emphasize how the DOs and ENDs are matched. When the year is equal to 11 (one greater than the 10 specified), the monthly routine is executed, then the yearly-routine. Control then returns to the main-control module and the termination module is invoked which in turn causes the print-10-year-total module to be executed.

USING NASSI-SHNEIDERMAN OR WARNIER-ORR CHARTS Count-controlled loops can be shown on either the Nassi-Shneiderman or Warnier-Orr chart by indicating the number of times that the loop will be executed. Figure 4–8 illustrates how the calculate-interest-due module would be flowcharted for each type of chart.

Early exit from a count-controlled loop

Each customer's invoices are stored in a table. For each invoice is stored the following data: invoice number, invoice date, status-code, and amount of the invoice. Within the table 10 items are stored for each customer. The table is part of the customer's master file record.

When a customer makes a payment, the table is searched for the invoice number for the invoice being paid. When a match is found, the record-invoice-payment module will be invoked. If a match is not found, it indicates that an error has occurred. Either an invoice number was entered and stored in the table incorrectly or the number of the invoice being paid was entered incorrectly. The following pseudocode illustrates how the search for the matching invoice number would be conducted and how an invalid invoice number will be detected.

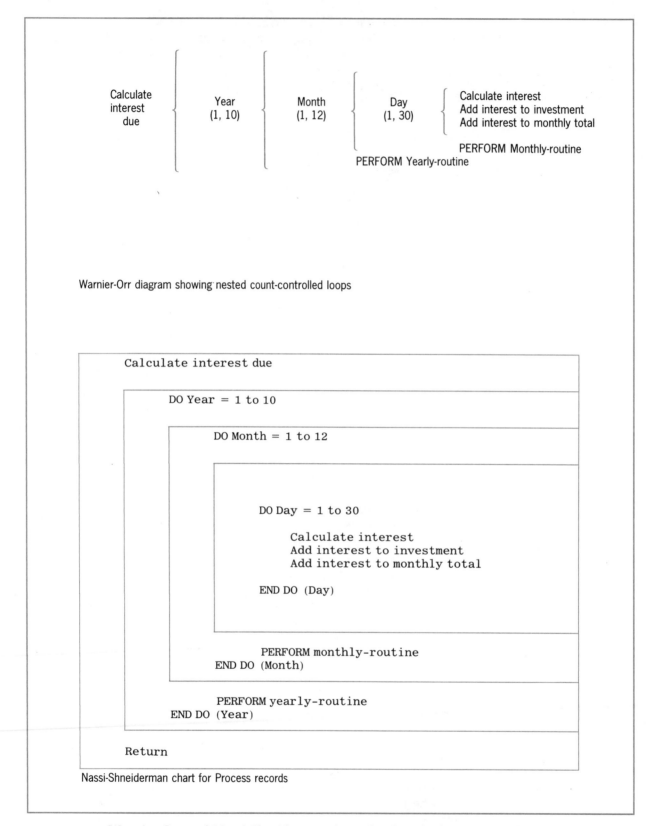

Warnier-Orr diagram showing nested count-controlled loops

Nassi-Shneiderman chart for Process records

Figure 4–8 *Warnier-Orr and Nassi-Shneiderman charts for the calculate-interest-due module*

© SRA 1988, 1983

```
* Search routine
  DO (counter = 1 to 10)
     IF TR-invoice-number = table-invoice-number(counter) THEN
        PERFORM record-payment-received
        counter = 12
     ELSE
        NULL
     END IF
  END DO
  IF counter = 11 THEN
     DISPLAY 'No match on invoice number ', TR-invoice-number
     No-more-processing = Y
  ELSE
     Null
  END IF
```

The pseudocode illustrated the following concepts:

1. A count-controlled loop that will be executed 10 times is established.
2. In doing the search, the loop's counter (called counter) is used as the subscript.
3. If the invoice number stored in table-invoice-number (counter) is equal to the invoice number read as input (TR-invoice-number), the following occurs:
   a. The record-payment-received routine is invoked. The required processing occurs.
   b. Counter is set to 12. This will cause the exit-test to be true as controls leaves the loop.
4. If counter = 11 an error message is displayed, and no further processing will occur for that particular invoice number.

If the entire table had been searched and the invoice number was not found, after the loop was executed 10 times *and counter is equal to 11*, a normal exit from the loop occurs. However, this represents an error condition and a message should be printed or displayed and normal processing suspended.

If the required invoice data is stored in the fifth area of the table, when counter is equal to 5 the "match" occurs, the required processing is completed, and the counter is set to 12 so that an exit will be made from the loop. Since the statement "IF counter = 11" is not true, the error routine will be bypassed.

A count-controlled loop was used as it provided:

- the subscript needed to search the table.
- an easy way of determining when an error condition occurred (no match).

CHECKPOINT QUESTIONS

9. When coding the statement required to execute a count-controlled loop, what three tasks are accomplished by the statement used to establish the loop?
10. In BASIC, when must STEP be used in establishing a FOR/NEXT loop?

11. For each of the situations described indicate if you would use WHILE, UNTIL, a count-controlled loop, or nested count-controlled loops.

    a. The statements within the enter-data module are to be executed at least once. If the value stored in VALID-DATA is a Y, an exit will be made from the loop.

    b. A table is searched to determine if it contains account number 42389. The table has 100 areas each of which is addressable.

    c. On your house loan you wish to determine how much interest will be paid each month for the next ten years, assuming that only the required monthly payments will be made. You also wish to know how much interest is paid each year and the ten-year total.

    d. The process-records module is to be executed as long as there are records within the transaction file that must be processed. However, the transaction file might be empty or the operator may wish to terminate the program in order to study the printed documentation.

    e. A table with 100 elements must be set to zero. In order to do this each individual area within the table must be set to zero.

    f. The date and beginning check number are to be entered from the operator's console. The loop will be executed at least once but will be terminated if the operator indicates that the data keyed in was correct.

12. What is a counter?

13. What symbol is used on a flowchart to show that a count-controlled loop is to be established? What information is shown within the symbol?

14. When nested count-controlled loops are used, how should the pseudocode be formatted?

15. Why might it be necessary to exit from a count-controlled loop before the maximum number of executions occur?

16. If the following BASIC code were used in a program, how many times would the statements within the loop be executed?

```
FOR COUNTER = 1 TO 10 STEP 4
     any required code
NEXT
```

17. How are nested loops shown on a Nassi-Shneiderman chart?

18. How are nested loops shown on a Warnier-Orr diagram?

19. What is the major difference between using a PERFORM/VARYING and a FOR/NEXT statement?

20. What similarities exist between a PERFORM/VARYING and FOR/NEXT statement?

SUMMARY
- The two major types of loops are count-controlled and conditional.

- DO WHILE, DO UNTIL, or PERFORM/UNTIL can be used to establish conditional loops.

© SRA 1988, 1983

- In a WHILE loop, the exit test occurs *before* any processing occurs.

- In a DO UNTIL loop, the exit test occurs *after* the processing statements are executed.

- When a PERFORM/UNTIL loop is established, the exit test occur *before* any processing occurs.

- In DO WHILE, DO UNTIL, and PERFORM/UNTIL compound conditions can be specified using logical operators.

- When a count-controlled loop is established, the code takes care of initializing the counter, incrementing the counter by the number specified, and testing to see if the exit condition is met.

- When a PERFORM/VARYING statement is used to establish a loop, the counter is established, checked, and incremented in one loop and the commands to be executed within the loop are in a subordinate loop.

- Count-controlled loops are used extensively in clearing, loading, and searching tables. Whenever statements within a routine are to be executed a specified number of times, a count-controlled loop should be established.

- The depth to which count-controlled loops can be nested is determined by the compiler. However, inner loops must be completedly enclosed within their outer loop.

- Less code is required when tables are used to store data than when individual fields are used to store related data items such as the names of all of an organization's sales representatives. A subscript is used to tell the computer which item is to be addressed.

DISCUSSION QUESTIONS

1. What is the major difference between a WHILE and UNTIL loop? Why is it sometimes better to establish a WHILE loop rather than an UNTIL loop?

2. How does a PERFORM/UNTIL statement differ from a DO UNTIL?

3. Give an example of a situation in which logical operators might be used in establishing either a WHILE or UNTIL loop.

4. Describe a situation in which nested count-controlled loops might be needed.

5. Give an illustration showing when it might be necessary to exit from a count-controlled loop before the exit condition specified is met?

6. When a count-controlled statement is coded using FOR/NEXT, what tasks are accomplished by machine-language commands generated from the statement? What is the purpose of the NEXT statement?

7. What guidelines should be developed and utilized for writing pseudocode for nested count-controlled loops?

8. How does a PERFORM/VARYING statement differ from a FOR/NEXT statement?

KEY WORDS

array	exit decision
conditional loop	PERFORM/UNTIL
count-controlled loop	PERFORM/VARYING
counter	roll totals
DO UNTIL	subscript
DO WHILE	table

© SRA 1988, 1983

PROJECTS

EXERCISE 4–1

You would like to invest $10,000 in a special account that pays an annual rate of .0855. Interest is compounded daily. You want to know how many months it will be before your account has a balance of $16,000 or more. In calculating interest use 30 for the number of days in all months and 360 for the days in a year.

Program specification

Input

Investment	In the initialization module, investment is set to $10,000 and interest
Rate of interest	is set to .0835.

Output

Number of months	Number of months before your initial investment is $16,000 or more.
Monthly interest	Each month's interest will be printed.
Processing	Use only the following modules: determine months, initialization, calculate-investment-value, termination, and print-monthly-interest.

Directions

1. Develop the detailed logic plan for all modules *except* print-monthly-interest. In the termination module, display the total number of months that will be needed. Make sure that you identify all the fields needed and set them to their initial values.

2. In this problem, why is it unnecessary to use nested count-controlled loops?

_____

_____

_____

PROBLEM 4–1

Your company has a large accounts receivable file. Your manager would like to know how many customers have not used their accounts since 88030 and have a zero balance in their balance-due fields. Starting with the first record in the file, the records will be processed sequentially. Name and address labels are to be printed for the first 1,000 customers who meet the conditions specified. However, it is possible that the end-of-file will be detected before 1,000 stickers have been printed.

You also wish to determine what percentage of the customers whose records were read, have a balance that is greater or equal to $10,000.

Output:	Name and address labels. These will be printed in a module called print-address-labels.
	Percentage of customers who owe your company $10,000 or more. This will be calculated on the basis of the total number of records read. If 5000 records were read and 500 had balances greater than or equal to $10,000, percentage would be 10% (500/5000 = .10).
Input:	
MF-name and MF-address	Used in printing the labels.
MF-balance	Contains the customer's balance.
MF-date-of-last-sale	The Julien date is recorded as YYDDD. January 10, 1987 would be recorded as 87010
Indicator:	
Read-more-records	If the end of file is detected before 1,000 stickers are printed, N will be stored in read-more-records. N will also be placed in the field as soon as 1000 stickers are printed.

Directions

1. Do a hierarchy chart using the following modules: print-labels (main control), initialization, process-customer-records, termination, read-customer-record, print-address-labels, and print-final-percentage.

2. Develop the detailed logic for all modules *except* read-customer-record, print-address-labels, and print-final-percentage.

INTERACTIVE EXERCISE 4–1

You are to execute the calculate-interest program that was used to illustrate the use of nested count-controlled loops. Before executing the program, review the program specifications, hierarchy chart, and flowchart which are on page 139–143.

Directions

1. Boot the system, load **BASIC,** press **F3** (or key in **LOAD**), key in Menu <**ENTER**>, press **F2** (or key in **RUN** <**ENTER**>).

2. Select menu **1,** option **5.**

   DO NOT return to the main menu until after you have completed the assignment listed under 4.

3. Displayed will be: ENTER INVESTMENT   //////.//
                       ENTER RATE OF INTEREST .////

   The slashes are used to illustrate the maximum size of the investment that can be entered. The decimal point serves as a reminder that decimal points are keyed in.

   Enter the following data: 10000.00   (space followed by 10000.00)
                              .1200   (decimal followed by 1200)

   If you have keyed in the data correctly, respond with a **Y** to the question DATA CORRECT? Y OR N?

   As the program executes, record the answers to the following questions:

   a. What is the interest for the fifth month of the first year?   _____

   b. What is the interest for the tenth month of the first year?   _____

   c. What is the interest for the first year?   _____

   d. What is the interest for the fifth year?   _____

   e. What is the interest for the tenth year?   _____

   f. What is the total amount of interest earned during the entire ten-year period? _____

   g. Why was it necessary to include a statement that made it necessary for the operator to press the ENTER key before additional data was displayed?

   _____

4. LIST statements 460-620 by entering **LIST 460-620** <**ENTER**>.

   What technique is used in writing the code that makes it easy to relate each FOR with its NEXT statement?

   _____

   _____

© SRA 1988, 1983

In writing the source code, was the guideline requring use of meaningful names followed? Explain your answer.

_____

_____

5. In order to illustrate that each time the month changes, the day loop is executed 30 times, add the following code to the program:

Statement Number   BASIC code
    561   PRINT USING "INTEREST FOR DAY ### IS ###.##";DAY, INTEREST

When you key in the source statements, make certain that the CAPS LOCK was pressed. The INTEREST and DAY field were defined using capital letters.

After you key in the statement, check it for accuracy, and then use the **ENTER** key. **Run** the program. Enter 10000 as the amount of the loan and .12 as the rate of interest.

What is the interest for day 19 of the first year? _____

What is the interest for day 30 of the second year? _____

Use **CTRL/BREAK** to exit from the program. When CTRL/BREAK is written with the slash between the two words, it indicates that both keys are pressed and held at the same time.

6. Because the only data entered is the amount of the investment and the interest rate, what steps would you take to test the program?

_____

_____

_____

_____

_____

INTERACTIVE EXERCISE 4–2

Program C4-2 simulates what will occur when a search is made within a table for a given value. Since the table in the example has 20 storage areas, the count-controlled loop must be executed 20 times. When the counter is greater than 20, an exit will be made from the loop. Immediately after the exit occurs, the counter will have a value of 21.

When the invoice number is found in the table, a branch occurs to the process-sales-invoice module. In this module normal processing will occur and the counter will be set to 22. Since the counter is set to 22, when control returns to the count-controlled loop, an immediate exit occurs.

When an exit is made from the loop and the counter is equal to 21, an error message will be displayed. The operator knows that a "match" did not occur and the invoice number is either incorrect or for some reason the data pertaining to the invoice was not stored in the record being processed.

Directions

1. Return to main menu, select menu **1**, option **6**, and press **F2** (RUN).
2. In response to: ENTER INVOICE NUMBER: ///// enter the following invoice numbers.

	Enter Number	MORE RECORDS TO BE PROCESSED? ENTER
a.	1046	Y
b.	1234	Y
c.	1048	Y
d.	1049	Y
e.	1055	N Do not return to menu.

3. **LIST 260–400**
   a. What controls the search loop?

   _____

   b. What terminates the process-sales-records loop?

   _____

   c. Initializing PROCESS$ to Y (or y) caused the process-sales-records loop to be executed when it was first invoked. When was the indicator originally set to Y?

   _____

4. Program C4-2 is not complete and stub testing was used to test the portions of the program that loaded the table, created the process-sales-records loop, executed a search for the invoice number entered, and transferred control at the proper time to the enter-sales-data module and the process-sales-invoice module.
   In entering the five invoice numbers listed under 2, did you test the items listed above?

   _____

   How did you know when control was transferred to the enter-sales-data module and the process-sales-records module?

   _____

5. List the source code on your printer by using LLIST. Read through the source code listed and then draw the hierarchy chart that was used to develop the logic for the completed modules and the stubs.

INTERACTIVE EXERCISE 4–3

Program C4-3 is not structured and is not a practical application. However, it does illustrate both a WHILE and count-controlled loop.

Directions

1. Select menu **1,** option **7.** Respond **N** to "RETURN TO MAIN MENU".
2. Use **LLIST** and list the program on your printer.
3. Run the program.
4. Answer the following questions.
   a. Why was the statement CONTROL IS NOW IN THE PROCESS-RECORDS LOOP displayed exactly 10 times?

   _____

   b. What caused the conditional WHILE loop to be terminated?

   _____

   c What will occur, and why will it occur, if statement 100
      IF J = 11 THEN PROCESS$ = "FINISHED" is changed to
      IF J = 10 THEN PROCESS$ = "FINISHED"

   _____

   _____

© SRA 1988, 1983

SELF-EVALUATION TEST 4

Name _____

Section Number _____

I. Write the term being defined in the space provided. A small blank within the statement indicates where the term is needed.

_____ 1. Another name for a table.

_____ 2. A conditional loop in which the exit decision is made before the statements within the loop are executed.

_____ 3. A whole, positive number used with the name of the table whenever an individual item stored in the table is to be retrieved.

_____ 4. The daily total is added to the monthly total. At the end of each month, the monthly total is added to the yearly total.

_____ 5. A conditional loop in which the statements are executed before the exit decision is made.

_____ 6. In the statement FOR J = 1 TO 100, J is called the _____.

_____ 7. When the exit decision is made and control leaves the FOR J = 1 TO 100 loop, what value is stored in J?

_____ 8. In BASIC, if J is to be incremented by 5 each time the statements within the loop are executed, _____5 is added to FOR J = 1 TO 100.

_____ 9. A statement sometimes coded in the main control module that causes the commands with the process sales records module to be executed until a stated condition is met.

_____ 10. FOR J = 1 TO 100 is an example of a _____loop.

_____ 11. When loops are nested, the inner loop must be completely _____the outer loop.

_____ 12. Establishes a count-controlled loop that controls the execution of commands in a second module.

II. Multiple Choice. Record the letter of the best answer in the space provided.

_____ 1. The two major types of loops are
   a. DO WHILE and DO UNTIL.
   b. conditional and unconditional.
   c. conditional and count-controlled.
   d. count-controlled and unconditional.

_____ 2. When DO WHILE or DO UNTIL is used,
   a. an IF statement must be coded for the exit decision.
   b. the exit decision coding is generated by the compiler from the WHILE or UNTIL statement.
   c. there are usually multiple entry points into the loop.
   d. the exit decision is made before any statements are executed.

_____ 3. When a loop is created to enter the date,
   a. the value of the indicator is initially set within the loop.
   b. the value of the indicator is set when the operator enters a value such as Y or N.
   c. the indicator is initially set before the loop is entered and may be changed by a value entered by the operator.
   d. it should be a count-controlled loop rather than a conditional loop.

_____   4. When a count-controlled loop is coded,
   a. the counter is set to its initial value.
   b. the exit-condition test is specified.
   c. each time the statements within the loop are executed, the value specified is added to the counter.
   d. a, b, and c are all true.
   e. none of the answers provided is true.

_____   5. When code is written for DO (counter = 1 TO 15 by 3), the statements within the loop will be executed
   a. 3 times.
   b. 4 times.
   c. 5 times.
   d. 6 times.

_____   6. A subscript can be
   a. a fraction.
   b. a negative number.
   c. greater than the number of items in the table.
   d. a, b, and c are all true.
   e. none of the answers provided is true.

_____   7. An early exit from a count-controlled loop should be achieved by
   a. using a GO TO statement.
   b. setting the counter at a value greater than the maximum number of times the statements within the loop would normally be executed.
   c. using a conditional loop located within the count-controlled loop.
   d. setting the counter equal to the maximum number of times the statements within the loop would normally be executed.

_____   8. When developing a series of totals such as a total for the month, year, and final total,
   a. the monthly total is accumulated in the daily-total loop and printed as part of the month-end activities.
   b. totals are accumulated in the same loop that invokes the print module used to print the totals.
   c. each individual amount is added to all three totals.
   d. the total fields are set to zero only in the initialization module.

_____   9. A nested loop is established. The outermost loop is executed 10 times, the middle loop 5 times, and the innermost loop 30 times. Within the innermost loop, INTEREST is added to TOTAL-INTEREST. That particular calculation is made
   a. 30 times.
   b. 150 times.
   c. 1500 times.
   d. 50 times.

_____   10. The ability to create
   a. loops is the most powerful tool used in developing the logic of a program.
   b. count-controlled loops is more important than creating conditional loops.
   c. count-controlled and conditional loops, as well as the ability to create complex IF statements, makes it relatively easy to write complex, but completely structured, programs.
   d. conditional loops is more important than being able to create count-controlled loops.

III. True or False. Record a T or F in the blank provided. For each false statement, indicate why the statement is false or make the changes needed to correct the statement.

_____   1. Commands are always executed in the sequence in which they are stored in the memory of the computer.

© SRA 1988, 1983

_____ 2. Usually the commands stored within the process-records module are only executed once each time the program is run.

_____ 3. The major difference between a DO WHILE and DO UNTIL loop is when the exit decision is made.

_____ 4. The value of the indicator used to control a conditional loop can only be changed by entering a new value from an online terminal.

_____ 5. The exit decision for a conditional loop can only be based on one evaluation such as DO WHILE end-of-file = NO.

_____ 6. Although DO WHILE and DO UNTIL have a single entry point, there are usually multiple exit points.

_____ 7. PERFORM/VARYING is a COBOL statement used to establish a count-controlled loop.

_____ 8. When showing a count-controlled loop on a flowchart, a rectangle is divided into three triangles. The triangles are used to show the initial value of the counter, the exit test, and by what value the counter is incremented.

_____ 9. When pseudocode is used, there is no way of knowing what value is used to increment the counter.

_____ 10. The following is a good example of a nested count-controlled loop.
```
FOR J = 1 TO 10
    any required code
    FOR K = 1 TO 100
        any required code
    NEXT K
NEXT J
```

_____ 11. In the example used in 10, the statements within the loop controlled by K will be executed a total of 100 times.

_____ 12. Only relational operators can be used in WHILE or UNTIL statements.

_____ 13. More coding is required when tables are used and when individual fields are established to store the individual items.

_____ 14. Count-controlled loops are used extensively in searching tables. When a "match" is found, an early exit is made from the loop.

_____ 15. When Nassi-Shneiderman charts are used for illustrating nested count-controlled loops, a statement similar to what is used in writing pseudocode shows the initial value of the counter and the number of times the loop will be executed.

EFFECTIVE USE OF TABLES

After reading the chapter and completing the learning activities, you will be able to:

- Describe the characteristics of a one-, two-, and three-dimension table.

- When given a description of the data and the problem, identify when a one-, two-, or three-dimension table should be used.

- When given a description of a problem, develop a detailed logic plan for clearing a table, storing data in a table, and utilizing data stored within a table.

- Identify the ways in which the values used as subscripts can be determined.

- Explain why and how the main-control module for the survey program differs from those used in previous illustrations.

- Explain how case entry, count-controlled loops, and conditional loops controlled by WHILE are used in the survey program.

Since it is almost impossible to discuss the use of count-controlled loops without mentioning tables, they were briefly introduced in Chapter 4. Tables can also be called arrays or matrices. Tables can be located within real memory or included as part of records stored on magnetic tape, magnetic disk, or diskettes.

When records, storage areas, total fields, and constants are being defined to the computer, the programmer must also describe the attributes of the table being used. By using subscripts, each individual area within a table can be individually addressed. Tables can usually have either one, two, or three dimensions. Some languages permit tables to have more than three dimensions. Figure 5-1 illustrates how a one-dimension table should be visualized. Within memory, the areas within a table are adjacent to one another. Although each area in the three-dimension table illustrated in Figure 5-5 on page 166 is addressed individually by using the table row, and column number, the data is contiguous and not arranged as illustrated in Figure 5-5. However, in working with tables you must visualize them as having **rows** and **columns**.

In table processing, the areas within the table can be accessed sequentially or randomly. In **random access** processing, a unique subscript is used to go directly to the area within the table that contains the required data. In **sequential processing** each area within the table is accessed in the order it is located within the table.

In working with tables, programmers must know how to:

- establish tables. Usually tables can be defined as having either 1, 2, or 3 (and sometimes more) dimensions. Figures 5-1 through 5-3 illustrate how each type of table should be perceived.

- clear tables to zero or to spaces. Tables used to store numeric data are cleared to zero; tables used to store alphanumeric data are cleared to spaces.

- load tables. Tables can be loaded by using data stored within the program, keying in data, reading data stored in files, or by executing mathematical expressions. Subscripts must be used in order to determine where each item will be stored.

- retrieve data stored in a table sequentially. A count-controlled loop is often created. Each time the commands within the loop are executed, the loop's counter used as the subscript is incremented by 1. Therefore, each time the commands within the loop are executed a different area of the table is accessed.

- retrieve data from a table randomly. When data is accessed or stored randomly, a subscript entered from a terminal or from a transaction record is used in determining which area of the table is to be addressed.

- perform mathematical calculations using data stored within tables. Depending on the language being used, it may be possible to multiply the contents of Table 1 times the contents of Table 2 and store the results in Table 3.

How easy it is to work with tables depends on the programming language being used. While some languages permit the programmer to clear the table when it is initially defined, other languages make it necessary to create a count-controlled loop that sets each individual area to zero. While some versions of BASIC support MAT (short for matrix) statements that can be used to perform mathematical operations on the contents of the entire table, other versions of BASIC do not support MAT statements.

© SRA 1988, 1983

Address of Area	Data Stored in Area
Name-Table (1)	George Sharp
Name-Table (2)	Maurice Lockard
Name-Table (3)	Lloyd Abbott
Name-Table (4)	Roger Stimpson
Name-Table (5)	Cecile Peterson
Name-Table (6)	Helen Poggemeyer
Name-Table (7)	Donna Garcia
Name-Table (8)	Barbara Preston
Name-Table (9)	Jennifer Whitthorne
Name-Table (10)	Margaret Del Favero
Name-Table (11)	Nadine Lenham
Name-Table (12)	Grace Nexsen
Name-Table (13)	Paula Mitchell
Name-Table (14)	Jack Van Orden
Name-Table (15)	Wayne Danielson
Name-Table (16)	Morrie Hoff
Name-Table (17)	Virginia Husby
Name-Table (18)	Lorraine Barton
Name-Table (19)	Tomoke Damon
Name-Table (20)	Rupert Diefendorf
Name-Table (21)	Fred Greenway
Name-Table (22)	Betty Whitfield
Name-Table (23)	Gwyneth Kersten
Name-Table (24)	Marvin Krumweide
Name-Table (25)	Jack Sturdivant
Name-Table (26) thru Name-Table (50)	contains spaces

Figure 5–1   *A one-dimension table containing the names of sales representatives.*

TYPES OF TABLES

One-dimension tables

A one-dimension table is illustrated by Figure 5–1. The table would have been defined as an alphanumeric table that can contain 50 different names. Assume that you wish to print Virginia Husby's name on a check. In the print statement table-name (17) would have to be used. Using 17 as the subscript generates an address that permits the data stored in the seventeenth area of the table to be retrieved. Usually a variable read from a record or entered from a terminal would be used as the subscript rather than a number such as 17.

Assume you are the programmer responsible for developing the sales system for a medium-sized organization that has 25 sales representatives. Each sales representative is assigned a given territory and works with certain clients. In a number of different reports you wish to print the name of the sales representative that calls on each client. You could decide to put the name of the sales representative in each customer's master file record. However, this would take more space than if the sales representative's number were recorded in the record.

WORKING WITH THE ONE-DIMENSION TABLE   Figure 5–2 illustrates the pseudocode needed to establish the table, clear the table, load the table, and utilize the data stored in the table. When the table is defined, it is usually necessary to indicate the number of dimensions, the size of each area in the table, and the type of data that will be stored within the table. How this is done differs with each programming language. When the table is defined, space is reserved within real memory for the table.

Sometimes more areas are defined than are needed. In the illustration the table used for storing the sales representative's names was defined as a table containing 50 elements. If the table had been defined as one containing space for 25 names, when the 26th sales representative was hired, the table would have to be redefined. The program would have to be modified and recompiled. If the table is defined initially to provide space for 50 names, 25 additional sales representatives can be hired before the program requires modification.

The table will be loaded by using data stored in a disk file. Therefore to clear the table is not absolutely necessary. When the record is read from disk, the subscript used is the sales representative's number. The record is read into the memory of the computer and the name of the sales representative is moved into the table. Where it is located depends on the value of the subscript. Any data previously in that area of the table is replaced by the name of the sales representative.

Nonetheless, to clear the table is considered wise. Assume that when a new record was created, the sales representative's number was recorded as 29 rather than 19. Since we only loaded 25 names into the table, if the number 29 were used as a subscript and if the table was not cleared, then whatever was in the memory at the time our program was loaded would be printed. If the table had been cleared to spaces (blanks), nothing would be printed.

SUBSCRIPTS   Take a good look at the subscripts used in the example. Subscripts must also be enclosed in parentheses and separated by commas. A subscript must be a whole, positive number that is within the range of the table. If the number 27 is used as a subscript for a table defined as having 25 items, a statement such as "**Subscript out of range**" may be displayed and the job may abort. Or, depending on the language used, the job may continue but would produce invalid results when an invalid subscript is used.

© SRA 1988, 1983

Figure 5–2 Pseudocode required to establish, clear, load, and retrieve data stored in a one-dimension table.

Pseudocode	Explanation
`DECLARE table-name  (50)`	A table that will hold 50 names is established. Although we only have 25 sales representatives this allows for expansion.

`DO (counter 1 to 50)`
`    table-name (counter)`
`        = ' '`
`END DO`
	The loop's counter is used as a subscript. Spaces will be moved into each area of the table.

`PERFORM 3000-read-reps-name`
`DO-WHILE (end-of-file = N)`
`    table-name (WF-rep-number) =`
`        WF-sales-reps-name`
`    PERFORM 3000-read-reps-name`
`END DO-WHILE`
	The table is loaded by reading a sequential file that contains the name and number of each sales representative. When the end of the file is reached, an exit will be made from the DO-WHILE loop.

`PRINT . . .` `    table-name (TR-salesman)`	The sales record being processed contains the number of the representative who made the sale. In this case the field was called salesman. The name of the representative will be randomly retrieved from the table.

Either a number or a variable can be used as a subscript. When a variable, such as a counter, is used, it is the numeric value stored within the field that determines the address where the data is stored within the table. Within an application, the names of the variables used may change. When the table is being loaded, ROW and COL might be used as the subscripts. When the data is being accessed, two different variables may be used. Although meaningful names should be used, it is the data stored within the field that determines what area of the table will be accessed.

When data is retrieved randomly from a table, the subscript is usually:

- part of a record read from an online file
- keyed in by an operator
- generated by executing some type of mathematical expression
- determined by using case entry.

OTHER EXAMPLES If your college is a comprehensive two-year college, the majority of the students may come from 150 area high schools. Often reports are printed that include information pertaining to the school from which the students graduated. A three-digit school code recorded in each student's master file record can be used to retrieve the name of the school and other pertinent information from a table stored within real memory.

In printing invoices that include the cost of raw materials and certain basic charges falling into such categories as labor, travel time, consultation fees, and so forth, the description of the charges can be stored in a table in real memory. To retrieve the description from the table, the data entry operator would key in a two-digit code to be used as the subscript.

ADVANTAGES OF USING TABLES FOR STORING DATA There are many reasons why tables are used. In the example given, the advantages of using a table to store the name of the sales representatives are:

1. Less space is required in each customer's master file record. Only two digits are needed to record the number of the sales representative.

2. Less time is required to record the data in the file. Only two keystrokes are needed whereas twenty or more may be needed to record the name of a sales representative.

3. Easier maintenance of individual master file records. If a new sales representative replaces a former representative, only one change is required. The new name is stored in the file used to load the table. None of the individual master file records will be changed. However, if the names of the sales representatives were stored in the master file records, all of the individual records that contain the former representative's name would need to be **updated.**

4. Data stored within real memory can be accessed faster than by reading records stored on magnetic tape or disk.

WHEN TABLES ARE NOT USED Although very large tables can be located within real memory, the number of items and the amount of data which must be stored determines if a table should be created within memory or if the data should be retrieved randomly from an online disk file. For example, when sales invoices are prepared, the inventory master file record must be read for each item. The record contains the product description, selling price, and quantity on hand. All of this data must be used to process the sales data and to prepare the invoices. Since the record for each item must be retrieved, there would be no reason to store product descriptions in a table.

Conversely when relatively few items are required, and each item is used a number of times, it may be more efficient to establish tables within real memory rather than retrieving the same record from disk a number of times.

When errors occur during processing, the messages could be stored in a table within real memory and printed out after all of the good data has been processed. Another option is to store the messages in a file, then print them as needed. If the messages are to be retained and used in some type of error-analysis report in the future, it would be better to record them in a file. However, if only a few errors are detected and the messages are only used to print the initial error-report, an analyst or programmer might elect to store the messages in a table rather than in a file.

Two-dimensional tables

A two-dimension table is to be used to store the commission rates to be paid to the sales representatives. Two factors determine the commission rate:

1. The type of product sold. Our company sells six different types of products. Some are low-profit items, on which less commission is earned than on items with a higher profit margin.

2. The amount of the sale. As the amount of the sale increases, the rate of commission increases.

© SRA 1988, 1983

Figure 5–3 A two-dimension table used to store commission rates.

Subscripts	Row Based on Volume	Column—Type of Product					
		1	2	3	4	5	6
1,1–1,6	1	.10	.15	.18	.20	.22	.25
2,1–2,6	2	.11	.16	.19	.21	.23	.26
3,1–3,6	3	.12	.17	.20	.22	.23	.27
4,1–4,6	4	.135	.185	.215	.235	.245	.285
5,1–5,6	5	.15	.20	.23	.25	.26	.30

Figure 5–3 illustrates how the commission rates are stored in the table. The five rows represent the percentage paid based on the amount of the sale; the six columns represent the six types of products sold. When addressing an area within the table, two subscripts must be used. The first subscript identifies the row and the second subscript identifies the column.

WORKING WITH A TWO-DIMENSION TABLE   The table must be defined for the computer as a two-dimension table that has five rows and six columns. Thirty (5 × 6) individual commission rates can be stored in the table. The table should be cleared to zero and then filled with the commission rates. In this example the 30 commission rates will be stored within the program and during initialization the rates will be loaded into the table.

When the table is utilized, the type of product sold is part of the transaction sales record. However, the row subscript is determined by using the following information:

Amount of Sale
Less Than:	*Subscript*
10,000.01	1
20,000.01	2
50,000.01	3
100,000.01	4
over 100,000.00	5

Figure 5–4 illustrates how the table will be established, cleared to zero, filled, and utilized.

One disadvantage of loading tables with data stored within the program is that if the commission rates change, the appropriate changes must be made to the program. The program should be put into a test library, the changes made, and the program tested before it is put into the operational library. The documentation for the program should also be updated to reflect the changes.

When only a small quantity of data is needed, loading tables by using data stored within the program is more efficient than opening a file, reading the

Pseudocode	Explanation
DECLARE rate-table (5,6)	The table identified has 5 rows and 6 columns.

DO (row = 1 to 5)
   DO (column = 1 to 6)
      rate-table (row,column) = 0
   END column
END row
	Nested count-controlled loops are needed to places zeros throughout the entire table.

DO (row = 1 to 5)
   DO (col = 1 to 6)
      READ rate-table (row,col)
   END col
END row
	The thirty rates stored within memory are loaded into the table. In BASIC the rates would be stored as part of the program in data statements and a READ statement would be used to fill the table. In other languages, it might be unnecessary to create a loop to load the table.

IF sales $\langle$ 10000.01 then row = 1
ELSE IF sales $\langle$ 20000.01 then row = 2
   ELSE IF sales $\langle$ 50000.01 then row = 3
      ELSE IF sales $\langle$ 100000.01 then row = 4
         ELSE row = 5
ENDIF
commission = rate-table (row,type) * sales
	Case entry is used to determine the row subscript (based on volume of sales); the product type is read from the sales record.

Figure 5–4   *Pseudocode needed to establish, clear, load, and use data stored in a two-dimension table.*

records, and closing the file. Also, if the data is stored within the program and the program has been completely tested, the data within the table will also be correct.

CHECKPOINT QUESTIONS

1. When accessing data stored within a table, how does accessing information randomly differ from accessing data sequentially?

2. What advantages are often associated with storing data in a table?

3. What rules apply to the value stored in a variable used as a subscript?

4. If a field called WHICH is used as a subscript, in what ways might the data stored in the field have been obtained?

5. Assume that a company sells 20,000 different items. When the sales invoices are being prepared, would you recommend that a table containing the description of each item be stored within real memory? Explain your answer.

6. The percentage of state income tax to be paid is based on the number of exemptions and the amount of earnings. The tax table provides for from

© SRA 1988, 1983

zero to ten or more exemptions and there are 20 different earning brackets. The earnings determine the row subscript; the exemptions determine the column subscript.

   a. How would the table be defined? Describe how the data will be arranged, in regard to rows and columns, within the table.

   b. Write the pseudocode needed to clear the table to zero.

   c. What technique will be used to determine the value of the subscripts? Employee earnings are computed within the program and the number of exemptions are stored in the records stored in the payroll master file.

   d. What advantage is there in using a table for storing the percentages rather than storing the percent in each person's payroll master file record?

Three-dimension tables

Figure 5–5 illustrates a three-dimension table. In the illustration the single numbers represent the total number of men and women that answered the question in the same way. A survey was taken to determine the answer to five questions.

1. Each question has four possible answers, represented by the columns. The question answered is represented by the row. If a woman selected the second answer for question 1, the value of the total in the area for table 1, question 1, answer 2 would be increased by 1. In the figure, 14 women answered question 1 with answer 2; 85 women chose answer 3 to question 1.

2. If the respondent did not answer or gave an invalid answer, column 5 is used to record the data. Six males gave an invalid answer to question 4. The subscripts showing the area that records those results show table 2, question 4, answer 5 or RESULT (2,4,5). The increment is shown as RESULT (2,4,5) = RESULT (2,4,5) + 1.

3. A woman might have entered an incorrect answer to question five. One would be added to the area for invalid answers by the statement: RESULT (1,5,5) = RESULT (1,5,5) + 1.

Since the surveyor wants to know if men and women answer the questions in the same way, table 1 records the answers given by women and table 2 the answers by men. In working with the tables, three subscripts must be used. For example, if the name of the table is RESULTS, the address RESULTS (2,3,4) indicates that

1. Table 2 is used—the respondent is a man.

2. The question answered is number 3 (row subscript).

3. The respondent selected the fourth answer (column subscript). One will be added to the location in memory reserved for RESULTS (2,3,4).

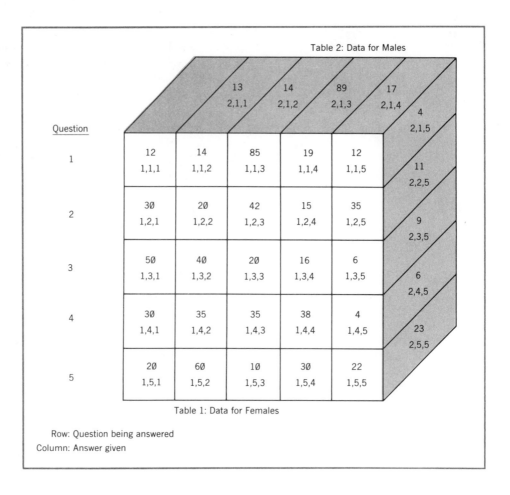

Figure 5–5 A three-dimension table used to store the results of a questionnaire.

The modules for the survey program which require a three-dimension table will be developed, and the program specifications and hierarchy chart will be illustrated. After the specifications are determined, the hierarchy chart and flowchart will be developed. The specifications for the survey program are illustrated in Figure 5–6.

Figure 5–7 illustrates how data is stored in the transaction file. In defining the records stored within the file, the programmer must specify the fields needed to record the questionnaire number, the answers to the five questions, and the sex of the respondent. The captions at the top of the illustration are for your benefit and are not part of the file.

The data listed shows the woman who sent in questionnaire number 1 answered the questions as follows:

Question	Answer
1	2
2	3
3	3
4	3
5	1

© SRA 1988, 1983

PROGRAM SPECIFICATIONS FOR THE SURVEY PROGRAM

Output

Printed report

Totals

Input

Transaction file

Explanation

The report will illustrate how each question is answered by both males and females as well as the percentage of people answering each question with a valid answer of 1, 2, 3, 4, or an invalid answer.

The total number of males and females who answered the questionnaire is to be printed.

A separate record is read for each questionnaire and it contains the following data:

TF-questionnaire-number
TF-answer-question-1
TF-answer-question-2
TF-answer-question-3
TF-answer-question-4
TF-answer-question-5
TF-sex-code (M if male; F if female)

Major processing tasks

Establish fields and indicators
Declare and zero tables
Read records and fill tables
Determine the percentages
Print the report

Editing

If the character recorded in the sex field is not an M or an F, a message is to be displayed and normal processing of the record will be bypassed.

If the digit recorded for an individual question is less than 1 or greater than 4, one will be added to the invalid-answer total accumulated for the question.

Figure 5–6 Specifications for the survey program.

The second questionnaire was answered by a man and since question 3 was answered with a 7, one will be added to the invalid-number total for question 2. Therefore, the subscript will not be the number of the answer but will be converted to a 5. Remember the fifth column is used for invalid answers.

Figure 5–7 Data stored within the transaction file.

Questionnaire number	Answers for the five questions					Sex
	1	2	3	4	5	
1	2	3	3	3	1	F
2	1	4	7	3	2	M

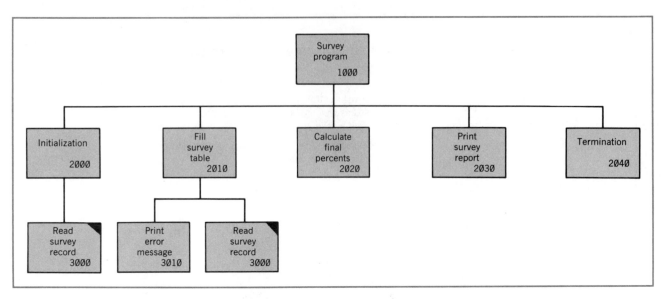

Figure 5–8 *Hierarchy chart for the survey program that utilizes a three-dimension table.*

Hierarchy chart for the survey program

The hierarchy chart illustrated in Figure 5–8 is somewhat different from the previous ones. This problem comprises five major tasks:

1. Getting started — Establish files, total areas, tables, and indicators. The transaction file is opened and the module which reads the records is invoked.

2. Filling the table — Store data read from the transaction record within the table. If a male answered question 3 with the fourth answer provided, the subscripts would be (2,3,4)—table 2, question 3, answer 4. One will be added to this area of the table.

3. Calculating percents — After all of the records are processed, use the data stored in the three-dimension table to calculate the percentages. The answers will be stored in another three-dimension table that has the same attributes as RESULTS.

4. Printing the report — After the percentages are calculated, the print-survey-report module will be invoked.

5. Termination — The file will be closed.

In addition to the major tasks represented by the initialization, fill-survey-table, calculate-final-percents, print-survey-report, and the termination modules, two support modules are needed. The first is used to read records and the second to generate an error message.

This problem is unusual in several respects. In most problems a record is read, calculations made, and the results of the calculations stored in a file, displayed, or printed. The **data processing cycle** of input-processing-output occurs. In the survey program all records are read and the information stored within the table *before* the percentages can be calculated and survey results printed.

© SRA 1988, 1983

Since the percentages were placed in a table, the detail printing can also be controlled by a count-controlled loop. The loop's counter is one of the subscripts used to retrieve information from both the results and percent tables.

Flowchart for the survey program

Figure 5–9, Part 1 through Part 3, illustrates the detailed logic required to develop this program. Although part of the material has been covered before, it provides a good review of basic techniques.

SURVEY MODULE—1000   The survey module controls execution of the other major modules. Control branches to initialization, the commands within the module are executed, and control returns to the survey module. Control then branches to fill survey table. Control remains within that module until all records have been processed. When control returns to the survey module, the calculate-final-percent module is invoked. Control remains within this module until the commands within the nested count-controlled loops are executed. After returning to the survey module, control branches to the print-survey-report module. After the commands within the module are executed, the termination module is invoked, files are closed, and the job ended.

INITIALIZATION MODULE   The detailed flowchart for the Initialization module is on page 170. As you study the flowchart, observe that:

1. Total areas are defined for the total number of men and women who completed the survey.

2. Two indicators must be used. More-data is used to control the execution of the fill-survey-table module. The indicator is initially set to Y and as long as Y remains in the field, the commands within the module will be executed. The value stored in the more-data changes when the end-of-file condition is detected in the transaction file.

    Valid-data controls the execution of the WHILE loop located within fill-survey-table. Valid-data initially contains a Y. However, if a record with an invalid sex code is read, an N will be stored in the field. This causes the commands stored within the WHILE loop to be bypassed.

3. Three tables are needed. The first table, illustrated in Figure 5–5, contains the total number of valid answers (columns 1 through 4) and invalid answers (column 5) given for each of the five questions. The second table will be used to store the percentage of the men and women that answered each question with a 1–4 answer or an invalid answer. When the questionnaire is filled out, the number of the answer selected must be placed in the blank provided. The third table is used to store the answers recorded in each transaction record. The answers remain in the five-area one-dimension table only until the next record is read.

4. The transaction-records file is opened. It is a sequential file that contains one record for each questionnaire.

5. Nested count-controlled loops are needed to clear the tables. The outermost loop provides the subscript for the table to be accessed; the middle loop provides the subscript for the row to be accessed; and the innermost loop provides the subscript for the column. While table = 1 and row = 1, the innermost loop is executed 5 times. Zeros are placed in

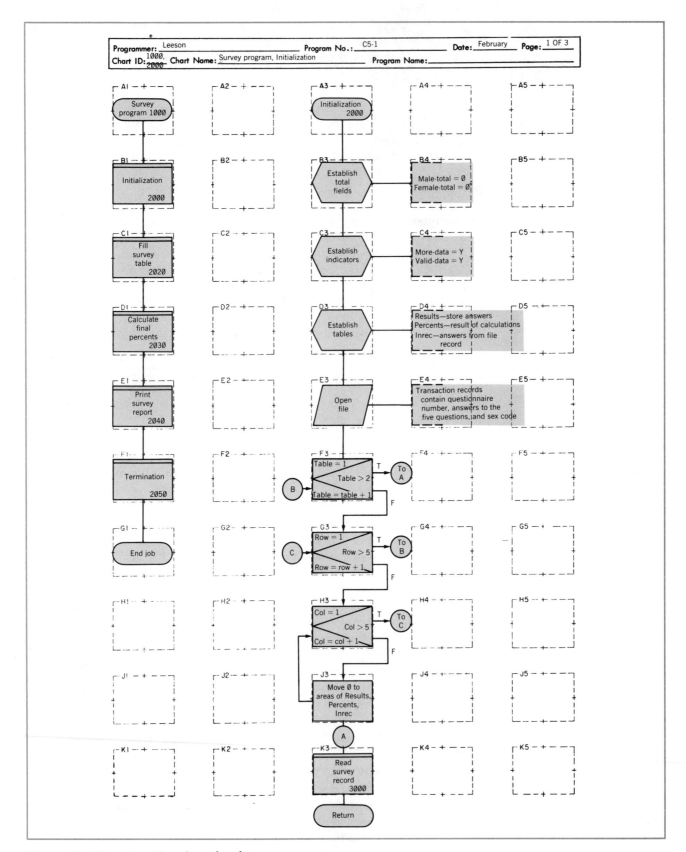

Figure 5–9 Part 1   Flowchart for the survey program

© SRA 1988, 1983

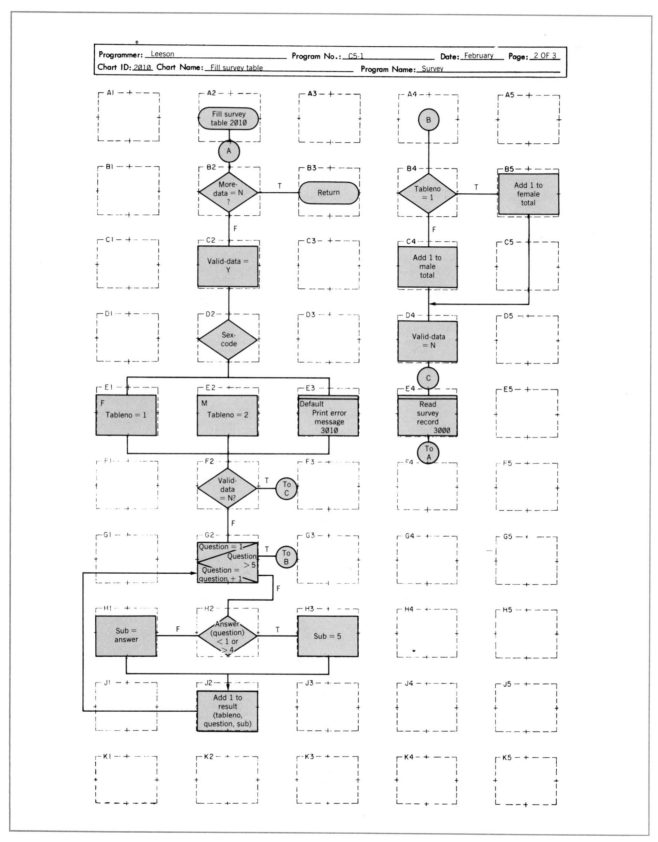

Figure 5–9 Part 2   Flowchart for the survey program

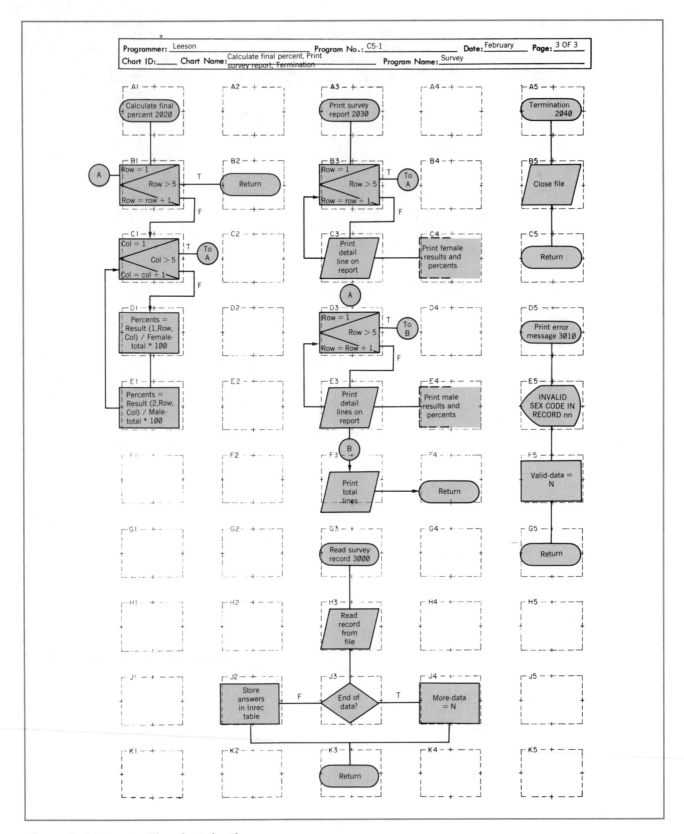

Figure 5–9 Part 3 Flowchart for the survey program.

© SRA 1988, 1983

the five areas located in the first row. Row changes to a 2 and the innermost loop is again executed 5 times. The commands within the rectangle that state, "Move 0 to areas of Results, Percents, and Inrec" will be executed 50 times.

6. The read-survey-record module is invoked. If the file is empty, N would be moved into more-data. Since an evaluation for a WHILE loop is made *before any commands are executed*, none of the statements within the fill-survey-table module will be executed.

This should also answer the question "Why not just invoke read-survey-record at the top of the WHILE loop?" If you did, when the end-of-file was detected, the commands within the loop have started to be executed and the last record read may be processed twice, invalid results will be achieved, or the job may abort. What occurs depends on the language being used.

In the initialization module, the first three blocks represent tasks that are referred to as "housekeeping details," and declarative statements may be used when the program is coded. The remainder of the blocks represent imperative commands that are executed at the beginning of the program in the "let's get started" phase.

FILL TABLE The fill-survey-table module provides an excellent example of each type of loop covered in Chapter 4. The first diamond that states "more-data = N" represents the decision made to determine if control should remain within a WHILE loop. As long as more-data contains an N, the commands within the loop will be executed. The second diamond that contains "sex code" illustrates case entry. The commands within one of the three rectangles will be executed.

The third diamond which contains "valid-data = N" represents a WHILE loop. If error-in-record, module 3010, is executed, valid-data will contain an N and the commands within the WHILE loop will be bypassed. Within the WHILE loop is a count-control loop. Although a three-dimension table is used to store the answers, only a single count-controlled loop is needed. The first subscript (Tableno) is determined by the sex of the respondent. The second subscript (Question) is determined by the value of the counter "Question" which represents the question being answered. The third subscript (sub) is determined by the way the question was answered.

This one module requires the use of two WHILE statements, IF/THEN/ELSE statements for case entry, and a count-controlled loop. Without the ability to use tables and count-controlled loops, the source coding for this problem would require many more statements than are used in writing the code for Interactive Exercise 5–1.

At the bottom of the loop controlled by valid-data, note that valid-data is set to N. This was done so that commands will be executed only once. In this case an IF statement could have been used rather than establishing a WHILE loop controlled by the value stored in valid-data.

CALCULATE FINAL PERCENT Figure 5–9, Part 3, on page 172 illustrates the calculate-final-percent module. A nested count-control loop controls the execution of the statements shown within the processing symbols. The calculations must be made separately for the data stored in the men's and women's tables. Each of the calculations shown will be executed 25 times. The answers will be stored in the percent table which also is a three-dimension table.

Some languages may support the use of statements that would permit the mathematical operations to be made on data stored in the result table and the answers placed in the percent table without using nested count-controlled loops. However, the logic executed by the computer will be similar to what is shown in the illustration.

READ SURVEY RECORD—3000   If end-of-file is not detected, the answers to the five questions are stored in the one-dimension table. This is done to make the processing of the information easier. The end-of-file is detected *after* the last transaction record stored on the disk has been read and processed.

Other modules   It is not necessary to explain what occurs in the termination or error-in-record modules. Since the data to be printed is stored in two separate tables (results and percents), a count-controlled loop is used to print the information stored in the tables. The loop's counter is one of the subscripts used to access randomly the data stored within the two tables. Since separate detail lines are printed for the men and women respondents, two separate loops are used. In the first loop, the report lines for women are printed; in the second loop, the men's-report lines are printed.

CHECKPOINT QUESTIONS

7. In the example TABLE (J,K,L), what does each of the three subscripts identify?

8. Why does the main control module for the survey program differ from the ones used in previous examples?

9. Why was a three-dimension table used for storing the results of the survey?

10. Why were the tables cleared in the initialization module rather than in the fill-survey-table module?

11. Why are there usually two statements within a program that invoke the read-survey-record module? If fill-survey-table is controlled by a WHILE statement, what is wrong with placing the statement that invokes the read-survey-record module as the first one within the WHILE loop?

12. What are the advantages of storing the questionnaire results in one table and the percentages in a second table?

SUMMARY

- While some languages support other types of tables, most programming languages support the use of one-, two-, or three-dimension tables that can be used to store either alphabetic or numeric data.

- Data stored in tables can be accessed either randomly or sequentially.

- Storing data in tables reduces the:
  amount of coding needed to store and retrieve data.
  number of keystrokes needed to enter data into a master file.

© SRA 1988, 1983

amount of space needed to store data within a master file.

amount of maintenance needed to keep records stored within files current.

- The value of a subscript can be computed, keyed in by an operator, entered from a transaction or master file, or generated by a count-controlled loop.

- In working with tables, programmers must understand how to describe the table to the computer, clear the table, load the table, and retrieve data from the table.

- While declaring, clearing, and loading tables are similar for most of the problems encountered, the methods used to retrieve data from tables differ from program to program. Retrieving data sequentially, such as when the report was printed, is different than when the value of the subscripts must be determined in order to retrieve data randomly from a table.

DISCUSSION QUESTIONS

1. What should be considered in determining if data is to be stored in a table or included as part of master file records?

2. In the survey program, why were five 2000-level modules used rather than three?

3. Refer to the flowchart for the fill-survey-table module on page 171. What would occur if the statement valid-data = N were omitted? After a new record was read, why was valid-data reset to Y? Could the use of valid-data be eliminated if an IF statement were used to determine if the data was to be processed rather than a WHILE statement?

4. Why was a count-control loop needed to determine the value of the row subscript and to add 1 to the appropriate area of the table? How were the value of the subscripts used for the table and column determined?

5. Give an example of when data stored within a table should be retrieved sequentially rather than randomly.

6. Give an example of when data stored within a table should be accessed randomly. In your example indicate how the value to be used for the subscript would probably be determined.

KEY WORDS

column	sequential access
data processing cycle	subscript out of range
random access	update a record
row	

PROJECTS

EXERCISE 5–1

In a program you are designing, a data entry clerk must enter the date in the MMDDYY format. For example, January 1, 1989 would be entered as 010189. You have been told to edit the date in every way possible. When the date has not been carefully edited, errors such as entering the month as 24 and a February date as 023189 go undetected. The date entered is the date of the first order received from the customer; it will be retained in the master file record and used in a number of different programs.

The date is entered from a terminal and is part of the data keyed in when new records are added to the customer master file. Although the date is keyed in as one six-digit number, it is stored within the record as three individual fields: month, day, and year.

You have decided to create a table called DAYS-OF-MONTH that contains the days of each month. Visualize the table as:

Area of Table	Days in the month
1	31
2	28
3	31
4	30
. . .	
12	31

Directions

1. Write the pseudocode required to create the loop needed to enter and verify the date. Until the date is entered correctly, control is to remain within the loop. Check to see if:
   a. the month entered is valid.
   b. the day entered is correct. Use the table to do this. While this will detect an error such as using 31 for a date in February, it will not detect an error such as keying in the day as 14 rather than 15.

2. In a second program, the master file records that contain the date as MMDDYY are used as input for a program that will print a report. However, on this report you wish to print the date as January 1, 1989. In writing the pseudocode refer to the date fields as month, day, and year. Write the pseudocode needed to:
   a. Declare the table. Call the table "name-of-months". In working with the table, you will visualize it as follows:

Location	Data stored in table		Location	Data stored in table
1	January		7	July
2	February		8	August
3	March		9	September
4	April		10	October
5	May		11	November
6	June		12	December

© SRA 1988, 1983

b. Clear the table to spaces.

c. Load the table from data stored within the program. Assume that language such as BASIC is being used that permits data stored within the program to be read into a table.

d. Utilize the name of the month stored in the table as part of the printed report.

EXERCISE 5–2

A new billing program is being developed for a physician. His patients have complained in the past that they do not know what they are being charged for. The doctor has 30 different charge categories. Codes are used such as 01 for an office call, 02 for an X-ray taken in his office, and so forth. The patient charges are keyed in daily and include the patient's number, code for the charge, and the cost. At the end of the month the statements are prepared that will have the reason for the charge printed in full.

Directions

Write the pseudocode needed to:

a. Declare the table.

b. Clear the table to spaces.

c. Load the table. Assume that a language such as BASIC is used and that the reasons for the charges are recorded in DATA statements within the program and can be read and stored in the table.

d. Utilize the data stored in the report to print the information on the statement. The charge code is read from the patient's transaction file.

PROBLEM 5–1

Develop the logic for a program that will analyze the results of a questionnaire. The following specifications are developed for the program:

Output Report	Listing of each question and the number of persons who answered the question with a 1, 2, 3, 4, 5, 6, or invalid response.
	Total number of valid questionnaires; total number of questionnaires with errors.
	Total number of questionnaires received from people living within the city, out of the city but within the county, and total living outside of the county.
Input Transaction file	Records contain the number of the questionnaire, the answers to questions 1–10, and the location code. For each question, the respondent can select one of six possible answers. The location codes are: 1 if within the city; 2 if within the county; or 3 if outside of the county.

Major Processing

Establish totals and indicators.

Fill table.

Print detail lines.

Print total lines.

Directions

1. Develop the hierarchy chart for the required program.

2. Develop the detailed logic for all modules *except* print-survey-report and read-survey-data.

INTERACTIVE EXERCISE 5–1

Program C5-1 reads the transaction file and executes the logic illustrated for the survey program. Assume that you were the programmer and the transaction file contains the test data.

Directions

1. Boot the system, load **BASIC,** depress **F3** (LOAD), key in **menu** <ENTER>, press **F2.**
2. Select **menu 2,** option **8,** press **F2,** or key in **RUN** <ENTER>.
3. After the program executes, answer **Y** to Main menu? Y OR N?
4. Save the printout, as you will need it in order to complete some of the other assignments.
5. Select **menu 2,** option **9,** press **F2,** or key in **RUN** <ENTER>. After the program executes, return to the main menu.

    The check program reads the transaction records and prints the data. The next five fields are the answers to questions 1–5, and the last field printed is the sex code.

6. Refer to the program specifications for the survey program. Using the listing of the test file records and the report printed, answer the following questions pertaining to the survey program:

    Does the data adequately test the conditions listed in the specifications and those detailed in the logic plan? Refer to the test data by questionnaire number and give the rationale for your answer.

    _____

    _____

    _____

    _____

7. Select menu **2,** Option **8.** Do not Return to main menu. **LIST 550–690.** Answer the following questions pertaining to the code.
    a. Why is statement 570 outside of the WHILE VALIDDATA$ = "Y" loop?

    _____

    _____

    b. What will occur if statement 640 is deleted from the program?

    _____

    _____

INTERACTIVE EXERCISE 5–2

A small but very significant change has been made to the survey program.

Directions

1. Select menu **2,** option **10.** Run the program.
2. The same input file was used as when C5-1 was run. Compare the output from the two programs.
    a. Based on the information provided within the chapter, what change do you feel was made in the program that produced the invalid results?

    _____

    _____

© SRA 1988, 1983

LIST 540–690. Does the source code listed support your answer? By comparing the source code to the logic plan, determine exactly what changes were made.

_____

_____

b. In testing the survey program using this version, how would the programmer know that a logical error had occurred in the design of the program?

_____

_____

INTERACTIVE EXERCISE 5–3

Only one statement was deleted from the program. Two display statements were added to the program to help you to determine what occurs as the commands within the program are executed. Note that several compiler-generated errors are displayed during the execution of the program.

Since the information displayed will scroll on the screen, you may cause a pause to occur by depressing Ctrl/NumLock (Ctrl and NumLock) at the same time. To continue execution of the program, press any key *other than* the shift key, Break, or Ins (insert).

Directions

1. Select menu **2**, option **11**.
2. Execute C5–1B several times and then answer the following questions. To answer some of the questions you may want to refer to the flowchart for the survey program.

   When testing a program that does not provide valid results, the technique that should be used is to review the logic and then determine what did produce valid results. After this is done, you determine what did NOT work and then find the problem.

   a. What evidence is there that the main control module controlled the execution of each of the four major modules and control passed back and forth as was expected?

   _____

   _____

   _____

   b. If only one record was processed, why were all of the records stored in the transaction file read?

   _____

   _____

   c. Refer either to the detailed logic plan for the fill survey table module or **LIST 540–690** and determine what statement was omitted. Describe what occurred because the statement was omitted.

   _____

   _____

d. Explain why the error message "Divide by zero" was repeatedly displayed on the screen. Refer to the detailed flowchart before you answer the question.

_____

_____

_____

e. Since BASIC was used to write the program, when an attempt is made to divide by zero the program continues to execute. However, an overflow condition occurred since the resulting number was too large in magnitude to be represented in number format. When the program executed, what evidence was there that an overflow condition occurred?

_____

_____

_____

INTERACTIVE EXERCISE 5–4

When testing a program, a programmer usually knows what should occur and approximately how long the program will take to execute. Sometimes there is no physical evidence that the program is in an infinite loop. If the programmer feels the program is in an unrecoverable loop, an interrupt (job abort) can be created by using the CTRL/BREAK keys. In this version of the survey program some display statements were added to the program to assist you in determining what was occurring within the program.

Directions

1. Select menu **2**, option **12**.
2. Describe what occurred.

_____

_____

3. **LIST 540–690** and compare it with the flowchart for the fill-survey-table module. Explain why the program was in an infinite loop.

_____

_____

4. Why didn't the statement RETURN TO MAIN MENU? Y OR N? display on your screen?

_____

_____

_____

INTERACTIVE EXERCISE 5–5

Program C5-5 loads a table by using data statements stored within the program. Besides the main control module, there are only three modules—initialization, display-employees-names, and termination. In the initialization module, the table is defined and loaded. The display-employee-names module permits the operator to enter the two subscripts and then retrieves the required information from the table that contains the following data:

© SRA 1988, 1983

JOE	MARY	PHIL	RON	FRANK
GLEN	GARY	ANN	SUE	LOIS
ELLEN	MANUAL	KIM	PETER	RITA
SALLY	DENNY	MIKE	ALFRED	STAN
ROSE	JENNY	PAUL	WILSON	TERRY

You are to enter the subscripts needed to retrieve the required name from the table. Each time you enter the row and column subscripts, the name your retrieved from the table will be displayed. In response to the question DO YOU WISH TO CONTINUE? Y OR N, enter a **Y.**

Directions

1. Load menu. Select Menu **2,** Option **13.**

2. Enter the subscripts that will enable you to retrieve the following names from the table:
    a. STAN
    b. MIKE
    c. PHIL
    d. SALLY
    e. TERRY

3. In response to DO YOU WISH TO CONTINUE, enter an **N.**

4. Run the program again and enter 10 for each of the two subscripts.
    What occurred?

_____

_____

Revise the logic for the display-employee-names module so that when a subscript is out of range, the operator will have an opportunity to rekey the subscript and the program will not abort. Write the required pseudocode for the module in the space provided below.

© SRA 1988, 1983

SELF-EVALUATION TEST 5

Name _____

Section number _____

I. Record the term defined or the one needed to complete the sentence in the space provided.

_____ 1. Tables can be located within real memory or included as part of a _____ stored on magnetic tape or disk.

_____ 2. When a count-controlled loop is used to access data stored within a table, the data is usually being accessed _____.

_____ 3. When the subscript used to access the data stored in a table is read from a transaction record, the data is usually being accessed _____.

_____ 4. In the statement "Table (J,K), K is used to reference the _____.

_____ 5. In the statement "Commission-rates (sale,type)", sale and type are _____.

_____ 6. When one or more fields within records stored in a master file are changed, the file is being _____. In the case of personnel records, one employee may have moved and another has a pay increase.

_____ 7. Declaring the attributes of tables, total fields, and indicators is sometimes referred to as _____ and may require the use of declarative rather than imperative statements.

_____ 8. The _____ is usually thought of as input, processing, and output. As each individual record is read, the data is processed, and the results are displayed, printed, or recorded in a file.

II. Multiple choice. Record the best answer in the space provided. For each of the following situations, indicate if you would use a one-, two-, or three dimension table or would recommend that a table should not be used.
   a = one-dimension
   b = two-dimension
   c = three-dimension
   d = use of a table is not recommended

_____ 1. The results of a survey that has 20 questions with 5 answers each is to be analyzed. The results are to be evaluated on the basis of how city residents answered the questions compared to persons residing outside the city.

_____ 2. Our organization has 100,000 customers and each can be identified by his or her customer number. The transaction file being used to process sales contains their numbers but not their names. The report to be printed will contain their names, unpaid invoices, and balances.

_____ 3. A description of the services provided by a dentist is to be included on the statement sent to the customer.

_____ 4. Tax rates are based upon the amount of earnings and the number of exemptions.

_____ 5. In each student's master file record is a three-digit code that identifies the school from which the student graduated. A list is to be printed of all students who have over a 3.5 grade point average. The report is to include the name of the schools from which each student graduated.

_____ 6. In processing sales data, the transaction record contains the number of the item sold, to whom it was sold, and the quantity sold. The sales invoices printed must include the description and price of the product. Our organization stocks 40,000 different items.

———— 7. A list is to be printed of all people who sent in reservations for a conference to be held on May 12. The reservation forms submitted contain names, addresses, phone numbers, and occupations.

———— 8. A table contains commission rates that are based on the amount of the sale and the type of item sold. We sell 20 different types of products and there are 10 different classifications based on the amount of the sale.

———— 9. In a health center there are 20 professionals who perform services for patients. The statement sent to the customer includes the name of the professional who performed the service.

———— 10. A hotel has 500 rooms. Employees who have access to terminals, and a need for the information, want to be able to retrieve randomly the name of the individual staying in the room by entering the room number. For each room a file which contains the billing charges is maintained.

III. True or False. Record a T or F in the space provided. If the statement is false, indicate why it is false or make the required correction to make the statement true.

———— 1. In clearing a table to zeros or spaces, a count-controlled loop is often used.

———— 2. When a table is used to store the names of sales representatives, more *file maintenance* is required than when the names are stored within the master file records.

———— 3. When tables are defined it is not necessary to indicate the size of the table or the type of data to be stored within the table.

———— 4. When subscripts are entered from a terminal or from records stored within a file, a test should be made to determine if the subscript is within range.

———— 5. If an organization has 27 sales representatives, the programmer should establish a table that can store 27 names. When sales representative 28 is hired, the program can be changed. The file is loaded by reading in names stored in a file.

———— 6. When a record is read, the data is stored within real memory. When a field of data located within the record is moved into an area within the table, the old data stored in that area is replaced with the new data. In many languages a statement such as "nametable (N) = name-from-record" is used to move data from one location to another.

———— 7. One disadvantage of loading tables by using data stored within memory is that the program must be changed and tested in order to update the data.

———— 8. In the survey program, the exit decision for the fill-table module was made based on the value of the counter used in a count-controlled loop.

———— 9. The reason the hierarchy chart for the survey program has five major control modules, rather than three, is that the transaction data is stored in a file rather than being entered from a terminal.

———— 10. In determining whether the respondent was male or female, a simple IF/THEN/ELSE statement was used.

———— 11. If the values of indicators used to control loops are not changed at the proper time, an infinite loop is created that may require operator action in order to terminate the program.

———— 12. WHILE more-records = "Y" is used to control process-sales-records. A transaction file that contains 88 records is to be read. A total is kept of the number of records processed. If the statement used to invoke the read-sales-records module is the first one within the loop, the total may indicate that 89 records were processed.

———— 13. The value stored in the field used as a subscript can only be keyed in by an operator, read from a file, or computed by using a mathematical expression.

———— 14. In the survey program two three-dimension tables were used. One was used to record the respondent's answers and the other was used to store the results of the calculations. Using

© SRA 1988, 1983

two tables saved a great deal of coding as the calculations could be made within a loop rather than coding 25 calculations for both the male and female percentages.

_____ 15. In testing the survey program, at least one record should have an invalid sex code and one or more records should have answers that are less than one or greater than four. A small quantity of data should be used and hand-calculated results should be compared to the printed or displayed output.

PRINTING REPORTS

6

After reading the chapter and completing the learning activities, you will be able to:

- Identify the difference between:
  Scheduled and on demand reports.
  Full and exception reports.
  Internal and external reports.

- Utilize a print layout form in designing a report.

- Describe the types of print lines that are often included on reports.

- Utilize line counters to determine when headings are to be printed.

- Explain how edit masks are used to suppress zeroes and insert special characters into numeric print fields.

- Identify the characteristics of a typical report-producing report.

- List the tasks included in a typical print-detail or heading module.

- List the tasks that must be completed in a module invoked when a level break occurs.

- Identify the information recorded on a typical report specification form.

- Explain why data is often extracted from a large file before it is sorted and used as input for a report program.

- Explain why error messages might be recorded in a file and printed after all of the data is entered.

- Develop a detailed logic plan for a full, exception, multilevel, or external report.

An application program can usually be classified as **transaction processing, file maintenance, information retrieval** and display, or as a report program. Because of the decreased cost in telecommunications and online storage, as major systems are revised, batch jobs are often changed to online, transaction-processing applications. As data is generated, it is processed in time to influence the transaction.

Vital to the success of any transaction-processing application are master files that provide current, reliable information. Most master files are extremely volatile and in order to assure the integrity of the data stored within the files, programs must be available to add, delete, and change records. Records may need to be changed because of errors that occurred in recording the data or because of what are considered normal changes. For example, in the payroll-personnel master file changes may be required because an employee moves, has a salary increase, or a change in marital status.

When designing an application, the information required, when it is needed, and how it should be formatted all must be considered. When processing a sales order, sales representatives need immediate access to the customer's credit history and to the inventory record of the item requested. The customer's balance and the quantity on hand must be available **on demand.** Sales representatives should be able to use terminals to retrieve the required records and display their contents. The ability to display information on demand has decreased the need for many reports printed on a scheduled basis.

Although many organizations are attempting to decrease the number of printed reports and to control the paper explosion, many organizations still find that more reports are required and faster **line printers** are needed. These are centrally located "workhorses" used to print large batch reports printed on either a regular schedule or on demand. Line printers can print anywhere from 300 to 3,000 lines per minute. Organizations that print a tremendous number of reports may use **page printers** that accumulate an entire page of printing in a **buffer.** A buffer is a temporary storage area reserved for a particular task or function. Although the number of lines printed is determined by the length of the line, many large online page printers can print anywhere from 10,000 to 30,000 lines per minute.

The demand for **letter-quality printers** is also growing. Letter-quality printers are distributed and found in offices, warehouses, and locations where goods are produced. They are often used to print answers to queries and exception reports. Although much slower than line printers, some letter-quality printers can print 300 or more lines per minute.

TYPES OF REPORTS

Reports can be classified in many different ways. The terms most often used in describing reports are:

1. **Scheduled** — Time is allocated on a regular basis for printing reports such as the payroll register, payroll summary, budget report, or accounts receivable statements.

2. **On demand** — In order to control the requests for printed reports, reports once printed on a scheduled basis may be changed to on demand. If an accountant, manager, supervisor, or auditor needs a report, a written request for the report is sent to the CIS department.

© SRA 1988, 1983

3. **Listing**   A listing, or full report, might include all items currently in stock or names of all the employees.

4. **Exception**   Rather than listing the quantity of all products on hand, only items below the reorder point are listed. Or, only customers who have exceeded, or are very close to, their credit limit are listed. Top- and middle-management usually prefer reports that list the exceptions rather than detailed information for each account, item, or person.

5. **Multilevel**   The records used to print the reports are sorted on one or more fields. Assuming that the file was sorted on person, department, and store number, totals are printed for each of the three levels.

6. **Error**   As data enters the system and is processed, a certain percentage of the records will be rejected because part of the data is invalid. In transaction processing, errors in data entering the system are usually detected immediately and are corrected so that only valid data enters the system. However, when applications are batch-processed, errors in input records may not be detected until later. An error report is printed so that the invalid records may be studied, the cause of the error determined, and the necessary correction made. It may be necessary to rerun the batch job.

7. **Internal**   The information printed on the report is intended for the use of managers, supervisors, accountants, and auditors within the organization.

8. **External**   The information is printed for distribution to customers, stockholders, creditors, or the government. The contents and format of some external reports, such as those submitted to the Internal Revenue Service, are governed by laws or policy.

9. **Mailing labels**   Master files containing names, addresses, and classification codes are frequently used to print mailing labels. The program used to print the labels permits the user to enter the classification codes of the records to be used in printing the labels. For example, if labels are to be sent to all attorneys and CPAs, codes 14 and 18 might be entered.

10. **Form letters**   Computer-generated form letters are printed. Master files are used to supply the information needed to personalize the letters.

An increasing number of external reports are being submitted on an electronic medium such as magnetic tape rather than being printed. When an organization such as a bank submits tax information to the Internal Revenue Service on magnetic tape, the specifications developed by the IRS must be followed.

DESIGNING REPORTS

In designing reports, programmers and analysts must understand the characteristics of both the printer and the programming language being used. While letter-quality printers usually have both uppercase and lowercase letters, high-speed line printers may only have uppercase letters. How data can be formatted and characters such as dollar signs and commas inserted into numeric information is language-dependent. The number of special characters that can be printed depends on the physical characteristics of the printer and the programming language used to write the source code.

Some printers have **carriage tapes** that help control the vertical movement of the forms in the printer; others have commands that simulate the use of a carriage tape. While some languages permit the programmer to specify the line number where information is to be printed, other languages only permit the use of statements which single, double, or triple space before or after printing. The characters that can be printed depend upon the characteristics of the printer being used and the language used to write the source code.

Some desk-top laser printers, as well as large page printers, print both the form and the variable data on the form. Logos and other types of graphics can be printed along with the required information. Although once considered too costly, color now can be used effectively in printing either internal or external reports.

A print layout form is developed before designing the program and writing the source code. In developing the print layout form, the analyst must consider what information is needed, how the information should be presented to make the form easy to read and understand, and the characteristics of the printer and language being used.

PRINT LAYOUT FORMS

Once decisions are made regarding the type of report to be produced and the exact information to be included, the analyst designs the report. Then the design is submitted for *suggestions* and approval to the person who requested the report. If approved, the analyst feels confident it contains the required information and is in an easy-to-use format. Also, if the print layout form is dated and signed by the user, future controversy regarding the report format is usually avoided. Figure 6–1 illustrates an internal exception report designed for an inventory control department.

In studying the print layout form illustrated in Figure 6–1, you can determine what headings, detail, and total lines are required. When the information, such as INVENTORY EXCEPTION REPORT is printed on a layout form, it is constant information that must be printed on each page. The character X shows each space where the variable data is to be printed; 9s are sometimes used to show where variable numeric data will be printed. In the inventory exception report, three heading lines and as many detail lines as the paper will accommodate are to be printed on each page. On the final page of the report, the total number of items below the reorder point and the percentage that this represents of the total number of items in stock are to be printed.

Many reports also have **page footings** at the bottom of each page that provide the page total. After the page total is printed, the total is added to the final total for the report and the page total is set to zero.

The inventory exception report is an internal report that will be used by the inventory manager and the purchasing department. Internal reports are usually printed on **stock paper**. Most organizations have on hand one-part

© SRA 1988, 1983

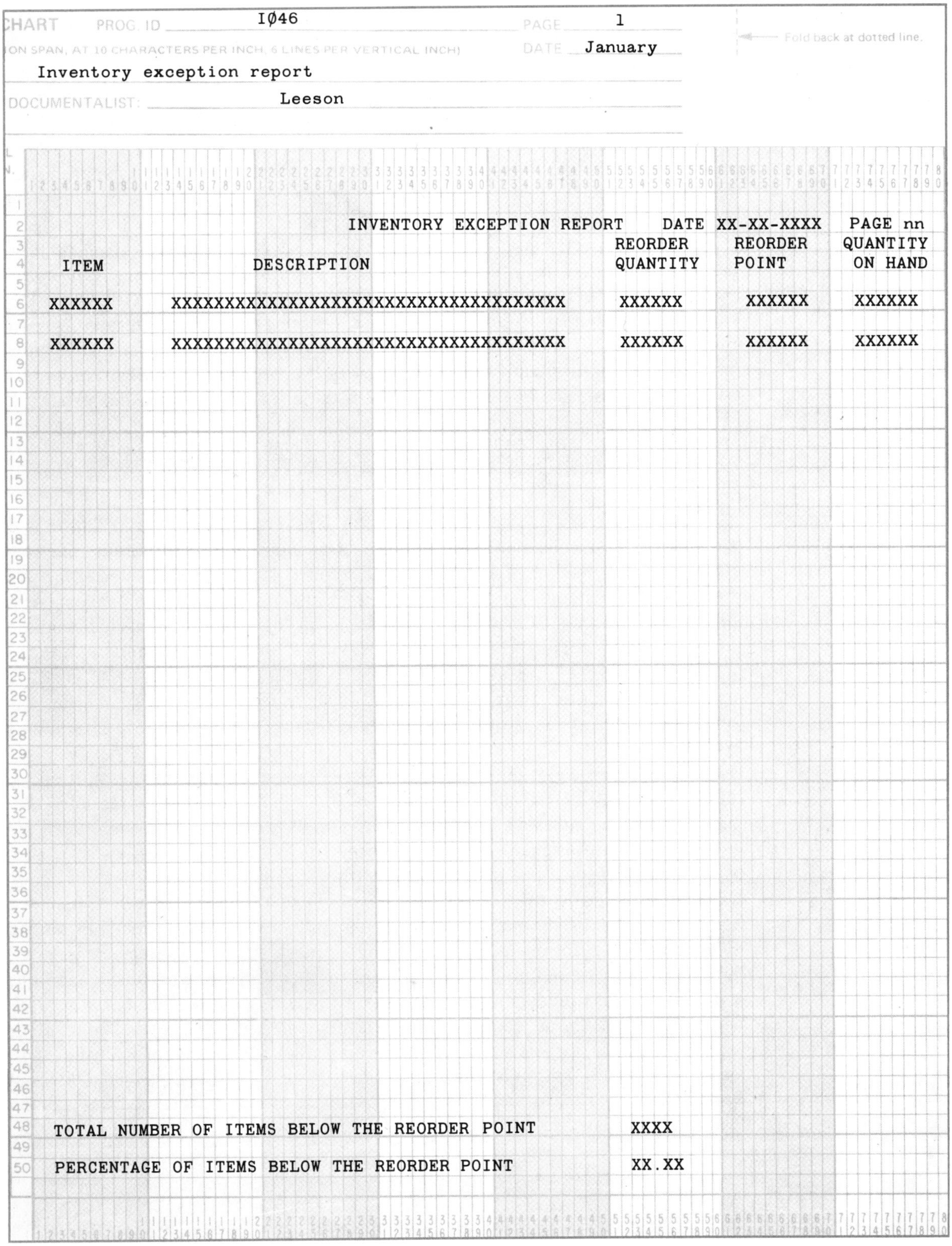

CHART   PROG. ID _____ IØ46 _____   PAGE ____ 1 ____   ◄── Fold back at dotted line.
ON SPAN, AT 10 CHARACTERS PER INCH, 6 LINES PER VERTICAL INCH)   DATE __ January __

Inventory exception report _____

DOCUMENTALIST: _____ Leeson _____

```
                                    INVENTORY EXCEPTION REPORT    DATE XX-XX-XXXX    PAGE nn
                                                                  REORDER    REORDER     QUANTITY
      ITEM               DESCRIPTION                              QUANTITY    POINT       ON HAND

     XXXXXX    XXXXXXXXXXXXXXXXXXXXXXXXXXXXXXXXXXXXXXXX           XXXXXX      XXXXXX      XXXXXX

     XXXXXX    XXXXXXXXXXXXXXXXXXXXXXXXXXXXXXXXXXXXXXXX           XXXXXX      XXXXXX      XXXXXX



     TOTAL NUMBER OF ITEMS BELOW THE REORDER POINT         XXXX

     PERCENTAGE OF ITEMS BELOW THE REORDER POINT           XX.XX
```

Figure 6–1   Print layout for the inventory exception report.

through six-part **continuous form paper** of varying sizes that is referred to as stock paper. Six-part paper causes one original and five copies to be printed. Continuous form paper has pin-feed holes that are used in mounting the forms in the printer. Since the forms are continuous, once they are properly positioned in the printer, the entire report can print without operator intervention.

Although stock paper may have colored horizontal bands or lines, headings or information about the firm or report is not preprinted on the paper. When an internal report is printed, the required headings are printed along with the detail and total lines.

External reports, such as sales invoices and checks, are printed on preprinted forms that include the organization's name and address, phone number, and other pertinent information. Often a logo or some type of artwork is included to enhance the form and create a more favorable impression. Figure 6–10 on page 211 shows how an external report is designed. The print layout will be used by the company that supplies the preprinted sales invoices and by the programmer who writes the source code for the sales invoice program.

Carriage control tapes

The numbers at the top and bottom of the print chart illustrated in Figure 6–1 tell the programmer what print positions are to be used in formatting the five types of lines needed. To the left of the print layout grid is a replica of a carriage control tape. While a few printers still use carriage control tapes to help control the vertical movement of forms in the printer, newer printers do not require their use. When carriage tapes are used, a command within the program starts the form skipping. A punch (or hole) in a designated **carriage control tape channel** stops the skipping. A carriage control tape, such as the one illustrated on Figure 6–1, has twelve channels which are designated by rectangles.

Standard list tapes are often used when internal reports are printed. A punch in Channel 1 is used to indicate the top-of-the-form where the first heading will be printed. Channel 12 is usually reserved for forms overflow. When an attempt is made to print past the **forms overflow position**, the form is automatically positioned to the top of the next page. Although a new page will be advanced in the printer, the headings will not be printed. When carriage tapes are used, many programmers still prefer to use line-counters to determine when the headings should be printed. A line-counter is a field established by the programmer that is used to keep track of the number of lines printed. In counting the number of lines printed, blank lines are also counted.

If preprinted forms, such as paychecks and sales invoices, are to be printed, each will usually have its own carriage tape. The carriage tape is designed to accommodate the length of the form and to control the skipping of the form in the printer.

Detail lines per page

The stock paper to be used for the inventory exception report is 8½" by 11". The paper is actually wider than 8½" as the space required to provide the pin-feed holes is not included in the measurement. To accommodate the design of the report, the printer must be set so that 6 lines per vertical inch and 10 characters per horizontal inch will be printed. Many printers can be adjusted so that either 6 or 8 lines per inch can be printed vertically and either 10, 12, or 15 characters horizontally.

When stock paper is used, usually one inch is reserved at the top and bottom of the page for margins. If there are 66 lines per page (11 × 6) and 12 are reserved for margins, 54 lines can be used for headings, detail, and total lines. Since the exception report has two headings, each of which is followed by a blank line, 50 lines can be used for printing the detail lines. Taking into consideration the top and bottom margins as well as the headings that must be printed on each page, 25 detail lines can be printed on each page of the inventory exception report. Each time a detail line is printed, one will be added to the line-counter. When the counter reaches 25, a new form will be advanced in the printer and the headings will be printed.

The documentation for the operator indicates what paper is to be used and how the forms are to be positioned in the printer. The documentation should indicate if the printer must be adjusted. Once the paper is positioned in the printer, the vertical spacing of the forms in the printer is usually controlled by the program. In the examples, the headings are to be printed in a single-space format. Then a space (blank line) is to occur before each detail line. The lines for the totals are to be printed one space below the last detail line. This could mean that one or both of the total lines could be printed in the space normally reserved for the bottom margin.

The decision to single- or double-space a report is based on its intended use. Reports that are frequently referred to for information regarding a particular subject should probably be double spaced. However, if the report is to serve only for occasional reference, then print time, paper, storage space, and money can be saved by single spacing it.

Types of print lines

Regardless of the language used, to print the report illustrated in Figure 6-1 requires six different print formats: three heading formats, one detail line, and two total line formats. When data is to be printed, the formatted line that may contain both constants and variables is moved from main memory into an area designated as an output buffer. From the output buffer, the formatted line of data moves either to a file used to store information to be printed or directly into the buffer of the printer. The operating system software transfers information into the output buffer and then to the file or printer. However, the programmer is responsible for setting up the print lines. As you can see, most lines contain both constant and variable data.

How print lines are formatted depends on the language used. With COBOL, for instance, declarative statements are used to format lines. Then before a line can be printed, the variable information must be moved into the formatted print structure by using a MOVE statement. In BASIC and many other languages, a move statement is not required. For example, assume that the detail line is to be printed and that the field containing the product description is called DESCRIPTION. By using DESCRIPTION in the print line, the computer will move the data from the input area into the location where the data for the print line is being formatted.

CHECKPOINT
QUESTIONS

1. What are the four major classifications associated with application programs?

2. Why are master files considered volatile?

3. In designing an application, how can a programmer best determine the type and amount of output printed or displayed?

4. What three techniques are used to decrease the number of reports printed?

5. If an inventory manager wanted to know which stock items were below or close to the reorder point, would he request a full or an exception report?

6. What are the differences in printing and use between internal and external reports?

7. Will more printing or less usually occur when reports are listed as being printed on demand rather than on a scheduled basis?

8. On a print layout form, what technique is used to show where variable information is to be printed?

9. Why should the print layout form be submitted to the person who requested the report before developing the detailed logic plan or writing the source code?

10. What is a standard list tape?

11. If a line printer uses a carriage control tape, what type of reports usually requires the use of a special tape rather than a standard list tape?

12. How does a programmer determine how many vertical spaces are available for printing detail lines?

13. What determines if a report should be single or double spaced?

14. What three types of print lines are illustrated on the print layout form for the inventory exception report?

15. Regardless of the language used, print lines are always formatted by the programmer in the same way. Explain why this statement is true or false.

**DETAILED LOGIC PLAN
FOR THE INVENTORY
EXCEPTION REPORT**

In working with the inventory department manager, the analyst responsible for designing the program has developed the specifications listed in Figure 6–2. The report specifications should be developed before the print layout chart is completed. Although the inventory exception report does not specify a requirement that date and page number be printed on each page, most organizations have such a policy.

Notice that the specifications do not indicate how input will be verified or edited. When the master file records were created, all five fields that will be used in printing the report were visually verified and the numeric fields were checked to make certain that only numeric data was entered. The programs used to maintain the master file records also contain a number of edit routines.

Programmers and analysts *must not* assume that data stored in master file records is accurate. The nature of the data and the way it was recorded in the

© SRA 1988, 1983

Figure 6–2
Specifications for the
inventory exception
report.

SPECIFICATIONS FOR THE INVENTORY EXCEPTION REPORT

Output

Printed report	The report will list the item number, description, reorder quantity, reorder point, and quantity on hand of each item that has a quantity on hand equal to or less than the reorder point. The detail lines are to be double spaced.
	The total number of items below the reorder point and the percentage the number represents of the total inventory are to be printed.

Input

Inventory master file	The following fields of data located within the master file records must be identified and used in printing the report: MF-item-number, MF-description, MF-reorder-quantity, MF-reorder-point, and MF-quantity-on-hand.
System date	The system date is to be retrieved and formatted as mm-dd-yyyy.

Required calculations

Totals are to be accumulated for the number of records read and the number of items with a quantity on hand equal to or less than the reorder point. The page number and line number must also be incremented.

Figure 6–3 Hierarchy
chart for the inventory
exception report.

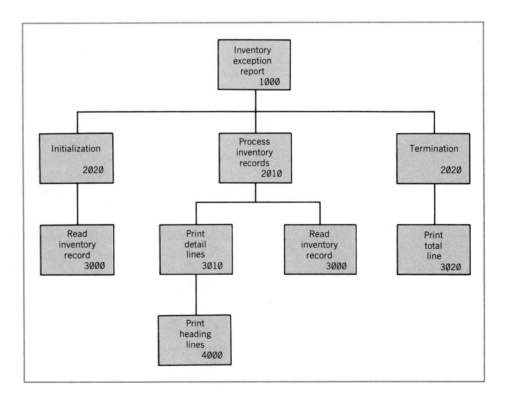

records determine whether or not data should be edited during the execution of a report-producing program. In this case, it would be difficult to determine if the reorder quantity, reorder point, and quantity on hand contain errors that have not been detected when the records were created or updated.

Hierarchy chart

The hierarchy chart illustrated in Figure 6–3 is typical of programs that read records sequentially from an existing file and use the data primarily for printing a report. Although totals are accumulated and a few IF/THEN/ELSE decisions might be made, most report programs require very little logic. Separate modules are usually used for the statements required to print detail, headings, and totals. The loop created for process inventory records continues to execute until the end-of-file condition is detected. Remember, at that time the last input record was processed and, if required, a detail line printed.

Flowchart for the inventory exception report

The initialization module illustrates several new tasks that must be performed when reports are printed. Fields must be established for a page number and a line counter.

LINE COUNTERS AND PAGE NUMBERS Although the page number and line counter can be handled differently, in this text in order to be consistent they will always be used in the report programs as follows:

1. Line counter
   a. In the initialization module, the field is defined and set to the *maximum number of detail lines* to be printed on a single page.
   b. *Before* a detail line is printed, the line counter is checked to see if headings should be printed. Since the line counter was initially set to 25, headings will be printed before the first detail line is printed.
   c. In the print-heading-lines module, the line counter is reset to 0.
   d. In the print-detail-line module, one is added to the value stored in the line-counter field.
   Rationale: Setting the line counter initially to the maximum number of lines to be printed makes it possible to treat all detail printing in the same manner. Also, the total lines will be printed on the same page as the last detail line.
2. Page number
   a. In the initialization module a zero is stored in the page-number field.
   b. *Before* a heading is printed, one will be added to the value stored in the page-number field.
   Rationale: At the end of the job the page-number field will contain the number of pages printed.

EXTERNAL SUBROUTINES Note that the symbol for calling in an external subroutine is shown with the caption "Format Date" inside. The date subroutine stored in an online library will be called into the program. The call statement used often contains a code that indicates how the date is to be printed. Since complete

© SRA 1988, 1983

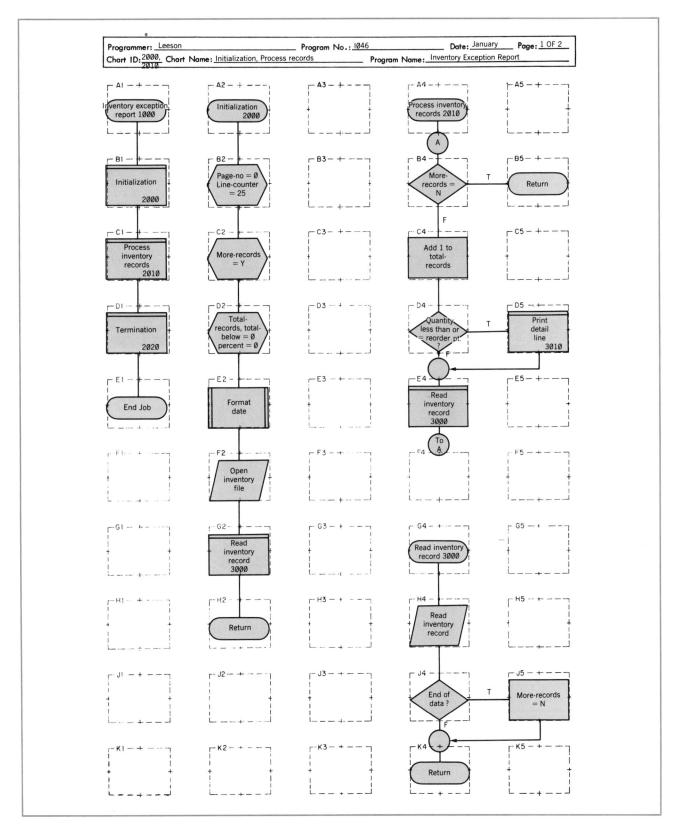

Figure 6–4 Part 1   Flowchart for the inventory exception report.

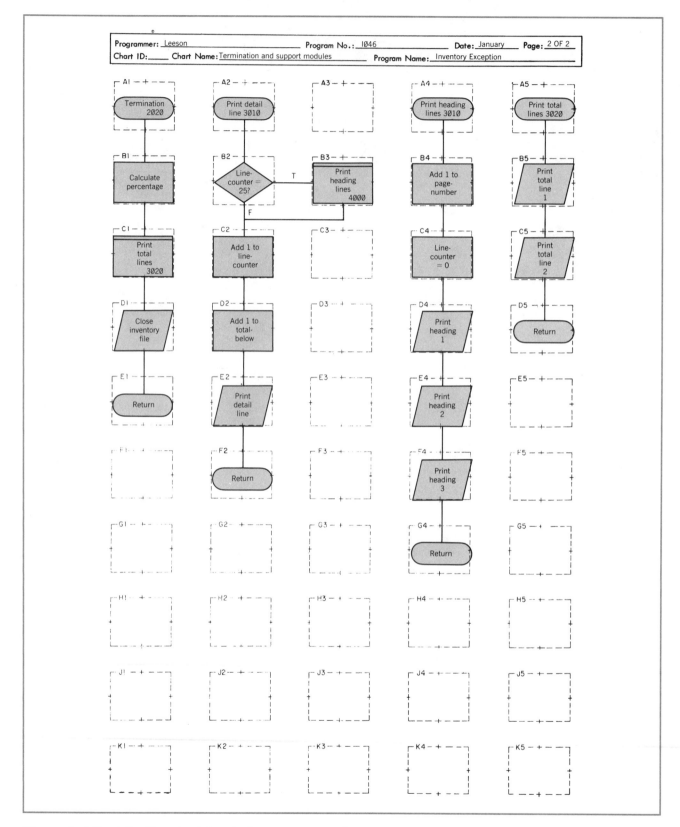

Figure 6–4 Part 2   *Flowchart for the inventory exception report*

© SRA 1988, 1983

documentation regarding how the subroutine is used is available, the logic is not detailed on the inventory exception report flowchart. In some languages a prewritten routine that can be incorporated into other programs is referred to as a **function**.

PRINT-DETAIL-LINE MODULE In the print-detail-line module, the line counter is checked, one is added to the line counter, one is added to the total-below field, and the detail line is printed. If COBOL is used for writing the source code, another processing block might be included just above the print-detail-line symbol and would contain a statement such as "MOVE DATA TO PRINT LINE." Also, when COBOL is used it is normally recommended that one location be used for all printing. Therefore, a statement such as "MOVE FORMATTED PRINT-DETAIL-LINE TO REPORT-LINE" will be included. When BASIC, or many other high-level languages, are used, it is not necessary to write statements to move data read as input or calculated to the output structure.

Some individuals might also feel that the "ADD 1 TO TOTAL-BELOW" does not belong in the print-detail-line module. Certainly the statement could have been included as one of the compound statements used when the IF condition was true. However, it is logical to include it within the print-detail-line module as the field total-below contains the number of lines printed.

EDITING DATA TO BE PRINTED When a field of data is defined as containing numeric data, it can only contain the digits 0–9. If you try to key in data such as 10,948.56, a **data exception** occurs. In BASIC if a comma is keyed in, the statement "REDO FROM START" appears and the operator has a second chance to key in the data correctly. If the program is coded in a language other than BASIC, the programmer usually has to write an error-routine that will identify the non-numeric data in the field and cause an appropriate error message to be displayed. When the numeric field is checked for non-numeric data, the input field is said to be *edited*. The term *edited* is also used to denote the addition of print characters to numeric data.

Although only digits *and a sign* are stored in the field containing the data, it is possible to set up an **edit mask** that provides for the insertion of commas, decimals, dollar signs, minus signs, and so forth. Unless a minus sign is included, all numeric data entering the computer is considered to be positive. If the resulting answer is negative when a mathematical operation occurs, the sign position of the field used to store the answer will be negative. Figure 6–5 illustrates how the data is stored within the computer, how the edit masks are coded, and how the data will be printed. In the illustration, a # is used to represent a numeric print position. When a language such as COBOL is used, 9s rather than #s are used to represent the numeric print positions.

The print layout chart shows how the printed output is to be edited. The printed output must comply with the installation's standards. For example, the guidelines might indicate that dollar signs are only printed on checks and financial statements used as external reports such as stock reports and position statements.

Whenever a field could become negative, the edit mask should provide for printing a minus sign. When dollar signs, commas, and other insertion characters are used in the mask, enough space must still be provided for the data. For example if a field contains eight digits and a dollar sign, comma, and dec-

Figure 6–5 Frequently used edit masks.

EDIT MASKS

Data	Mask	Edited Data	What Occurred
000123ˆ48	###,###.##	123.48	Lead zero suppression and insertion of decimal. Comma will not print unless there is a significant digit to the left of the comma.
000123ˆ48	$$##,###.##	$123.48	Since 2 dollar signs were used, the dollar sign floats up to the first significant digit.
000123ˆ48	$###,###.##	$ 123.48	A dollar sign is printed in the location specified. Lead zero suppression and the insertion of a decimal still occurs.
00012ˆ348	###,###.##	12.35	The ˆ symbol is used to show where the assumed decimal is located. The mast with two places beyond the decimal causes the output to be rounded up.
007976ˆ65	++##,###.##	+7,976.65	A + sign is printed and a comma is inserted. If the amount stored is negative, a − sign will print.

imal are added, the print layout chart must provide for eleven print positions rather than eight.

Figure 6–5 only shows a few examples of how data might be edited before it is printed. Programmers must know how to use masks and how to write source code to accomplish the editing required.

PRINT-HEADING-LINES MODULE   In the print-heading-lines module, the line counter must be reset to zero. If this is not done, the headings will only be printed once. If the page number had initially been set to 1, the statement "ADD 1 TO PAGE-NUMBER" would appear after the headings are printed rather than before.

Interactive Exercise 6–1 can be executed to see how the inventory exception report would be printed. The source code can also be listed and compared to the flowchart illustrated in Figure 6–4.

CHECKPOINT QUESTIONS

16. Why is it unnecessary to verify the input used to print the inventory exception report?

17. How did the hierarchy chart illustrated in Figure 6–3 differ from those used in previous examples?

18. In the initialization module, why is the line counter set to the maximum number of detail lines that will be printed on a single page?

© SRA 1988, 1983

19. When is the line counter set to zero?

20. Why isn't the logic for the date subroutine shown in a support module?

21. When numeric data is stored within a field defined as numeric, does it include commas, dollar signs, and other print characters?

22. What method is used to insert print characters into numeric data, such as in the net-amount field used in printing paychecks?

23. Why might the inventory exception report program be considered typical of many report-producing programs?

MULTILEVEL REPORTS

A sales analysis report might be designed as illustrated in Figure 6–6. Since the individual sales for each sales representative are listed, the report is considered a detailed report. In order to print the multilevel report illustrated, the sales transaction records must be sequenced by sales representative, department, and store. A **utility program** is used to sort the records stored in the sales transaction file. Utility programs are either purchased or developed in-house and are used to perform tasks such as sorting records, copying files, or listing records.

The documentation for the sales analysis report will indicate the file to be used as input for the sort program. Parameters are used to tell the computer the number of fields to be sorted, where each field within the record is located, the length of each field, and the type of data stored in the field. In this example, the sales representative is the minor field, the department the intermediate field, and the store the major field. The names (minor, intermediate, and major) indicate that sales representatives work within departments that are within stores.

Program specifications for the sales analysis report

The program specifications should be more detailed concerning how the report is to be printed. If you study Figure 6–6 you will observe the program must provide for the following print options:

1. Two headings are required. The first lists the name of the store, the date, and the page number. Since there could be several pages for each store, the pages are numbered separately for each store. A blank space is left between the first and second headings.

2. Each representative's sales are listed. When the sales representative's number changes, the total for the representative is printed and added to the total being accumulated for the department. Also observe that information such as the name of the sales representative, the representative's number, the department number, and the store number is only printed once. Printing the identifying information only once is often referred to as group printing.

3. When the department number changes, the sales representative's total is printed and added to the department total *before* the department total is printed and added to the store total.

CHART   PROG. ID _____ c6-2 _____   PAGE _____ 1 _____   ◄— Fold back at dotted line.

ION SPAN, AT 10 CHARACTERS PER INCH, 6 LINES PER VERTICAL INCH)   DATE _____

Sales analysis report

DOCUMENTALIST: _____ Leeson _____

```
 1  SALES REPORT FOR  XXXXXXXXXXXXXXXXXXXXXXXXX  XX-XX-XXXX      PAGE X
 2
 3  STORE      DEPARTMENT              SALES REPRESENTATIVE
 4    X           XX         X   XXXXXXXXXXXXXXXXXXXXXX  XXX,XXX.XX
 5                                                       XXX,XXX.XX
 6                                                       XXX,XXX.XX
 7                                                                   XXX,XXX.XX
 8                           X   XXXXXXXXXXXXXXXXXXXXXX  XXX,XXX.XX
 9                           X   XXXXXXXXXXXXXXXXXXXXXX  XXX,XXX.XX
10                                                                   XXX,XXX.XX
11                               DEPARTMENT TOTAL                    XXX,XXX.XX
12
13                XX         X   XXXXXXXXXXXXXXXXXXXXXX  XXX,XXX.XX
14                               XXXXXXXXXXXXXXXXXXXXXX  XXX,XXX.XX
15                                                                   XXX,XXX.XX
16                           X   XXXXXXXXXXXXXXXXXXXXXX  XXX,XXX.XX
17                               XXXXXXXXXXXXXXXXXXXXXX  XXX,XXX.XX
18                                                                   XXX,XXX.XX
19                               DEPARTMENT TOTAL                    XXX,XXX.XX
20
21                               STORE TOTAL                         XXX,XXX.XX
22
23                               REPORT TOTAL                        XXX,XXX.XX
```

Figure 6–6   *Print layout for the multilevel sales analysis report.*

© SRA 1988, 1983

Figure 6–7 Program specifications for the multilevel sales analysis report.

Sales Analysis Report Specifications

Output

Multilevel report
: The report is to be printed as specified on the report layout form. Totals are to be accumulated for each sales representative, department, and store. A report total for all stores is also to be printed.

Input

Transaction file
: The sales file must be sorted by sales representative within department within store number. The fields used in printing the report are: the representative's name and number, department number, store number, and sales amount.

Store name table
: Since there are only 20 stores, their names are stored in a table and retrieved by using the store number.

System date
: The date subroutine is used to obtain and format the date.

Calculations

Accumulate totals
: As level breaks occur, the totals are rolled, printed, and the total fields reset to zero. Totals must be accumulated for each sales representative, department, and store. In addition, a total for all stores is to be printed.

---

4. When the store number changes, the sales representative's total is printed and added to the department total. The department total is printed and added to the store total before the total line for the store is printed.

5. Headings are to be printed each time the store number changes or when the line counter is greater than 47. In this example, up to 54 lines (including spaces) can be printed on a page. Each time a heading, detail line, or total line is printed, the appropriate number must be added to the line-counter. When a sales representative's total is printed, 1 should be added to the counter. When a department total is printed, 2 is added to the line-counter—1 for the department line and 1 for the blank space which occurs before the next line is printed.

6. The line counter is checked in the print-detail-line module. It could happen that the counter was at 47 when the number of a different sales representative was read. If the department number also changed, both totals would be printed on the same page as the detail lines for the sales representative.

   Figure 6–7 illustrates the specifications that are developed for the multilevel sales analysis report.

Hierarchy chart for the sales analysis report

When you first look at the hierarchy chart for the multilevel sales analysis report it looks extremely complex. However, as you study the chart you will observe that many of the modules are repeated. For example, the print-sales-rep-change module is shown four times. To explain why this occurs and how a multilevel report program must be designed, consider the following test data

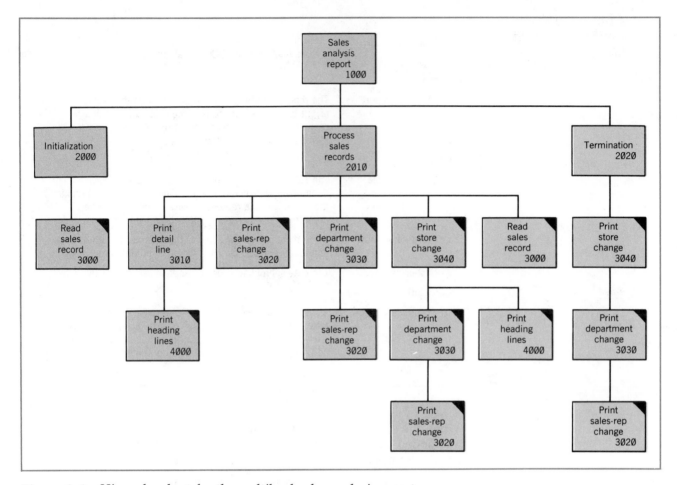

Figure 6–8 *Hierarchy chart for the multilevel sales analysis report.*

which has been sorted by representative number within department number within store number:

RECORD	STORE	DEPT	REPRESENTATIVE	AMOUNT OF THE SALE
1	1	1	1	500.00
2	1	1	1	100.00
3	1	1	2	1000.00
4	1	1	2	500.00
5	1	2	3	600.00
6	1	2	3	300.00
7	1	2	3	400.00
8	2	1	4	1000.00

1. After the first sales record is read, *and before processing occurs*, the numbers for the store, department, and sales rep are stored (or saved). This is done by moving the numbers from the input record to the areas defined as the storage areas. In many languages this is done by using statements such as:

    Save-store = TR-store-number
    Save-dept = TR-department-number
    Save-rep = TR-sales-rep-number

© SRA 1988, 1983

After the commands are executed, the numbers are in both locations within the memory of the computer.

In our example, the save areas and input record number areas all contain ones—for store number, department number, and sales representative number.

2. In the process-sales-records loop the first statement compares the values stored in the save fields with the values read in from the sales-transaction record. The pseudocode for the required IF/THEN/ELSE statement is:

```
IF Save-store NOT = TR-store-number THEN
    PERFORM 3040-print-store-change
ELSE
    IF Save-dept NOT = TR-department-number THEN
        PERFORM 3030-print-department-change
    ELSE
        IF Save-rep NOT = TR-sales-rep-number THEN
            PERFORM print-sales-rep-change
        ELSE
            NULL
END IF
```

If there is no change in any of the values being compared, all conditions tested are false and none of the modules specified is executed.

3. When record 3 is read, save-rep is equal to 1 and TR-sales-representative-number is equal to 2. Therefore, the third test (IF save-rep NOT = TR-sales-rep-number) is true and the print-sales-rep-change module will be executed and the following tasks are performed:

a. The total (600) is added to the department total.

b. The sales-rep total line is printed.

c. One is added to the line counter.

d. The new sales representative's name and number are moved to the print areas so that the name and number of the second representative will be printed. After the first line is printed for a sales representative, spaces replace the sales representative, store, and department numbers as well as the name of the representative. This is done so that the information for a sales representative, department, or store will only be printed once.

e. The total sales for the first sales representative is set to zero.

When control returns to the process-sales-records module, normal processing for record 3 (the first record for a new sales representative) will take place.

4. When record 5 is read, a department break occurs. The hierarchy chart or the flowchart shows that *before* the tasks in the department-change module can be executed, the print-sales-representative-change module must be invoked.

5. When record 8 is read, a store break occurs. As illustrated on the hierarchy chart, the print-department-change module is invoked which in turn invokes the print-sales-representative-change module. After the commands in these three modules (3020-print-sales-representative-change, 3030-print-department-change, and 3040-print-

store-change) are executed, control returns to the process-sales-records module and the 8th record is processed.

6. When the end-of-file condition occurs and control leaves process-sales-records, total lines for the first sales representative, department, and store must be printed. In each of the three modules, the totals are rolled so that the final total is accurate.

The hierarchy chart also presents a strong argument in favor of using a structured, modular approach to designing and implementing programs. Although several of the modules are invoked from two or more locations within the program, each module is coded only once.

Flowchart for the sales analysis program

The flowchart provides an excellent review of many topics that were presented in previous chapters. By studying the initialization module on page 207 you will note that the indicator more-records is again used and will be set to N when the end-of-file condition is detected. The third symbol illustrates the storage areas that are defined to save, or store, the sales representative, department, and store number. This must be done so that the **level breaks** can be determined by comparing the numbers from each new record to those saved from a previous record.

Areas are also defined for the print fields for each of the numbers and the sales representative's name. By referring to the print layout chart on page 202 you will note that the store, department, and sales representative's number are only printed once. Printing the information on each detail line would make the report less attractive and harder to read. To avoid printing this information more than once, spaces are moved into those areas in the print-detail-line module *after the line is printed*. The spaces remain in those fields until a level break occurs. In each of the level-break modules, the appropriate data from the new record which has not been processed is moved in the print fields and the data will be printed one time.

A count-controlled loop is used to load the store names in the table. In the print-heading-lines module, the store number is used as the subscript to retrieve the name from the table. Including the store names in the program and loading them into a table is far less time consuming and expensive than recording the store name in each transaction record.

The process-sales-records module, shown on page 208, is relatively short. Since a WHILE loop is used, the decision-exit test is made at the top of the loop. In the initialization module the first record was read and the numbers stored so that the first record can be treated the same as any other record. In our example, when the first record is processed, all of the tests are false and the sales amount in the first record is added to the total for the representative, the detail line is printed, and the second record is read.

In the print-detail-line module on page 209 note that the print-heading-lines module will be invoked whenever the line-counter is greater than 47. Since either 1 or 2 is added to the line-counter depending on the line printed, a true test might never occur if the statement had been "IF line-counter = 48 ". The line counter could go from 47 to 49. Headings would only be printed initially and again when a level break occurred on a store number change. In the print-heading-lines module the line-counter is set to 3 since all lines printed—including the blank lines left between the headings and after a department total is printed—must be counted.

© SRA 1988, 1983

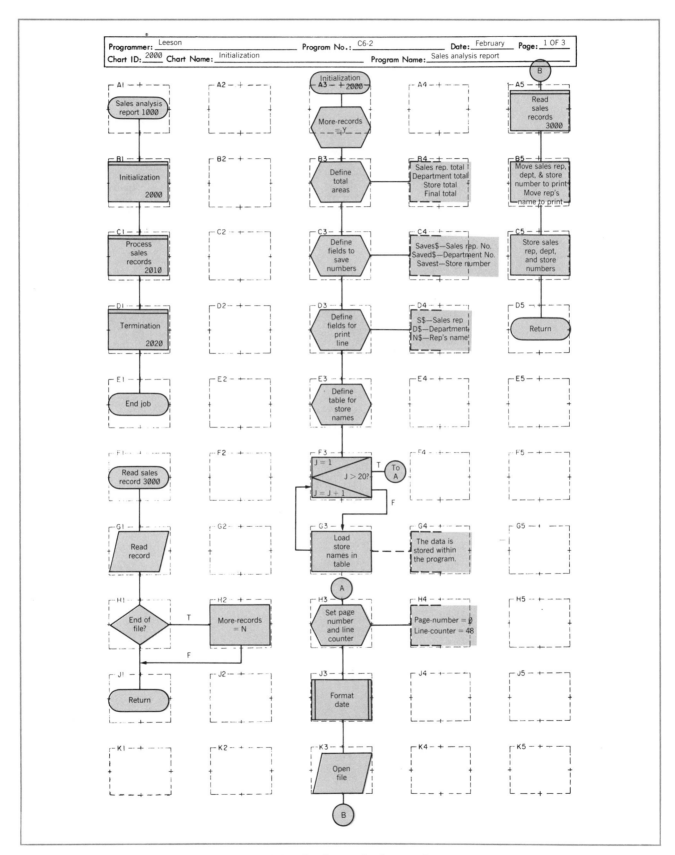

Figure 6–9 Part 1   Flowchart for the multilevel sales analysis report.

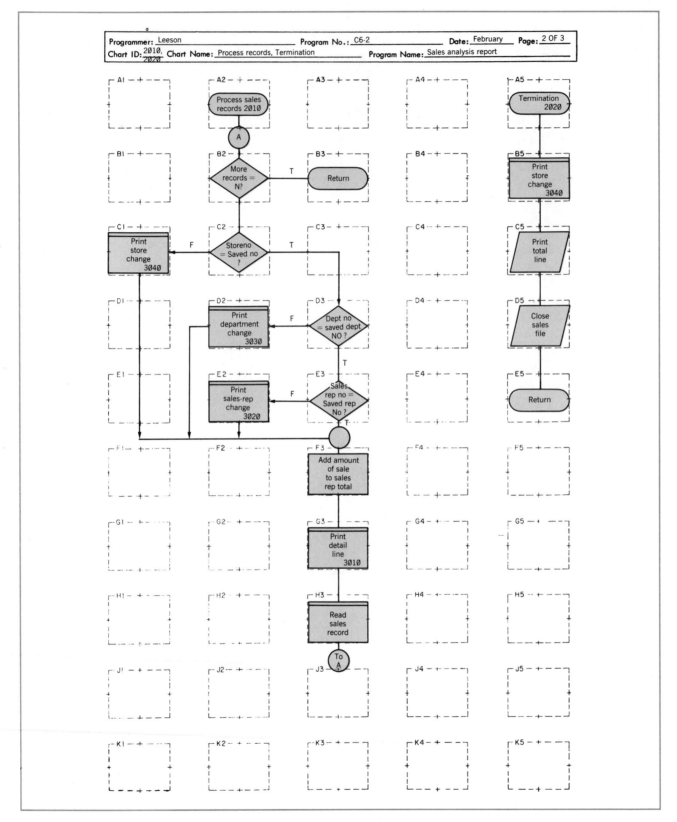

Figure 6–9 Part 2 Flowchart for the multilevel sales analysis report.

© SRA 1988, 1983

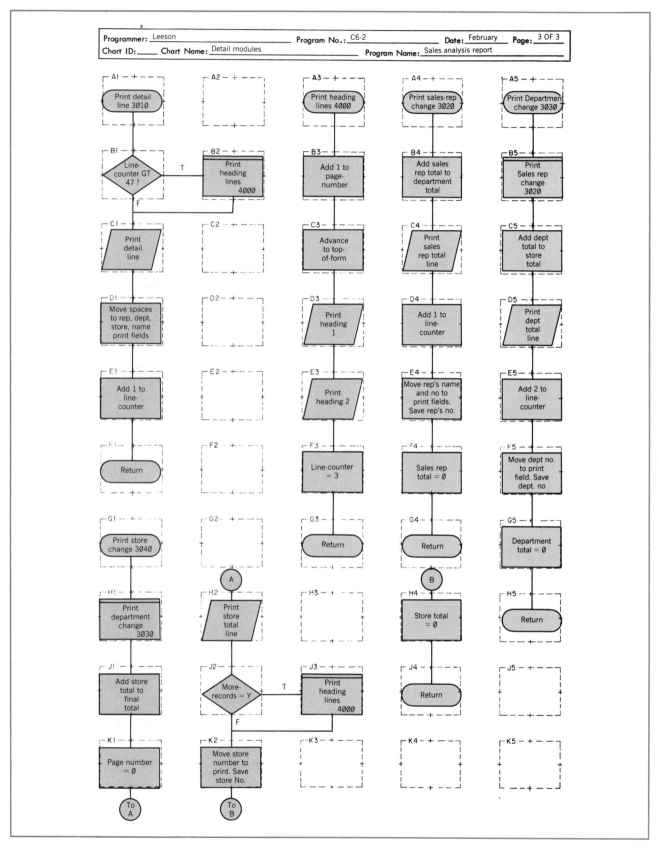

Figure 6–9 Part 3   Flowchart for the multilevel sales analysis report.

Summary of required tasks

The multilevel report could have been a group-printed or a summary report that provided one line of output for each sales representative rather than listing each sales transaction. Also the way the information is printed on the report differs, depending on the standards of the installations and the requirements specified by the individual who requested the report. There are, however, a number of tasks that must be performed within the print program whenever a multilevel report is printed. These tasks are:

1. The fields used in determining when a level break occurs must be saved. The data in the storage field is compared to its counterpart which is part of the input record.
2. The IF/THEN/ELSE statement tests first for a major, second for an intermediate, and finally for a minor level break.
3. When a level break occurs, normal processing of the new record is suspended until after the commands included in the level-break change modules are executed.
4. When a level break occurs, the total accumulated for that level is added to the next highest total, the total line is printed, the total field cleared to zero, and a new number is stored in the save field.

A multilevel report can have more than three levels. A file containing historical data could be sorted by decade, year, month, and day. The day total would be the lowest level and the decade would be the highest. When a change occurred in decade, the day-, month-, and year-change modules would be executed before the decade-change module statements could be executed.

CHECKPOINT QUESTIONS

24. How many different types of print formats are required to print the multilevel sales analysis report?
25. Is the report illustrated in Figure 6–6 an exception report or a detail report?
26. On a multilevel report when will the sales representative total line be printed?
27. Is the statement "When the first record for a new department is read, normal processing is suspended until after the commands in the print-sales-representative-change and print-department-change modules are executed" a valid assessment of what occurs?
28. Why is the comparison made between the save-store-number and the store number read from the input file before comparing the department numbers?
29. When the end-of-file condition is detected, what must occur before the final total can be printed?
30. Why are special print fields used for the sales representative's name and number as well as the department and store numbers?
31. Why are the store names retrieved from a table rather than being read from the records stored in the sales transaction file?

© SRA 1988, 1983

32. Why is the statement IF LINE-COUNTER > 47 used rather than the statement IF LINE-COUNTER = 48?

33. In spite of the variations in ways that multilevel reports are printed, certain tasks must be executed in order to obtain a report like the one illustrated in Figure 6–6. List them.

EXTERNAL REPORTS

Although the sales analysis and inventory reports are internal reports printed on stock paper, sales invoices are external reports. The invoice forms are preprinted with the organization's name, address, phone number, and logo. Field titles, column headings, other information, and both horizontal and vertical

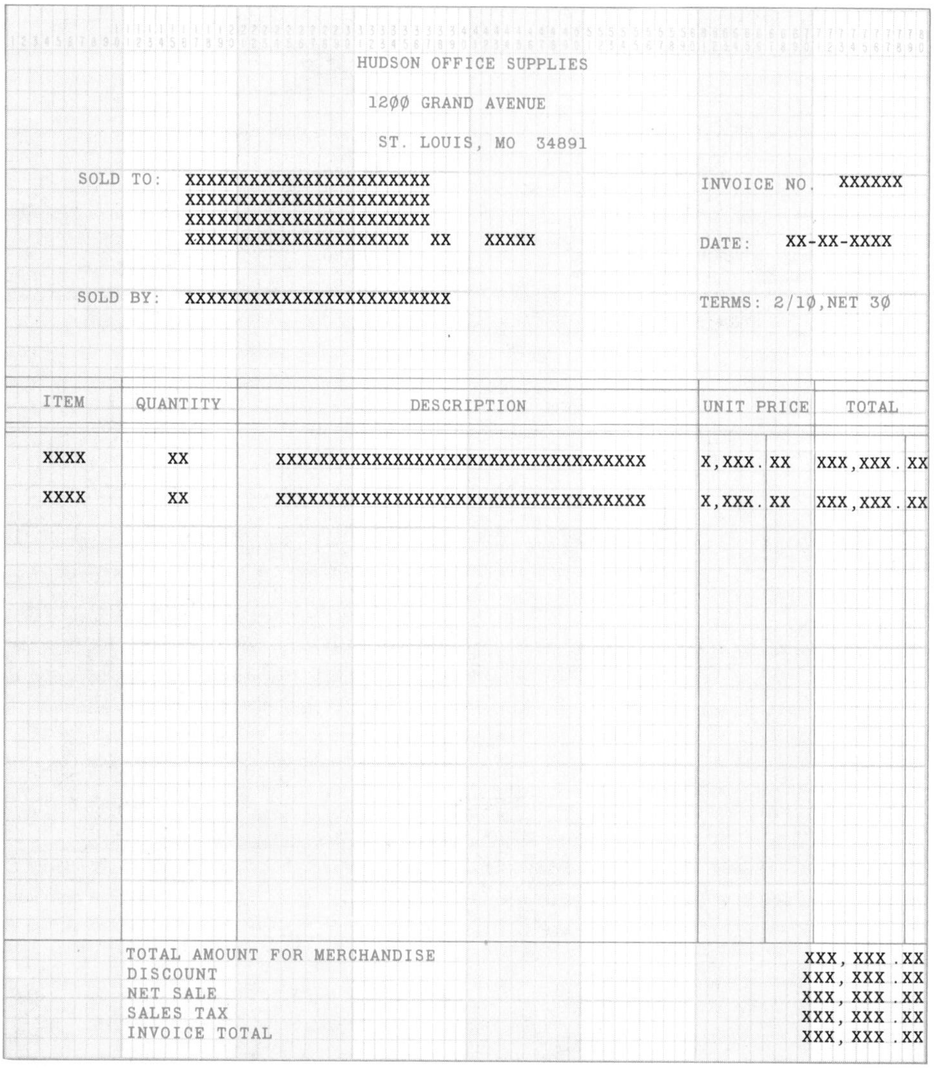

Figure 6–10   Preprinted sales invoice form.

```
                    HUDSON OFFICE SUPPLIES

                     1200 GRAND AVENUE

                    ST. LOUIS, MO   34891

    SOLD TO:  XXXXXXXXXXXXXXXXXXXXXXXX        INVOICE NO.  XXXXXX
              XXXXXXXXXXXXXXXXXXXXXXXX
              XXXXXXXXXXXXXXXXXXXXXXXX
              XXXXXXXXXXXXXXXXXXXXX XX   XXXXX  DATE:   XX-XX-XXXX

    SOLD BY:  XXXXXXXXXXXXXXXXXXXXXXXXXXX      TERMS: 2/10,NET 30


  ITEM    QUANTITY           DESCRIPTION          UNIT PRICE    TOTAL

  XXXX      XX     XXXXXXXXXXXXXXXXXXXXXXXXXXXXXXXX  X,XXX.XX   XXX,XXX.XX

  XXXX      XX     XXXXXXXXXXXXXXXXXXXXXXXXXXXXXXXX  X,XXX.XX   XXX,XXX.XX







          TOTAL AMOUNT FOR MERCHANDISE                        XXX,XXX.XX
          DISCOUNT                                            XXX,XXX.XX
          NET SALE                                            XXX,XXX.XX
          SALES TAX                                           XXX,XXX.XX
          INVOICE TOTAL                                       XXX,XXX.XX
```

Report Specifications

Field Name	Source	Special Requirements
MF-customer-name	Customer master file	
MF-customer-address-1	Customer master file	
MF-customer-address-2	Customer master file	
MF-city	Customer master file	
MF-state	Customer master file	
MF-ZIP-code	Customer master file	
SYSTEM-date	Formatted date from system	
TABLE-rep-name	Name retrieved from table	Subscript is SNUMBER from Customer master
TR-sales-invoice-number	Sales transaction file	
TR-item-number	Sales transaction file	
TR-quantity-sold	Sales transaction file	
MF-description	Inventory master file	
MF-product-price	Inventory master file	
Item-total	Calculated	Price × quantity.
Invoice-total	Calculated	Add item totals.
Invoice-discount	Calculated	Rate used is stored in the Customer master file.
Invoice-net-sales	Calculated	
Invoice-sales-tax	Calculated	Rate used is stored in the Customer master file.
Invoice-net-amount	Calculated	

Figure 6–11   Data requirements for the sales invoice program.

rules are also preprinted on the form. In writing the source code the programmer must control both the vertical movement of the form in the printer so that the information is printed on the right lines and the horizontal positioning of the data. In writing the source code, the print layout form will be used to determine where the data must be printed.

For each sales invoice, the form is first positioned at the location where the customer's name and the invoice number are to be printed. The next three lines are single spaced and then two blank lines are printed before the SOLD BY line. Seven blank lines occur before the first detail line is printed. A variable number of detail lines are printed; then skipping occurs, so the five total lines are printed at the bottom of the form.

When the program is in its test phase, a transparency of the sales invoice can be placed over the sales invoices that are printed on stock paper. The programmer can easily see if the information is printed in the right locations. If a transparency is used, testing can be done using stock paper rather than putting the sales invoices in the printer each time a test run occurs.

© SRA 1988, 1983

Since the sales invoice program described is a batch job, the invoices are printed on the computer's high-speed printer. The documentation for the program must include directions for the operator regarding how the forms are to be positioned in the printer and how the printer is to be adjusted.

Report specifications for the sales invoice program

The information printed on Figure 6–10 will be preprinted on the form by the company from whom the forms are obtained. The Xs indicate where the variable data is to be printed. Before the sales invoice is designed, a report specification form similar to the one illustrated in Figure 6–11 may be completed. Listed on the form is the required data, the source of each field of data, and any special requirements or instructions. Frequently the form also shows the length of each field and the type of data stored within the field. Before a print layout form can be completed, the analyst must know the size of each field and the maximum number of digits that will be required for each total field.

Program specifications

Atlhough the format is somewhat different than has been used previously, the data-requirement form illustrated in Figure 6–11 and the sales invoice shown in Figure 6–10 provide most of the information needed to design and write the program. The sales transaction records contain the following fields: invoice number, customer number, item number, and quantity purchased. The records are in sequence by invoice number; one or more records may be included for each invoice number. The customer number and item number fields will be used to retrieve randomly the required master file records from the customer and inventory master files.

The layout form for the sales invoice shows that up to thirteen detail lines can be printed on each form. The analyst assigned to the project has determined that in the past ten years from one to five items have been listed on invoices. Therefore, providing for invoices that require two pages will not be necessary.

When data is needed and information is printed

The programmer assigned the task of developing the logic for the program must determine *when* the information must be available and *when* each line will be printed. When analyzing how the data is to be printed on the sales invoices, it might be wise to still think in terms of heading, detail, and total lines.

Headings	Printed initially and *after* the totals for the previous invoice are printed. The customer's master file must be available. The five lines above the first double line are considered as headings.
Detail	One line is printed for *each* different item purchased. For each different item, the corresponding inventory master file record must be available.
Total	Printed *after* the first record for a new invoice is read but *before* the new headings are printed.

Control will exit from the process-sales-records module when the end-of-file condition is detected for the sales transaction file. The required inventory and customer master file records are randomly retrieved by using the item number and the customer number. In the next chapter, random retrieval of records will be covered in more detail. In studying the hierarchy chart for the sales invoice program, do not be concerned with the details concerning how the inventory and customer master file records are retrieved.

The hierarchy chart shown in Figure 6–12 has a number of modules duplicated. The modules must be thought of as functional modules. Tasks closely related to the major function will be included in the module. For this reason, some of the print modules might contain one or two calculations. This is a realistic approach to developing modular programs that are easy to maintain. However, when a number of calculations are required to complete the processing for an invoice, a separate module should be developed for required calculations.

To determine what tasks should be performed in each module, you should:

1. Study the information provided including the print layout form and the report specifications.

2. Make a detailed list of the tasks that must be accomplished and when each task must be performed. Consider carefully how the computer will know when a "break" in invoice numbers occurs.

3. Using the hierarchy chart provided, make a list of the tasks that will be performed within each module.

The detailed logic plan can then be developed and tested by using records that would produce three or four invoices with one to five items. If you are assigned Problem 6–1, you will be asked to develop the logic for all of the modules except the read-sales-records, read-customer-records, and read-inventory-records modules.

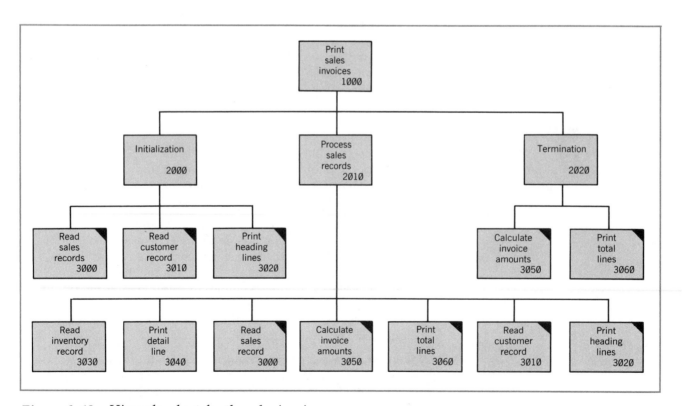

Figure 6–12   *Hierarchy chart for the sales invoice program.*

© SRA 1988, 1983

When you develop the logic for the program, assume that a standard list tape will be used. If the operator positions the forms in the printer correctly, before the headings are printed, the form will skip to the position identified as top-of-form (TOF) or top-of-page. The rest of the spacing of the form is controlled by the program that prints the invoices. After the sales representative's name is printed, seven lines are left blank and then the first detail line is printed. One technique that can be used is to create a loop:

```
DO (J = 1 TO 7)
    PRINT ' '
END DO
```

From the location where the first detail line is printed, there are 25 print lines to where the first total is to be printed. To complicate the problem, an invoice can have one or several detail lines. The following technique can be used to position the form to the location where the total lines will be printed.

- Print-detail module

```
PRINT detail line
lines = lines + 2        (The detail lines are double spaced.)
```

- Print-totals module

```
DO (line-counter = lines TO 25)
    PRINT ' '
END DO
```

In a count-controlled loop, the variable line field is used to initialize the line counter rather than a constant. If the value stored in lines is 6 (3 detail lines were printed), 20 spaces will be left before the totals are printed.

CHECKPOINT QUESTIONS

34. When special forms are used rather than stock paper, what factors in regard to writing source code become more critical?

35. Assume that a new payroll system is being designed and the programmer wishes to test the paycheck program. How can the placement of the information on the check be tested when the information is printed on stock paper rather than the checks?

35. What information is provided on the report specification form?

36. When will the customer's name and address be printed on the top of the sales invoice?

37. Why must the invoice number be saved each time a record with a new invoice number is read?

38. When the invoice number is different from the one read from the previous record, what modules will be invoked and what tasks must be performed?

39. In developing the logic for the process-sales-records module, why will there by an outer loop controlled by more-records and also an inner conditional loop that is controlled by a statement such as WHILE (SAVE-sales-invoice-number = TR-sales-invoice-number)?

**EXTRACTION
PROGRAMS**

Of the fields stored within a record, often only a small portion are used in the report-producing program. Assume that the payroll department has requested a report that provides the following information:

Name of Field	Length
MF-Credit-union-number	4
MF-employee-name	30
MF-social-security-number	9
MF-current-deduction-amount	8
MF-YDT-credit-union-contribution	8

The detail lines are to be printed in credit-union number sequence. The payroll master file records are in employee-number sequence.

Figure 6–13 Sort/write report and extract/sort/write report concepts.

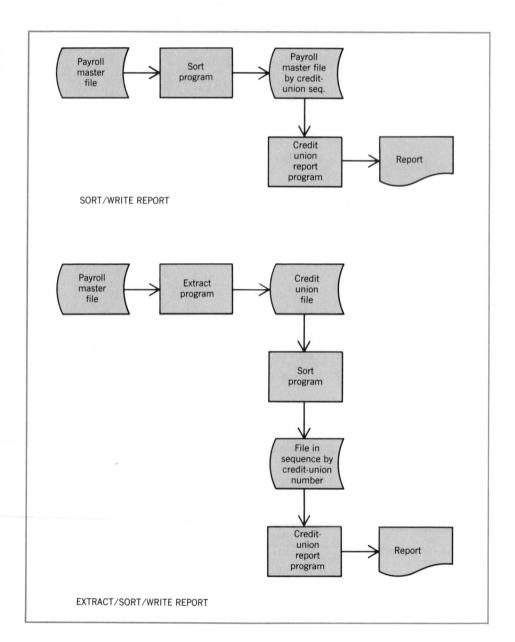

© SRA 1988, 1983

Adding the numbers listed under the field length shows that only 59 bytes of data are used to print each detail line. All the required information is available in the records stored in the payroll master file. The records stored within the payroll master file are 600 bytes long and there are 9,500 records in the file. Only 10 percent of the employees are members of the credit union. If the employee is not a member of the credit union, zeroes are stored in the credit-union field.

The analyst or programmer must make a decision. Should the entire master file be sorted on the credit-union number or should the required data be extracted, stored in a file with fewer and smaller records, and then sorted? The *system flowchart* in Figure 6–13 illustrates both concepts. A **systems flowchart** illustrates the flow of data, the input, and the output produced. The logic of the program specified in the processing block representing the computer is not explained. Systems flowcharts are frequently used to graphically illustrate the input needed and the output generated by executing the program.

Using an extract/sort/write program

Although the second concept illustrated, Extract/Sort/Write report, requires one additional step, it is far more efficient than using the Sort/Write report method. The second method is more efficient because far fewer, and shorter, records will need to be sorted than when all of the master file records are sorted. However, if a language such as COBOL is used, one program can be developed to do all three steps. The programmer:

1. Specifies the conditions under which the data stored in the master file records is to be extracted and specifies the fields that will be transferred into the output records.
2. Provides the parameters for sorting the records stored in the new file.
3. Develops the logic for the report-producing phase of the program.

Although the language used may support data extraction and internal sort statements, the programmer for a number of reasons may want or need to develop his or her own extraction program.

Developing separate extract and report programs

An extraction program tests each record to see if the conditions specified are true. When they are true, the required fields are transferred into an output record and recorded on a medium such as disk. The logic for the program which formats the credit union records is as follows:

```
*Process-master-file-records module
DO WHILE (more-records = Y)
    IF MF-credit-union-deduction > 0 THEN
        PERFORM write-credit-union-record
    ELSE
        NULL
    END IF
    PERFORM read-master-record
END DO
```

In the program which reads the records sequenced by credit-union number, the following logic is needed:

```
*Process-credit-union-records
DO WHILE (more-records = Y)
   PERFORM write-detail-line
   any required mathematical statements
   PERFORM read-credit-union-record
END DO
```

Since a detail line is printed for each record, the report is considered a full report, or listing program, rather than an exception report.

OTHER TYPES OF REPORTS

An organization may have hundreds of programs to produce reports. These may be printed either on a scheduled basis or on demand, either for external or for internal use. Some of the techniques used to print exception reports, multilevel reports, and external reports using special forms have been illustrated.

Error reports

Frequently error reports are printed. When data is entered into an online, transaction-processing system, input errors must be corrected immediately. However, if a transaction file is being created to be used as input for a batch-processing application, it is more efficient to accumulate all the error messages in a file. After all the data is entered, the error messages are printed. Each error is analyzed and the proper action is taken to correct the error. Often in order to correct the error, sales representatives or department heads may need to be contacted. Or it may be necessary to make a search of other online files or to use printed reports. In Chapter 9 some of the techniques used to accumulate errors and print error reports will be illustrated.

Condensed reports

Situations also arise where data stored in a file is used to create both a full report and a summarized version. Assume that each supervisor receives a detailed payroll distribution report for his or her department. The payroll distribution report shows how the costs associated with payroll are charged to each account and to the department. While supervisors need detailed reports, the controller and department managers are only interested in department totals. The records are sorted by the account number to be charged within each department.

Each time the department number changes, a total is printed for the first department and headings are printed on a new page for the second department. While the full report is being printed, the total for each department is written into an online file. After the first report is printed, the output file is closed, reopened as an input file, and used to print a condensed report. If a large file is used, it saves computer time to create a second file containing the condensed information. When the condensed report is printed, it is not necessary to read all the records in the larger file. To apply the principle "keep it simple," a programmer would design and implement two separate programs that will be executed as a single job. The first program prints the full report

© SRA 1988, 1983

and creates a file with the information needed to produce a condensed report. The second program prints the condensed report.

If a large computer system is being used that supports SPOOLing, two or more different reports can be generated and printed within a single program. Under SPOOLing, the data to be printed is stored in a file and then printed according to a predetermined priority. However, many minicomputer and microcomputer systems do not support the utilization of two or more print files within a single program.

CHECKPOINT QUESTIONS

40. How does a system flowchart differ from the structured flowcharts illustrated throughout the text?

41. Under what circumstances is it more efficient to extract the required data from a master file, sort the data, and then utilize the sorted data in a report-producing program rather than sorting the records in the master file?

42. In the program used to extract the necessary records from the master file, what criteria were used in determining if a record was to be written in the credit-union-report file?

43. How would you classify the report printed by using the credit-union file?

44. Give an example of an instance when data stored in the student master file might be extracted, sorted, and then used to print a report.

45. In a transaction-processing system, why are input errors usually corrected as they occur rather than printing an error report after all the data is entered?

46. If a transaction file is being created that will be used in a batch-processing application, why is it more efficient to store the error messages in a file, print a report, and then solve all of the problems at one time?

47. If both a full and a condensed report are required, what technique can be used to avoid reading all of the records in a large file twice?

48. If a full report is available, why is it necessary to print a condensed report?

SUMMARY

• Application programs are often classified as transaction processing, file maintenance, information retrieval and display, or as report programs.

• When a request for information is received, the analyst must determine when it is needed and how it will be used. The basic questions is: "Should a report be printed or should immediate access to the information be available by using an information retrieval and display program?"

• In order to control the "paper explosion," reports are printed on demand rather than on a scheduled basis and information previously printed as part of a report is displayed on a VDT.

• The type of report to be printed and its contents must be based on the purpose of the report and the needs of the individuals who will be using the report.

- Forms design requires the cooperative effort of an analyst working along with the individual who requested, and will utilize, the report. Decisions must be made regarding the number of lines per inch, the number of horizontal characters per inch, and the spacing of the information on the report. The characteristics of the printer and programming language to be used must be considered when the report is designed.

- External reports are often printed on preprinted forms and a higher quality of paper may be used than when internal reports are printed. An image of the organization may be created based on the quality of the report.

- Internal reports are printed on stock paper and both the headings and the information are printed by either a centrally located line printer or a smaller printer which may be remotely located from the computer center.

- When a full report or listing is printed, one line is printed for each record that is read from an online file or keyed in by an operator.

- Exception reports list only information that requires immediate attention. For example, only items that must be reordered or customers who have not used their accounts in over two years are listed.

- In order to print a multilevel report, the records containing the required data are sequenced by using a utility sort program. Multilevel reports can list all records or can summarize the data and print only totals.

- Some languages, such as COBOL, support data extraction and internal sorts. This makes it possible to write one program that extracts the data, sorts the data in the new file, and then prints the desired report.

- When records must be sequenced before being used as input for a report program, the analyst must determine what percentage of the records will be used. If only a small percentage of the records contain data that will be used in printing the report, the records should be extracted, sorted, and then used as input for the program that prints the report.

- While printing a full report, information can be summarized, written into a file, and then used to create a summarized report.

- When data to be used in a batch application is recorded in a transaction file, error messages may be accumulated in a file and then used to write an error report.

DISCUSSION QUESTIONS

1. What are the four types of application programs frequently designed and developed in-house?

2. Although the increased use of computers has caused more information to be printed, what steps are being taken to reduce the amount of printed output?

3. At one time all reports printed on centrally located line printers were printed in black uppercase letters, 10 characters per inch and 6 lines per vertical inch. Is this true today? Depending on the printer and programming language being used, what options are available?

4. In designing a report, why is it necessary to consider the characteristics of the printer and the programming language?

© SRA 1988, 1983

5. The CIS manager has made the statement, "In order to conserve paper, all reports will be single spaced." Tell why you would agree or disagree with the manager's statement.

6. What are the characteristics of a typical report program?

7. Give three or four examples of when an exception report rather than a full report should be printed.

8. Although there are different types of multilevel reports that can be printed, what factors must be provided for, or considered, when a multilevel report such as the one illustrated in Figure 6–6 page 202 is to be printed. Give two or three other examples of when a multilevel report would be printed.

9. The report specification form for the sales invoice program listed the required data and its source. How, or where, does the information printed on reports originate? What is probably the most frequently used source?

10. If functional modules are developed and used to design structured programs, how can a mathematical statement such as LINECOUNTER = LINECOUNTER + 2 be justified in a print module? Would you recommend that a separate module be created for the mathematical statement?

11. The manager of the sales department has requested that every day a full report showing the credit status of all customers be printed. To justify his request he indicates that at least four or five times a day calls are received from sales representatives requesting information regarding the credit status of a customer. How would you respond to his request? What might be a better solution to the problem? Justify your answer.

12. The CIS manager has asked you to do an analysis of all reports printed. Your response must include the information printed on each report; when each report is printed (scheduled or on demand); and who receives the report. You discover that there are approximately 1,000 different report programs and that many contain duplicate information. Many of the full reports are listings that are from 400–500 pages in length. Thirty-five different reports are submitted to either the federal or state government. What recommendations might be made? Who should be consulted before the report of your findings and recommendations is submitted?

KEY WORDS

buffer	letter-quality printer
carriage control tape	level break
carriage control tape channel	line printer
continuous form paper	on demand report
data exception	page footings
edit mask	page printer
exception report	standard list tape
file maintenance	stock paper
forms overflow position	system flowchart
function	transaction processing
information retrieval	utility program

PROJECTS

EXERCISE 6–1

When the payroll distribution report is printed, the records in the file are sorted by account number within department. The file contains approximately 5,000 records. A multilevel report is printed that lists the total for each account number within the department and the department total.

At the end of the report, a total is printed that must agree with the gross paid for the month for all employees. In addition, 16.7 percent of the total for each account number is also charged to the account number for the federal and state payroll taxes paid by the employer. The final total for the fringe benefits paid must also equal the sum of all fringe benefits paid to or for employees during the month.

The payroll transaction records contain a great deal of information that is used to print several different reports. The data contained in the payroll records needed for this report includes the following fields:

TR-account-number	Number to which the expense will be charged.
TR-department-number	Department to which the expense will be charged.
TR-gross-earnings	Gross earnings of employee.
TR-fringe-benefits	Total fringe benefits paid to employee.

The detail line on the report contains the following information:

Account number	A 12 position numeric field
Gross pay	XXX,XXX.XX The field contains 8 digits—6 to the left of the assumed decimal and 2 to the right.
Fringe benefits paid	XXX,XXX.XX
State and Federal taxes	XXX,XXX.XX
Total charged to account	XXX,XXX.XX

The total charged to the account is computed by adding gross pay, fringe benefits, and the state and federal taxes. There may be one or more records for each account.

The charges for each department are listed on a separate page and the heading must contain both the department number and name. Within our organization we have 50 departments and 100 different accounts. The totals for each department are printed at the bottom of its report.

Directions

1. Prepare a print layout form that illustrates the headings, detail line, and total line. Assume that 8½″ × 11″ paper will be used. Twenty-five detail lines are printed on a page. Each department's report starts with page 1.
2. Prepare a hierarchy chart.

EXERCISE 6–2

Using the hierarchy chart prepared in Exercise 6–1, develop a detailed logic plan for the program needed to produce the payroll distribution report. You need not develop the logic for the read-payroll-records module.

EXERCISE 6–3

The controller has asked that a summary report be printed listing the department number, name of the department, gross pay, fringe benefits, payroll taxes, and total charge for each department.

Directions

1. Modify the hierarchy chart you did for Exercise 6–1 to include a write-condensed-file module. A record will be written for each department that contains the data required to print the report.

© SRA 1988, 1983

2. Develop a print layout form, a hierarchy chart, and a detailed logic plan for the program that will print the report the controller has requested.

   The records in the file will be read sequentially and the job will be terminated when the end-of-file condition is detected.

   It is the policy of the company that all reports have headings that include a date and page number. Whenever possible totals are to be printed that can be used to check the validity of the report.

3. What would the totals printed for this report equal?

PROBLEM 6–1

Review the material provided in the section covering external reports and develop a detailed logic plan for the print sales invoice program.

Directions

1. Follow the steps listed in the text and list all the tasks that must be performed.

2. Using the modules identified in the text, list the tasks under the appropriate module. For example:

   3000-Read-sales-records

   1. Read a record from the sales transaction file.

   2. IF end-of-file, move N to more-records.

   Do not be concerned with the tasks associated with reading the inventory master file records.

3. After you have listed the tasks under each module, check to see that they are in the proper sequence. For example, net sales must be calculated after the customer's discount is determined.

4. Complete the detailed logic plan for all modules except read-sales-records, read-customer-record, and read-inventory-record.

INTERACTIVE EXERCISE 6–1

A test file with the data needed to execute the inventory exception program is provided and identified by the name INVT.DAT. The records in the test file only contain the fields used as input and do not contain the information usually available in inventory master file records.

Since the test file contains a limited number of records, the line counter is initially set to 5. In the print-detail module the IF statement is also changed to read "IF line-counter = 5 THEN . . .". The change was made so that the heading routine could be tested. Also the percentage of records that are listed on the report is much greater than would normally occur.

Directions

1. Boot the system, load **BASIC,** and then load **Menu.** Select Menu **3,** Option **14.**

   The test data for the inventory exception report will be listed on the printer. Listed for each inventory item is the item number, description, reorder point, quantity to reorder, and the quantity on hand.

2. Return to the main menu. Select Menu **3,** Option **15.**

   Before selecting Option 15 position the paper in the printer so that there is a one-inch top margin. Depending on the printer you are using, after you position the paper you may need to press keys such as **TOF** (top of form) and **LF** (line feed).

3. After the program is executed, do not return to menu until you have answered the following questions.

a. Examine the flowchart provided in Figure 6–4 and the listing of the test data. Was the test data sufficient to test all conditions that could occur? Explain your answer.

_____

_____

_____

_____

_____

b. Although the percentage of items below the reorder point that printed is very high, how would you check the validity of the total lines?

_____

_____

4. **LIST 520–570** and statement **190**. Note that a LPRINT USING statement is used to format the data line and to edit the numeric data. After the print format is established, the variables to be listed are printed.

   a. Change statement 530 to **IF LINECOUNTER = 25 THEN** . . .

   b. Enter **RUN** and execute the program.
   Why didn't the headings print?

   _____

   _____

5. **LIST 610–680.** The LPRINT CHR$(12) causes a form feed to occur and makes it possible to print the heading at the top of a new page.

   a. Refer back to the flowchart for the print-heading-lines module on page 198 and determine if the source code follows the detailed logic plan.

   What would occur if statement 630 were moved down and renumbered 675?

   _____

   What other change would need to be made if statement 630 is renumbered and executed after the headings are printed?

   _____

   _____

   _____

6. Return to main menu.

INTERACTIVE EXERCISE 6–2

Exercise 6–2 provides the software for the multilevel sales analysis report. A small file, SDATA.BAK, is used to test the program. The records in the sequential file only contain the five fields of data needed to test the program.

Because of some of the limitations of the BASIC subset used to create the program for this exercise, the source code for the print-detail-line module differs slightly from the flowchart. If the program were an operational program used on a scheduled basis, the print-detail-line module would be modified to agree with the program.

© SRA 1988, 1983

Directions

1. Select Menu **3**, Option **16**.
   The records stored in the test file will be listed.

2. Return to the main menu.

3. Position the paper in your printer so that the sales report will have a one-inch top margin.

4. Select Menu **3**, Option **17**. The multilevel sales analysis report will be printed. Do not return to menu.

5. Compare the print layout form on page 202 with the report printed on your printer. Also compare the printed report with the listing of the test file data printed when Option 16 was selected.

   a. How would you prove the validity of the output?

   _____

   _____

   _____

   b. Because of the limited amount of data for each store, what conditions are not tested?

   _____

   _____

6. **LIST 820** and change the statement to read:
   820   IF LINECOUNTER > 16 THEN
               GOSUB 950

   Enter **RUN** and execute the revised version of the program.

   What additional features of the program were tested?

   _____

   _____

   _____

7. a. Do not return to the menu. You will execute a second version of the sales analysis program which is not included in the menu.

      LOAD C6-2A

   b. **Enter CLS**   CLEAR SCREEN AND THEN LIST THE STATEMENTS.

      LIST 270–300   THESE STATEMENTS IDENTIFY THE NAME OF THE FIELDS USED TO STORE THE NUMBERS IDENTIFIED.

      LIST 600   INPUT # 2 READS THE RECORD AND IDENTIFIES THE FIELDS CONTAINED WITHIN THE RECORD.

      Either copy the information down or use your **PrtSc** and print the statements.

   c. Enter **RUN** to execute the second version of the sales analysis program.

   d. Compare the results with those obtained when Option 17 was selected.

   e. **LIST 660–760.**

      On a separate sheet draw a flowchart based on the code listed and compare it with the one provided for the process sales records module on page 208.

   f. Walkthrough the code listed, or your flowchart, using the test data listed by running Option 16 which is the program which displays the test data for the sales analysis report.

      Determine *exactly* what occurred, what information on the second report is invalid, and why the output is invalid. Record your findings on the bottom of your flowchart.

8. **LOAD C6–2B.** This is another version of the sales analysis report program which is not included in the menu.

a. **LIST 1030–1100.**

   Compare the source code with the flowchart for the print sales rep change module which is listed on page 209.

b. Compare the output produced by running Option 16, the first version of the sales analysis report program, with the output obtained by running C6–2B. What caused the report printed by running C6–2B to be invalid?

   _____

   _____

   _____

c. When should the error in the source code have been detected?

   _____

d. Enter **SYSTEM** to exit to DOS.

© SRA 1988, 1983

SELF-EVALUATION TEST 6

Name _____

Section Number _____

I. Record the term being defined or the one needed to complete the sentence in the space provided.

_____ 1. A report listing only the items that are below the reorder point.

_____ 2. When commas or dollar signs are to be added to a numeric field, an _____ must be constructed that might be similar to $$##,###.##.

_____ 3. Some printers have _____ that are used to help control the vertical movement of the forms in the printer.

_____ 4. A temporary storage area used to store data before it is transferred to the printer is called a _____.

_____ 5. When internal reports are printed, stock paper is used. The programmer must write the source code to print the _____, detail lines, and total lines.

_____ 6. When _____ paper is used, pin-feed holes are located on each side of the form. The holes are used in positioning the forms in the printer.

_____ 7. A _____ shows input, processing, and output. However, only the name of the program or function is shown in the processing block and the logic of the program needed to process the input is not explained.

_____ 8. A sort program is an example of a _____ program.

_____ 9. When _____, such as the one that formats the system's date, are used a detailed logic plan is not provided for the module.

_____ 10. If the inventory manager and other members of the department need to gain immediate access to information stored within the inventory master file, a _____ program should be designed and implemented rather than a report program.

II. Multiple choice. From the description provided, indicate which type of report is being produced. Record the *best* answer in the space provided.

a. scheduled   e. multilevel
b. on demand   f. internal
c. listing   g. external
d. exception

_____ 1. Daily, monthly, and yearly totals are printed.

_____ 2. A report is printed that includes all of the inventory items in stock.

_____ 3. A payroll register is printed on stock paper and used as a reference by the controller and members of the payroll department.

_____ 4. A quarterly report is submitted to the federal government which shows the amount deducted from each employee for social security.

_____ 5. The payroll register is printed at 10:00 a.m. every Wednesday.

_____ 6. All accounts with expenditures that equal or exceed 85 percent of their budgeted amount are listed.

_____ 7. Financial statements are printed for the stockholders.

_____ 8. On an average of three or four times a month a listing of all overdue books is printed for the librarian. Whenever her staff has time to send out notices, the list is printed.

_____ 9. When _____ reports are printed, preprinted forms are often used rather than stock paper.

_____ 10. Several times during the year the sales manager would like a comparative analysis report printed showing how the current month sales compared to the same month last year.

III. Multiple choice. Record the letter of the best answer in the space provided.

_____ 1. Printers that print anywhere from 10,000–30,000 lines per minute are called
   a. line printers
   b. page printers
   c. letter-quality printers
   d. laser printers

_____ 2. When designing a printed report
   a. the analyst determines what information is needed.
   b. the user who requested the report determines what information is needed and how the report should be formatted.
   c. the analyst works with the user in determining what information is needed, when it is needed, and the format in which it will be displayed or printed.
   d. the analyst designs the report and develops the detailed logic plan before consulting with the user.

_____ 3. When a field such as the product description is read from a master file record,
   a. the programmer must use a MOVE statement to transfer the data into the print line.
   b. the programmer never has to move the description from the input area to the output area.
   c. whether or not the programmer must use a MOVE statement to transfer the data into the print line is language-dependent.
   d. and moved into the print line the information is no longer in the input field.

_____ 4. When a subroutine is called into an application program, the programmer should
   a. read the documentation in order to determine the name of the subroutine, what options are available, and what parameters are required.
   b. develop a detailed logic plan for the subroutine and include it with those developed for the other modules.
   c. refer to it by a unique name that is meaningful.
   d. write the required source code to implement the functions executed by the subroutine.

_____ 5. When a line counter is used, it is
   a. set to zero in the initialization module.
   b. reset to zero each time a detail line is printed.
   c. incremented whenever headings are printed.
   d. set to the maximum number of lines to be printed on a page in the initialization module.

_____ 6. In order to print a multilevel report by account number within department,
   a. the records must be sorted on account number within department.
   b. each time a new account number is read, the number must be stored and compared with the one from the next input record.
   c. whenever a department change occurs, the statements in the account-change module will be executed and the department line will be printed.
   d. the statements in a, b, and c are all true.

_____ 7. When a level break occurs on the minor field, the
   a. total accumulated for the level is added to the next highest total.
   b. total line is printed.
   c. total field is reset to zero.
   d. new number for the minor field is saved.
   e. tasks identified in items a through d are executed.

_____ 8. External reports
   a. are usually printed on stock paper.
   b. include items such as paychecks, sales invoices, and federal report.
   c. contain less information than internal reports.
   d. today are usually printed rather than being recorded on an electronic medium such as tape.

© SRA 1988, 1983

_____ 9. Extract/sort/write programs should be used when
   a. the majority of the data stored in the original file will be used in writing the report.
   b. a large percentage of the records stored within the master file will be needed as input for the report program.
   c. few of the records stored within the master file will be needed as input for the report program.
   d. a limited amount of the data stored in the master file will be needed and only a small percentage of the records will be listed on the report.

_____ 10. Most report programs
   a. use information stored in online files.
   b. require a great many calculations and complex decisions.
   c. print external reports since very few internal reports are required.
   d. print reports on preprinted forms.

IV. True or False. Record either a T or F in the space provided.

_____ 1. Because of the availability of faster printers, fewer reports are submitted on an electronic medium such as magnetic tape.

_____ 2. Some laser printers print both the form and the information.

_____ 3. The Xs on the print layout form indicate where constants will be printed.

_____ 4. Stock paper is always single-part forms that are 8½" by 11".

_____ 5. The programmer is not responsible for formatting the information printed in either the heading or detail lines.

_____ 6. The print layout chart should be completed prior to developing the program specifications.

_____ 7. It is unnecessary to edit input read from a master file.

_____ 8. If the page-number field is initialized to zero, after the headings are printed one is added to the field.

_____ 9. In the print-detail module after the detail line is printed the line counter is checked to see if the heading module should be invoked.

_____ 10. If an operator keys in $10,000.00 in a field which has been defined as numeric, a data exception may occur and the program may cancel.

_____ 11. If a field contains −45.78 and the edit mask was coded as +####.##, the number will be printed as +45.78.

_____ 12. Only the digits 0–9 are stored in a field which has been defined as numeric.

_____ 13. Dollar signs are usually printed on internal reports such as the inventory exception report.

_____ 14. In the multilevel sales analysis report program after the department line was printed, the sales representative's total was added to the department total.

_____ 15. In the process-sales-records module of the sales analysis report, the record was processed before an IF statement was used to determine if a level break occurred.

_____ 16. A multilevel report is limited to three levels.

_____ 17. A report specification form often contains the name of the field, its origin, length, and type of data contained within the field.

_____ 18. In a transaction-processing application the error messages are usually accumulated in a file used to produce an error report that is printed after all of the transactions are processed.

_____ 19. Today the majority of the printers used can only print 6 lines per inch vertically and 10 characters per inch horizontally.

_____ 20. If both a full report and a condensed report are required, the information for the condensed report may be stored in a table and printed after all of the data for the full report has been processed.

FILE PROCESSING

7

After reading the chapter and completing the learning activities, you will be able to:

- Identify the media used to store online files and databases.

- Identify the characteristics of the four major types of file organization.

- When given a description of an application, determine if the records stored within the file should be sequentially or randomly accessed.

- Describe the information recorded on a file specification form and how it is used.

- Describe how the content of a master file is determined.

- Distinguish between alphanumeric, zoned numeric, and packed numeric data.

- Identify the data stored in a typical data dictionary.

- Explain why and how the backup file for the old payroll master file was used to create the new master file.

- Explain why it may be necessary to define the printer as a file and open and close the print file.

- Identify when the invalid-key routine will be invoked during the creation of a new ISAM master file.

- Explain how an end-of-file mark is recorded in a file and how it is used.

- Identify the steps needed when modification in a system requires new fields to be added to the master and transaction files.

- Identify the steps required to add the stock deduction data to the payroll master file records.

- Identify how data entered from a terminal is used to create a sequential disk file.

- Describe the logic used in developing a random-update program.

- Explain when an invalid-key condition will occur during the execution of a random-update program.

- Explain why the execution of a random-update program should be aborted if an invalid-key condition occurs while rewriting the updated record.

The information printed in reports and written into files can be read from a transaction or master file, keyed in by an operator, calculated, or retrieved from a table. In typical business-oriented programs, the majority of the input is retrieved from records stored in online files. Records can be stored on diskettes, hard disk, cassette tape, reel-to-reel tape, or in a **mass storage system**, **hard-card system**, or **laser-optical disk subsystem.** While records stored on some media can only be accessed sequentially, there are several types of **direct access** devices. The records stored in files on a direct access device can be retrieved either randomly or sequentially.

RECORD STORAGE

Diskettes

Eight-inch diskettes, or floppy disks, were initially developed for use with minicomputer and word processing systems. When microcomputer systems were developed, 5¼" diskette subsystems were widely used for storing files and databases. As hard disks became less expensive and able to store more information in a smaller area, many microcomputer systems were configured with both hard disk and diskette drives. Although data is stored less densely on diskettes and it takes longer to retrieve than when stored on hard disk, records can be accessed both sequentially and randomly. Diskettes are still widely used as an input, output, and storage medium.

Magnetic tape

Cassette tapes, similar to the ones used on voice recorders, were first used on terminals and minicomputer systems. Larger versions of cassette tapes are used with some minicomputer systems for tape backup. The tapes are approximately the size of a videotape and can store a large amount of data. Smaller cassette tapes are used with microcomputer systems to back up files stored on diskettes and hard disk.

In 1984 IBM introduced its 3480 tape drives which use ½-inch tape stored in cartridges. The cartridge is about one-fourth the size of a reel of standard tape and the tape stored within the cartridge can hold 20 percent more data. As many as 38,000 characters of data can be stored on one inch of tape. Large organizations use the 3480 system for storing historical data, backup copies of databases, files, and software, and for offloading infrequently used files.

When the term *magnetic tape* is used, the reference is usually to reel tape. One-half-inch reel tape is standardized in regard to how it is manufactured and the amount of data that can be recorded per inch. Reports are usually submitted on ½-inch, 1600 character-per-inch tape to the federal and state governments. Large organizations, such as banks, credit unions, and insurance companies, also accept reports submitted on standardized tape.

Within an organization, magnetic tape is used for backing up files, application programs, and the operating system. When many medium- and large-size computer systems are configured, at least one magnetic tape drive must be obtained.

The major disadvantage of using magnetic tape as a medium for storing files is that records can only be accessed sequentially. However, storing information on magnetic tape requires less space and is less expensive than when the same amount of information is stored on magnetic disk. When files are offloaded to magnetic tape, the disk file may be recreated from the tape before the file is used as input or is updated.

© SRA 1988, 1983

Direct access storage media

HARD DISK Records stored on hard disk, diskettes, or laser-optical disks can be accessed either sequentially or randomly. Reference to a magnetic disk usually signifies hard disks mounted on drives that can hold one or several disks. Each magnetic disk consists of a thin, circular metal plate. One or more disks are stacked on a vertical shaft and separated by a small amount of space. Figure 7–1 illustrates how read/write heads are positioned over hard disks.

Although disk subsystems differ in the amount of data that can be stored on the individual disks and in how rapidly records can be retrieved, the densities of data stored on disk is increasing while the retrieval time is decreasing. When selecting a computer system, the type of disk drives and organization methods supported must be considered very carefully. Although laser-optical disk systems and hard-card systems are becoming more popular, in medium and large organizations the majority of online files and databases are stored on hard disk. In a hard-card system, data is stored in RAM (random-access memory) chips.

LASER-OPTICAL DISKS Data is recorded on laser-optical disks, also called video or optical disks, by using low-intensity laser beams to record images on the plastic disks. Early disks could only be used to record data and to read the data stored on the disks. Later developments permitted the data recorded on disks to be

Figure 7–1 Read/write heads are positioned over cylinders composed of surfaces located on ten different tracks.

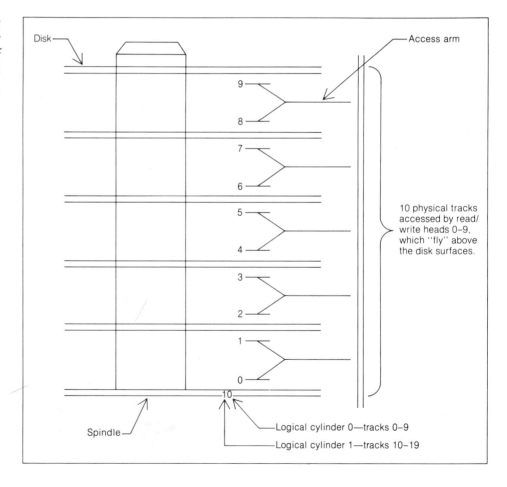

read as input, updated, and then rewritten on the disks. The laser-optical systems that permit records to be updated are not yet in full-scale production as their market acceptability has not yet been established.

MASS STORAGE SYSTEMS   As the demand for data increased, more tape and disk drives were added to computer systems. Mass storage systems (MSSs) were developed that permitted massive amounts of data to be stored online. These systems combined the low cost of magnetic tape with the random access capabilities of disk. Files are written on magnetic tape which is stored in a tape cartridge. When a request is received for the information, control software provides for obtaining the cartridge, opening the cartridge, and transferring the records to magnetic disk for processing. Although an MSS system would not be appropriate for storing files required for transaction-processing, an MSS system does provide excellent storage for backup, historical, and infrequently used files. Since it is an automated system, operators are not required to load and unload the tape cartridges.

FILE ORGANIZATION

Selecting the right hardware is important to minimize access time and provide enough online storage. However, when application software is designed, analysts and programmers are more concerned with the organization and access methods supported by the operating system and the language being used. The development of transaction-processing systems became feasible when the cost of storing master file records online decreased and operating systems supported direct access storage devices.

The programmer or analyst determines how files are organized and protected, the content and size of the records, the size of each field within a record, and the type of data stored within each field. Files, as well as programs, can be protected from unauthorized use by **passwords**. A password is a unique combination of characters that must be used to gain access to a file or program. The file-organization methods supported are a function of the operating system software and not of the disk hardware. A brief summary of the four most popular methods is provided.

Sequential

When a sequential file is created, the records are written on the file as they occur. An index is *not* maintained on the record level by the operating system, and the records can only be accessed sequentially. When the records within a file can be accessed only sequentially, the file cannot be used for storing records needed for an online transaction-processing system. Although records can be added to an existing file, the records cannot be inserted into their proper location within the file. For example, if records were stored in sequence for customers 10 and 20, when customer 15 was added to the file the record will be recorded at the end of the file and not in its proper location between records 10 and 20.

It is more time consuming and difficult to update a record stored within a sequential file than one stored within direct access files. When updating a record a search is made for it. To make a sequential search, it is necessary to read and compare all records until the desired one is found. When the record is found, the data is changed and the record rewritten. Some languages do not support updating sequentially organized files.

© SRA 1988, 1983

Since an index is not required or maintained, records stored in a sequential file can be sequentially accessed faster; they require less storage space than records stored in a direct access file. Records in transaction files are usually accessed sequentially, seldom updated, and used for a limited period of time and in a limited number of applications. For these reasons, transaction files stored on magnetic disk are often organized sequentially. Files used to back up online files and databases are also organized as sequential files. Because they are widely used, some of the ways sequential files are created and utilized are illustrated.

Random or direct

Although the records stored in a direct file can be accessed randomly, an index is not maintained by the system software. Either an algorithm or a key is used to write a record on disk or to retrieve a record. The absolute address needed to retrieve records can be supplied directly by the user or can be generated by the system from the data supplied by the user. Although records can be randomly retrieved faster than when some other organizational methods are used, file maintenance is more difficult than when ISAM or VSAM files are used. Records cannot be inserted into their proper storage location in, or deleted from, a direct file.

Indexed sequential access method (ISAM)

When an **ISAM** file is initially created, the input records *must* be arranged in key sequence. If a record is out of sequence, a programmer-generated message that the record was not added to the file is usually printed or displayed. If the programmer has not provided for sequence-error handling, the system causes the file-create program to abort.

An ISAM file requires several areas on disk. One area is used for maintaining an index. When direct access to a record is required, the request for the record contains the key for the record. The index is checked to determine where the record with that key is located. The index of a file might be compared to the index of a book. When information is required, the index is checked to determine where it is stored within a book or file. The records are stored in an area referred to as the **prime area.** The programmer must also indicate how much file space is to be reserved for the **overflow area.**

When additional records are added to the file, the operating system software inserts the new records into the file so that all records are still in sequence. When new records are inserted into the file, some of the records stored in the prime area may be relocated in the overflow area. Unless the file is reorganized, the overflow areas can become full and a message such as "OVERFLOW AREA FULL. JOB ABORTED" will be displayed. When a file is reorganized, it is first copied to a sequential file. When this occurs, the operating system software inserts the records from the overflow area into their proper location. The second step is to use the sequential file to recreate the master file. Since this is considered as file maintenance, the logic required to reorganize an ISAM file will be covered in Chapter 8.

Each record in an ISAM file must have a unique **key**. The field used for the key is generally an identifying field, such as a student's name or Social Security number, or an employee or item number. Each record is stored in its key-sequence within the file. The operating system software maintains an index of where each record is stored.

Each time the records in an ISAM file are to be accessed, the programmer or analyst determines whether they should be accessed sequentially or randomly. If only a small percentage of the records is to be updated, the file should be accessed randomly. When only selected records are to be processed based on data (other than the key) stored in a field *within the records to be processed*, the records will be accessed sequentially. For example, assume you would like to print a report of all customers who are within 10 percent of their credit limits. Each record is read sequentially and each customer's balance is compared with 90 percent of his or her credit limit. If the figure is less than the balance, the required information for the customer will be printed on the report. Usually report programs access records in a file sequentially whereas maintenance programs access the records randomly. Examples will be provided of how ISAM files are created, accessed sequentially and randomly, and backed up.

Virtual storage access method (VSAM)

Records stored in **VSAM** files can be accessed either randomly or sequentially. A VSAM file can be organized as a key-sequenced file, an entry-sequenced file, or a relative-sequenced file. The key-sequenced system, which is similar in many ways to ISAM, is used most often and will be the method discussed.

Data sets stored within a VSAM file are divided into **control intervals.** The length of the control interval is determined either by the VSAM software or by the analyst. A control interval is a storage area reserved for storing certain records. Each control interval has an assigned location on disk. Control intervals are independent of the device upon which the records are stored. Once the file is created, the control-interval size cannot be changed without recreating the data set.

When records are added to the file, the new records are inserted into the correct location within the file. If there is not enough space within a control interval to insert a new record, a control-interval split occurs. Half of the records stored in the old control interval will be moved into the new control interval. Figure 7–2 illustrates what occurs when a control-interval split occurs.

Retrieval of VSAM records is considered to be one-and-a-half to three times faster than retrieval of ISAM records. The index structure of VSAM files is more efficient than the structure used for ISAM files. Along with being faster and more efficient, VSAM files have the following advantages:

- multiple keys can be used for retrieving records. For example, a record could be retrieved by using the student's name, number, or Social Security number.

- in a single program, records can be retrieved both sequentially and randomly from a single file. The customer's master record is accessed randomly and the supporting transaction records located within the file for the customer are accessed sequentially. (This concept will be illustrated when **variable length records** are discussed in Chapter 10.)

- obsolete records are physically deleted from the file. A delete code is used within the record and when the file is reorganized the records flagged for deletion are excluded.

- files are automatically reorganized. When a control interval becomes full, the records are divided between two new control intervals.

© SRA 1988, 1983

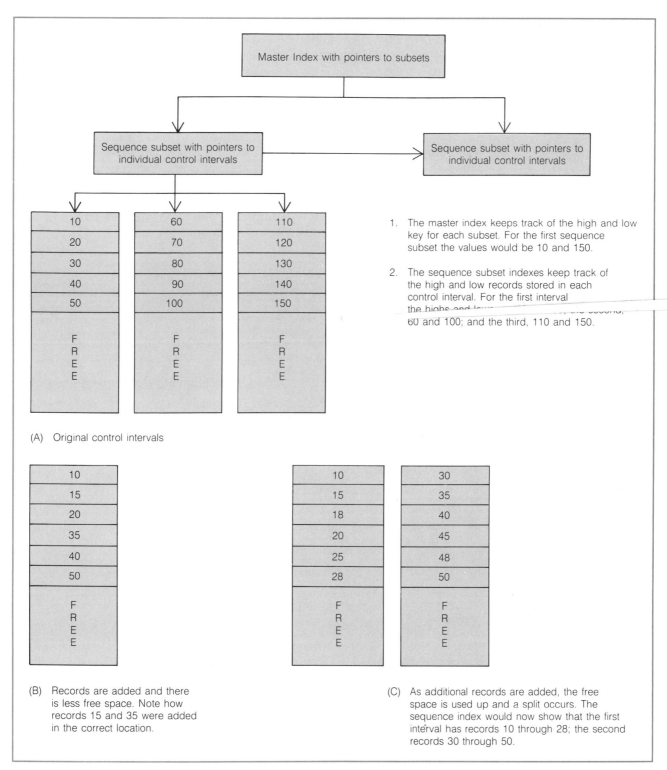

Master Index with pointers to subsets

Sequence subset with pointers to individual control intervals

Sequence subset with pointers to individual control intervals

| 10 |
| 20 |
| 30 |
| 40 |
| 50 |
| F R E E |

| 60 |
| 70 |
| 80 |
| 90 |
| 100 |
| F R E E |

| 110 |
| 120 |
| 130 |
| 140 |
| 150 |
| F R E E |

1. The master index keeps track of the high and low key for each subset. For the first sequence subset the values would be 10 and 150.

2. The sequence subset indexes keep track of the high and low records stored in each control interval. For the first interval the highs and lows ~~~~~~~~~~~~, the second, 60 and 100; and the third, 110 and 150.

(A) Original control intervals

| 10 |
| 15 |
| 20 |
| 35 |
| 40 |
| 50 |
| F R E E |

| 10 |
| 15 |
| 18 |
| 20 |
| 25 |
| 28 |
| F R E E |

| 30 |
| 35 |
| 40 |
| 45 |
| 48 |
| 50 |
| F R E E |

(B) Records are added and there is less free space. Note how records 15 and 35 were added in the correct location.

(C) As additional records are added, the free space is used up and a split occurs. The sequence index would now show that the first interval has records 10 through 28; the second records 30 through 50.

Figure 7–2   As additional records are added to a VSAM file, the records are inserted into their proper location. Eventually a split will occur.

Because less maintenance is required and records can be retrieved faster, many ISAM files are being converted to VSAM files. Although the files are defined differently within the program, the logic needed to utilize VSAM and ISAM files is usually the same. A major difference occurs when the master file has both master records and shorter transaction records. The master record is randomly accessed and the transaction records stored in the file will be accessed sequentially.

The customer master file record contains information regarding the customer's billing address, shipping address, credit history, and credit limit. Following each customer's master file record are one or more records used to record data regarding individual sales invoices and cash receipts.

Despite the many advantages of VSAM files, not all operating system software support them. Therefore, computer operators, programmers, and analysts should know how to utilize both ISAM and VSAM files.

CHECKPOINT QUESTIONS

1. What are the four major sources of data used for reports, for display, or for output files?
2. What are the advantages of using hard disk rather than diskettes?
3. How is magnetic tape stored in cassettes or cartridges used?
4. Under what circumstances would you recommend that standardized magnetic tape be used?
5. Does the storage medium or device being used have more or less impact than the file access method on the design of an application?
6. Under what circumstances should a sequential rather than an ISAM or VSAM file be used?
7. What four advantages are obtained by using VSAM rather than ISAM files?
8. If an organization converted its ISAM files to VSAM files would the logic of the majority of the programs need to be changed?

FILE SPECIFICATION FORM

A master file was defined as one containing permanent and updated information for use in one or more application programs. In a typical payroll system the master file is used in from 50 to 100 different display, maintenance, update, and report programs.

When a new system is being created, the analyst determines which programs are needed. Each program is analyzed to determine what input is necessary to generate the required output. The analyst must then decide whether the data should be entered as the transaction occurs or stored in a transaction file, master file, or table.

By analyzing the needs of each individual program, a list of items that must be included in the master file is compiled. From this list, the file specification form is completed. In completing the form, the analyst must determine the name for each field, the size of the field, the type of data stored within the field, and the location within the record.

© SRA 1988, 1983

File Specification Form

System: Payroll   File Name: PAYMAST—Payroll master   Organization: ISAM

Key: MF-NUMBER   Record size: 352   Blocking factor: 20   Block size: 7040   Page 1 OF 2

Location	Length	Type		Data
1	1	AN	MF-DELETE-CODE	Blank or D.
2–7	6	AN	MF-NUMBER	Employee number.
8–23	16	AN	MF-LAST	Last name.
24–35	12	AN	MF-FIRST	First name.
36	1	AN	MF-Middle	Middle initial.
37–60	24	AN	MF-ADDRESS1	First address line.
61–84	24	AN	MF-ADDRESS2	Second address line.
85–108	24	AN	MF-ADDRESS3	Third address line.
109–113	5	AN	MF-ZIP1	Five digit zip code.
114–117	4	AN	MF-ZIP2	Four digit zip code.
118–118	1	AN	MF-STATUS	S = salaried, H = hourly, P = part-time.
119–124	6	NZ	MF-HIRED	Date hired—MM/DD/YY
125–130	6	NZ	MF-TERMINATED	Date terminated—MM/DD/YY
131–135	5	NP	MF-SALARY	Salary as XXXXX.XX for salaried employees only.
136–137	2	NP	MF-TIMES	Number of payments salary is distributed over.
138–140	3	NP	MF-HOURLY-RATE	Hourly rate for hourly and part-time employees—XX.XXX.
141–144	4	NP	MF-STOCK-DED	Stock deduction per pay period.
145–148	4	NP	MF-STOCK-BAL	Balance in stock deduction account.
149–151	3	NP	MF-STOCK-SHARES	Total number of shares purchased for the employee.
152–156	5	NP	MF-STOCK-TOTAL	Total amount contributed by the employee to the stock plan.
157–160	4	NP	MF-CREDIT-UN	Amount deducted for credit union each pay period.
161–164	4	NP	MF-TERM-INS	Term insurance deducted during the second pay period of each month.
165–168	4	NP	MF-UNITED-FUND	Total amount of United Fund pledge.
169–170	2	NP	MF-INSTALLMENTS	Number of installments United Fund pledge is to be paid over. The deduction is made the first pay period of each month.

Figure 7–3 Part 1   *Specifications for the payroll master file.*

File Specification Form

System: Payroll	File Name: PAYMAST—Payroll master		Organization: ISAM		
Key: MF-NUMBER	Record Size: 352	Blocking Factor: 20	Block size: 7040	Page 2 OF 2	

Location	Length	Type		Data
171–172	2	NP	MF-INSTALL-MADE	Number of installments made.
173–176	4	NP	MF-UNITED-DED	Total amount of pledge deducted.
177–179	3	NP	MF-UNION-DUES	Deducted the first pay of the month from the earning of hourly employees.
180–181	2	NP	MF-ACCOUNT-NO	Although there are 150 different account numbers, the payroll account numbers range from 41–65.
182–183	2	NP	MF-COST-CENTER	The cost centers are numbered from 1–69.
184–192	9	NZ	MF-SOCIAL-SEC-NO	Social Security number.
193–194	2	NP	MF-NO-EXEMPTS	Number of exemptions declared for federal tax.
195–195	1	NZ	MF-TAX-STATUS	1 = single status; 2 = married status.
			Quarterly Deductions and Earnings	
196–199	4	NP	MF-QTR-FICA	Social Security deducted.
200–203	4	NP	MF-QTR-FEDTAX	Deduction for federal income tax.
204–207	4	NP	MF-QTR-STATE-TAX	Deduction for state income tax.
208–211	4	NP	MF-QTR-GROSS	Gross paid earned.
			Year-to-date Earnings and Deductions	
212–216	5	NP	MF-YTD-GROSS	Gross earnings.
217–221	5	NP	MF-YTD-FEDTAX	Federal income tax.
229–226	5	NP	MF-YTD-STATETAX	State income tax.
227–231	5	NP	MF-YTD-FICA	Social Security deducted.
231–236	5	NP	MF-YTD-STOCK-DED	Total stock deduction for the year.
237–241	5	NP	MF-YTD-CREDIT-UN	Total credit union deduction.
242–246	5	NP	MF-YTD-TERM-INS	Total term insurance deduction.
246–251	5	NP	MF-YTD-UNITED-FD	Total United Fund deduction.
252–352	101	AN	MF-FILLER	When the file is created, this area will be filled with spaces. This area might be referred to as the "expansion area."

Figure 7–3 Part 2   Specifications for the payroll master file.

© SRA 1988, 1983

Understanding the information recorded on the form

The payroll master file specification form should be included as part of the documentation for the payroll system. As you refer to Figure 7–3, located on pages 239–240, you may find some unfamiliar terms. Although some of the information needs no explanation, some of the data recorded on the form is described here.

Record size:
: Although only 251 bytes are used when the file is created, as changes are made to the payroll system additional fields may be added. Therefore, 101 bytes of filler are used as an expansion area.

Blocking factor:
: When files are stored on magnetic disk, a table supplied by the hardware manufacturer is used to determine what blocking factor should be used. In this case 20 was used. This means that during a READ or WRITE operation a **physical record** of twenty **logical records** will be read from, or written on, disk. In developing the logic of the program, the programmer is only concerned with logical records. Records are read into, or written out of, buffers. The blocking and unblocking of records is taken care of by the operating system software. Figure 7–4 illustrates the concept of unblocking a physical record for processing.

Block size:
: The number of records in the physical block is multiplied by the size of the record.

Location:
: Within the record each field has an assigned location.

Length:
: The length is given in **bytes**. A byte usually contains eight bits plus a parity bit. Within an eight-bit byte, one character of data can be stored. However, if numeric fields are packed, two digits may be stored within a byte.

Type:
: AN denotes an alphanumeric field that can contain letters of the alphabet, digits, or special symbols.

: NZ is used to designate numeric zoned (unpacked) data. Each digit occupies one byte.

: NP is used to designate a packed field. In a packed field two digits are recorded in each byte. However, the last byte of the field contains only one digit plus the sign. If the field changes from positive to negative, the value used to denote a negative field will be stored in the sign position.

While the blocking factor used does not impact the design of a program, it is the responsibility of programmers and analysts to determine what blocking factor should be used so that optimum use can be made of storage space. Also, a large file with a blocking factor of 20 can be processed faster sequentially than if a blocking factor of 10 is used.

In Figure 7–4 the blocking concept is illustrated. A physical record is read from a disk or tape into a buffer. When the buffer becomes full, the records are unblocked into logical records and processed. While this is occurring, a second input buffer is being filled. Processed logical records are blocked and stored in an output buffer. After the buffer becomes full, the block of records is written out to disk or tape. While the contents of the first buffer are written out to tape or disk, a second output buffer is filled.

Figure 7–4 A physical block of records is read into a buffer and then unblocked so that a single logical record can be processed.

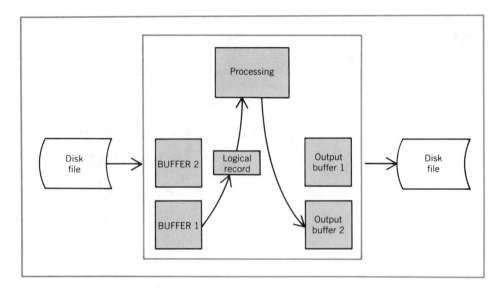

Determining data types

In determining the logic to be used in creating a new program, the way data has been defined in the master file has a direct impact on the logic of the program. In Figure 7–3 you will note that the Social Security number field is a nine-position zoned field. Usually an edit mask can be established that will cause dashes to be inserted so that the number will be printed as 123-45-6789. Or, it may be necessary to insert blanks between the series of digits that make up the Social Security number. In order to do this the programmer may have to move the nine-digit numeric field into one that has been defined as an alphanumeric field.

String functions are available that can separate a number such as a Social Security number into its three components. Many languages support a number of string handling functions that permit part of the data to be extracted from a string or two or more fields to be combined into one field. In COBOL, numeric zoned or alphanumeric fields can be divided into their various components without using a string function.

Packing numeric fields saves file space and requires less conversion. Fields used in mathematical statements should be packed or defined as **binary fields**. Binary data is stored within a field using bits which may be either ON or OFF. The location of the bit within the field determines its value. Within some computers a numeric zoned field is packed and then converted to binary before being used in a mathematical computation. Comparisons and arithmetic commands are usually performed on binary data. However, if conversions to and from binary must be made, the conversions are made by the operating system.

Programmers must determine how each field of data will be used and then determine how it will be defined and stored within the file. The limitations of the language must also be considered. Programmers must be aware of restrictions imposed on the use of certain types of data. Although alphanumeric data can be used in IF statements and compared with other string data, it cannot be used in mathematical operations. Also, while numeric data can be converted to and treated as alphanumeric data, a field originally defined as alphanumeric usually cannot be converted to a numeric field.

© SRA 1988, 1983

Field size   In determining the number of bytes required for a packed field, the programmer must add one digit to the field size and divide the number of digits by 2. For example, the analyst has determined that the salary field must contain six whole numbers and two digits beyond the decimal (XXXXXX.XX). The data has eight digits plus one for the sign. Since 9 divided by 2 is 4.5, and data cannot occupy a half byte, the field size is determined to be 5 bytes.

In designing a file, programmers and analysts are responsible for determining field size. Assume that the the credit union field was established as XXX.XX (three whole numbers and two beyond the assumed decimal). What would occur if an employee wants to have $1,000 a month deducted? Will it be necessary to change the file structure and recreate the file? In order to determine field size, the programmer must:

1. Know the data. What was the largest salary earned or the largest order placed? What will be the total gross paid to all employees for the entire year?

2. Allow for expansion. If we have 987 employees at the present time, a three-digit employee number field is probably not large enough to allow for future needs.

3. Follow some simple rules. When two four-digit fields are multiplied, the number can be as large as the sum of the digits in the mutiplier and multiplicand. In division, the number of whole numbers in the answer area should be as large as the dividend, and the places beyond the decimal should be as large as the divisor.

4. Know the default options of the language being used. Some languages round up while others truncate. When an overflow occurs and the answer will not fit into its allotted area, will the job abort, will an error message be displayed, or will an invalid answer go undetected?

Copy statements   Many programming languages include a copy statement which permits the source code identifying the fields within a record to be copied from an online library into the program being developed. The copy statement may also be called an **APPEND** or **CHAIN** statement. Copying data structures saves coding time and also helps to prevent errors. Once a field is defined within a record, its size, type, or *location* cannot be changed without recreating the file. What would happen if, in an update program, the location of the year-to-date gross pay field and the year-to-date federal income tax field were accidentally reversed?

If a field within a record needs to be enlarged or relocated, the file will need to be recreated. When a file is recreated the programmer or analyst may also elect to change the size of the record and the blocking factor. Changing the size of the record or the blocking factor will make it necessary to recompile all of the programs that use the file.

Data names   Many organizations have standards based on the programming language being used that must be followed when determining field names. For example:

1. All names must describe the contents of the field. Using short names to save time in coding may create problems when programs need to be modified.

2. The file name should be used as part of the data name. For example, PAYMAST-ENUMBER. Or, MF can be used to designate a master file and TR to designate the transaction file.

3. If the language employed permits dashes, a dash should be used to separate the words used in identifying individual fields. For example, MF-CREDIT-UNION-DEDUCTION.

4. Each field must have a unique name. For example: MF-LAST-NAME from the payroll master file record; CF-LAST-NAME from the current or transaction file record.

While many early languages did not permit data names to be more than six characters in length, today most languages permit data names to be much longer. Although the data names used do not impact the design of the program, when meaningful names that also identify the source of the data are used, programs are much easier to understand and to maintain.

If you have listed the code used in writing the programs for the Interactive Exercises, you may have observed that in BASIC, dashes cannot be used as part of the data name. Also, an alphanumeric field name must end in a dollar sign.

Data dictionaries

A **data dictionary** is a centralized file that contains data about data. In addition to the information shown on the file specification form, the dictionary also keeps track of the programs in which each field of data is used. Most dictionaries contain information about and maintain the relationships between entries in the following categories:

1. fields within master and transaction file records
2. file and record type
3. file organization
4. statements in which master and transaction records are used
5. source documents where data originates
6. programs and reports that utilize the data stored within the files
7. users that can retrieve information concerning the information stored within online files

Some data dictionaries permit listing all the programs and statements within each program in which any given field is used. When it is necessary to modify a program, the information maintained by the data dictionary is very useful.

Data dictionary software includes programs for entering new information into the dictionary, modifying or deleting entries from the dictionary, and producing reports pertaining to information stored in the dictionary. When a dic-

© SRA 1988, 1983

tionary is used, the organization's standards usually require that the data names used when the file was created should also be used in all future programs.

The data dictionary should be checked whenever modifications are made to either transaction or master file records. For example, the file specification report indicates that the status field must contain either an S, H, or P. What if a new category were developed for temporary help that required a T status code? The dictionary should be checked to determine in which programs the MF-Employee-status or TR-Employee-status field is used. Each program and statement identified as containing either of the two fields should then be checked to determine if changes are needed.

RECORD LAYOUT

The record layout illustrated in Figure 7–5 is a graphic and condensed version of the file specification form. All of the alphanumeric data is located in the first part of the record while the numeric information is at the end of the record illustrated. Because of the way the record is organized, it may be possible to move spaces into all of the alphanumeric fields with one statement and zeroes into the numeric fields with a second statement. Also, since the quarterly and yearly total fields are grouped, at the end of a quarter, a single statement will reset all of the quarterly fields to zero.

How the fields within the record are organized has a direct impact on how easy it is to clear fields and do routine file maintenance.

CHECKPOINT QUESTIONS

9. How does an analyst determine what data should be stored in the payroll master file records?
10. What information is recorded on the file specification form?
11. In designing and coding programs, how would the file specification form be used?
12. What is the difference between a logical and a physical record?
13. In developing the logic of a program, is the programmer concerned with logical or physical records?
14. What is a byte?
15. If a field is defined as an alphanumeric field, what restrictions may be placed upon its use in a program?
16. If copy or append statements are supported, why should they be used in coding an application program?
17. Suppose the law regarding how the state income tax is to be calculated and remitted to the state is changed. How might the maintenance programmer use the data dictionary?
18. In designing the record layout, why are all the quarterly and year-to-date fields adjacent to one another?

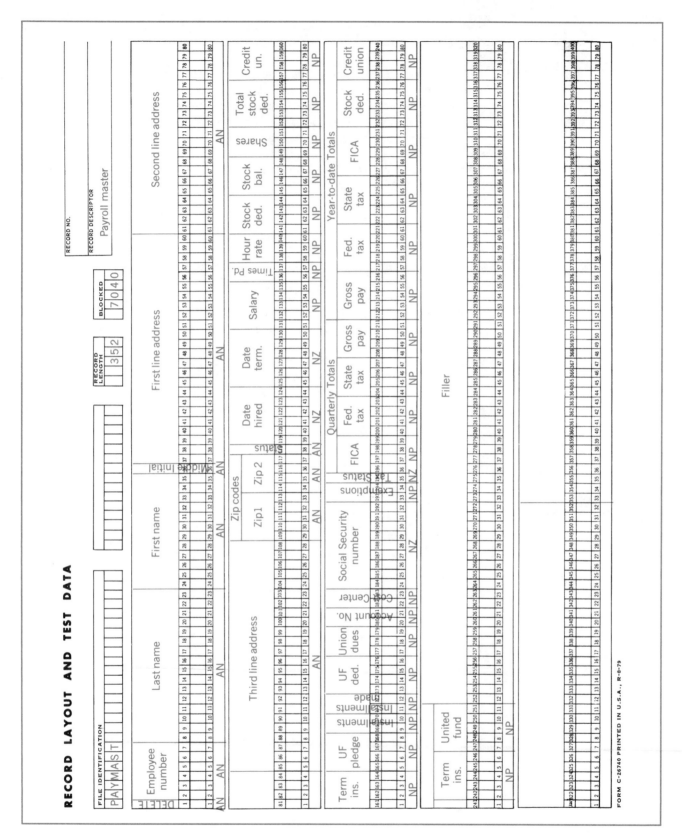

Figure 7–5   Record layout for the payroll master file.

© SRA 1988, 1983

CREATING THE PAYROLL
MASTER FILE

After the file organization method is determined and the payroll master file record is designed, the analyst must determine:

1. what information is available in existing files;
2. what additional information is needed; and
3. how the additional information will be entered into the master file.

Unless the file is being created for a small organization obtaining its first computer, files are already available that contain most or all of the information needed to create the master file. For the organization obtaining its first computer, the required data may need to be keyed in. However, assume that our organization has a computerized payroll system. Since the present computer system is being replaced with one that is faster and has more online storage, the payroll system was redesigned. The new payroll system will be phased in on the new computer on January 1. Therefore, all of the quarterly and yearly fields will be set to zero.

In analyzing what data is needed to create the new master file, the programmer determined that all of the information described on the file specification form is available in the old master file except the stock deduction information. Under the current payroll system, the amount employees contributed to the stock plan was not a payroll deduction. Since approximately 45 percent of employees contribute to the stock deduction plan, contributions should be deducted from gross earnings and the additional data maintained in the payroll master file.

The new payroll master file must be available for the first pay period in January. The programs required to create the file must be designed, tested, and documented *prior to that time.* Our organization will use a four-step approach to creating the master file:

1. After the last pay period in December, use the old payroll system maintenance programs to make the required changes to the old master file such as adding new employees, changing salaries, or flagging records for deletion.

2. Copy to magnetic tapes the updated existing payroll master file stored on disks mounted on the old computer's disk drives. A program used to back up the master file onto magnetic tape is available. Transport the magnetic tape to the new computer system and create the payroll master file on the new system.

3. Develop a program that will write the stock information into a sequential disk file. The records will contain the employee number, stock deduction per pay period, balance in the deduction account, total number of shares purchased to date, and total amount the employee has contributed to the stock deduction plan. The five fields of data will be keyed in by an operator, visually checked, and then written into the stock deduction file.

4. After the data recorded in the stock deduction file is confirmed, the sequential file will be used as input to randomly retrieve the required records and transfer the information into the master file.

When a new system is designed, every effort should be made to use existing files and to avoid rekeying data. Since the old system creates standardized magnetic tapes that can be used on the new system, the majority of the data

Figure 7–6 System flowchart for the file-create program.

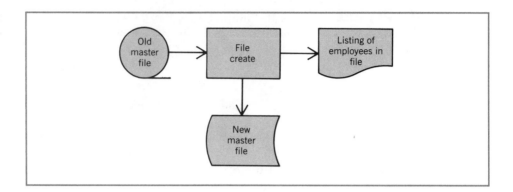

can be transported to the new system. The master file conversion must be completed after the last pay period in December and before the first pay period in January.

Program specifications for the file-create program

Figure 7–6 provides a graphic presentation of the program needed to create the new payroll master file. The file will be created by using the magnetic tape that contains all of the fields except those pertaining to the company's stock deduction plan. When the source code is written, statements will be included to indicate the file organization, the record size, and the blocking factor to be used. Other statements will be required that describe the data structure of the records stored within the file.

When an ISAM or VSAM file is created, an error routine will be invoked if two records have the same key (employee number) or if the records are out of sequence. Since the magnetic tape contains the records stored in the old master file, it is unlikely that either error will occur. Nevertheless the error routine should be included.

The specifications provided in Figure 7–7 should be followed in developing the logic for the program needed to create the payroll master file. Since the specifications call for an error report to be printed after all the records are processed, assume that the system being used does not support the creation and simultaneous printing of two separate reports. When developing program specifications, the characteristics and limitations of the hardware, control software, and programming language being used must be considered.

Hierarchy chart for the payroll master file-create program

In studying the hierarchy chart illustrated in Figure 7–8, you will observe that it has many of the modules included on the charts illustrated for other programs. As you study the flowchart illustrated in Figure 7–9, note there is little change in the write-payroll-report and write-heading-lines modules. Again these modules are typical of what occurs when a report is printed. The data for the report is obtained from the employee records stored in the tape file. The heading would contain an appropriate caption, the date from the system, and a page number. The report would be sent to the payroll department and it would be checked to determine if each employee has a record in the new payroll file.

© SRA 1988, 1983

Figure 7–7 Program specifications for the payroll master-file-create program.

Program Specifications

Output

Payroll master file — The file specification form provides a detailed explanation of the file organization and record layout.

Report listing — All employees added to the file will be listed. Each employee's number, name, status, account number, and cost center will be printed. The total number of employees in each category will also be included as part of the report.

Error report — The employee number and name of records out of sequence or those with duplicate keys will be stored in a table.

After the report listing is printed, either the statement NO DUPLICATE RECORDS OR RECORDS OUT OF SEQUENCE or a listing of the records that created the invalid-key error will be listed.

Input

Payroll backup tape — Since the old master file was updated before it was copied, the tape file contains permanent and updated information for all employees.

Processing — Quarterly, year-to-date, and stock deduction fields must be set to zero. The data from the input tape structure must be moved into the record structure for the disk master file records. An error routine should be provided for records out of sequence and duplicate records.

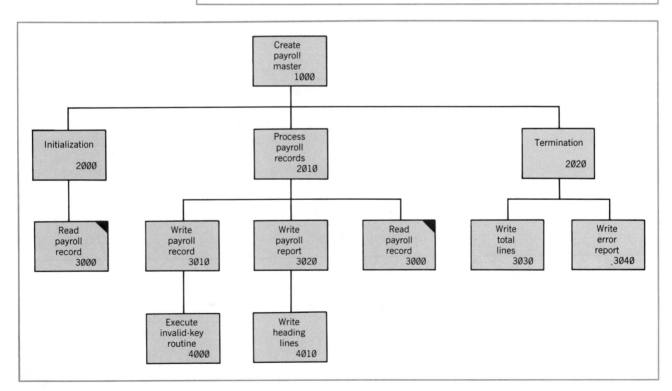

Figure 7–8 Hierarchy chart for the payroll master-file-create program

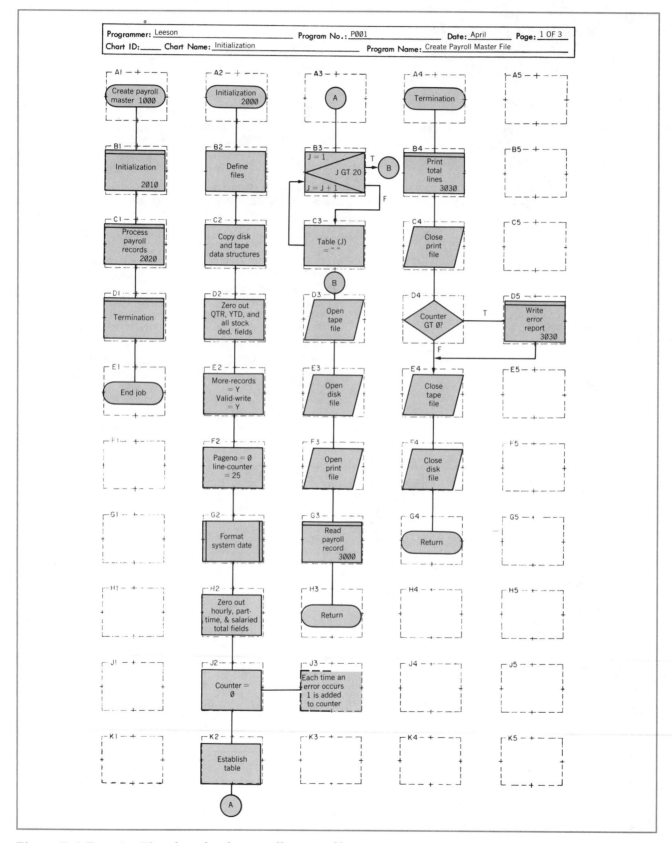

Figure 7–9 Part 1 Flowchart for the payroll master-file-create program.

© SRA 1988, 1983

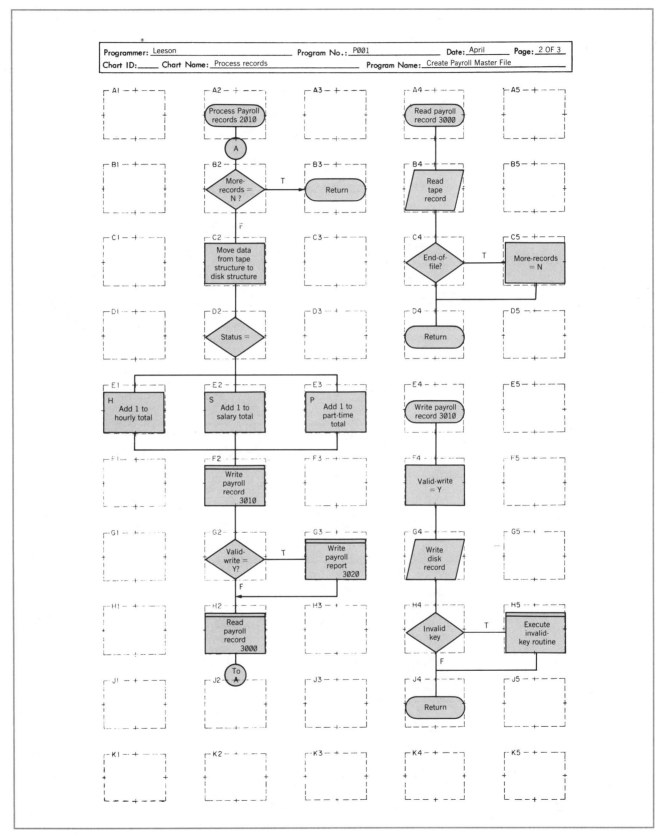

Figure 7–9 Part 2 Flowchart for the payroll master-file-create program.

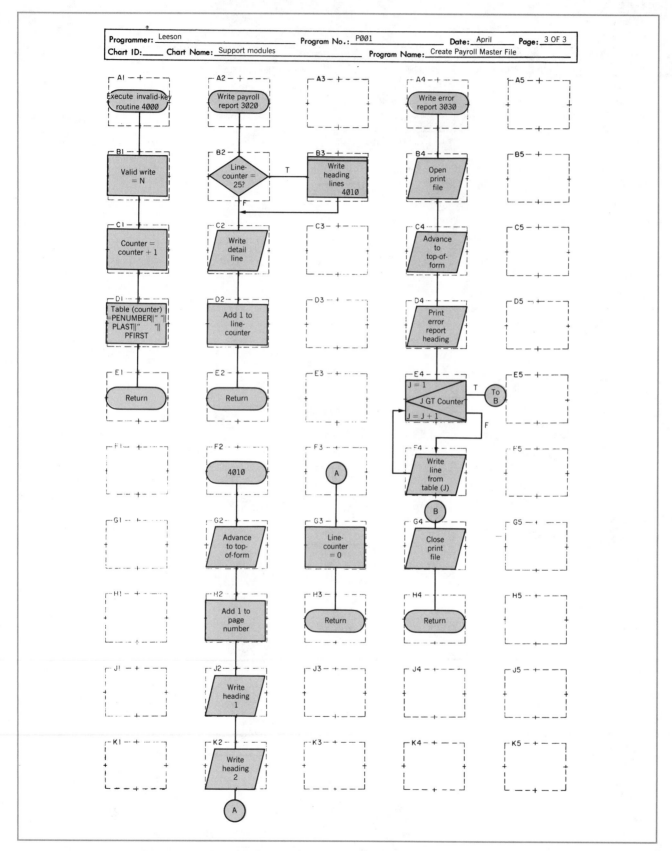

Figure 7–9 Part 3 Flowchart for the payroll master-file-create program.

© SRA 1988, 1983

As you review the initialization module, note that one of the input/output symbols contains the statement "Open print file." Depending on the language being used, the print file may also be opened and closed by default. However, in this example, we wish to print two different reports. The first is the listing of the individuals who have records in the new payroll master file and the second is an error report. In order to get the last line of the totals on the right report it may be necessary to close the file which forces the last line of the first report to be printed. Usually a print line remains in the buffer until a new line of information enters the buffer. The second line "pushes" the first line out to the printer.

Although it may not be necessary to declare the printer as a file and open and close the file, when this is not done the default options for the printer are in force. If the programmer wishes to increase the size of the print line or to change the page size, the printer usually has to be declared as a file.

INVALID-KEY ROUTINE   When an ISAM or VSAM file is being created, an invalid-key routine module will be invoked whenever a record is out of sequence or an attempt is made to create a record that has the same key as a previous record. In this routine, the field called *counter* will be incremented by 1 and used as a subscript to store the employee's name and number in a table. Since the fields are alphanumeric, the number, first name, and last name will be **concatenated** and stored in the error table. On the flowchart within the rectangle is the statement "Table (counter) = PENUMBER||" "||PLAST||" "PFIRST. The symbol || is used to indicate that the data stored within the three fields is to be treated as one field and stored within the table at the location specified by the value of the counter. Note that blank spaces are concatenated along with the values stored in the MF-NUMBER, MF-LAST, MF-FIRST.

Also, when the invalid-key routine is invoked valid-write is set to N which causes the write-payroll-report routine to be bypassed. The names listed on the report are only those whose records have been written in the disk payroll master file. In the write-payroll-record module, VALID-WRITE is always reset to Y before an attempt is made to write the record. In the execute-invalid-key routine the indicator is set to N. Since N is stored in the field, the write-payroll-report module will not be invoked.

If the programmer does not indicate what action is required when an invalid-key condition occurs, the **standard system action (SSA)** is usually to abort the job and to display a statement such as JOB ABORTED DUE TO SEQUENCE ERROR OR DUPLICATE RECORD.

END-OF-FILE MARK   When a tape or disk file is being created, an end-of-file mark is recorded in a trailer record that *follows* the last record that contains data. This occurs when the file is closed. Whenever a tape or disk file is processed sequentially, commands from the operating system software check to see if the end-of-file mark is detected. When the mark is detected, the options specified by the programmer will be executed. Consistently in this text N is moved into the field called more-records.

If the programmer does not determine what action should occur when the end-of-file mark is detected, the standard system action is to abort the job and print a message such as JOB ABORTED DUE TO READING PAST THE END OF FILE.

WRITE ERROR REPORT   In the write-error-report module the print file is reopened. An appropriate heading is printed, and then the information stored in the first location of the table is printed. In pseudocode, the loop created within the write-error-report module would be illustrated as follows:

```
DO (Error-subscript = 1 to Counter)
   Print table (Error-subscript)
END DO
```

When the data was concatenated and stored in the table, *counter* was used as the subscript. If ten names and numbers were stored in the table, counter would equal 10 and the last name and number were stored in the tenth location of the table. When the data is to be printed, error-subscript is used as the counter. An exit will be made from the loop when error-subscript is greater than the value (10) of counter.

If an error report is printed, records have not been created for the employees listed. Since a file maintenance program must be developed for adding new employees to the existing file, the add-new-employees program will be used to add the employees listed on the report to the file. The add-new-employees program will be be discussed in more detail in Chapter 8.

CHECKPOINT QUESTIONS

19. Why should existing data stored in files be used to create a new master file rather than rekeying all of the data?
20. When might it be necessary to key in all of the data needed for a new master file?
21. Why was the old master file updated before the data was transferred to the new master file?
22. Why was a listing of employees included in the new master file printed and transmitted to the payroll department?
23. When an ISAM file is created, what causes the invalid-key routine to be executed?
24. Although the printer can sometimes be used without declaring it as a file and opening the file, why is it sometimes necessary to declare the printer as a file?
25. What happens when two or more fields are concatenated?
26. Why is an end-of-file mark written at the end of a disk or tape file?
27. How was the field called counter used when an invalid-key condition was detected? How was it used when the error report was printed?

ADDING NEW FIELDS TO AN EXISTING MASTER FILE

Often it is necessary to add one or more fields to an existing file. Assume that the city in which our organization is located has just passed a city income tax. The law states that 1 percent of an employee's taxable income is to be withheld for city income tax. Since $54 is deducted for each exemption, city tax would be calculated as follows:

```
TR-city-tax = (gross-pay − MF-tax-exemptions × 54) × .01
IF TR-city-tax < 0 THEN
   TR-city-tax = 0
```

© SRA 1988, 1983

The following changes must be made to the existing payroll system:

1. The record structure for the payroll master file must be changed to include fields for the quarterly and year-to-date city income tax fields. Some of the space previously labeled "filler" will need to be used for the new fields.

2. The record structure of the sequential payroll transaction file will need to be changed to include the current and year-to-date (YTD) city tax. The transaction file is created during the execution of the program that calculates the employee earnings, deductions, and net pay. The transaction file will be used to update the master and to print the paychecks. It will also be used as input for several report programs.

3. The program which calculates the gross and net pay, as well as several maintenance programs, will need to be changed.

4. A report program used to submit the required reports to the city will need to be designed, tested, and documented.

In the city tax example, both the transaction and master file structures must be changed. However, before the new fields can be used to accumulate the city tax data, zeroes must be moved into the fields. Usually some type of utility program is available that sequentially reads a record from disk, moves zeroes into the new fields, and then rewrites the record. The program would be identified as a sequential-update program. The main processing module would be as follows:

```
*process-payroll-records module
 DO WHILE (more-records = Y)
      MF-QTR-city-tax = 0
      MF-YTD-city-tax = 0
      PERFORM rewrite-disk-record
      PERFORM read-disk-record
 END DO
*end process-payroll-records module
```

Although the payroll master file is organized as an ISAM file, access will be sequential and the job will be terminated when the end-of-file mark is detected. The rewrite-disk-record module is very similar to the write-disk-record module illustrated in Figure 7–9, Part 2, on page 251. When files are sequentially updated, each record is retrieved, one or more fields changed, and the record is rewritten in its assigned location on disk. An invalid-key condition will occur *if the value stored in the key field (employee number) changes before the record is rewritten.*

The program used to store zeroes in the new fields was referred to as a utility program. Once the program is created, it can be used whenever a similar situation exists. The statements that zero out the city tax fields would be replaced with statements that zero out, or move spaces into, the new fields added to the structure.

In order to determine what other programs need to be modified, the programmer might use the data dictionary to determine in what programs the state tax fields are used. Any program that used the state tax fields would probably need to be modified to include statements for the newly created city tax fields.

ADDING THE STOCK DEDUCTION DATA TO THE FILE

When the new payroll system was being designed, it was decided that the payroll master file would be created by using the final and updated version of the old payroll master file which is stored on magnetic tape. The data structure of the payroll master file records included the four stock deduction fields that will be used to record information that is available but was not included in the old payroll master file. In order to add the stock deduction information to the master file, two programs, create-stock-file and add-stock-amounts, will be needed.

One program, a random-update program, could have been used. The record for each employee that contributes to the stock deduction plan would be retrieved, the data entered directly into the data structure by the operator, and the record rewritten. The two-program approach was used so that the report created when the create-stock-file program was executed could be verified before the data was added to the payroll master file. Using the two-program approach leads to greater accuracy and greater confidence that the data stored in the payroll master file records is accurate.

Create-stock-file program

The create-stock-file program is a good example of a sequential file create program. The data structure for the stock file must be determined and defined within the program. The operator keys in and visually verifies the five fields of data. When the *enter* key is depressed, the field of data is stored in its proper location within the data structure. When the *write* command is executed, the record is stored in the output buffer, blocked into a physical record, and then written into the file.

Figure 7–10 illustrates the hierarchy chart for the create-stock-file program. When you study the chart you will observe that many of the modules are familiar and have been used in many different programs. In earlier chapters and in interactive exercises, a module similar to the enter-stock-data module has been illustrated. In the create-stock-file program three modules are used for entering data. The enter-data module invokes the format-operator-screen module. In this module the prompts are printed and then control returns to enter-stock-data. The cursor is repositioned to the correct location so that the data replaces the slashes that indicate the field size. If the operator keys in one or more fields incorrectly, the enter-data-correction module is invoked.

Modules similar to the print-stock-report and print-stock-heading modules have also been illustrated several times. The only module that has not been explained in detail is the write-stock-record module.

When sequential files are created on diskettes, disks, or magnetic tape, a key is not defined for the file. Therefore, an invalid-key condition does *not* occur. The pseudocode for the module would be as follows:

```
*Write-disk record module
WRITE stock record
*End module
```

When the write command is executed, the record is stored in the output buffer reserved for the file. When the buffer is full, the physical record is recorded on the disk. If a blocking factor of 30 were used, 30 records would be stored in the output buffer before its contents are recorded on the disk. Although the programmer or analyst determines the blocking factor, only logical records are considered when the logic of the program is developed.

© SRA 1988, 1983

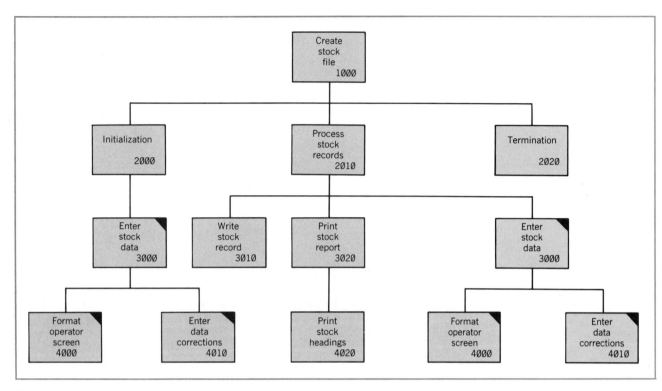

Figure 7–10   Hierarchy chart for the create-stock-file program.

In the termination module, the file will be closed. When the file is closed, an end-of-file marker is placed after the last record and the last block of records is written from the buffer into the file.

Figure 7–11 illustrates the specifications for the create-stock-file program; Interactive Exericse 7–1 contains additional information about the program. The source code for the program is written using the modules shown on the hierarchy chart illustrated in Figure 7–10.

Add-stock-amounts program

After the file containing the stock data has been created, verified, and corrected if necessary, the information will be added to the payroll master file records. Since only 45 percent of the employees participate in the stock plan, their records will be randomly retrieved, updated, and rewritten. To determine if it would be more efficient to access the records in the master file sequentially and update only if a match occurs, the program would have to be written both ways. The time required to execute both programs would be recorded and compared.

For the sequential update program, the stock records must be in sequence by employee number. A match is determined by using an IF statement to compare the employee number in the stock record with the employee number from the master file record. Since this program will only be executed once and only 45 percent of the records will be accessed, the analyst has decided it would probably be more efficient to develop a random-update program.

Figure 7–11
Specifications for the
create-stock-file program.

Specifications for the Create-Stock-File Program

Output

Disk file

A sequential disk file with records containing the employee number, stock deduction per pay period, account balance, number of shares of stock obtained, and the total amount contributed to the fund will be created.

Printed report

The printed report will list the information written into the sequential disk file.

Input

Keyed in by operator

A formatted screen will be displayed that provides prompts and illustrates the size of each field.

Verification

Before the data keyed in by the operator is entered, it must be visually verified. The program will also edit the data to determine that only numeric data was entered.

The printed report will be audited by the accountant responsible for the stock deduction plan. If errors are detected, a utility program will be used to make the necessary changes in the sequential stock file.

The logic of a sequential-update program is different from a random-update program, and therefore a sequential update program will be illustrated in Chapter 8. The specifications for the random-update add-stock-amount program, utilized in Interactive Exercise 7–1, are as follows:

Specifications for the Add-Stock-Amounts Program

Output

Updated payroll master file records

The information stored in the stock file is transferred to the master file records and the records are rewritten into the file.

Input

Stock deduction file records

After the stock deduction report is approved, and the necessary corrections made to records with incorrect data, the data stored in the file is used to update the master file records.

Payroll master file records

The employee number stored in the stock deduction records is used to retrieve the corresponding master file record randomly.

The add-stock-amounts program is typical of a random-update program. As illustrated in Figure 7–12, the initialization module invokes the read-stock-record module and the read-master-record module. The employee number in the stock record is used to retrieve the employee's master file record. When a command is executed to read a master file record, the index is used to determine where the employee's master file record is stored. If the number is not found in the index, an invalid-key condition exists. If the programmer does not pro-

© SRA 1988, 1983

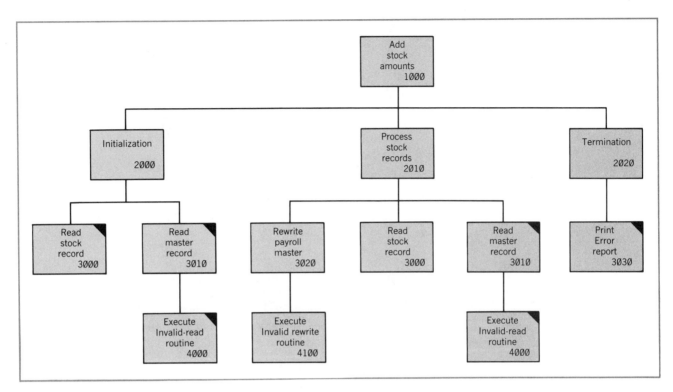

Figure 7–12   Hierarchy chart for the add-stock-amounts program:

vide an error routine, standard system action will cause the job to abort and a message such as RECORD NOT FOUND will be printed.

Invalid-key condition on random retrieval

The pseudocode for the read-master-record and the invalid-read modules might be written as follows:

```
*3010-Read-master-record module
     Valid-read = Y
      READ disk-file KEY stock-file-employee-number
           INVALID KEY
                PERFORM 4000-Execute-invalid-read-routine
 *End of module
*4000-Execute-invalid-key-routine
    ·Valid-read = N
     Appropriate code either to print messages,
     store error messages in a table,
     or write messages in a sequential file.
*End of module
```

Since a master file record was not read, the data from the stock record would not be transferred to the master file record and the rewrite-master-record module would not be executed. The pseudocode for the process-stock-records module would be as follows:

```
*2010-Process-stock-records
 DO-WHILE (more-records = Y)
     IF Valid-read = Y
          MF-stock-ded = TR-stock-ded
          MF-stock-balance = TR-stock-balance
          MF-stock-shares = TR-stock-shares
          MF-stock-account-total = TF-stock-account-total
          PERFORM 3020-rewrite-payroll-master
     END IF

     PERFORM 3000-Read-stock-record
     IF More-records = Y THEN
          PERFORM 3010-Read-master-record
 END DO
*End module
```

As long as there is a corresponding master file record for each record in the stock file, valid-read will equal Y. However, if an invalid-key condition is detected, an error message will be printed and valid-read will equal N. The rewrite-payroll- master module will be invoked only when a new master is read and the information from the stock file record is moved into the corresponding fields in the master file record.

Invalid-key condition on rewrite commands

If the key changes before a record is rewritten, an invalid-key condition occurs. Only if there is an error in the program logic will the invalid-key condition occur while a record is being rewritten into an existing file. If the invalid-key condition does exist, a message should be displayed and the job aborted. The problem is due to a logic error in the program. The error must be found, the program changed, and testing resumed. Since a copy of the master file is used when the program is being tested, the analyst or programmer is not concerned that the data within the master file has been affected because of the error in the program.

The pseudocode for the rewrite-payroll-master and execute-invalid-key-routine modules might be coded as follows:

```
*3020-Rewrite-payroll-master module

    REWRITE payroll master file record
        INVALID KEY
            PERFORM 4100-execute-invalid-rewrite routine
*End of module
```

```
*4100-Execute-invalid-rewrite routine
    PRINT 'Invalid key while rewriting record ', MF-number
    PRINT 'Job canceled. Notify programmer of error.'
    CLOSE stock file
    CLOSE payroll master file
    END or STOP
*End of module
```

© SRA 1988, 1983

The invalid-rewrite module is an excellent example of providing for an "it-should-never-happen" error. Because it represents an abnormal situation caused by a programming error, control did not return to the rewrite-payroll-master and then to process-payroll-records modules. The decision was made to abort the job before any more records were read. An alternative to using END or STOP that will cause the job to end, would be to use an additional indicator such as STOP-PROCESSING. In the initialization module STOP-PROCESSING would have been set to N. When the error is detected, STOP-PROCESSING will be set to Y.

If the second approach is used, the process-stock-records module will need to be changed as follows:

```
*2010-Process-stock-records module
 DO WHILE (more-records = Y)
    IF Valid-read = Y
        MF-stock-deduction = TR-stock-deduction
        MF-stock-balance = TR-stock-balance
        MF-stock-shares = TR-stock-shares
        MF-stock-account-total = TR-stock-account-total
        PERFORM 3020-Rewrite-payroll-master
    END IF
    IF STOP-PROCESSING = N
        PERFORM 3000-Read-stock-record
        IF More-records = Y THEN
            PERFORM 3010-Read-master-record
    END IF
 END DO
*End of  module
```

The execute-invalid-key-module would be changed as follows:

```
*4000-Execute-invalid-rewrite module
    PRINT 'Invalid  key  while  rewriting  record ',  MF-NUMBER
    PRINT 'Job canceled. Notify programmer of error.'
    STOP-PROCESSING = Y
    More-records = N
*End of module
```

After the statements in the execute-invalid-rewrite module are executed, control returns to the rewrite-payroll-master module. Since all the commands have been executed, control returns to process-stock-records. Since STOP-PROCESSING is equal to Y, the commands within the read-stock-record and read-master-record modules will not be executed. Control returns to the top of the loop and the exit test is made. Since more-records is equal to N, control returns to the main control module, control branches to the termination module and the files are closed. When the control returns to the main control module, the job is terminated.

While the first example violates the guidelines of "single entry, single exit" to a module or a *program*, it does seem to be a much cleaner and less complicated way of achieving the same results. It would seem that the "keep it simple" principle has been followed.

CHECKPOINT QUESTIONS

28. Using the payroll master file illustrated in Figure 7–3 on page 239–240, as an example, give an illustration of when one or more new fields may need to be added to the master file records.

29. If a new field containing numeric data is added to the record, why must a program be executed that places zeroes in the new field?

30. In a file created using information keyed in by an operator, when is the data entered into the data structure? When is the record recorded on disk?

31. When the logic of a program is developed, does the blocking factor used influence the way the program logic is developed?

32. Describe how a random-update program differs from a sequential-update program.

33. Are guidelines available that determine when a sequential-update program should be developed rather than a random-update program?

34. If an invalid-key condition occurs on a rewrite command, why should the job be aborted?

35. If the files are closed and the job is aborted in the execute-invalid-rewrite-routine module, what structured programming guideline is violated? In this case why might the decision to display a message and immediately abort the job be justified?

SUMMARY

- Information printed on reports or written into files can be read from transaction or master files, keyed in by an operator, calculated, or retrieved from tables.

- Files can be stored on magnetic tape, diskettes, magnetic disks, hard-cards, laser-optical disks, or in a mass storage system.

- A file can be organized as a:

Sequential file	Records are accessed in the sequence in which they are stored within the file; an index is not maintained.
Direct file	An absolute address, or algorithm that calculates the address, is used to randomly retrieve records. Records cannot be inserted into their proper place within the file or deleted from the file.
ISAM file	Indexes are maintained that provide the disk-address of each record. A unique key must be included as part of the record. New records can be inserted into their proper location and file maintenance is relatively easy. To avoid running out of space in the overflow areas, the files must be reorganized.
VSAM file	Indexes are maintained that provide the address of the control interval where each record is stored. Multiple keys can be used and within a program records can be accessed both randomly and sequentially. When a control interval is filled, a split occurs and the file is reorganized.

© SRA 1988, 1983

- Magnetic tape files can only be organized and accessed sequentially. Standardized tape is used for submitting reports and transmitting information from one computer system to another. Backup and historical files are often maintained on magnetic tape.

- Files stored on diskettes, hard disk, hard cards, and laser-optical disks can be organized so that records can be retrieved randomly or sequentially.

- Master files are usually organized as ISAM or VSAM files; transaction files are often organized as sequential files.

- When records are written on or retrieved from a medium such as disk, a data structure must be identified for the file. The data structure identifies the location of each field, the size of the field, and the type of data stored within the field.

- The programmer or analyst designing the file determines the size of the record, the size and location of the fields, and the type of data to be stored within each field. When the file is created, extra space is provided that can be used for new fields that must be added due to changes in laws or policies, or the need for additional information.

- When data stored in an old file is used to create a new file, two data structures are usually needed. The data from the old file (perhaps a tape file) is read into one structure, moved field-by-field into the second structure, and then written on the output medium. If the input and output data structures are identical, one statement can usually be used to move the entire record from the input structure into the output structure.

- When a new system is developed, the majority of the data needed for the master file may be available in existing files. In order to reduce cost and to avoid keyboarding errors, data from existing files should be used to create the new file.

- A data dictionary is often maintained that contains data about the contents of files and about the programs in which each field of data is used. When a dictionary is used, each field must have a unique name. Once a field is defined and named, it should always be referred to by its original name.

- Copy, append, or chain statements can be used to bring data structures stored in an online file into an application program. This saves coding time, forces programmers to use proper field names, and reduces the possibility of errors in coding the structure.

- Record layouts are graphic presentations of the data recorded on file specification forms. Both documents become part of the documentation for the system.

- Invalid-key conditions occur:

    During the the creation of a program, when an attempt is made to write a record into the file that is out of sequence or has a duplicate key.

    When an attempt is made to randomly retrieve a record with a key that is not in the index maintained for the file.

    When an attempt is made to rewrite a record whose key has a different value than when the record was read as input.

- When a file is created, or additional records are added to an existing file, an end-of-file mark is placed behind the last record written into the file.

- When new fields must be added to an existing master file, it may be necessary to:

  Change the data structure to include the new fields.

  Zero out, or move spaces into, the new fields.

  Create a program, or modify an existing program, to add the new data to the data structure.

- When new data is to be added to a file, it may be advantageous to key the data into a sequential file and print a report. After the report is audited, the master file records are retrieved, the data from the sequential file is stored within the master file's data structure, and the master file records are rewritten.

- Since master file records are utilized in many different programs, it is essential that the data stored within the records is current, accurate, and protected from unauthorized use. Several types of maintenance programs must be developed to maintain the integrity of each record stored within the master file.

DISCUSSION QUESTIONS

1. On what media can direct access files be stored? Which medium is used the most often?

2. What are the advantages and disadvantages of using magnetic tape rather than magnetic disk as a storage medium?

3. For each situation described, indicate what type of file organization you would recommend for the accounts receivable master file and give the rationale you used in making your decision:
   a. When payment is received from a customer, the customer's master file record must be randomly retrieved. It is then necessary to do a sequential search to find the invoice that is being paid.
   b. Since there are few additions or deletions from the accounts receivable master file, you would like the file organized so that records can be retrieved randomly in the least amount of time.
   c. Although support is not provided for VSAM files, some programs require the master file records to be accessed sequentially while others require direct access to the records.
   d. The records stored within the file will always be accessed in the order in which they are recorded within the file.
   e. In some direct access programs the records are retrieved by using the account number of the customer as the key, and in other programs the name of the customer is used.
   f. The accounts receivable master file is copied to a backup file stored on magnetic tape.

4. In terms of content and of how the data can be used, what differences are there in alphanumeric, zoned numeric, and packed numeric fields?

5. Why should a copy statement be used to bring the data structure into a new program rather than rekeying the required source code?

© SRA 1988, 1983

6. What information regarding the accounts receivable master file would be recorded in a data dictionary? Although the same information regarding the file or database could be maintained manually, what are the advantages of having an online data dictionary?

7. You are responsible for developing a new accounts receivable/sales system. How would you determine what data should be recorded in the accounts receivable master file? What is your responsibility in regard to its organization and in defining its attributes?

8. During a random-retrieval program using the accounts receivable file, describe when an invalid-key condition might occur and how the problem should be handled.

9. In the discussion regarding how an invalid-key condition occurred while rewriting a record, two solutions regarding how the error should be handled were provided. Indicate which one you would use and give the rationale for your decision.

10. The accounts receivable master file record has a field that contains a five-digit Zip Code. Although we don't have to, our company would like to use the nine-digit Zip Code. The problem is that the Zip Code field only provides space for five digits. At the end of the file there are 36 bytes of unused space called "filler." There are 100,000 records in the accounts receivable master file that represent customers throughout the world. What steps would you take to add the last four digits of the Zip Code to each customer's record? Usually when the Zip Code is printed, it is in the following format: XXXXX-XXXX.

11. Why is the integrity of the information stored within the master file or database critical to the success of the accounts receivable system?

12. Using the payroll master file described in the text, describe two programs that are part of the payroll system that would require direct access, and two that would require sequential access, to the records.

13. If a print file can be opened by default, why is it sometimes necessary to define the printer as a file, open the file, and close the file?

14. Prior to this time, our company has not permitted payroll deductions for United Fund. The employees have requested that United Fund contributions be deducted from their gross earnings over one or more pay periods. Some employees might elect to have the contribution spread over five periods while others might elect to have the deduction spread over all twenty-six pay periods.
    a. What new fields will need to be added to the payroll master file records?
    b. How would you identify the other programs that might need to be changed?
    c. What procedure would you recommend for adding the new fields to the existing records and entering the data into each employee's record? Approximately 95 percent of our employees contribute to United Fund.

KEY WORDS

append
binary
byte
chain
concatenated
control interval
data dictionary
direct access
hard-card storage system
indexed sequential access
    method (ISAM)
key

laser-optical disk system
logical record
mass storage system (MSS)
overflow area
password
physical record
prime area
standard system action (SSA)
variable length records
virtual storage access method
    (VSAM)

© SRA 1988, 1983

PROJECTS

EXERCISE 7–1

Using the hierarchy chart provided in Figure 7–10 for the create-stock-file program and the information provided in the text:

1. Develop the report layout for the printed report.
2. Develop a detailed logic plan for the program.

EXERCISE 7–2

Using the hierarchy chart provided in Figure 7–12 for the add-stock-amounts program and the information provided in the text:

1. Develop the report specification for the error report. Since there should be few, if any, detail lines on the report, you need only print the headings one time. If there are no error messages, print the message NO ERRORS IN THE EXECUTION OF THE PROGRAM.
2. Develop a detailed logic plan for the random-update version of the add-stock-amounts program. Assume that you will be using an ISAM file.
3. In your invalid-read routine, you may either store the error messages in a table or create a file and store the messages in a sequential output file. If you store the messages in a file, you will need to close the file and then reopen it.

   Closing the file records an end-of-file mark after the last record and opening the file will permit the first READ statement to access the first record stored within the file.

PROBLEM 7–1

The payroll master file is to be used to create a program that prints a report providing the following information:

1. A list of all salaried employees. For each employee, the following data is to be listed.

   Name. (Call in a subroutine that will format the name as Smith, Joan. The formatted name is treated as one field of data on the report.)

   Date hired.

   The amount of salary paid each pay period. Our employees are paid every two weeks.

   The amount and percentage of their bi-weekly salary that are put into the stock deduction plan.

   The amount and percentage of their bi-weekly salary that are put into their credit union account.

2. After all the detail lines are printed, the following information is to be printed.

   Total number of salaried employees.

   Total amount paid to salaried employees each pay period.

   Average amount contributed to the stock deduction plan.

   Average percent of salary contributed to the stock deduction plan.

   Average amount of credit union deduction.

   Average percent of salary contributed to credit union.

3. Design the report.
4. Develop a hierarchy chart and a detailed logic plan for the program.

INTERACTIVE EXERCISE 7–1

A payroll master file has been created that you will use in several exercises. Unfortunately the version of BASICA used to create the master file does not support either ISAM or VSAM files. However, random files are supported and the records stored within those files can be accessed either randomly or sequentially. This version of BASICA also requires the programmer to write source statements that will put the data read from a file or entered by an operator into the buffer reserved for the *random file*. Random files also use GET to read a record and PUT to write a record. When sequential files are created, INPUT and PRINT (or WRITE) are used rather than GET and PUT.

Not all of the fields described in the file specification form illustrated on pages 239–240 are included in the file. However, the fields are included that will be needed to calculate each employee's gross and net earnings. Also, there are enough fields to demonstrate the programs needed to maintain the integrity and currency of the records stored within the file.

The program that created the payroll master file was very similar to the one described in Figure 7–9. Although the fields needed for the stock deduction plan are established and filled with zeroes, the create-stock-file and add-stock-amounts programs need to be executed before the master file records are complete. At present there are only six master file records.

The first program you will execute is a utility-type display program. If all the fields had been included in the file, the program would probably display two screens of data for each employee. Within most systems there are retrieval programs that can be used to gain access to information stored within master files. The display program can also be used to determine the validity of other programs. For example, when the add-stock-amounts module is executed, the only visual evidence that the program executed correctly is the message "STOCK DEDUCTIONS WERE JUST ADDED TO MASTER FILE RECORDS" which prints just before the files are closed.

The first time you display the employee's records you will note that all of the stock deduction fields contain zeroes. After the add-stock-amounts program is executed, the amounts you entered from the keyboard should be included in those fields. However, you will follow good procedure and copy the PAYMAST file *before* you test the programs.

Directions

1. Boot the system, load **BASIC,** and load **menu, Press F2.** Select menu **3,** option **19.**

2. When the prompt ENTER EMPLOYEE NUMBER appears, **enter** each of the following numbers:

Employee Number	Name Displayed
1	Smith, Joan
2	Brown, Ben
3	Benson, George
4	Neal, Tobby
5	Lockard, Fred
6	Brody, Lila

   If you have the **PrtSc** feature, print the screen of data that is displayed for each employee. *Retain the printouts for future use.*

3. After all six records are displayed, enter **N** in response to RETURN TO MAIN MENU? Y OR N? You will need to display some of the source code and answer some questions before you return to menu.

4. **List statements 140–150.** These statements were brought into the program by using the **CHAIN MERGE** command. Regardless of how the records are accessed, these two statements will always be the same. Notice that when the file is opened, the name PAYMAST.DAT is used to identify the file. Also the record length is specified. In the version of BASIC being used, the records will be blocked so that as many as possible will fit in a 512 byte sector. A sector is a storage area on a diskette that contains 512 bytes.

   Each data structure is identified by using the field statement. The field statement provides the location of the field, the size of the field, and the name of the field. When BASICA is used to create random files, numeric fields will eventually be packed.

© SRA 1988, 1983

5. **LIST 230-280**

    Is a sequential or random file being accessed?

    _____

    How does the computer know which record is to be accessed?

    _____

6. Enter **RUN.** Enter **85** in response to ENTER EMPLOYEE NUMBER.
    What occurred?

    _____

    Why was the error message displayed?

    _____

    _____

7. Return to menu.

INTERACTIVE EXERCISE 7–2

You will now execute create-stock-file (STOCKF) which stores the information entered from the keyboard into a sequential file. A confirmation report that lists the data entered is also printed. After the report is confirmed, the sequential file will be used as input to the add-stock-amounts program (ADDSTOCK).

Directions

1. Select menu **3,** option **20** and enter **RUN** or press **F2.** Make certain that you have turned your printer on.
2. When the formatted screen appears, enter the following data:

Employee	Deduction	Balance	Shares	Total
1	13.	19.38	10	247.18
2	20.	14.78	100	2378.90
3	17.	14.98	52	1347.98
4	18.50	7.32	120	3245.98
5	19.	14.57	80	1945.69

    Since Lila Brody, employee number 6, is a part-time employee, she cannot participate in the stock deduction plan.

3. How would the programmer who wrote the program know that the program worked properly and that both the printed output and the information recorded in the disk is correct?

    _____

    _____

4. Do not return to MENU as you will run the program several more times.

    When the statement DATA CORRECT? ENTER Y OR N is displayed, enter **N.** In response to ENTER NUMBER OF THE FIELD TO BE CORRECTED enter a **7.**

    Why did the error message print? To answer the question, you may wish to **LIST 640-700.**

    _____

    _____

    In response to MORE DATA? Y OR N? enter **N,** return to the main menu, and select option **6.**

5. When new employees are added to the payroll master file, the stock deduction information will be added to their records. Will this program ever be used again?

_____

_____

_____

6. After you have returned to the system, key in the following command:
   COPY STOCK.DAT PRN <ENTER>

   The copy statement will cause the data stored in STOCKD.DAT to be displayed on your printer. Check the data that is listed with the information you were asked to enter. Why should the data stored in the file be listed before the program is considered operational?

   _____

   _____

INTERACTIVE EXERCISE 7–3

Add-stock-amounts (ADDSTOCK) reads the records stored in the sequential stock file. The employee number from each record is used for random retrieval of the employee's payroll master file record.

Since this is a random-update program, when the program is being tested, a copy of the master file should be used. In a random-update program, records are retrieved, the contents of one or more fields changed, and the updated record rewritten into the file.

Directions

1. Before you load BASIC and menu, key in **COPY PAYMAST.DAT STUDENT.DAT <ENTER>**. You now have a copy of the payroll master file to which you can add the values stored in the stock file.
2. Insert the operating system diskette and in response to > key in **BASICA**. Insert the program diskette.
3. Load **menu.** Select menu **3,** option **21.**
4. In testing the program before it is operational, how would the programmer know that the right information had been placed in each of the records?

   _____

   _____

   What indication was there that the program executed correctly and that all records stored in the transaction file were processed?

   _____

   _____

6. Return to the main menu.

INTERACTIVE EXERCISE 7–4

1. Select menu **3,** option **19.**
2. Display the record for employee number 1.
3. Enter **N** in response to "MORE RECORDS? Y OR N?"
4. Do not return to the main menu.

© SRA 1988, 1983

5. **LIST statement 140.**

   OPEN "PAYMAST.DAT" AS #2 LEN = 128 will be displayed.

   Move your cursor to PAYMAST and change it to STUDENT. Press **ENTER.**

   The statement will now read: OPEN "STUDENT.DAT" AS #2 LEN = 128.

   Enter **RUN** or press **F2.**

6. Display the records for employees 1, 2, and 3.

   Use **PrtSc** and print the information displayed on the screen. Compare the results with those obtained the first time you executed option 19.

7. Once it has been determined that the stock deduction information was correctly stored within the payroll master file, which file STUDENT.DAT or PAYMAST.DAT will be retained, backed up, and used in future payroll programs?

   _____

   _____

8. Return to menu and exit to the system.

© SRA 1988, 1983

SELF-EVALUTION TEST 7

Name _____

Section Number _____

I. Record the term being defined, or the one needed to complete the statement, in the space provided.

_____ 1. A direct access storage device that uses low-intensity laser beams to record images on plastic disks. Although widely used as a mass storage medium, the ability to update records is still experimental.

_____ 2. An accounts receivable file may have _____ records. The master record contains constant and updated data and the supporting records the detail of individual transactions. Usually the master records are larger than the supporting records.

_____ 3. _____ are used as a means of limiting access to files and programs.

_____ 4. If an invalid-key routine is not provided, the default or _____ may cause an operating-system generated message to be displayed and the job to abort.

_____ 5. When two or more fields containing alphanumeric data are joined together to form one field they are _____.

_____ 6. When a VSAM file is created, records are stored in _____.

_____ 7. A _____ numbering system is based on two possibilities. A bit can either be on or off.

_____ 8. When a new record is added to the prime area of an ISAM file, it may cause one of the existing records to be moved into an _____ area.

_____ 9. Online transaction-processing systems became feasible when the cost of storing information in online _____ access files decreased. The time needed to retrieve the records has also decreased dramatically.

_____ 10. Because ½-inch reel tape is _____, a tape written on one computer system can be read by many other computer systems.

II. Multiple choice. For each situation described, indicate the medium or device that would be used.
  a. 5¼″ diskettes   d. magnetic reel tape
  b. hard disk   e. laser-optical disks
  c. cassette tapes   f. mass storage system

_____ 1. The medium used most frequently for storing online master and transaction files.

_____ 2. Widely used for submitting reports to the government and to private organizations.

_____ 3. Are primarily used to store files and programs that will be processed by a microcomputer.

_____ 4. Although they are utilized to store massive amounts of information, the ability to update information stored within records is still being tested.

_____ 5. Used to provide file backup for small systems using microcomputers or minicomputers.

_____ 6. Although records can be retrieved sequentially or randomly, access is slower and data is less dense than when hard disks are used.

III. Multiple choice. For each situation, indicate the file organization that should be used or is being described.
  a. sequential   c. ISAM
  b. direct   d. VSAM

_____ 1. The analyst feels that multiple keys should be available for retrieving records.

_____ 2. To prevent the overflow area from becoming full, the file must be reorganized by the computer operations personnel.

_____ 3. The records in the file will only be used to update the master file and to print listings.

_____ 4. An algorithm is used to calculate the addresses of records.

_____ 5. Records are stored in control intervals. When a control interval becomes full a split occurs so that additional records can be inserted into their proper location within the file.

_____ 6. The organizational method usually used when backup files are created.

_____ 7. Within a single program, records within a single file can be accessed both sequentially and randomly.

_____ 8. The file organization method that usually provides the fastest and most direct access to the records stored within the file.

IV. True or false. Record a T for true or an F for false. Either change the statement so it is true or indicate why the statement is false.

_____ 1. Since the way data is stored on disk is standardized, a disk created on an IBM system can be used on an NCR system.

_____ 2. Because the speed and density of magnetic tape is improved, online files should be stored on tape.

_____ 3. If a file stored on hard disk is seldom used, it should probably be offloaded to magnetic tape so that the file space can be used more productively.

_____ 4. When ISAM or VSAM files are used as input files, the programmer must determine if the records should be accessed randomly or sequentially.

_____ 5. It is always faster to process the records stored in an ISAM file sequentially than randomly.

_____ 6. In a VSAM file, obsolete records are automatically deleted from the file.

_____ 7. Usually a master file is created for each program within a system.

_____ 8. Alphanumeric data fields can be edited and also used in arithmetic statements.

_____ 9. When a field is packed, two digits can be stored in a single byte.

_____ 10. Processing zoned numeric data is more efficient than processing data stored in packed fields.

_____ 11. Passwords are only used to control the access to programs.

_____ 12. If a field is packed, an eight-digit number can be stored in four bytes.

_____ 13. Copy statements can be used to bring an existing data structure into new programs. This reduces the possibility of making errors.

_____ 14. A data dictionary can be used to determine in what programs each field within a record is used.

_____ 15. In each program in which the payroll master file is used, the organization of the file is changed.

_____ 16. If a file specification form is created for the payroll master file, the documentation will not include a record layout form for the file.

_____ 17. If the record for Sam Long is to be randomly retrieved from the payroll master file, his name will be used as the key to obtain the correct record.

_____ 18. If the programmer wants to print a constant and the data is stored in two alphanumeric fields as one string of data, the data is concatenated.

_____ 19. When a file is being created, the invalid-key condition only occurs when the transaction records used to create the file are out of sequence.

_____ 20. When an invalid-key condition occurs during the creation of a master file, the job should be aborted.

_____ 21. When new fields are added to the payroll master file to provide for United Fund deductions, it is unlikely any of the operational programs will need to be changed.

© SRA 1988, 1983

_____ 22. Ten percent of the student population lives in Midland. If a report is to be printed listing their names and addresses, the records should be accessed randomly.

_____ 23. Five percent of the employees receive a pay increase. The program used to make the changes will access the records sequentially.

_____ 24. When an existing file is used to create a new file, the size of the records, the blocking factor, and the location of the fields within the record may be changed.

_____ 25. In a random update program, records from a sequential file are used to retrieve and update the master file records. If an invalid-key condition occurs on a rewrite, an indicator, such as valid-rewrite, may be used to suspend normal processing.

_____ 26. In order to assure the integrity of the records, a number of file maintenance programs are needed for each master file.

_____ 27. If an entirely new system is created, it may be necessary to key in all of the data needed to create the required master files.

_____ 28. Depending on the language being used, if an invalid-key routine is not provided, the SSA may be to print an error message and abort the program.

_____ 29. End-of-file marks are only recorded at the end of a sequential file.

_____ 30. Since the person responsible for the stock deduction funds wanted to audit the information before it was added to the master file, two programs were required rather than one.

File Maintenance

After reading the chapter and completing the learning activities, you will be able to:

- Identify the types of maintenance programs needed to maintain the currency and integrity of an online master file.

- Describe the specifications developed for the payroll CHANGE program.

- Explain how the change codes entered by the operator are used within the CHANGE program.

- Identify the statements needed to check the validity of responses keyed in by an operator.

- Explain how an ON statement is coded and executed.

- Explain why two different print formats are needed to print the CHANGE program detail lines.

- Identify the source code needed in a typical change module.

- Identify the controls built into the CHANGE program.

- Describe how an operator's response to a question such as "RIGHT REC-ORD? Y OR N?" is validated.

- Describe the technique used to print the master file correct report.

- Explain how records are retrieved and updated in the payroll master file UPDATE program.

- Describe how a "lock" is placed on the payroll master file and when it will be removed.

- Identify the differences between random-update and sequential-update programs.

- Explain why a file should be backed up whenever the data stored within the file is changed.

- When given a description of a file, identify the changes that might be made when the file is recreated from the backup file.

Every computerized system needs one or more online master files or databases that contain updated, current, and reliable data. When files are used in interactive systems, provision must be made for the required maintenance. For example, in a file of stock items, new products must be added, products no longer in stock deleted, and new shipments of merchandise added to the appropriate records. Unless these and other changes are made regularly, the sales/inventory/receivable system will not provide relevant, timely information.

The payroll master file described on page 239–240 is an excellent example of a file that requires constant maintenance. Changes are required to add new fields, change or correct existing fields, delete and add records, and to zero out quarterly and yearly totals. In addition, because files may be destroyed due to operator error or to hardware or software malfunction, or to catastrophe, they must be backed up.

When the payroll system is designed, one of the tasks is to determine what maintenance programs are required. The analyst, working with the payroll department, must determine for each program whether it will be run in an interactive transaction-processing or a batch-processing mode. Next, the most efficient way of accessing the required records must be determined. An equally important consideration is to determine what controls can be built into each program to assure that correct data is entered and that output is valid.

MAINTENANCE PROGRAMS FOR THE PAYROLL SYSTEM

The payroll system is used as only one example; similar programs would be needed for any typical master files or databases. Inventory, accounts receivable, personnel, accounts payable, and many other types of master files require the same type of maintenance programs. A decision has been made to create the following maintenance programs for the payroll system:

Program	Description
ADD NEW	Data will be entered from the terminal and stored in the master file record structure. If an ISAM or VSAM file is used, the records will be inserted into their proper location within the file.
CHANGE	Normal changes, such as an address or salary change, must be made on a regular basis.
CORRECT	Although a number of controls are built into the system, entries of amounts such as an employee's gross pay may be incorrect. When this occurs, a number of corrections to the quarterly and year-to-date fields may be needed.
ADD-FIELDS	Because of changes in laws, policies, or the information requirements of management, new fields and data may need to be added to the master file. Each change must be individually analyzed to determine the most effective way to create the new fields and add the required data.
UPDATE	The data recorded in the payroll transaction file concerning the current payroll period is used to update the master file records.
BACKUP	When changes are made to the master file, it should be copied to a sequential backup file.
RECREATE	After the current version of the master file is backed up, the RECREATE program is used to recreate the master file.

© SRA 1988, 1983

During the execution of the program the record size and blocking factor can be changed, obsolete records can be deleted, and the fields used for quarterly and year-to-date totals reset to zero.

CHANGE, CORRECT, and ADD-NEW will be designed as interactive transaction-processing applications. Since all changes to the payroll master file must be authorized, a source document is used to record the required information. Once the change is approved, a member of the payroll department uses an online terminal to retrieve the required program and to key in the changes.

The other maintenance programs are designed as batch applications and will be executed by computer operations personnel. The one exception is that when new data is to be added to the existing records, each case must be considered on its own merits. Three utility-type programs may be available that can be modified to make the required changes. The first sequentially retrieves all master file records and moves zeroes or spaces into the fields that were added to the data structure. The second program is used to create a transaction file that contains the new data. The third program reads the transaction file records and updates the corresponding records in the master file.

CHANGE PROGRAM

Although the CHANGE and CORRECT programs could be combined into one program, using the "keep it simple" guideline, two programs are developed. The CHANGE program permits the operator to make normal changes such as entering new data in the address, name, status, or salary field. In an organization of 1,000 employees, an amazing number of records may need to be changed before their current pay can be calculated.

How often it is necessary to run the CORRECT program is directly related to the number of **controls** built into the system and the accuracy of the data submitted by department heads and payroll personnel. A control is a method used to ensure the accuracy of the input and output. If adequate controls are built into the payroll system and each employee is careful to complete his or her assigned tasks, perhaps only once or twice a year will corrections need to be made to the quarterly and year-to-date totals.

Program specifications

The program specifications illustrated in Figure 8–1 were developed by the analyst. Although several approaches can be used to design the program, the specifications described in Figure 8–1 must be followed.

Since the CHANGE program will be coded and executed in completing Interactive Exercise 8–1, only the changes made on the modified version of the employee master file will be illustrated. In addition to the changes described in Figure 8–2, a provision would be needed to change the address, Zip Code, termination date, account number, exemption, and tax status fields.

APPROACHES THAT MAY BE USED   There are several different approaches that could be used to develop the CHANGE program. The one illustrated requires the operator to enter the employee number, change **code**, and the new value for the field being changed. Codes are used to condense data. For example, a 1

Figure 8–1
Specifications for the
change program.

Specifications for the Change Program

Output

Updated master file records	Records will be retrieved randomly, updated, and rewritten.
Printed report	A confirmation report listing the employee number and name, field changed, and both the former and new contents of the field will be printed.
Visual display	The name of the person, as well as the description of the change to be made, must be displayed and confirmed.

Input

Master file records	Records will be randomly retrieved.
Data entered from keyboard	The operator will key in the employee number, change code, and new value.
Table containing field names	The change code will be used to retrieve the name of the field being changed.

Controls

When a record is retrieved, the employee's name will be displayed and the operator will determine if the correct record was retrieved. When the change code is entered, a description of the change will be retrieved and visually verified by the operator. The printed report will be attached to the source documents and returned to the person who authorized the change. If a change was not made, or was made incorrectly, a notation will be made on the document and it will be returned to the operator. Whenever possible, each field of data should be edited before being stored in the master file data structure.

represents a change in the delete field and a 2 denotes a change in the employee's name field. A separate module will be developed for each type of change. Using this approach will encourage stub testing. Each change module can be tested as it is added to the program. Also, when a new field that is subject to change is added to the file, a new module can be inserted into the CHANGE program.

CHANGE CODES   The change code will be used to determine which module should be executed and to retrieve the description of the change from the table. The field names, or description of the change, will be coded within the program and loaded into a table.

Figure 8–2 illustrates the change codes that will be used and also explains the relationships that exist among the various fields. These relationships must be considered when the logic for each of the change modules is developed.

Flowchart for the CHANGE program

Figure 8–2 lists the 10 codes that will be entered in order to invoke the correct change module. Figure 8–3, Part 1, shows the **ON statement** that will be executed to determine which of the 10 change modules will be executed. When an ON statement is used, the value stored in the parameter (such as change-

© SRA 1988, 1983

Change Codes and Interfield Relationships

Code	Data Field	Description
1	CF-DELETE-CODE	When a record is to be deleted a D must be stored in the field.
2	CF-NAME-CHANGE-CODE	An individual's name may have changed or a previous error is being corrected.
3	CF-STATUS-CHANGE	The status of an employee is changed to part-time, hourly, or salaried. If changed to part-time or hourly, the hourly rate field must be changed. When the change is for a salaried employee, data must be entered for the salary and pay-periods fields.
4	CF-SALARY-CHANGE	A change is also required for the field that contains the number of pay periods over which the salary is paid.
5	CF-TIMES	The number of payments over which an employee's salary is spread must be changed.
6	CF-HOURLY	The employee's hourly rate is decreased or increased.
7	CF-STOCK-DEDUCTION	The amount an employee contributes to his or her stock deduction account is decreased or increased.
8	CF-CREDIT-UNION	The amount an employee contributes to his or her credit union account is decreased or increased.
9	CF-TERM-INSURANCE	The amount an employee pays for term insurance is increased or decreased.
10	CF-UNITED-FUND	The amount pledged for United Fund is entered. The number of installments over which the pledge is to be paid must also be changed. The other two United Fund fields are set to zero.

Figure 8–2   Codes used in the payroll master file CHANGE program.

code) determines which module will be executed. If change-code is equal to 4, the fourth module listed will be executed. Using an ON statement is an easier way to implement case structure than is using compound IF/THEN/ELSE statements.

Since the ten modules 3010 through 3100 are very similar, two were selected and illustrated in Figure 8–3, Parts 3 and 4, which are on pages 284–285. Because the flowcharts illustrate both old and new concepts, some of the concepts are explained. As the modules are explained, please refer to the flowcharts on pages 282–285.

INITIALIZATION MODULE   Module 2000, Initialization, on page 282 illustrates the following concepts.

1. A statement must be provided to explain the type of file being accessed, its record size, blocking factor and so forth. Also the data structure must be included to show the name, size, and location of each field.

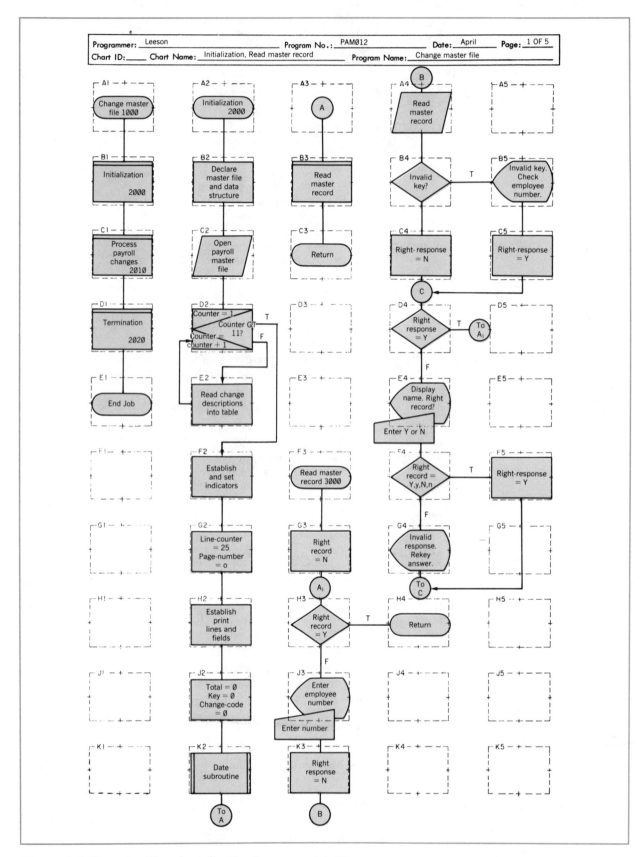

Figure 8–3 Part 1   *Flowchart for the change-master-file program.*

© SRA 1988, 1983

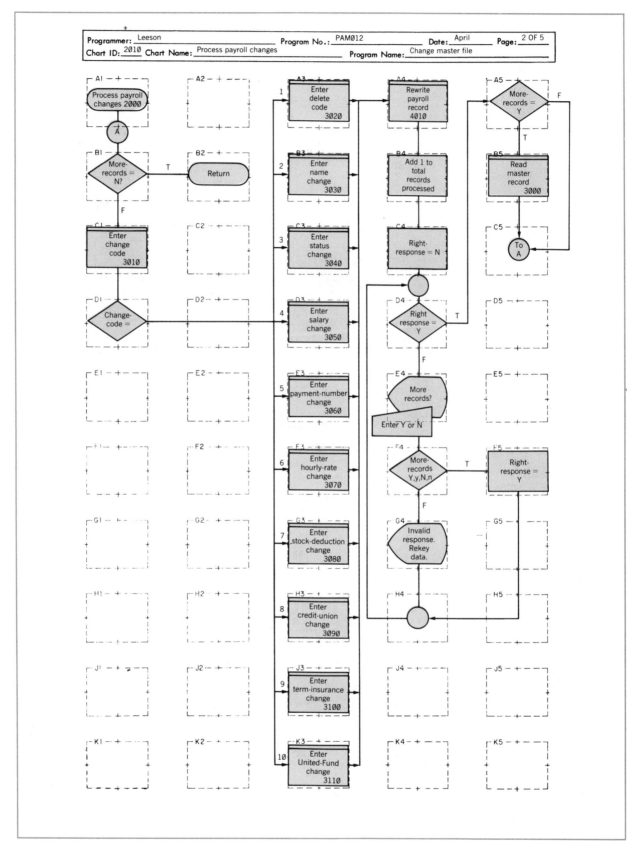

Figure 8–3 Part 2   *Flowchart for the change-master-file program.*

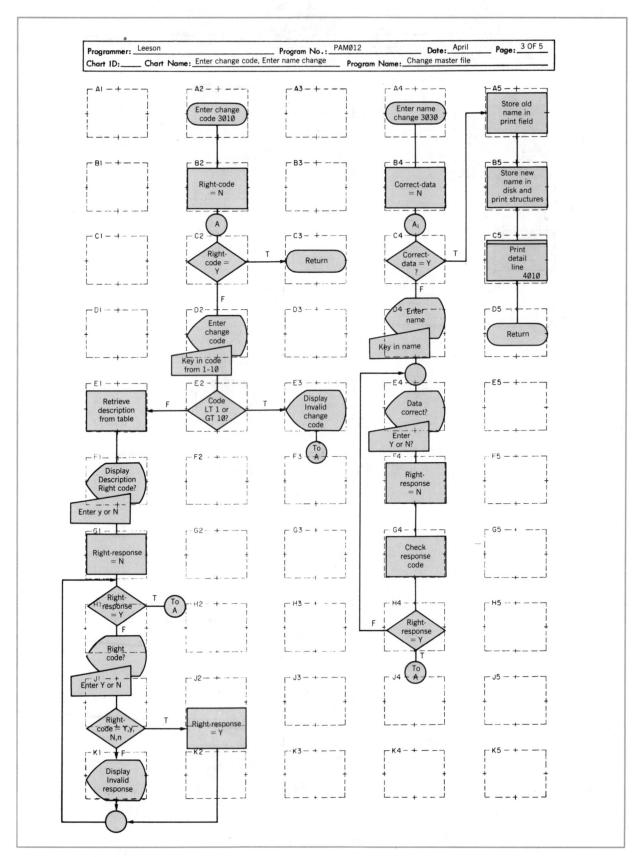

Figure 8–3 Part 3   *Flowchart for the change-master-file program.*

© SRA 1988, 1983

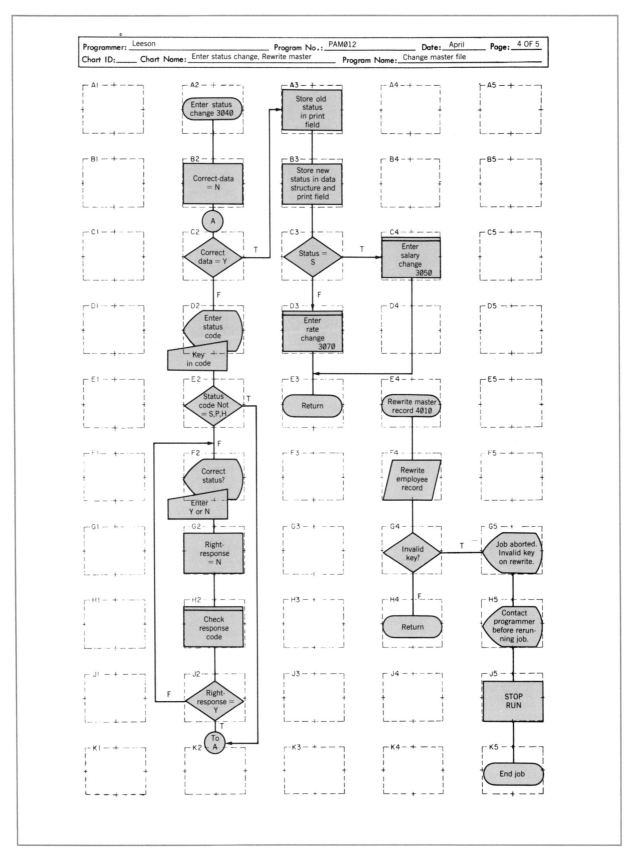

Figure 8–3 Part 4 *Flowchart for the change-master-file program.*

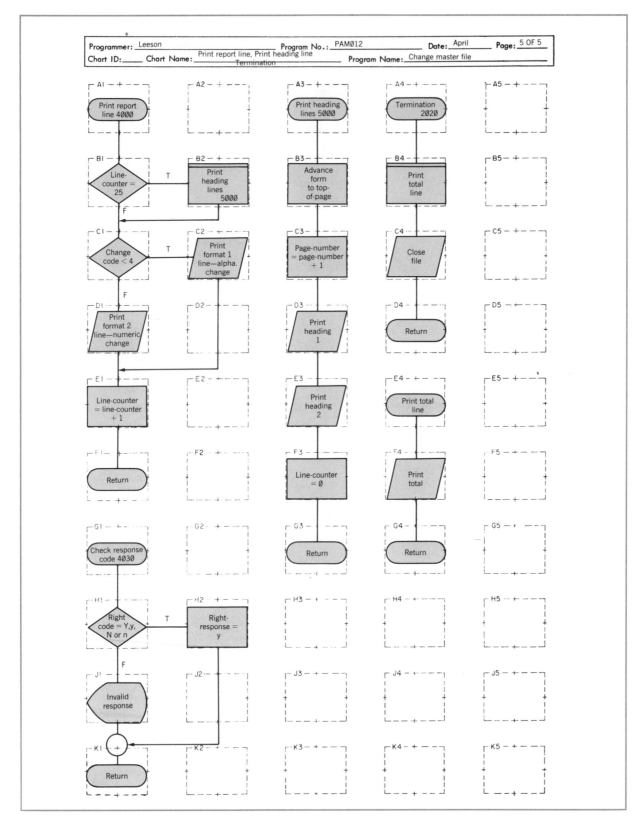

Figure 8–3 Part 5   *Flowchart for the change-master-file program.*

© SRA 1988, 1983

2. A table is used to store descriptions of the changes being made. Eleven titles will be stored within the table. When a new pledge is entered for United Fund, the number of installments must also be entered. When Table(11) is used in a print statement, the eleventh title prints as "U.F. Installments."

3. It is considered good practice to have a separate indicator to control each type of loop. The following indicators are used:

More-records. Initially a Y is stored within the field. After each change is made, the operator is asked "MORE CHANGES? Y OR N?" When the operator enters an **N,** control leaves the process-payroll-changes WHILE loop.

Right-record. Right-record is initially set to N. The operator keys in an employee number, a record is randomly retrieved from the master file, and the employee's name is displayed. The operator is asked "RIGHT RECORD?" If the operator enters a **Y,** control leaves the loop.

Right-code. The enter-change-code module is controlled by right-code. The operator keys in the change code, the description is retrieved from the table and displayed, and the operator is asked "RIGHT FIELD? Y OR N?". If a **Y** is entered, control leaves the loop and returns to the process-payroll-changes module.

Correct-data. Each of the 10 change modules has a WHILE statement controlled by correct-data. After the operator keys in the data for the change being made, DATA CORRECT? Y OR N? is displayed. If an **N** or **n** is entered, control remains in the WHILE loop, the prompts are displayed again, and the operator rekeys the data.

Right-response. Each time a response is entered it is checked to determine if a **Y, y, N,** or **n** was entered. Any other response will cause an error message to be displayed and the operator is given another chance to respond with either a **Y** or **N.**

4. When the print module is explained, the use of the print line fields will be covered in more depth.

READ-MASTER-RECORD MODULE   The read-master-record module, illustrated on Figure 8–4, Part 1, is composed of nested WHILE loops. The outer loop is controlled by right-record. Initially the indicator is set to N. If the operator enters a **Y** or **y** in response to the question RIGHT RECORD? Y OR N?, control returns to the module which invoked the read-master-record module. The inner WHILE loop checks the response entered by the operator to make certain it is either a **Y, y, N,** or **n.** If an invalid response is entered a message is displayed and the operator has an opportunity to rekey the response.

The pseudocode for the read-master-record module, illustrated in Figure 8–4, illustrates how the indicators are used and how the validity of the response to RIGHT RECORD? is checked.

PROVIDING DELAYS FOR READING SCREENS   You may wonder how you can provide a delay so that the operator can read the message before it is replaced with the prompt "RIGHT CODE? Y OR N?". A delay can be achieved in many different ways. One way is to write a statement that tells the operator to PRESS THE ENTER KEY or PRESS ANY KEY

Pseudocode for the Read-Master-Record Module

```
* Read-master-record module.
    Right-record = N
    DO WHILE (Right-record = N)
        DISPLAY 'Enter employee number.'
        ACCEPT employee number (key for random retrieval of record)
        Right-response = N
        READ payroll-master-file-record
            INVALID KEY
                DISPLAY 'Invalid key. Check employee number.'
                Right-response = Y
                PERFORM execute-invalid-key-routine
        DO WHILE (Right-response = N)
            DISPLAY employee's name from file and 'Right record? Y or N?'
            ACCEPT right-record
                IF Right-record = N,n,Y,or y THEN
                    Right-response = Y
                Else
                        DISPLAY invalid response.   Rekey data
                END IF
        END DO WHILE
    END DO WHILE
* END MODULE
```

Figure 8–4   Pseudocode for the read-master-record module.

TO CONTINUE. Until the operator presses a key, the information remains on the screen and the execution of the program is suspended. If available in the language being used, a **SLEEP** or **PAUSE statement** may be available. The length of time that the terminal is to "sleep" is provided in the SLEEP statement.

A third approach is to establish a loop that does nothing but consume time. For example, if you ran the Interactive Exercises you have observed that the SRA logo remains on the screen for a brief period of time. A loop created by coding FOR J = 1 TO 1000: NEXT J causes the pause to occur. Each time the loop is executed 1 is added to J and J is compared with 1000. When J is greater than 1000, control goes to the statement following NEXT J. The length of the delay created by using the statement is directly related to the internal speed of the computer being used. It might be necessary to execute the loop more than 1000 times. However, if the pause is much longer than it takes for the operator to read the message, the operator may respond negatively and it will take longer than necessary to enter the changes.

INVALID-KEY ROUTINE   If the payroll master file is an ISAM or VSAM file, an invalid-key routine should be established for both the read and the rewrite statements. The invalid-key routine for the READ statement should display a message and create a loop which permits a valid key to be entered and a record retrieved. When an invalid-key condition occurs on a REWRITE statement, a message should be displayed and the job aborted.

The source code for Interactive Exercise 8–1 was written in BASIC. Although random (direct) files are supported by the version of BASIC used,

© SRA 1988, 1983

```
                    Pseudocode for the Process-Payroll-Changes Module
*Process records module
 DO WHILE (More-records = Y)          (Indicator was set in initialization)
      PERFORM 3010-Enter-change-code
      ON change-code PERFORM              (Code was entered and confirmed)
          3020-Enter-delete-code
          3030-Enter-name-change
          3040-Enter-status-change
          3050-Enter-salary-change
          3060-Enter-payment-number-change
          3070-Enter-hourly-rate-change
          3080-Enter-stock-deduction-change
          3090-Enter-credit-union-change
          3100-Enter-term-insurance-change
          3110-Enter-United-Fund-change
      PERFORM 4010-Rewrite-payroll-record
      Right-response = N
      DO WHILE (Right-response = N)
          DISPLAY "More records? Y or N?"
          ENTER Y or N
          IF More-records = Y,y,N,or n THEN
              Right-response = Y
          ELSE
              DISPLAY "Invalid response.  Rekey data."
          END IF
      END DO WHILE
      IF More-records = Y or y THEN
          PERFORM 3000-Read-master-record
      ELSE
          NULL
      END IF
 END DO WHILE
 *End module
```

Figure 8–5   Pseudocode for the process-payroll-changes module.

ISAM or VSAM files are not supported. However, records can be retrieved randomly from a direct file. Since an index is not available, an invalid-key option is not available on READ or REWRITE statements. Therefore, the programmer needs to execute additional editing routines to make certain the employee number enter as the key is valid.

PROCESS PAYROLL CHANGES   Since records are randomly retrieved from the payroll master file, the end-of-file condition cannot be used to terminate the job. When the operator enters an **N** in response to MORE RECORDS? Y or N?, control leaves the outer WHILE loop. The inner WHILE loop is controlled by right-response. The pseudocode for the process-payroll-change module would be coded as illustrated in Figure 8–5.

ON STATEMENTS   Most programming languages permit users to use an ON statement rather than using the more typical IF/THEN/ELSE case entry statements. When an ON statement is used, the value of the field specified determines which *one* of the routines will be executed. In the example, if a **3** is entered by the operator as the change code, control goes to the third module specified (enter-status-change); if a **7** is entered, control goes to the seventh module specified (enter-stock-deduction-change). How ON statements are coded depends on the language being used. In BASIC, the line number of each module is used in the statement rather than the name of the module; in COBOL, the name of the module (called a paragraph name) is used.

PRINT REPORT LINE   Having a visual concept of the change report helps to provide a better understanding of how the program must be designed. When the report is printed, the data printed on the detail line comes from the following sources:

Field	Source
Number	Entered and confirmed by operator. It is also the key used to retrieve the employee's record.
Name	Retrieved from the payroll master file record.
Change Made	The change code entered by the operator is used to access the area of the table in which the description of the change is stored. It is also used in the ON statement to determine which change module will be executed.
Old Data	The information is retrieved from a field stored within the employee's record.
New Data	Keyed in and confirmed by the operator.

Since the data in the last two fields varies depending on the change being made, the data must be extracted from the employee's record and moved to the print field. The data keyed in is also moved to the print field. If the data were not moved into the print position within the change module being executed, a separate print format would be needed for each type of change made.

However, by using only two print formats, a substantial amount of coding is saved. Format 1 is used for the first three changes that require alphanumeric data to be printed in the last two print fields. Format 2 is used in printing the numeric changes made for codes 4–11. If COBOL is used, one print format can be established that redefines the alphanumeric fields as numeric. However, separate names are used for the alphanumeric and numeric fields. Where did code 11 come from? When an employee makes a new United Fund pledge, the U.F. installment field must also be changed.

By looking at the report, you will also note that when a status change from an H (hourly) to S (salaried) occurs, the enter-salary-change and enter-pay-

```
                          CHANGE REPORT            04-18-88           Page 1
    NUMBER      NAME        CHANGE MADE      OLD DATA           NEW DATA
      10    Long, George    Delete Code                        D
      20    Green, Mary     Employee Name    Green, Mary        Garcia, Mary
      30    Benson, George  Status Code      H                  S
      30    Benson, George  Salary Change              .00           36,345.67
      30    Benson, George  No. of Payments            .00               10.00

    TOTAL NUMBER OF RECORDS CHANGED:     3
```

Figure 8–6   Illustration of the payroll-master-file-change report.

© SRA 1988, 1983

ment-number-change modules are also executed. This is a good example of **interfield relationships** that should be considered when designing a program. Three lines will print on the report. However, only 1 is added to the total number of records changed field. Two other facts are illustrated by the report: alphanumeric data is aligned to the left of the print field and numeric data is aligned to the right of the print field. Most computer languages align data to be printed or displayed in that manner.

Since the report is an internal report to be used only to confirm the validity of the changes made to the payroll master file, the payroll department head would probably approve the report format. The report is designed for 8½″ × 11″ standard stock paper and the information printed on the report is easy to identify and read.

A TYPICAL CHANGE MODULE   Figure 8–3, Parts 3 and 4, on pages 284–285 illustrate what occurs in the enter-name-change and enter-status-change modules. The status change module is somewhat unique since it also invokes either the enter-salary-change or enter-hourly-change module. Also, since seven of the ten modules can use the same check-reponse routine, the check-response module is called rather than repeating the same code seven times.

The pseudocode illustrated in Figure 8–7 for the enter-hourly-rate-change is typical of the code needed for the other change modules. The pseudocode shows that not all of the statements are within the WHILE loop. Only after valid data is entered and confirmed will the data be stored in the master file record and moved to the print-old field.

The pseudocode for the check response routine is as follows:

```
*Check-response module
 IF correct-data NOT = Y, y, N, or n THEN
      position cursor
      DISPLAY invalid response
      cause delay to occur
 ELSE
      Right-response = Y
 END IF
* end module
```

If the operator had entered a valid response, when control returns to the invoking module, then right-response will be equal to Y. If the operator's response was incorrect, control remains in the DO-WHILE (right-response = N) loop.

Structured programming guidelines utilized in the change-master-file program

Sometimes it is wise to take stock of the goals in learning to design structured programs. Refer to Figure 1–6 on page 16 which lists the characteristics of a well-written program. If you were to list the source code developed for the change-master-file program, you would probably agree the program meets the characteristics specified.

One problem with using BASIC to code the programs is that the total length of a statement is somewhat limited. Therefore, some of the field names had to be shortened to code the statement describing the fields located within the payroll master file. Because hyphens or dashes are not permitted in field names, some of these are less readable and meaningful than they would be in another language.

Enter Hourly Rate Change

```
* Hourly Rate Change Module
    Change-code = 6                          (If this module was invoked by
                                             the enter-status-change
                                             module the change-code
                                             entered was a 3 and must be
                                             changed to a 6.)

    Correct-date = 'N'                       (Indicator is set so the loop
                                             will be executed at least once.)

    DO-WHILE (Correct-data = N)
        Clear screen
        Position cursor
        DISPLAY enter hourly rate
        ACCEPT new-amount                    (This will be moved to print
                                             field and to data structure.)

        Right-response = N
        DO-WHILE (Right-response = N)
            Position cursor
            DISPLAY data correct?   Y or N?
            ACCEPT response
            PERFORM check-response module    (If the response is valid, Right
        END DO-WHILE                         response is set to Y.)


        Print-old-field = MF-hourly-rate
        Print-new-field = new-amount
        MF-salary = 0
        MF-times = 0
        MF-hourly-rate = new-amount
        PERFORM 4000-Print-report-line
    END DO WHILE
* end of module
```

Figure 8–7   *Pseudocode for the enter-hourly-rate-change module.*

Controls built into the program

Editing will be discussed fully in the next chapter. However, at this point it seems wise to determine whether the program meets the requirement of building controls into the system (Figure 8–1). Controls built into the program are briefly summarized.

- The employee number is confirmed by displaying the employee's name on the VDT.

- The change code entered is verified by retrieving and displaying the description of the change.

- Whenever data is entered, the operator is asked to reply to RIGHT DATA? or a similar statement. The operator's response is checked to see that it is either a **Y, y, N,** or **n.**

- Each numeric field entered is checked to see that only the digits **0–9** are entered.

© SRA 1988, 1983

- Since only 10 change codes can be entered, an IF statement is used to determine if the code entered is greater than 0 and less than 11.

- Since a status code must be either a P, S, or H, an IF statement is used to determine if the code is a P, S, or H.

- Since there are only 26 pay periods a year, the number entered in the enter-payment-number-change module cannot be greater than 26.

- The statement NUMBER OF RECORDS UPDATED followed by the number is displayed as part of the termination routine. The number printed must agree with the total number of source documents submitted.

While the program was being coded and the code tested, stub testing was used. As each change module was added, the module was tested using valid and invalid data.

CHECKPOINT QUESTIONS

1. What are the seven types of programs required to maintain and protect a typical master file program?

2. Which of the programs specified in question 1 would be run in an interactive mode?

3. Why is it considered better to have a CHANGE and CORRECT program rather than combining the two programs into one?

4. When making changes in the payroll master file, how much data will be keyed in by the operator?

5. By studying the specifications for the program and the program flowchart, determine the approach used in developing the CHANGE program.

6. Why are the descriptions of the changes stored in a table?

7. If the operator enters change codes ranging from **1–10,** why are eleven titles stored in the table?

8. What occurs when an operator keys in an invalid response to the message MORE RECORDS? Y OR N?

9. What three techniques may be used to provide a delay so that the operator can read the information displayed on the screen?

10. Assuming that the operator entered a **2** in the change-code field, what module would be executed when the following ON statement was executed?

    ON change-code
        salary-change, stock-deduction-change, name-change.

11. What alternative method can be used to code the pseudocode statement illustrated in question 10?

12. Contrast how alphanumeric and numeric fields are justified.

13. Five fields of data were printed in each detail line of the change-master-file report. Where did each field of data originate?

14. Of what value is the printed report? What will occur if someone detects an error on the report, such as that Sam Smith's new pay rate is incorrect?

15. In reviewing the program specifications, flowcharts, and pseudocode provided for the CHANGE program, would you recommend that the content of any of the modules be changed? For example, you might recommend that the United Fund module be divided into two separate modules.

16. What controls are built into the CHANGE program?

CORRECTING THE PAYROLL MASTER FILE RECORDS

The CORRECT (correct-master-file) program would be similar to the CHANGE program. Since the program is designed to correct the quarterly and year-to-date totals, more data will be keyed in by the operator. Although more data is recorded on each of the two formatted screens, fewer modules are needed. Assuming that an ISAM or VSAM file is being used, the program should provide for an invalid key condition. Figure 8–8 illustrates the program specifications and 8–9 the hierarchy chart for the correct-master-file program.

In designing the program, the programmer or analyst must keep in mind that a computer works algebraically. In the example A = 1000 and B = −300, if the statement A = A + B is executed within the program, A will equal 700. When a command to add is given and one of the fields is negative, the smaller number is subtracted from the larger and the answer carries the sign of the larger.

The source document must indicate if the field to be entered is positive or negative. In absence of a sign, the field entering a computer will be stored as a positive value. If a negative amount is to be entered a minus sign (−) must

Figure 8–8 Specifications for the correct-payroll-records program.

<table>
<tr><td colspan="2" align="center">CORRECT MASTER FILE</td></tr>
<tr><td colspan="2">**Output**</td></tr>
<tr><td>Updated master file records</td><td>Records are retrieved randomly, updated, and rewritten into the payroll master file.</td></tr>
<tr><td>Confirmation report</td><td>A separate report, listing the employee's name and number and both the incorrect and correct quarterly and year-to-date totals, is printed for each correction.</td></tr>
<tr><td colspan="2">**Input**</td></tr>
<tr><td>Master file records</td><td>The employee's number is entered as the key and used to randomly retrieve the required record.</td></tr>
<tr><td>Data keyed in by an operator</td><td>Formatted screens must be used that provide a prompt and the size of each field. Separate screens should be provided for the quarterly and year-to-date corrections.</td></tr>
<tr><td colspan="2">**Controls**</td></tr>
<tr><td colspan="2">The data entered by the operator must be visually verified. If any field is incorrect an opportunity must be provided to make the necessary change. The printed report will be submitted to the payroll department for confirmation that the necessary corrections were made.</td></tr>
</table>

© SRA 1988, 1983

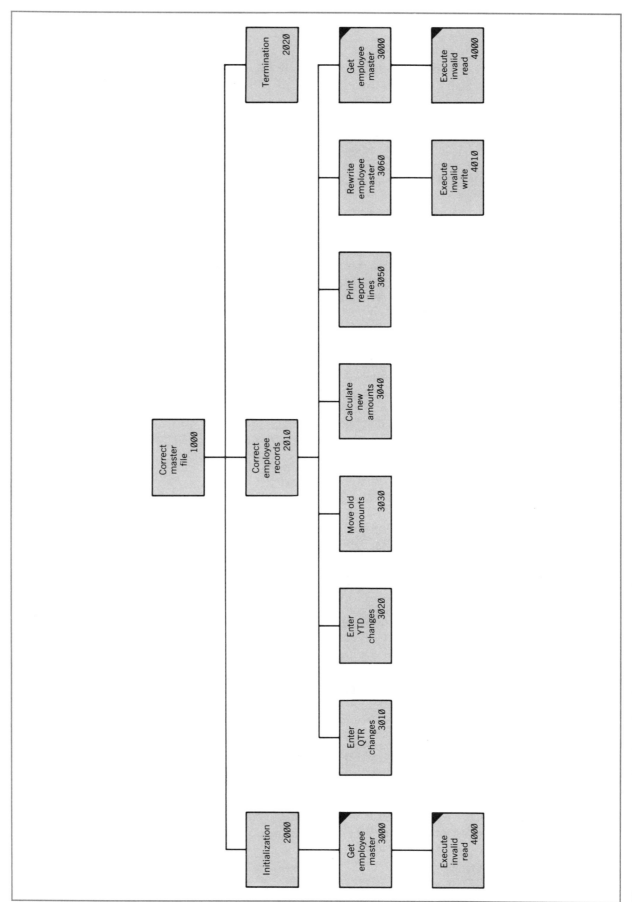

Figure 8–9 Hierarchy chart for the correct-master-file program.

precede the number. An operator keys in -300.00 to represent a negative 300. This is an important factor in designing the correct-master-file program.

The analyst might feel that requiring a minus sign to precede a negative amount could cause problems. In this case, the program could be designed so that the correct value—rather than the amount of the correction—would be entered for each field. The correct value would then replace the value stored in the field. If only the amount of the adjustment to a field is entered, less data will need to be keyed in by the operator. For example, only the gross pay and FICA need to be adjusted. Zeroes will be entered in the remainder of the fields, and the statements to add the value entered from the terminal to the value stored in the master file record can still be used.

Hierarchy chart for the correct-master-file program

All the techniques necessary to develop a detailed logic plan for the CORRECT program have been presented. It is important to realize that another analyst might develop a hierarchy chart somewhat different from the one illustrated. The primary objectives for any program are to produce valid output, to provide a user-friendly environment for the operator, to keep the amount of data that must be entered to a minimum, to provide as many internal program controls as possible, and to create a program that is easy to maintain.

Earlier in the text, it was suggested that the tasks a program must accomplish should be listed. The next step is to group the tasks into modules and determine the sequence in which the tasks must be accomplished. Assuming this was done, the analyst has determined that the modules illustrated in Figure 8–9 will be needed. A brief explanation will be provided for some of the modules. For this program, the main control and initialization modules require no explanation.

GET EMPLOYEE MASTER   In the get-employee-master module, the screen will be cleared and a prompt displayed for the operator to enter the employee's number for whom the record must be retrieved. A read statement is used to obtain the record. If an invalid key condition occurs after the entry of an employee number not in the index, an error routine must be provided.

If a record is obtained, the name of the employee will be displayed and the operator asked RIGHT RECORD? Y OR N?. The operator's response must be checked to make certain it is either a **Y, y, N,** or **n.** The WHILE loop is controlled by the indicator right-record. Until the operator responds with a **Y** or **y** to the question RIGHT RECORD? Y OR N?, control remains in the WHILE loop.

ENTER QTR CHANGES AND ENTER YTD CHANGES   Refer to Figure 7–3 (page 239–240) and determine the quarterly and year-to-date fields that may need to be corrected. The screen for the quarterly changes displays four prompts while the year-to-date screen displays eight prompts. Screen layout forms are available that can be used to indicate where the prompt will be displayed and where the data will be entered. The form usually provides for 25 rows and 80 columns. If forms are not available, a print layout form can be used. As illustrated in Figure 8–10, the print layout form provides the line number (row) and the horizontal position (column). In looking at the design, you can see that the first prompt will be printed on row 7, column 11. In positioning cursors, the first number is always the row and the second the column.

© SRA 1988, 1983

Figure 8–10 Screen design for quarterly-total corrections.

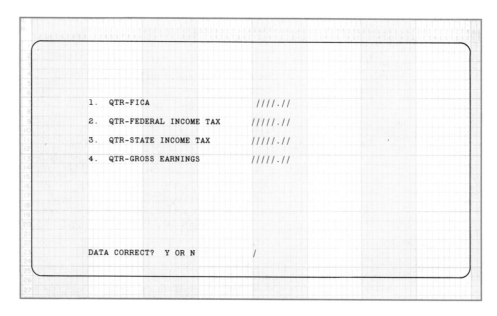

```
1.   QTR-FICA                    /////.//

2.   QTR-FEDERAL INCOME TAX      /////.//

3.   QTR-STATE INCOME TAX        /////.//

4.   QTR-GROSS EARNINGS          /////.//



     DATA CORRECT?  Y OR N            /
```

The technique usually used is to display the entire screen. The cursor is then repositioned to where the first field of data is to be entered (row 7, column 42). After the answer is keyed in, visually confirmed, and the enter key pressed, the cursor moves to row 9, column 41.

The operator's response to DATA CORRECT? Y OR N must be checked. If the response is **Y** or **y,** the WHILE loop controlled by valid-data will not be executed. If the operator responds with **N** or **n,** the operator is asked which field is wrong and must answer with a 1, 2, 3, or 4. The digit keyed in is stored in a field called ANSWER. An IF/THEN/ELSE statement, similar to the one illustrated in Figure 8–11, is coded within the loop to determine where the cursor will be positioned so that the operator can rekey the data. If ANSWER is not equal to 1, 2, 3, or 4, the default option is executed. Figure 8–11 illustrated how the pseudocode for the IF/THEN/ELSE statement would be coded.

Figure 8–11 Pseudocode for entering the correct amount to change a quarterly total.

```
            PSEUDOCODE FOR THE IF/THEN/ELSE STATEMENT
IF answer = 1 THEN
   position cursor to 7,42
   ACCEPT qtr-fica-amount
ELSE IF answer = 2 THEN
        position cursor to 9,41
        ACCEPT qtr-federal-income-tax amount
     ELSE IF answer = 3 THEN
             position cursor to 11,41
             ACCEPT qtr-state-income-tax amount
          ELSE IF answer = 4 THEN
                  position cursor to 13,41
                  ACCEPT qtr-gross-earnings amount
               ELSE
                  DISPLAY 'INVALID ANSWER.'
                  VALID-ANSWER = N
END IF
```

Figure 8–12 Pseudocode for the enter-QTR-change module.

```
            PSEUDOCODE FOR ENTER QTR CHANGE

*Enter-qtr-data module
 FORMAT screen
 Position cursor
 Enter data
 Right-response = N
 DO WHILE (right-response = N)
     DISPLAY data correct?  Y or N?
     ACCEPT valid-data
     IF valid-data NOT = Y, y, N, or n THEN
          position cursor
          DISPLAY 'invalid response.  rekey response'
          cause delay for message to be read
     ELSE
          right-response = Y
     END IF
 END DO WHILE
 DO-WHILE (valid-data = N or valid-data = n)
     DISPLAY 'Enter number of field to be corrected.'
     ACCEPT answer
     IF/THEN/ELSE statement to determine where to position
          cursor and what data is to be entered.
     DISPLAY data-correct? Y or N?
     ACCEPT valid-data
     IF valid-data NOT = N, n, Y, OR y THEN
          Valid-data = N
   END DO WHILE
   * end of module
```

If the operator responds with a valid number, the cursor returns to the locations where the incorrect data was entered. Once the cursor is at the correct location, the data can be rekeyed by the operator. Some analysts might wish to add more code so that the old data is replaced by the correct number of slashes and then reposition the cursor so that the data may be entered. Control must remain in the correct-data-loop until all the necessary corrections have been made.

PSEUDOCODE FOR ENTER QTR CHANGE   The pseudocode in Figure 8–12 illustrates the general concepts of the Enter-qtr-data module. Control will remain in the first WHILE loop until a **Y, y, N,** or **n** is entered in response to the message DATA CORRECT? Y or N? The answer in response to DATA CORRECT? is stored in the valid-data field which controls the second WHILE loop.

An experienced analyst once remarked that anywhere from 40 to 50 percent of the source code required for a program is devoted to providing controls, editing, and other types of error detection. Experienced operators who are well-trained and conscientious seldom make mistakes. However, it is far less costly and time consuming to correct an error before it enters the system than after it results in invalid information being stored in a file, printed as part of a report, or worse yet, producing invalid paychecks.

PRINT REPORT   The report, illustrated Figure 8–13, must be printed *before* the master file record is rewritten. If the report were printed after the record was

© SRA 1988, 1983

```
                    PAYROLL MASTER FILE CORRECTION REPORT      MAR-27-1988
     EMPLOYEE NAME:    James Brown              Employee Number:   1245


                    FIELD NAME              OLD AMOUNT         CORRECTED AMOUNT
     QTR-FICA WITHHELD                         630.42                560.52
     QTR-FEDERAL WITHHOLDING TAX             1,325.67              1,242.57
     QTR-STATE WITHHOLDING TAX                 110.00                 99.67
     QTR-GROSS EARNINGS                     11,367.89             10,487.19
     YTD-FICA WITHHELD                         630.42                560.52
     YTD-FEDERAL WITHHOLDING TAX             1,325.67              1,242.57
     YTD-STATE WITHHOLDING TAX                 110.00                 99.67
     YTD-GROSS EARNINGS                     11,367.89             10,487.19
     YTD-STOCK DEDUCTION                       300.00                300.00
     YTD-CREDIT UNION DEDUCTION                250.00                200.00
     YTD-TERM-INSURANCE                         48.00                 48.00
     YTD-UNITED FUND CONTRIBUTION               60.00                 60.00



     REPORT CONFIRMED BY:    _____


                             _____
                                              Date
```

Figure 8–13   Payroll master file correction report.

rewritten, only the corrected values would be available. The incorrect amounts are replaced with the value calculated as follows:

MF-QTR-FICA = MF-QTR-FICA + TR-QTR-FICA-AMOUNT

The field called MF-QTR-FICA is retrieved from the master file record, updated by performing the arithmetic operation, and restored to its proper location within the data structure. Therefore, the following sequence of events must occur in order to print the report:

1. Advance to top-of-form
2. PRINT heading line and data   (Format 1)
3. PRINT line with employee's name and number   (Format 2)
4. PRINT captions for column headings   (Format 3)
5. MOVE "QTR-FICA-WITHHELD" to print-account-title
6. MOVE MF-QTR-FICA to print-old-amount
7. MF-QTR-FICA = MF-QTR-FICA + TR-QTR-FICA-AMOUNT
8. MF-QTR-FICA to print-new-amount
9. PRINT detail line   (Format 4)

The statements illustrated in lines 5 through 9 would be repeated, using different field names, for each of the quarterly and year-to-date print lines. Print-account-title, print-old-amount, and print-new-amount are the names of the fields that are established in the format 4 print line.

Note that in some cases the amounts were not changed. Also because the change is for the first quarter, the quarter and year-to-date amounts are the same.

Since an entire page is printed for each record corrected, it is not necessary to maintain a line-counter or to increment a page number.

REWRITE EMPLOYEE MASTER   Since the new amount had to be calculated for the report, the new values are already stored in the master file data structure. In the rewrite-employee-record module, all that remains to be done is to write the record out to disk and to provide for an invalid-key routine. If an invalid-key condition occurs, a message for the programmer should be printed and the job aborted.

ADDING NEW EMPLOYEES TO THE PAYROLL MASTER FILE

If the original master file was created by keying in data from a terminal, only a slight modification in the program is needed to create the add-new-employee program (ADDNEW). The way the WRITE statement is constructed is one of the few changes that must be made. If a new employee's number is the same as one that already exists in the file, an invalid-key condition will occur. A message will be printed and the information will need to be rekeyed using a unique number for the new employee.

Since, in the payroll example, the file was created using data stored in the old master file, a new program must be written. The specifications for the report are illustrated in Figure 8–14.

Although it depends on the size and type of organization, on a week-to-week basis very few new employees are hired. In seasonal industries there will be periods throughout the year when a number of temporary employees are hired. This might occur in a canning factory or in a large retail store during holiday seasons. Comparing the data written on the source document with the information displayed on the VDT is much better than printing a report. If the data displayed is correct, it has to be recorded correctly in the record. However, a full report listing the data entered might agree with the source documents, while the information displayed directly from a new employee's record might disagree due to a programming error. If the program is well tested, this should not occur.

Initialization and enter data modules

Refer to Figure 7–3 on pages 239–240, and determine what fields of data must be entered. Fields that need not be keyed in can be set to their proper value in the initialization module. Looking at the fields listed on Figure 7–3, the following fields can either be set to blank or zero: delete code, termination date, stock balance, stock total, stock shares, the United Fund fields, and all of the quarterly and year-to-date fields. With those fields eliminated, the screens designed will need to provide for entering twenty-four fields of data. Although only one module is shown on the hierarchy chart, three screens should be designed.

© SRA 1988, 1983

Figure 8–14
Specifications for the
ADDNEW program.

SPECIFICATIONS FOR THE ADD-NEW-EMPLOYEES PROGRAM

Output

Payroll master file records | The records will be added to the existing file.

Printed report | The report will list each employee's number and name. The total number of employees added to the file will be printed at the bottom of the report.

Visual display of prompts | A prompt indicating the name and size of each field.

Input

Data keyed in by the operator. | After each screen is displayed and the data entered, the operator must confirm each field visually.

Controls

Visual confirmation of data keyed in by the operator. The relationships that exist among the fields and the data stored within each field must be evaluated in order to determine what additional editing can occur.

The printed report will be sent, along with the new employee source documents, to the payroll department employee responsible for filling out the source documents. Using the numbers listed on the report, the DISPLAY program will be run. The information displayed on the formatted screen will be compared with the data listed on each of the source documents.

Figure 8–15 Hierarchy
chart for the add-new-
employees program.

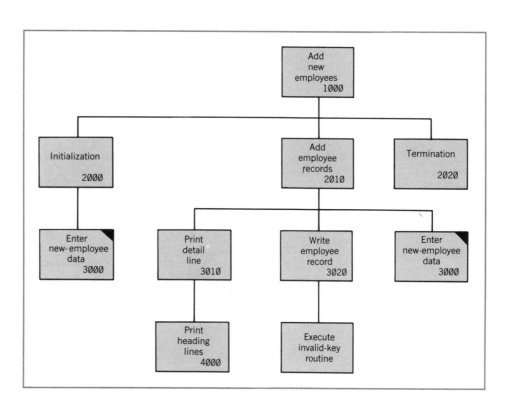

The technique used in verifying and correcting the data would be identical to the logic illustrated for the CORRECT program.

Also, depending on the language being used, the data keyed in by the operator may be entered directly into its field within the payroll master file structure.

Other modules

The hierarchy chart is typical of many interactive programs that are used to enter data, print a report, and either update existing records or create new records. If the data is entered and used to create a sequential file that will be used in a second program to update the master file records, an invalid-key module will not be needed in the original program.

MASTER FILE UPDATE PROGRAM

The payroll transaction file created when the payroll register program was run contains all of the data relating to the current payroll period. Very little data was keyed as most of the data in the transaction file was either calculated or transfered from the payroll master file.

The records stored within the sequential transaction file contain the employee's gross pay, voluntary deductions, and deductions for taxes and FICA. The transaction file may also contain some year-to-date information that will be needed when the paychecks are printed. Once the validity of the information printed on the payroll register is determined, the transaction file will be

Figure 8–16
Specifications for the
payroll UPDATE
program.

SPECIFICATIONS FOR THE PAYROLL-UPDATE PROGRAM

Output

Updated master file records   The selected data from the transaction file records will be added to the master file records.

Input

Transaction file   The records stored within the transaction file are in sequence by employee number and the file is organized as a sequential file.

Master file   Since a large percentage of the records have corresponding transaction file records, the records will be accessed sequentially.

Controls

After all of the transaction file records are processed, a statement MASTER FILE UPDATED ON MMM-DD-YYYY will be printed along with the statement TOTAL NUMBER OF RECORDS UPDATED: xxxxx. The number of records updated must agree with the total number of employees listed on the payroll register and the number of checks printed.

The updated payroll master file is used to print the payroll summary. The summary totals must agree with the previous payroll summary totals *plus* the total printed on the payroll register.

When the master file is updated, a **"lock"** must be placed on the records so that they cannot be updated again until after the file is backed up and recreated.

© SRA 1988, 1983

used to print the paychecks. The transaction file will also be used as input for the payroll UPDATE program that adds the current values stored in the transaction records to the payroll master file records. The specifications for the programs are provided in Figure 8–16.

Hierarchy chart for the payroll update program

Since a large percentage of the records stored in the master file will be updated, the records in the master file will be accessed sequentially. Although it might be possible to have an unmatched transaction file record, in the payroll update program this should never occur. Remember, the transaction file was created during the execution of the payroll register program and the records within the transaction file are in the same sequence as the payroll master file records.

As illustrated in the flowchart (Figure 8–18), when a transaction record is read, the indicator read-trans is set to N. Until there is a match, another transaction record will not be read. When a match occurs and the update-employee-master module is invoked, read-trans is reset to Y. The job will be terminated when the end of the transaction file is detected. When this occurs, read-master indicator is set to N so that additional master file records will not be read.

When the master file records are rewritten, the word LOCK is moved into a field called L$. In the initialization module, once the first master file record has been read, an IF statement is used to determine if L$ is equal to "LOCK". If the condition is true, the job is terminated because the file has already been updated. In each pay period, the payroll master file update program can only be run once. If the file was updated twice, the employee's year-to-date and quarterly totals would be incorrect. When the file is backed up and recreated, the lock is removed by moving spaces into the lock field.

Figure 8–17 Hierarchy chart for the payroll-update program.

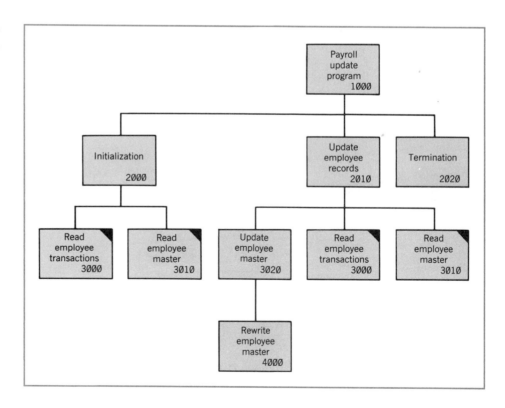

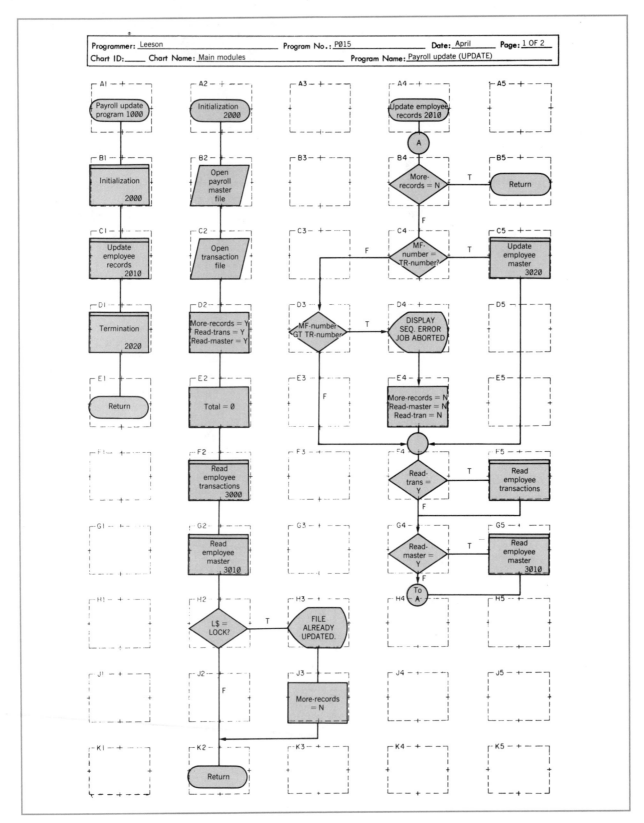

Figure 8–18 Part 1   Flowchart for the payroll-update program.

© SRA 1988, 1983

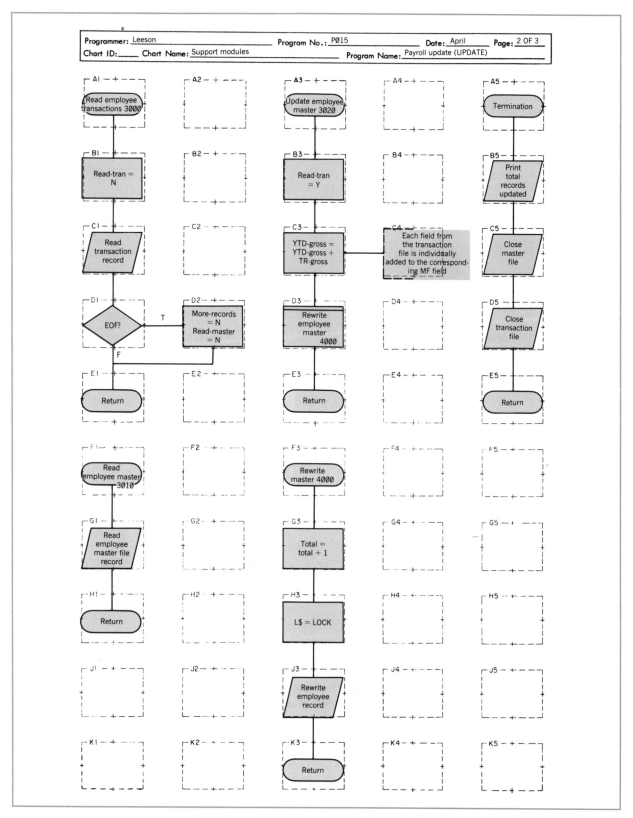

Figure 8–18 Part 2 Flowchart for the payroll-update program.

Figure 8–19 System flowchart for the backup and recreate programs.

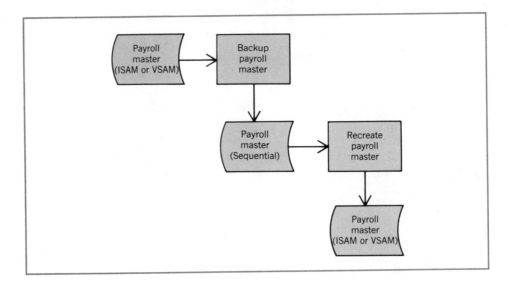

BACKING UP AND RECREATING THE PAYROLL MASTER FILE

When the file is backed up, two files are described and opened. The data in either an ISAM or VSAM file is read into its data structure located within the memory of the computer. The record is then recorded in a sequentially organized file. When the new file is created, the blocking factor may be changed. Since indexes are not required, less space is required to store records in a sequential file than in a VSAM or ISAM file. While backing up the file, *changes should not be made in any of the records.*

In many installations an additional backup file may be created and stored in an offsite location. If an organization loses a file that is not backed up, it is time consuming and expensive to recreate the file. In many organizations today it would be a disaster if the master files and databases were destroyed.

Recreating the master file

In most installations a utility program is available that can be used to back up files. When the file is recreated, changes may be made in the file that make it necessary to write a program designed to recreate the file. Pseudocode is provided in Figure 8–20 to show how the initialization and recreate-master-file modules might be constructed.

If the quarter-number is greater than zero, the quarterly totals will be set to zero. Also if the quarter-number is equal to 4, the year-to-date totals as well as some additional fields will be reset to zero. These changes cannot be made until the final payroll summary and some of the other year-end reports are printed. If the reports are not printed before the first pay period of the following year, the changes will be made and an additional master file will be created from the year-end backup file. The same program can be used as long as zero is entered in the quarter-number field and a new name and location on disk is provided for the file.

The two tasks, backing up the original master file and creating the new master file, may be run as one job. The batch job will require the execution of two separate programs. Whenever changes are made in the master file records, the file should be backed up. Therefore, a separate job will also be set up that will only back up the file. Although the backup and backup/recreate programs

© SRA 1988, 1983

PSEUDOCODE FOR THE INITIALIZATION AND RECREATE-MASTER-FILE MODULES

```
*Initialization module
 OPEN sequential backup file
 OPEN ISAM or VSAM file
 More-records = Y
 DISPLAY 'If last pay in quarter enter a 1,2,3, or 4 else enter a 0'
 Valid-quarter-number = N
 DO WHILE (valid-quarter-number = N)
     ACCEPT quarter-number
     If quarter-number < 0 OR quarter-number > 4 THEN
         DISPLAY 'Invalid quarter number. Reenter data.'
     ELSE
         valid-quarter-number = Y
     END IF
     END DO
 PERFORM read-master-backup

*End Initialization module

*Backup-employee-master module
 DO-WHILE (more-records = Y)
     IF quarter-number > 0 THEN
         PERFORM Quarterly-change-routine
     ELSE
         NULL
     END IF
     IF quarter-number = 4 THEN
         PERFORM Yearly-change-routine
     ELSE
         NULL
     IF delete-code = ' ' THEN
         PERFORM write-master-backup
     ELSE IF year-to-date-salary > 0 THEN
             PERFORM  write-master-backup
         ELSE
             NULL
     END IF
     PERFORM read-master-backup
 END DO
 * End update-employee-master module
```

Figure 8–20 Pseudocode for the initialization and recreate-master-file modules.

are batch jobs, they may be initiated from a terminal by a member of the payroll department. If this is the case, the jobs would be described as remote-batch jobs.

CHECKPOINT QUESTIONS

17. If only twelve items need to be corrected, why are two screen formats used?

18. What occurs when a negative number is added to a positive value?

19. In the CORRECT program, when will an invalid-key condition occur when an attempt is made to read a record?

20. Why should the operator's response to a question such as RIGHT RECORD? Y OR N? be checked?

21. Why is it important that errors are detected before incorrect data is incorporated into a report or added to a file?

22. Why should a detail line be printed on the report before the master file record is rewritten?

23. Why is a separate page printed for each correction made to a payroll master file record?

24. When the ADDNEW program is executed, is the operator required to key in data for all of the fields described on the file specification form?

25. Why is a "lock" placed on the payroll master file after the records are updated to include the values stored in the payroll transaction file?

26. Since a new transaction record is to be read only when a "match" occurs, how is the read-trans indicator used to control the reading of transaction records?

27. What occurs when the end-of-file condition is detected on the transaction file?

28. How would you describe the UPDATE program?

29. How is the job aborted when the TR-employee number is smaller than the MF-employee number?

30. Why is a program usually developed to recreate the payroll master file rather than using a utility program?

31. Under what conditions will a record in the old master file not be included in the new master file?

32. What occurs at the end of the fourth quarter?

33. What is the difference between a batch job and a remote-batch job?

SUMMARY

- Programs must be available to add new records to the file, change existing records, correct records, add fields, update data by adding values stored in a transaction file, back up the file, and recreate the master file.

- Each program should be evaluated to determine if it should be executed in an interactive transaction-processing or batch mode. Remotely located terminals are often used for making changes, corrections, and additions to a master file or database.

- If a field can be checked for a numeric value, an ON statement may be used in place of a compound IF/THEN/ELSE statement. In the statement "ON code 5000, 6000, 3000" control branches to 5000 if code is equal to 1, to 6000 if code is equal to 2, and to 3000 if code is equal to 3.

- Separate indicators should be used to control each type of loop. For example, more-records controls process-records, and correct-data controls the loop used to check the validity of the operator's response.

- In order to provide time for the operator to read information displayed on the screen, several techniques can be used. A sleep or pause statement can

© SRA 1988, 1983

be used, a response from an operator may be required, or a loop created for the sole purpose of consuming time.

- A single print format may be used to print different information. Before printing the line, the required information, either constants or variables, is moved into predetermined print fields.

- Whenever data enters the computer and is used in calculations or as part of a report, file, or database, every precaution should be taken to make certain it is correct. Each field of data should be analyzed to determine how it can be validated.

- Computers work algebraically. When a negative value is added to a positive value, the smaller field is subtracted from the larger. The resulting answer carries the sign of the larger field.

- Unless preceded by a minus sign, data entering the computer is treated as a positive value.

- When the data structure is defined for the program designed to add new records to an existing file, zeroes can be moved into fields such as the year-to-date or quarterly total fields. Only the variable fields that differ from record to record need to be keyed in by an operator.

- When formatted screens are used, the entire format is usually displayed. The cursor is then positioned at each location where data must be entered. After all of the required data is displayed, the operator is asked to check its validity. An opportunity must be provided to correct data which was entered incorrectly.

- When new employees are added to an existing ISAM or VSAM file, an invalid-key condition occurs if a key which is already in the index is entered for a new employee.

- When data stored in a transaction file is used to update a master file, both files are usually accessed sequentially. When a match occurs, the master file is updated, rewritten to disk, and both a transaction and master file are read. When the end-of-file condition is detected for the transaction file, the job is terminated.

- When backing up a file, changes should not be made to the information stored within the records.

- Often two copies are made of an existing master file. One is stored onsite and the other stored in an offsite location.

- When recreating a file from the backup copy, records flagged for deletion can be omitted and year-to-date or quarterly totals fields can be reset to zero.

DISCUSSION QUESTIONS

1. In regard to the amount of data entered, the type of data entered, and the frequency with which the program is run, contrast the CHANGE and CORRECT programs.

2. When a field of data is entered, how does the computer know which field is to be changed? How does the operator determine that the right field will be changed?

3. In the CHANGE program, why should the relationships that exist between fields be determined?

4. In the ADDNEW program, 24 fields of data must be keyed in by the operator. Why is it a good idea to develop three formatted screens? What general technique is used to display the format, enter the data, and check the validity of the data keyed in by an operator?

5. A programming student remarked "If data is visually verified by the operator, there is no need to utilize other editing methods." Tell why you agree or disagree with the statement.

6. A manager who is unfamiliar with electronic data processing methods and procedures remarked "If the data used to create the master file is correct, it is unnecessary to run any of the maintenance programs." Tell why you agree or disagree with his statements.

7. Why were both the CHANGE and CORRECT programs run in an interactive mode and the master file accessed randomly?

8. In the CORRECT program why was it necessary to execute the print-report module before the rewrite-disk module?

9. Why is a two-task job executed when an ISAM or VSAM is recreated? Why aren't changes made when the sequential backup file is created?

10. For the sales/accounts receivable/inventory system, an accounts receivable and inventory master file must be online whenever any of the interactive sales programs are executed. Describe the maintenance programs that should be available and when they should be executed.

KEY WORDS

code	ON statement
control	PAUSE statement
interfield relationships	SLEEP statement

© SRA 1988, 1983

EXERCISE 8-1

Using the information provided concerning the payroll master file specifications in Figure 7–3, pages 239–240, and the information concerning the CORRECT program provided in this chapter, complete the following tasks:

1. Develop the layouts for the two formatted screens needed to display the prompts and input the required data.
2. Develop a detailed logic plan for the CORRECT program. In developing the logic plan, use one statement such as "Display Prompts" and a second one, "Enter Data," rather than describing each prompt and response. Use a loop and enter the amounts keyed into column one of a table that has 12 rows and 3 columns. Move the old amount from the master file into column two and the corrected amount into column three.

PROBLEM 8-1

Review the information in the text regarding the organization's stock deduction plan and the fields pertaining to the plan that are in the master file. After the master file is updated, the STOCK program is run to determine the number of shares that can be purchased for each employee who participates in the plan. The following specifications are to be used in developing the program:

Output

Updated master file records	The number of new shares purchased is added to the stock-shares field and the cost of the stock is subtracted from the stock-balance field.
Report	The stock-purchased report should list the name and number of the employee, the number of new shares purchased, the total shares the employee has, the old and new balance in the stock-balance field, the total value of the stock, and the total amount invested in the plan. The total number of shares purchased and the total market value of the stock are to be printed after all of the data is processed.

Input

Current value of the stock	The current market value of the stock is used to determine how many shares can be purchased, the current balance of the stock-balance field, and the current value of the employee's contribution to the plan.
Master file records	Although stock may not be purchased for all employees participating in the plan, each employee's record must be read in order to determine the status of their stock accounts. Only employees for whom stock is purchased will be listed on the report.

Controls

   Determine the validity of the market value of the stock entered by the operator.

Directions

1. Develop a print layout form for the stock deduction report.
2. Develop a hierarchy chart and a detailed logic plan for the stock deduction program.

INTERACTIVE EXERCISE 8-1

The specifications for the payroll CHANGE program are described in the text and a flowchart is available that illustrates the logic of some of the modules. In studying the interrelationships that exist between fields, it was determined that whenever a change in status occurs, either the salary or hourly rate field must also be changed. Also, whenever a salary is changed, the number of installments over which the salary will be paid must be entered. When a United Fund pledge is entered, the number of installments must also be entered.

When a status change occurs, control automatically branches to either the rate-change or salary-change module. This reduces the possibility of errors and saves rekeying the employee number and change code.

In the program, line-counter was initially set to 5. Each time it equals 5, the headings will be reprinted.

Directions

1. Before you load BASICA, copy the payroll master file to the student file by entering:

   COPY PAY2.DAT   STUDENT.DAT

   PAY2.DAT contains the six payroll master file records that have the original data plus the data entered when the ADDSTOCK program was executed. Since you no longer need the previous version of STUDENT.DAT you will replace it with a complete version of the payroll master file. STUDENT.DAT will be used in the CHANGE program. Your program diskette must be on drive A.

2. Load **BASICA.** Mount the program diskette.

3. Load **MENU.** Select menu **4,** option **22.**

4. Testing the program with valid data. Until you have entered all the data listed below, enter a **Y** in response to the question MORE CHANGES? Make the following changes:

Employee Number	Change Code	Data	
1	2	**Garcia, Jean**	
2	6	**17.425**	(Increase in pay)
3	8	**30.00**	(Increased deduction)
4	3	Status:	**S**
		Salary:	**33000.00**
		Pay Periods:	**26**
5	7	stock deduction	**20.00**
6	1	"D" is automatically entered for the delete code.	
1	4	Salary:	**27500.00**
		Pay Periods:	**26**
2	10	Pledge amount	**500**
		Installments	**10**

In response to MORE DATA? enter **N.**

Enter **N** in response to RETURN TO MAIN MENU? because you will execute the CHANGE program again to list some of the source code.

5. Testing the program with invalid data and responses. Enter **RUN** and enter the following data:

Employee Number	Change Code	Data	
1	13	Correct to a **4**	
		Salary:	35700
		Pay periods:	26
		In response to DATA CORRECT? enter a **Z.** Correct by entering **Y.**	
1	2	In response to RIGHT RECORD? enter a **T;** correct by entering **Y.** Name: Garcia, Jean	
1	5	33 Correct to **26.**	
1	3	**T** Correct to an **S.**	
		Salary:	99999.99
		Pay Periods:	26

In response to "MORE CHANGES?" enter an **F.** Correct to an **N.**

© SRA 1988, 1983

6. Refer to page 292 and review the material on controls built into the system. In completing 2 and 3, were all of the controls tested?

_____

_____

In response to RETURN TO MAIN MENU? Y OR N?, enter an **N**.

7. **LIST 830–980.**

   a. In the ON statement, what does N% represent?

   _____

   b. In the ON statement GOSUB (which causes a branch to a module and then back to the statement following the ON statement) is followed by a series of numbers.

   What do the numbers represent?_____

   If N% is equal to 5, what module will be executed? Where within the program is it located?

   _____

8. Since part of the normal testing procedure would be to display the records and determine if the changes made are recorded in the payroll master file records, you will display the records and compare the information displayed with the change report.

   a. Return to the **main menu**. Select menu **3**, option **19**. After displaying the record for employee 1, indicate there are no more records to be displayed. Do not return to menu.

   b. **LIST 140.** Displayed will be: OPEN "PAYMAST.DAT AS # 2 LEN = 128. Change the PAYMAST to **STUDENT**. The statement will then read:

   OPEN "STUDENT.DAT" AS # 2 LEN = 128

   c. Enter **RUN** and display the six records by entering as the employee numbers: **1, 2, 3, 4, 5, 6**

   d. As the records are displayed, compare the information displayed with your change report. Were the changes entered made in the employee master file records?

   _____

   e. What if _none_ of the changes made were shown in the records displayed? As a programmer you should check which module of your program first?

   _____

   _____

   f. What if all of the changes are reflected in the records except whenever a pay rate change is made the old rate is still displayed. What module would you check and what statement illustrated in the pseudocode on page 292 was probably omitted?

   _____

   _____

   _____

   g. Return to the main menu.

INTERACTIVE EXERCISE 8–2

The UPDATE program is an excellent example of reading two files sequentially. When the employee number from the master file matches the employee number from the transaction file, the values stored in the transaction file are added to appropriate fields in the master file records. If there is not a match, the program checks to see if the TR-number is less than the MF-number. If so, the transaction file records are out of sequence or there is a missing master file record. Although this should never occur because of the way the transaction file was created, provision is made for this occurrence. If the TR-number is greater, only a master file record will be read.

If you need to recreate the master file:

1. Return to the system.
2. Enter **COPY PAY .2 DAT STUDENT.DAT**
3. Load **BASIC.**
4. Load menu.

Directions

1. Select menu **4,** option **23.** You will be accessing the master file you used in the CHANGE program. However, none of the year-to-date totals have been updated. You are to assume that the transaction records for the first pay in January are used to update the master file.

2. As the program executes, watch the screen. Some display messages were added to the program so that you could see what occurs. Do not exit to the menu program as you will execute the program twice.

   What master file record is not updated?

   _____

   Why wasn't the record updated?

   _____

3. **LIST 470–570.** In looking at the code, CVS(E$) is the employee number from the master file and NUMBER is the employee number from the transaction file.

   When will control leave the loop?

   _____

   Under what two conditions will READMASTER$ be set to N?

   _____

   _____

   In the read-transaction-record module, READTRAN$ is set to N. When is it reset to Y in order to read another record?

   _____

   _____

4. Enter **RUN** and execute the UPDATE program again.

   What occurred and why did it occur?

   _____

   _____

   _____

© SRA 1988, 1983

SELF-EVALUATION TEST 8

Name _____

Section Number _____

I. Record the term being defined or the word or phrase needed to complete the statement in the space provided.

_____ 1. Rather than writing source code such as IF code = 1 THEN GOSUB 1000 ELSE IF code = 2 THEN GOSUB 1500 ELSE IF code = 3 THEN GOSUB 1800, an _____ statement may be used.

_____ 2. After the number and type of needed maintenance programs are determined, the next step is to determine in what mode each program should execute and how the master file records should be _____.

_____ 3. In the CHANGE program, the descriptions of the changes were stored in a table and randomly retrieved by using the _____.

_____ 4. When a data structure is described, the name, size, type of data, and _____ of each field within the record must be described.

_____ 5. A delay which permits an operator to read the data stored on the screen can be provided by a command such as sleep or pause, by requiring the operator to respond to a message, or by _____.

_____ 6. In printing the detail lines for the change program, two formats were used: one format for printing the alphanumeric variables and a second for printing the _____ variables.

_____ 7. When data such as an employee's status code or rate of pay is changed, the new data _____ the old data which was stored in the field.

_____ 8. How frequently the CORRECT program has to be executed is directly related to the number and type of _____ built into the program and how conscientiously employees perform their assigned tasks.

_____ 9. When formatted screens are used to display prompts and the size of the field, the _____ must be positioned before the operator keys in the data.

_____ 10. In the CHANGE program, the master file records were accessed _____.

II. Multiple Choice. Record the letter of the *best* answer in the space provided.

_____ 1. The CHANGE program is a
   a. sequential-update program.
   b. random-update program.
   c. sequential-report program.
   d. random-report program.

_____ 2. When indicators are used,
   a. the same one should be used to control all WHILE or UNTIL loops.
   b. the amount of coding should be reduced by assigning the indicators short names.
   c. a separate indicator should be used to control each type of WHILE or UNTIL loop.
   d. each module should have its own indicator.

_____ 3. An ON statement
   a. can always be used to replace a compound IF/THEN/ELSE statement.
   b. can be used to branch to one of several modules depending on the value of the parameter (such as code) used in the statement.
   c. can only be used if the parameter (such as code) is followed by GO TO.
   d. is less efficient than using a compound IF/THEN/ELSE statement.

_____ 4. In checking the operator's response to a question such as MORE DATA? Y OR N?, valid-response was set to Y
   a. when an error was detected in the check-response module.
   b. if an error was not detected in the check-response module.
   c. before control passed to the check-response module.
   d. after the check-response module was executed.

_____ 5. In developing a logic plan, the sequence in which certain tasks should be completed is to
   a. identify the required tasks, determine the input, then determine the output.
   b. determine the output required, determine the input and calculations needed to produce the required output, list the tasks required, determine the modules that should be developed.
   c. list the tasks required, determine the output required, determine the input and calculations needed, determine the modules that are required.
   d. determine the modules that are needed, the tasks to be performed, the output required, and the input needed.

_____ 6. When records for new employees are added to an existing file, an invalid-key condition
   a. cannot occur.
   b. occurs if the records added to the file are out of sequence.
   c. occurs if the employee number for a new employee is the same as one already used.
   d. only occurs when an alphanumeric key is specified.

_____ 7. When both the transaction and master file are accessed sequentially, processing usually occurs
   a. when the MF-number is greater than the TR-number.
   b. when the MF-number and the TR-number are equal.
   c. when the MF-number is less than the TR-number.
   d. after the end-of-file is detected.

_____ 8. When the master file was updated by using information stored in a transaction file,
   a. records stored in the master file were accessed randomly.
   b. a detailed report of the changes made in the master file was printed.
   c. there were no controls built into the program.
   d. the total number of records updated had to agree with the total number of checks printed and the number of employees listed on the payroll register.

_____ 9. In many organizations, a file such as the accounts receivable or inventory file that is used in a transaction processing system
   a. is seldom maintained because it is constantly in use.
   b. requires little maintenance because it is part of an interactive system.
   c. requires constant maintenance if the information produced from the system is to be accurate.
   d. is never backed up as it does not need to be reorganized.

_____ 10. Maintenance programs are
   a. usually executed in a batch mode.
   b. usually executed in an interactive mode.
   c. evaluated on an individual basis to determine the mode in which they should be executed.
   d. usually designed so that the records stored in the master file are accessed randomly.

III. True or False. Record a T or F in the blank provided. For each false statement, indicate why the statement is false or make the changes needed to correct the statement.

_____ 1. If data is edited or validated as it enters the system and becomes part of the data stored in an accounts receivable master file, it is seldom necessary to execute any of the maintenance programs.

_____ 2. Organizations often have a policy that states that all changes to a master file or database must be authorized.

© SRA 1988, 1983

_____ 3. The CHANGE program was executed as a remote-batch job.

_____ 4. In the CHANGE program, the operator keyed in the employee's number and name then visually verified the name by comparing it with the one listed on the source document.

_____ 5. In a typical correct-data module, the cursor is positioned by evaluating the operator response to a statement such as "ENTER NUMBER OF INCORRECT FIELD."

_____ 6. In editing the status field to determine if the right code was entered, the following statement should be used: IF STATUSCODE < > S AND STATUSCODE
< > H AND STATUSCODE < > P an appropriate error routine.

_____ 7. In the CORRECT program, the amount of the adjustment is entered and either added or subtracted from the amount stored in the field before the correction is made. Therefore, two statements are required. One is used when the amount is to be subtracted and the second when the amount is to be added.

_____ 8. When records are accessed randomly, an invalid-key condition is required only if it is a random-update program.

_____ 9. A screen layout form is used in order that the programmer knows the row and column in which the cursor is to be positioned.

_____ 10. When a report such as the payroll master file correct report is printed, a separate print format is used for each line.

_____ 11. When new records are added to the employee master file, the operator must enter zeroes for the year-to-date and quarterly total fields.

_____ 12. In a typical update program, an identifying number recorded in the transaction file is used to randomly retrieve the corresponding record in the master file.

_____ 13. When the records in a transaction file are used to update the corresponding records in a master file, control leaves the process-records module when the end-of-file condition is found on the master file.

_____ 14. Since the backup and recreate programs are sometimes processed as a two-task job, changes are made in the file as it is being backed up.

_____ 15. Both the master file and the backup file for the master file are usually organized in the same way.

© SRA 1988, 1983

EDITING DATA

9

After reading the chapter and completing the learning activities, you will be able to:

- Contrast editing in an interactive environment with editing techniques used in creating a transaction file.

- Identify the major advantages and disadvantages of interactive transaction-processing as contrasted to using a transaction file in a batch-processing application.

- Develop a logic plan for detecting:
    An invalid customer number.
    Data outside an allowable range.
    Nonnumeric data in a numeric field.
    An invalid item number.
    Errors using a reasonableness test.
    Errors using a limit test.
    An invalid code by sequentially searching a table.
    Invalid data by using a relationship test.
    A sequence error.
    An empty file and bypassing the statements within the termination module.

- Explain why a field may need to be redefined.

- Identifying when a binary search rather than a sequential search of a table should be conducted.

- Explain when a trailer record might be used and what impact it has on the statements used within a typical read-record module.

- Explain why error reports should be analyzed to determine what errors occurred and why the errors occurred.

- When given a detailed description of the system and program being designed, determine the control totals that can be used to determine the validity of the output.

- When given the description of the editing techniques used in preparing the transaction file and of the master files used in processing the data, determine what information should be provided in a typical confirmation report.

- Describe how two files can be processed sequentially when the editing module is only invoked when there are matching records.

Whenever possible, new data entering the system should be edited or validated. In an auditing text, it was noted that there are over 1,000 ways to validate data processed by a computer. Therefore a great deal of a programmer's time and effort is spent editing data. The CIS manager of one savings and loan company indicated that more than 40 percent of his programmers' time is spent writing routines for editing.

Whenever possible, a good programmer will edit all the variable data entering the system. While numeric data stored within a field can usually be edited in one or more ways, it is more difficult to edit alphanumeric data. Some fields of data, such as a customer's name or street address, can only be visually verified. If alphanumeric codes are entered, a table of valid codes can be searched to determine if the code is valid.

Fortunately errors in alphanumeric data are not as critical as errors in numeric data. For example, although management and the customer may be unhappy if the customer's name is misspelled, the sales invoice and shipment will still be delivered. However, if a wrong quantity or item number is entered and the error not detected, the wrong merchandise or an incorrect quantity will be shipped.

Whenever data is stored in a master file or transaction file, it must be edited. A programmer must think, "Errors will be made and I must make absolutely certain that those errors are detected." A programmer must assume that the data is invalid until it is proven to be valid; never should a programmer assume that data is valid. When new records are added to a master file, the record can either be displayed on the VDT or its contents printed and verified by the individual who submitted the source document. Once master files are created, the majority of the variable data entering the system is numeric and can usually be edited.

When data is not edited, jobs may abort and cause unnecessary and costly delays in processing vital data. In a well-managed installation, programming standards that require all variable data entering the system to be edited are usually followed. In the design walkthrough, members of the review team should check to make certain that all the variable data has been validated.

Although some editing techniques have been incorporated into the design of some of the applications illustrated, these along with other common techniques, will be explained. Since each program and each data structure is different, programmers must determine in each situation how the data can be validated.

EDITING IN AN INTERACTIVE ENVIRONMENT

When data is entered by an operator into an interactive transaction-processing application, it is edited as soon as it enters the system. If an error is detected, a message is displayed on the operator's VDT and the operator is provided an opportunity to make the necessary correction. An interactive sales-transaction system will be used in discussing some of the ways that the sales data can be edited *before* it becomes part of a report or part of the transaction file. In an interactive sales-transaction system, sales data is entered from remote locations and used to check the customer's credit, determine the availability of the items ordered, and to provide the data required to produce the sales invoice.

In a typical sales-transaction system, a limited amount of data must be keyed in by the operator. Usually any errors detected are corrected immediately. If for some reason the error cannot be corrected using the resources

© SRA 1988, 1983

Figure 9–1 Editing data entered in an interactive sales-transaction application.

INTERACTIVE SALES-TRANSACTION PROCESSING	
Data Entered	**Verification Methods**
Customer number	Edit for nonnumeric data in a numeric field. Random retrieval of record using an invalid-key routine. Display name and provide for visual verification. Unused credit is determined and displayed.
Item number	Edit for nonnumeric data in a numeric field. Random retrieval of record using an invalid-key routine. Display description and provide for visual verification.
Quantity ordered	Edit for nonnumeric data in the field. Apply a **reasonableness test.** Availability of item is determined.
Shipping code	Edit for nonnumeric data in the field. Use a **within range test.** **Sequential search** for code stored in a table within the customer's record.
Shipping date	Edit for nonnumeric data in the field. Relationship test. Limit test.

available, the operator or sales representative must be able to proceed to the next order. Figure 9–1 illustrates the data that must be entered and how each field can be verified or edited.

Invalid customer number

Whenever a key, such as a customer number, is used to retrieve randomly a record from an ISAM or VSAM file, an invalid-key routine should be included in the design of the program. In a transaction-processing application, an error message should be displayed and the operator or sales representative given a chance to enter a valid number.

Although a valid number is entered, the number might not be the one needed to retrieve the right record. Once a record is retrieved, the name stored in the customer-name field is displayed and visually confirmed. In several different applications this technique has been illustrated.

Sometimes additional proof, other than displaying the customer's name, is required. A bank may have several customers with the same first and last name. To be absolutely certain the correct account is being processed, the customer's address or balance may also be displayed and visually confirmed.

Limit check

Once the right record is obtained a **limit check** is performed. A limit check is used to test values stored in a numeric field against maximum or minimum values that may be either a variable or constant. In many online applications, such as when people wish to charge to their VISA or Master Charge accounts and the amount of unused credit must be determined. In each customer's master file record are two fields: MF-balance which is the amount the customer owes; and MF-credit-limit which is the customer's maximum credit allowed. The following pseudocode would be used to provide a limit check:

```
*limit-check routine.
IF MF-balance > MF-credit-limit THEN
    DISPLAY 'Contact credit manager before processing order.'
    Halt-processing = Y
ELSE IF MF-balance >  (.90 * MF-credit-limit) THEN
        DISPLAY 'Unused limit is:', MF-credit-limit - MF-balance
        DISPLAY 'Limit will be rechecked after order is entered.'
        Halt-processing = N
    ELSE
        Halt-processing = N
END IF
```

If after the limit-check routine is executed halt-processing is equal to Y, normally processing will be suspended and the operator will be asked to enter a new customer number. If sales representatives are supplied up-to-date information regarding the status of their customers' credit, it is seldom that an order will not be processed.

In order for the second credit check to be effective, the items and quantity ordered will need to be entered and the total cost of each item, as well as the total cost for the order, calculated before the customer's credit is rechecked. The following statement would then be used:

```
IF MF-balance + total-cost-of-order > MF-credit-limit THEN
    DISPLAY 'Credit manager must approve order.'
    Halt-processing  = Y
ELSE
    Halt-processing  = N
END IF
```

Although the inventory master file records are retrieved in order to determine the availability of the item on hand and its selling price, the amount ordered is only placed "on reserve" until it is determined that the entire order can be processed and the items are shipped.

In the majority of the cases where the last order received places the customer over his established credit limit, the sales invoice may still be printed and then reviewed, along with the customer's credit history, by the credit manager. If approval is given, the sales representative is notified and no further adjustments are needed.

If the credit manager decides that the order cannot be processed, a separate program will be used to reduce the quantity reserved for filling the sales order. A letter will also be sent to the customer and the sales representative will be notified.

In determining how to program a computer to handle the situation of the most recent order placing a customer over his predetermined limit, two factors must be considered. In terms of increased profit and sales, is the goodwill and convenience to the customer more important than the possible loss of income due to what is termed a "**bad debt**"? A bad debt occurs when a customer is unable or unwilling to pay the amount owed so that it must be written off as a loss. This is an excellent illustration of how the philosophy, objectives, and practices of an organization must be incorporated into the design of a program.

© SRA 1988, 1983

Invalid item number

After the correct master record is retrieved and the initial credit check is made, the operator keys in an inventory item number that is used as the key to retrieve the appropriate record from the inventory master file. Since the record is randomly retrieved from the file, an invalid-key routine must be provided.

Once the record is obtained, the description of the item is displayed. If the description does not match the one on the sales order, the operator can use the resources available to determine the correct item number. If the correct item number cannot be determined within a reasonable length of time, the order will not be processed until the information is obtained.

Editing for numeric data

When a program is coded, a programmer must indicate whether the data stored within a field is numeric or alphanumeric. Some languages, such as COBOL, also permit the programmer to indicate that the field is alphabetic. If a numeric field is used in a calculation or in an IF statement, the job will normally abort if nonnumeric data is stored within the field. However, this should never occur and it is up to the programmer to see that it doesn't happen. How easy it is to edit a numeric field is determined by the language used.

If you work with BASIC, you know that when the following occurs, a message such as REDO FROM START will be displayed:

- Nonnumeric data entered in a numeric field. Keying in an amount as $2000.00 or pressing a wrong key may cause this to occur.

- Too much data is entered. Keying in 10,000.00 rather than 10000.00 will cause the message to be displayed. Because commas are used to separate fields of data, the computer thinks two fields of data are being entered.

A programmer can make a BASIC program more user-friendly by defining the field in which numeric data is to be entered as an alphanumeric field. The data can then be checked for nonnumeric characters. If none are found, a function can be used to convert the string data to its numeric value.

- The operator is responsible for visually verifying the data entered.

- Other editing techniques are used to determine the validity of the information. For example, in using the menu program the menu selection number must be greater than zero and less than seven.

Class test

If COBOL is being used, numeric data entering the computer is not automatically checked. However, it is possible to use a **class test**. A class test is used to determine if the data stored in a field is numeric, alphabetic, or alphanumeric. In pseudocode, a COBOL class test would be coded as:

```
* class test
Nonnumeric-data = Y
DO-WHILE (Nonnumeric-data = Y)
    DISPLAY 'Enter quantity. '
    ACCEPT TR-quantity
    IF TR-quantity NOT NUMERIC
        DISPLAY 'nonnumeric data in field. Rekey data. '
    ELSE
        Nonnumeric-data = N
    END IF
END DO
```

REDEFINING FIELDS   In some languages it may be necessary to **redefine** a numeric field as an alphanumeric table and check each position to determine if it contains nonnumeric data. When a field is redefined, the same area within memory or on a storage medium such as disk can be treated as containing more than one type of data. The following pseudocode shows how a field might be redefined.

```
* redefining a field
  TR-quantity       PIC 9999
  TR-quantity-edit  (4) DEFINED
     TR-quantity  CHAR (1)
```

In the example, using PIC 9999 indicates that it is a four-position numeric field. In languages such as COBOL and PL/I 9s are used to indicate that a field is numeric. In the second illustration the (4) indicated that there is a table with four elements that contains alphanumeric data. CHAR (1) indicates the data stored in each of the one-position fields within the table can be alphanumeric.

If the second statement is coded as TR-quantity-edit DEFINED CHAR (4) it would indicate a four-position field containing alphanumeric data. Individual fields, as well as fields that are part of a data structure, can be redefined.

In the example, TR-quantity can be used in an arithmetic statement, compared in an IF statement with a numeric constant or a field containing numeric data, or moved into a field for printing which has edit-characters such as commas or dollar signs. Each area in TR-quantity-edit is compared to an alphanumeric field or to an alphanumeric constant. The data would also be moved into an alphanumeric print field which will cause the data to be aligned to the left and the unused area of the field filled with spaces. In contrast, numeric fields align to the right and the unused spaces are filled with zeroes which are normally suppressed by using an edit mask.

BINARY COLLATING SEQUENCE   Using the version of the redefined field that created a table, the following pseudocode illustrates how the data would be edited for nonnumeric data.

```
*   numeric edit routine for a field redefined as a table
nonnumeric-data = Y
DO-WHILE (nonnumeric-data = Y)
    DISPLAY 'Enter quantity.'
    ACCEPT TR-quantity
    DO (counter = 1 to 4)
       IF TR-quantity-edit (counter) < '0' THEN
           DISPLAY 'nonnumeric data entered in field.'
           counter = 6
       ELSE
           NULL
       END IF
    END DO
    IF counter <>  6 THEN
        nonnumeric-data = N
    ELSE
        NULL
    END IF
END DO-WHILE
```

© SRA 1988, 1983

In the statement "TR-quantity-edit (counter) < "0," the data stored in a single position of the table is compared to zero. If **EBCDIC** is used for storing data, then 0–9 have a higher value than special characters or letters of the alphabet. EBCDIC is a popular code used to store data in a computer or on a storage medium such as disk or tape. The acronym stands for Expanded Binary Coded Decimal Interchange Code. Most medium- and large-size computers use EBCDIC to store data. When comparisons are made within a computer, it is based on the **binary collating sequence.** The collating sequence is based on the pure binary value of a character. When EBCDIC is used, the binary collating sequence is as follows:

Type of data	Example	Collating Sequence
Special characters	#, $, or %	lowest
Alphabetic	A, B, or C	next higher
Digits	0–9	highest

In the editing illustration, counter value will equal 6 if nonnumeric data was found in the field. If the count-controlled loop is executed four times as specified, an exit will be made from the loop when counter is greater than 4. When an error is not detected, counter will equal 5 when an exit is made from the loop.

Reasonableness check

After TR-quantity is checked to determine that it contains only numeric data, it may be possible to provide a **reasonableness test.** For example, based on past history, it is unlikely that a customer would order more than three or four of a selected item at one time. This was determined by studying the orders previously placed for the particular item. Within the item's master file record is a field called MF-maximum-order and a 5 is stored in the field. The following pseudocode illustrates how a reasonableness test can be utilized.

```
*   reasonableness test.
Valid-quantity = N
DO-WHILE   (valid-quantity <> Y OR valid-quantity <> y)
    DISPLAY 'enter quantity ordered'
    ACCEPT quantity-ordered
    IF quantity-ordered > MF-maximum-order THEN
        DISPLAY 'Check quantity ordered.    O.K.? Y or N?'
        ACCEPT  valid-quantity
    ELSE
        valid-quantity = Y
    END IF
END DO
```

In the example, assume that the operator enters 6 as the quantity ordered. Since 6 is greater than the 5 stored in the MF-maximum-order field, the condition is true and the message will be displayed. If 6 is correct, the operator enters a **Y** and control leaves the WHILE loop. If 6 is incorrect, the operator enters an **N** and control remains within the loop and the operator enters the correct quantity. Note that control will remain within the loop *unless* the operator enters either a **Y** or a **y.** If the operator enters an invalid response to O.K.? Y or N?, control will still remain within the loop.

In order to use a reasonableness test for the quantity ordered, the field called MF-maximum-order would need to be included within the data structure for the inventory master file records. Each time a new item is added to the inventory, someone within the sales department determines the quantity to be stored within the field. If the message CHECK QUANTITY ORDERED continually appears and causes unnecessary delays, the CHANGE program would be used to increase the number. Although changes may be required for items as conditions change, the cost of designing and implementing a reasonableness test is minor when compared to the cost of shipping 50 items rather than 5, or 10 rather than 1. When more items are shipped than are ordered, the seller pays the cost of packaging the item and shipping the item, and revenue is lost because it cannot be sold to someone else while it is in transit or stored in the buyer's warehouse.

Reasonableness tests are used in batch jobs as well as in interactive applications. The federal government does much of its preliminary auditing of income tax returns by using maximums based on taxpayers' gross earnings. For example, if a person with a gross income of $10,000 indicates that $2,800 was given as charitable contributions, the amount probably would be flagged as being unreasonable.

Limit check for quantity

After determining that the quantity entered is numeric data and is within reason, the program must perform a limit check to determine if enough stock is on hand to process the order. In the master inventory record are two fields identified as (1) MF-quantity-on-hand, which is the quantity of the item in the warehouse ready to be shipped; and (2) MF-quantity-reserved, which is the quantity reserved to fill orders already processed. The limit check is based on the quantity-available. The pseudocode needed to provide the limit check is:

```
*limit check for quantity
 IF (MF-quantity-on-hand - MF-quantity-reserved) <
          TR-quantity THEN
    DISPLAY 'Insufficient quantity on hand to fill order'
    DISPLAY 'Backorder item?  Y or N?
    ACCEPT backorder-answer
 ELSE
    NULL
 END IF
```

In an interactive sales-transaction system, the person entering the data may be able to ask the customer if another item can be substituted or if they wish to have the item backordered. If the item is backordered, as soon as sufficient quantity becomes available it will be shipped to the customer.

Within range test

In our organization, there are 1,500 different shipping codes to indicate the shipping route and the mode of transport that will be used. Once the shipping code is entered and checked to make certain that the field contains only numeric data, the value stored within the field should be checked to determine if

© SRA 1988, 1983

it is within range. A **within range test** determines that the value entered is greater than the minimum and less than the maximum specified. For the shipping code, the following test would be made.

```
*  within range test
Range-test = N
DO-WHILE (range-test = N)
    IF TR-shipping-code < 1 OR TR-shipping-code > 1500 THEN
        DISPLAY 'Invalid shipping code entered.   '
        DISPLAY 'Enter shipping code===========>'
        ACCEPT  TR-shipping-code
    ELSE
        range-test = Y
    END IF
END DO
```

Range tests can be used to determine the validity of different types of data. For example, when the change code is entered, it must be greater than 0 and less than 11. Similarly, hourly rates within a department cannot be less than 4.82 or greater than 15.03. When range tests are used, the maintenance programmer must be aware of the programs in which the tests are used and of when conditions have changed sufficiently so that the test must be revised. If, for example, the employees within the department receive a 10 percent raise, the range test should be changed to less than 5.30 or greater than 16.53.

When a date is entered, the month must be greater than 0 and less than 13. The number entered for the day must be greater than zero and less than the maximum number of days plus one which are stored in a days-in-month table. The value entered for the months is the subscript used to retrieve the number of days in the month.

Sequential search

For each customer, only a limited number of routings or shipping codes may exist. Determining the routes and codes to specify the various routes is a function performed within an organization's traffic department. Each time a new customer is added to the customer master file, a determination is made regarding how merchandise can be shipped and which carriers should be used. The sales representative must know how to code the shipping information and with the customer must decide which alternatives should be used. Assuming a customer usually can select one of five or six different shipping alternatives, the computer must know which ones can be used.

When the customer's record is created, the acceptable shipping codes must be stored in it. The most efficient way to achieve these results is to store the acceptable codes for each customer in a table in their master file. To make certain there is enough room for the acceptable codes, eight areas are provided. A count-controlled loop can be established to do a **sequential search** and look for a "match." Once the data is stored within the customer's master file record, the following pseudocode could be used to determine if a valid code was entered *for the customer whose order is being processed*:

```
*Sequential search for a valid shipping code
 Good-shipping-code = N
 DO-WHILE (Good-shipping-code = N)
     DO (counter = 1 to 8)
         IF TR-shipping-code = table (counter) THEN
             counter = 10
         ELSE
             NULL
         END IF
     END DO
     IF counter < > 10 THEN
         DISPLAY 'Invalid shipping code entered. Check code.'
         ACCEPT TR-shipping-code
     ELSE
         Good-shipping-code = Y
     END IF
 END DO-WHILE
```

Manufacturing firms may list the raw materials needed to manufacture each product. A table containing the identifying numbers for the required raw material is established. When raw material is used in production and charged to a given product, the table is checked to determine if the number or code entered for the raw material is stored in the table. If the number cannot be found, either the wrong raw material number was entered or the table is incomplete. If a wrong code number is undetected, the wrong record will be updated to reflect the decrease in the quantity of the material on hand and the cost charged to the production of the product will be incorrect.

Relationship check

The last field entered by the operator is the date the items are to be shipped. In the initialization module, the transaction date is entered as month, day, and year. January 10, 1989 would be entered as 01101989. The shipping date is entered in the same format. Some customers may wish to have their orders shipped on the same day as the order is received; others may want the orders shipped on a future date. In either case, the shipping date must be equal to or greater than the transaction date. The shipping date would first be edited for non-numeric data, then edited to be sure it is equal to or greater than the transaction date. The logic is expressed in the following pseudocode:

```
*  Relationship test comparing shipping and transaction dates
Good-date = N
DO-WHILE (good-date = N)
    DISPLAY 'Enter date as mmddyyyy'
    ACCEPT TR-shipping-date
    IF TR-shipping-date NOT NUMERIC THEN
        DISPLAY 'Nonnumeric data in field.'
    ELSE IF TR-shipping-date < TR-transaction-date THEN
            DISPLAY 'Shipping date < transaction date.'
        ELSE
            Good-date = Y
    END IF
END DO
```

© SRA 1988, 1983

If nonnumeric data is entered in the field or if the shipping date is less than the transaction date, control remains within the loop and the operator is provided an opportunity to rekey the date.

Editing data effectively

To edit data effectively, an analyst must understand:

- How the field was defined initially and how it can be checked to determine if the correct type of data was entered.
- The minimum and maximum values that can be entered for the field.
- The precise relationship of the data being entered to the record being processed.
- Relationship of the data being entered to other fields within the record or within the program.

Unless analysts and programmers work closely with end users, errors may not be detected. End users usually understand the interfield relationships that exist and the restrictions relating to the processing of data for individual records.

CHECKPOINT QUESTIONS

1. As a general rule, is numeric data or alphanumeric data easier to edit?
2. Is it usually more serious to have invalid alphanumeric data or invalid numeric data enter a system? Use illustrations in explaining your answer.
3. In an interactive transaction-processing application, is data usually edited when it enters the system or after it is stored within a file?
4. Is displaying the customer's name always proof that the correct record was obtained?
5. When you wish to charge an item to your VISA account, what type of check is conducted before you are permitted to charge the item?
6. Why might a limit check be completed before the data for the order is entered as well as after all of the data is entered?
7. If a customer has a $100,000 credit limit and by processing the current order his account balance will reach $105,000, what factors should be considered in determining if the order will be filled?
8. What is a class test?
9. Assume that a field containing numeric data was originally defined as an alphanumeric field. What may the programmer be able to do so that the data can be edited to include commas and dollar signs?
10. When data is stored using EBCDIC, does a letter of the alphabet or a digit have a higher binary collating sequence?
11. In order to use a reasonableness test for checking the quantity of an item ordered, what data has to be stored in the item's master file record?
12. How does the Internal Revenue Service use a reasonableness test?
13. When reasonableness tests are used, why should the data used in making the test be reviewed and, when necessary, updated?

14. What type of test is used to determine if there is enough of an item in stock to fill an order?

15. In a payroll application, when might a range test be used?

16. Within each inventory master file record is a table that contains five elements. Stored within each element of the table is a vendor account number. Unless prior approval is obtained, new shipments must be ordered from one of the vendors listed. When an order is being placed, how can the validity of a vendor account number be determined?

17. How can a relationship test be used to check the shipping date entered for an order?

18. What should an analyst do in order to make certain that data entering the sales system is validated so that invalid data does not enter the system?

EDITING IN A BATCH ENVIRONMENT

One of the major advantages of interactive transaction-processing is that the majority of the errors will be detected *before* the input is processed and becomes part of the online database or part of a report. Depending on the application and the computer system being used, the following disadvantages may occur:

- The productivity of the operator is decreased. Time is spent in visually verifying data and in using the resources available to make the necessary corrections.

- If the terminal is online to a remotely located computer, the cost of transmitting data in an interactive mode may be prohibitive.

Although the speed with which data can be transmitted has increased, **connect time** to a remotely located computer can be expensive. In relationship to transmitting and processing data, keying in data is extremely slow. The entire input-process-output cycle is decreased due to the time it takes to key in data. When an application is designed, management must work with analysts to determine which method is more cost effective. Will the benefits of interactive transaction-processing produce increased revenues to offset the additional costs associated with online telecommunications?

CREATING A TRANSACTION FILE

Assume that a sales-transaction file is created by keying in data. After all the data is entered and stored in a file, the data is transmitted in a **burst mode** to the corporate computer for further processing and for the preparation of the sales invoices. When data is transmitted in a burst mode, it is transmitted from an online file without interrruption. Often data stored in a remotely located file is transmitted into a centralized computer, stored in a second file, and then processed after all the data is transmitted.

In business and industry today **nonprogrammable terminals** are being replaced with **programmable** or **smart** terminals. Often microcomputers are used **offline** by operators who key in the data recorded in the transaction file. The microcomputer or programmable terminal can be programmed to do most routine editing of numeric data. Figure 9–2 illustrates the data that will be keyed in to create the transaction file and how it can be edited when a microcomputer or smart terminal is used offline.

© SRA 1988, 1983

Figure 9–2 Editing data stored in a sales-transaction file.

EDITING DATA STORED IN THE SALES-TRANSACTION FILE

Field	Type of Data	Validation or Editing Method Used
TR-date	Numeric	Entered once for all transactions. Edited for data, limit check for month and day, and visually verified.
TR-order-number	Numeric	Edited for data and range test.
TR-customer-number	Numeric	Edited for data and visually verified. Table searched for valid customer numbers.
TR-item-number	Alphanumeric	Edited for data; a table is also searched for a corresponding number.
TR-quantity	Numeric	Edited for data.
TR-shipping-code	Numeric	Edited for data; a table is also searched for a corresponding number.
TR-shipping-date	Numeric	Edited for data and relationship check.

Verifying the order number

All of the sales orders are numbered and the beginning number and the ending number are entered *once* and used in a range test. If today's sales orders range from 10987–11432, the low-order-number will be 10987 and the high-order-number will be 11432. The statement needed for the range test is:

```
IF TR-order-number < low-order-number OR TR-order-
number > high-order-number THEN
     appropriate error routine
```

The order number is entered as part of the sales-transaction record in order to provide an **audit trail** that relates the record being created to the original source document.

Verifying the customer number

An organization distributing merchandise on a national basis may have thousands of customers, each of whom is assigned a unique number. If the number is only visually verified, there is a possibility that the number entered is for the wrong customer or that it is an obsolete number. The customer who had the number assigned no longer has a record in the customer master file.

Using a binary search

If the organization has only a few thousand customers, the valid customer numbers could be placed in a table and a search conducted to find a matching number. Some languages, such as COBOL, have a SEARCH statement that can be used to conduct a **binary search.** In a binary search, the same logic is used as when people are asked to guess a number and are told if the number guessed is higher or lower than the correct number. The table is divided in half and the search argument (the number being looked for) is compared with the mid-point number. If higher, the top half of the table is divided and the search argument contrasted with the mid-point number of the top half. If the second comparison produces a "lower-than" response, the second quarter of the table is divided and another comparison made. The table continues to be divided and comparisons made until either the number is found or it is determined that the number is not in the table.

Assuming that a table has 10,000 entries, if a sequential search is conducted an average of 5,000 comparisons will be made. In a sequential search a count-controlled loop is created and each element of the table is compared, in sequence, to the search argument. However, if a binary search is conducted the *maximum* number of comparisons made will be 14. A mathematical formula can be used to determine for each size table the maximum number of comparisons that will be made before the number is found. If a table has more than 50 entries, a binary search is more efficient than a sequential search.

Since a limited number of items are carried in stock, valid item numbers can be stored in a table and a binary search conducted to determine if the item number entered is valid. Although the number entered is a valid number, it may not be the correct number.

Accumulating control totals

A programmable terminal can also be programmed to accumulate totals. When each record is written into the file, 1 is added to the record-count field. Also, each time a quantity is entered, and edited, the quantity is added to a total-quantity field. These totals, along with the date field, are written into a record which might be identified as a **trailer record**. The record might have the following format:

Position	Data
1	"T" to identify the record as the total or trailer record rather than a record containing sales data.
2–8	Total orders entered.
9–15	Total quantity entered.

Although the quantity-entered total is meaningless, it will provide a means of determining if the total quantity ordered either resulted in items shipped, backordered, or not processed, either because the customer was over limit or due to some other type of error. The total-order-entered field contains the total number of orders in the transaction file.

CHECKPOINT QUESTIONS

19. If editing in an interactive environment is more effective than editing using an offline programmable terminal, why isn't all data edited in an interactive mode?

20. What is the difference between a programmable and a nonprogrammable terminal?

21. If sales orders are numbered and entered in a batch, how can the order number be verified?

22. Why does a binary search usually take less time than a sequential search?

23. When might a binary search be conducted as a means of verifying the validity of a code or numeric value?

© SRA 1988, 1983

PRODUCING THE SALES INVOICES

The system flowchart illustrated in Figure 9–3 provides an overview of how the data stored in the transaction file will be processed in order to print sales invoices similar to the one illustrated in Figure 9–4. The system flowchart illustrates the input required and the output produced. When a dataflow line has arrows at both ends, it indicates that the records in the file are read as input, updated, and rewritten.

The sales invoicing application introduces several new concepts: the use of a trailer record to contain control totals; the analysis of error reports to determine if additional editing or controls are needed; the need to transmit confirmation reports; and the ways that new data is created and added to an existing master file.

Error reports

Although the programmable terminals perform a number of editing tasks, the error report printed after the invoices are printed may still contain the following types of entries:

Order	Customer Number	Item Number	Problem
9875	10976		Credit limit exceeded.
9995	10965	1237	Insufficient quantity on hand.
10357	587		Invalid customer number.
13458	19436	9833	Item no longer in stock. Order 9835.

Figure 9–3 Systems flowchart for the sales invoicing procedure.

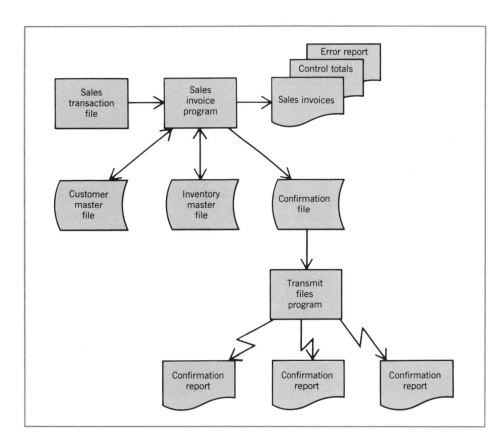

```
                    COMPUTER SUPPLY CENTER
                      1490 Explorer Drive
                    Wakefield, Kansas 92347
                       (720) 619-8346
```

Billing Address:	Computer Service Center 1948 Long Parkway Austin, TX 32987	Invoice Number:		23678
		Date of Invoice:		03/14/1989
Shipping Address:	Computer Service Center 1950 Long Parkway Austin, TX 32987	Shipping Date:		04/02/1989
		Ship Via:		**United Parcel**
		Due Date:		05/07/1989

Item	Quantity	Description	Unit Price		Total Price	
4278	10	Model 2000 Daisywriter	967.	52	9675.	20

Product Total	9,675.20
Shipping Charges	97.42
Sales Tax	.00
Invoice Total	9,772.62

Figure 9–4   Invoice produced after processing data in transaction file.

These errors were detected because information stored in the inventory and customer master files was available to further edit the data stored in the transaction file. Because of the editing techniques used when the transaction file was created, only a small percentage (perhaps less than one percent) of orders is likely to be "dropped out" and require additional processing. The first two errors listed, credit limit exceeded and insufficient quantity on hand, are considered normal conditions. The number of this type of error is recorded; management would become concerned only if the percentage increased.

© SRA 1988, 1983

If too many customer numbers are listed as "invalid," either the person inputting the data did not visually verify the entry or the person recording the customer number on the source document made a mistake. In either case, a person is accountable for the error. When the message "Item no longer in stock" appears, it is an indication that the table used in the binary search was not maintained and obsolete numbers were not deleted.

It is common to keep statistics regarding the type and number of errors detected when the sales invoices are prepared. The analyzed information determines whether or not additional verification methods should be used to catch the most frequent errors.

Control totals

Control totals are printed after the invoices to show that all records were processed and either resulted in output, such as a sales invoice, or were listed on an error report. In the sales-invoicing application, the following totals might be printed.

```
TRANSACTION FILE RECORD TOTAL:            XXXXX
TOTAL NUMBER OF ORDERS PROCESSED:         XXXXX
TOTAL NUMBER OF ORDERS NOT COMPLETED:     XXXXX
TRANSACTION FILE QUANTITY TOTAL:          XXXXX
TOTAL QUANTITY PROCESSED:                 XXXXX
TOTAL QUANTITY UNPROCESSED:               XXXXX
```

The first total is printed by using the number recorded in the transaction file trailer record. The next two totals are accumulated by the sales invoice program and the sum of the two totals must equal the first total. The computer can be programmed to add the two accumulated totals, then to subtract their sum from the trailer total. If the results are not zero, an additional message is printed.

When a trailer record is used, each time a record is read, a check must be made to determine if the control record rather than a data record has been read. When the trailer record is read, more-records will be set to N and control will branch to the termination module. The fourth total is printed by using the number recorded in the transaction file trailer record and it must be equal to the sum of the next two totals.

If transaction files are received from several locations, the files can be merged and processed as one large file or each can be processed separately. If the files are combined and processed as one large file, the individual transaction file totals are added together.

Confirmation reports

Another way of validating the data transmitted into the system is to transmit back to each remote location a confirmation report. Figure 9–5 illustrates a typical confirmation report.

CONFIRMATION REPORT OF ORDERS TRANSMITTED ON: MMM-DD-YYYY PAGE 1 OF 3						
DISPOS-ITION	ORDER NUMBER	CUSTOMER NUMBER	CUSTOMER NAME	ITEM NUMBER	DESCRIPTION	QUANTITY
P	12345	945	Johnson Brothers	426	IBM PCs	10
P	12346	10943	J. F. Hunt and Sons	927	DAISYWRITER	8
C	12347	19765	S. Brown and Assoc.	1937	20-MG DISK	5

Figure 9–5 *Confirmation report listing the disposition of orders transmitted from a remotely located terminal.*

The information for the confirmation report was obtained from the following sources:

Field	Source
DISPOSITION	Coded information. P for processed, C for unprocessed due to a credit check.
ORDER NUMBER	Transaction file record
CUSTOMER NUMBER	Transaction file record
CUSTOMER NAME	Customer master file
ITEM NUMBER	Transaction file record
DESCRIPTION	Inventory master file
QUANTITY	Transaction file record

Control totals showing the number of processed and unprocessed records, as well as the total quantity processed and unprocessed, will be included at the end of the report.

Under disposition, codes can be used such as P for a processed record and C for when a customer fails to pass the credit check. It is important that the confirmation report is compared with the data transmitted. Usually the report is received and verified *before* orders are shipped. If the wrong customer is listed or the description of the product is incorrect, the correct customer number or item number can be transmitted to the host computer and someone will be assigned the task of making the necessary corrections.

When a branch office did not receive confirmation reports for three days, a query was made and it was determined that due to a technical problem none of their orders had been transmitted into the system. Although telecommunication equipment is fast and usually reliable, problems along the network can occur and applications must be designed to catch errors that might cause data to be distorted or lost.

Updating the customer master file

When the data stored in the transaction file is processed and the sales invoices produced, data stored in the master file must to obtained in order to check the customer's credit limit and to obtain the customer's name, billing, and shipping addresses needed for the sales invoice.

The analyst designing the application must decide which information listed on the sales invoices will be needed to produce the end-of-month statements

© SRA 1988, 1983

Figure 9–6 System flowchart for updating the customer master file.

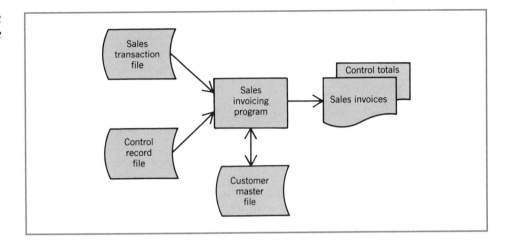

sent to the customer and to produce reports which indicate how many accounts are 30, 60, 90, or over 90 days past due. You may have observed that this information is often printed on the bottom of one of your monthly statements.

DATA FOR THE CUSTOMER'S DETAIL RECORDS   The following information from each invoice will be stored in the customer master file detail records.

Field	*Rationale*
Invoice Number	Provide an audit trail between the data stored in the master file and the printed invoice. It also serves to identify the record.
Date of Invoice	Further positive identification of the record.
Shipping Date	The information may be needed to answer queries from customers or sales representatives.
Due Date	Required to determine the "age" of accounts receivables.
Invoice Total	Required for billing the customer and for aging receivables.

Two types and two lengths of records will be stored in the customer master file. Each customer will have a *master record* with the firm's name and address, shipping information, beginning balance, and other such information. In addition, each customer's *detail records* will show information for current sales transactions, payments, and credit received. The concept of variable length records and the technique used in storing the sales invoice information in the customer master file will be discussed in Chapter 10.

CONTROL RECORDS   When the job is initiated, a **control record** contains the beginning invoice number and date to be used as the invoice date. Control records that provide such needed information as this can be entered ahead of time. Then the operator who initiates a job does not have to respond to a message displayed on the console, preventing unnecessary delay in the job's execution. Also, since computer operations personnel are less familiar with the data to be entered, errors are more likely than when someone in the sales department creates the control record.

DATA SOURCES   The shipping date was part of the transaction record and the due date was calculated using a formula based on the credit policy of the company. The product total, shipping charges, sales tax, and invoice total are all calculated. Once a program has been tested, documented, and evaluated, calculated data is usually valid.

VALIDATING DATA   The information stored in the customer master file as the result of processing the transaction data and information obtained from two on-line master files is an excellent example of why data must be validated. If any part of the information printed on the invoice and used to update the customer master file is incorrect, a CORRECT program will be needed to make the necessary corrections.

CHECKPOINT QUESTIONS

24. When the inventory and customer master files are available, what additional checks can be made on the data stored within the transaction records?

25. If a trailer record is used, what additional coding is required each time a record is read from the transaction file? When will more-records be set to N?

26. What type of errors listed on the error report were considered "normal"?

27. If the message "Invalid account number" occurs frequently, why should management be concerned?

28. Why are statistics kept regarding the type and frequency of errors that occur?

29. What is a control total?

30. How should the confirmation report be used?

31. Why should the confirmation be checked as soon as possible? What happens on detection of such errors as a mismatch between the customer's name on the report and the name on the sales order source document?

32. Why is it preferable to create a "control record" with such information as the beginning invoice number and invoice date rather than to key in this information from the operator's console?

33. Why does recording the sales invoice information in the accounts receivable master file emphasize the need for editing and data validation?

CREATING AN EDIT MODULE AND ERROR REPORT

In the sales invoice batch-processing application, techniques to help validate information to be processed and to determine the validity of the output were discussed. In the payroll register program, attention will be given to creation of an edit module and printing of the error report.

System flowchart for the payroll register program

Figure 9–7 illustrates the system flowchart for the payroll register program. The payroll master file contains the records described in Figure 7–3 (pages 239–240); review the information about the data stored in the payroll master

© SRA 1988, 1983

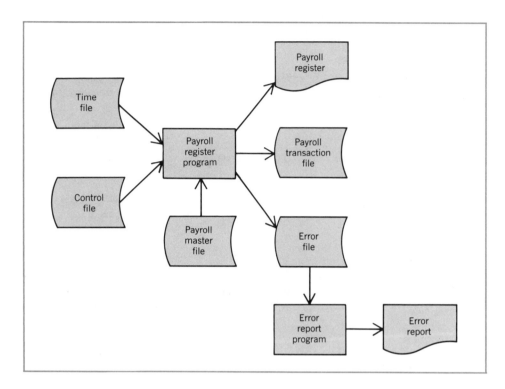

Figure 9–7 System flowchart for the payroll register.

file. The time file contains the variable data that must be used to determine which employees will be paid and to calculate the earnings for those employees. The time file is organized as a sequential file and the payroll master file will be accessed sequentially.

As indicated on the system flowchart, two sequential output files will be created. The payroll transaction file will be used in the UPDATE program and also to create the paychecks and other needed reports. The error file contains both error messages that describe the error and the data recorded in the time records with errors.

The payroll job is executed as a two-step or two-task job. The first program edits the time file data, calculates the gross and net pay for the employees to be paid, and produces the printed payroll register, the payroll current file, and an error file as output. The second program is used to print the error report.

If errors are detected during the execution of the PAYREG program by the edit routines, the error report will be used to determine the cause of the problem and appropriate action will be taken. After the time records are corrected, the PAYREG program will need to be rerun.

Although the payroll register job is used as an example of a comprehensive two-task job and documented in Chapter 11, detailed information is provided in this chapter regarding how the data stored in the time file is edited. It provides an excellent example of relationship checks. Relationship checks or editing is also referred to as **combination checking.**

Time file   The time file contains records that are in sequence by employee number and contain the fields listed in Figure 9–8. Figure 9–8 also explains the interfield relationships that exist and explains how the data must be edited. When the

Figure 9–8 Data recorded in the time file records.

Field	Editing Required
TF-Record-identification	A "P" is recorded in each record to indicate it is a time record rather than a control or trailer record.
TF-Employee-number	It is imperative that the records are sequenced by employee number in ascending order. If a record is out of sequence, an error message is generated and another time record will be read.
TF-Employee-status	The status must be an H, S, or P and must also agree with the status code recorded in the master file. An employee's status may have changed and the change was not reflected in the records stored in both files.
TF-Pay-code	If salaried employees are NOT to be paid, an N will be recorded in the field. If a P is recorded in the field, the employee will receive the pay indicated in the part-pay field rather than their normal salary. A P or N code can only be used for salaried employees. A B is used for hourly and part-time employees.
TF-Part-pay field	If a P is recorded in a salaried employee's pay code field, the part-pay field must be greater than zero.
TF-Regular-hours	A number greater than zero and less than 80.1 must be recorded for hourly workers; for part-time workers the hours must be greater than zero but less than 40.1. The payroll is based on a two-week pay period and part-time workers can work a maximum of 40 hours per pay period.
TR-Overtime-hours	Only hourly workers are permitted to work overtime and are limited to 20 hours per pay period.

file is created, numeric fields were checked for nonnumeric data and alphanumeric fields were edited to make certain the field is not blank.

In regard to the characters used in the TF-pay-code field, it is logical to use an N to represent NO-PAY and a P to represent PART-PAY. Only salaried employees have a pay code. Although the field could be left blank when a record is created for an hourly or part-time employee, to use a code is considered better than to leave the field blank. A blank field could be an error of omission rather than the required code. There is no reason why a B rather than an H or some other character was used.

Hierarchy chart for the payroll register program

The hierarchy chart for the payroll register program illustrates how the control record containing the date for the payroll register and the first check number will be invoked by the initialization module. Depending on the language used, the record could have been identified with a C for control record and included as the first record in the time file.

Initially both a time and master file record are read. Control remains within process-payroll-records until the end-of-file condition is detected for the master file. In the termination module files are closed and the print-payreg-totals module will be invoked. Control totals for the total records processed and the number of hourly, part-time, and salaried employees paid will also be printed.

© SRA 1988, 1983

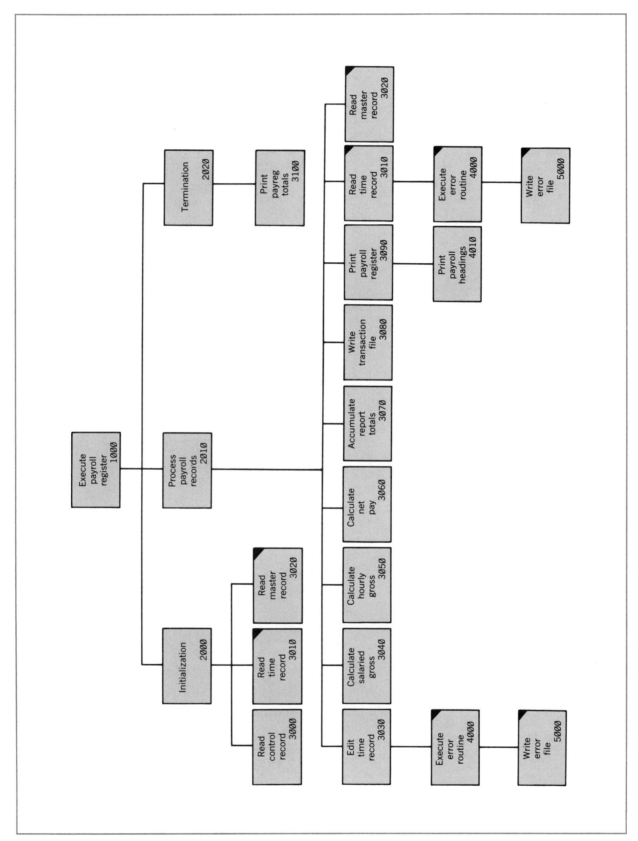

Figure 9–9 Hierarchy chart for the payroll register program.

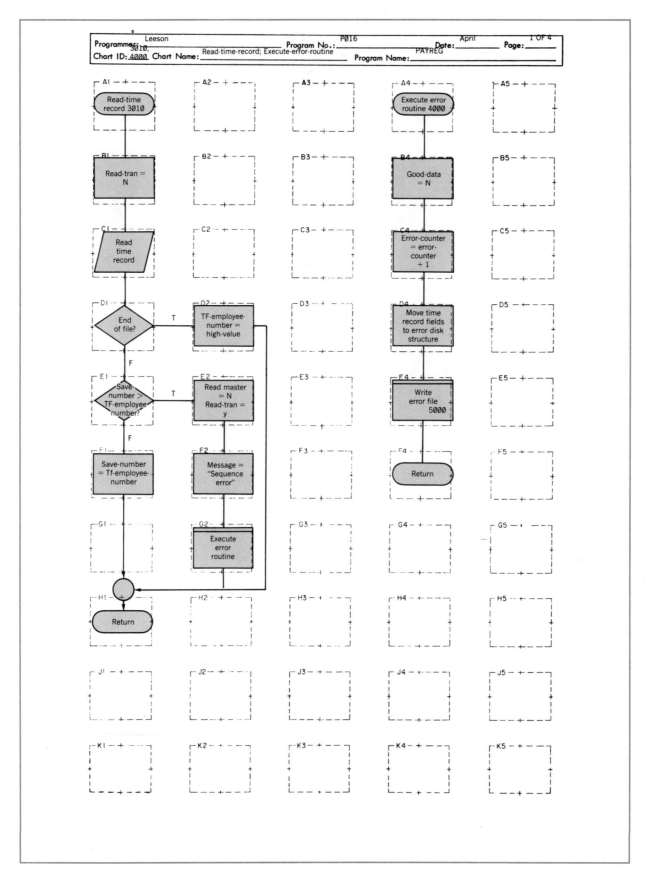

Figure 9–10 Part 1 Flowchart for the read-time-record and execute-error-routine modules.

© SRA 1988, 1983

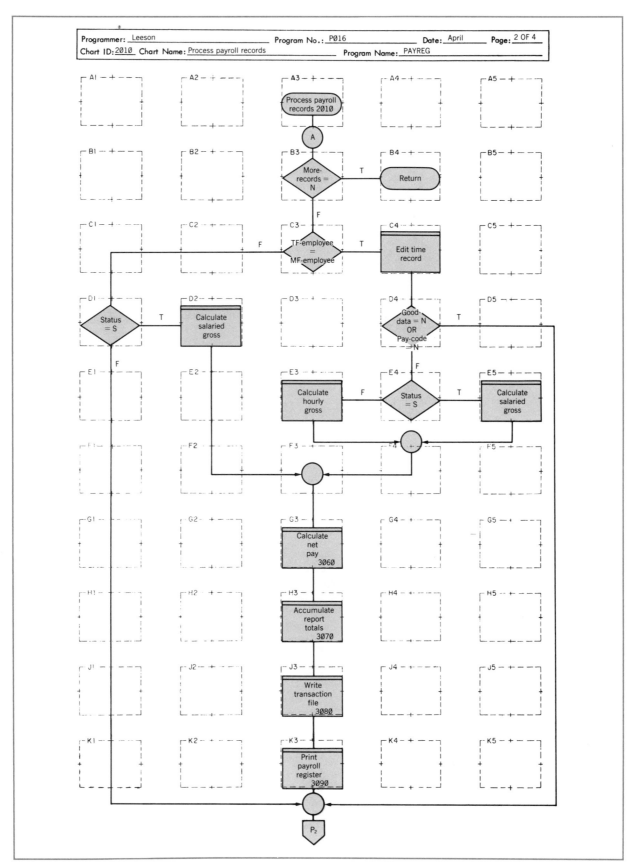

Figure 9–10 Part 2 Process-payroll-records.

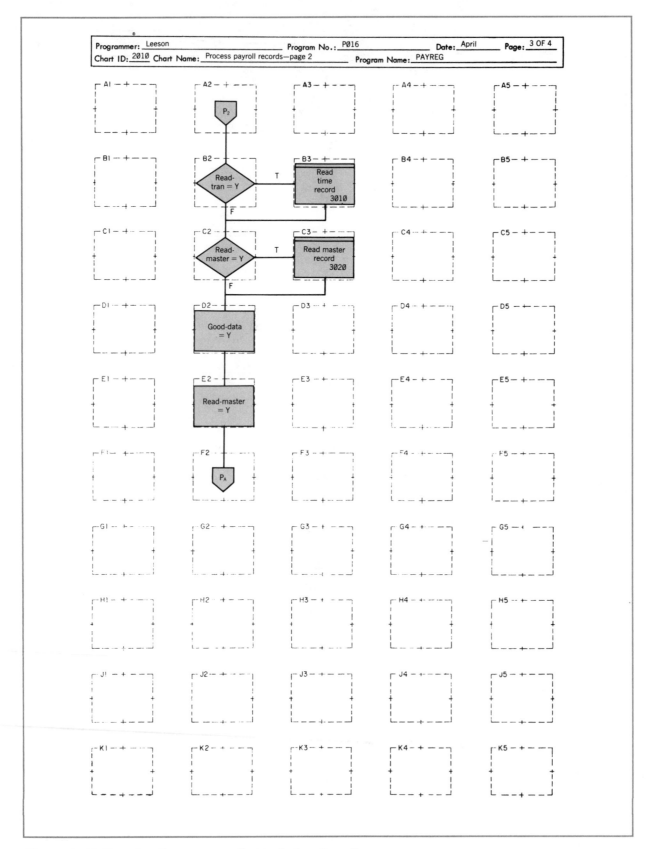

Figure 9–10 Part 3   Process-payroll-records (continued).

© SRA 1988, 1983

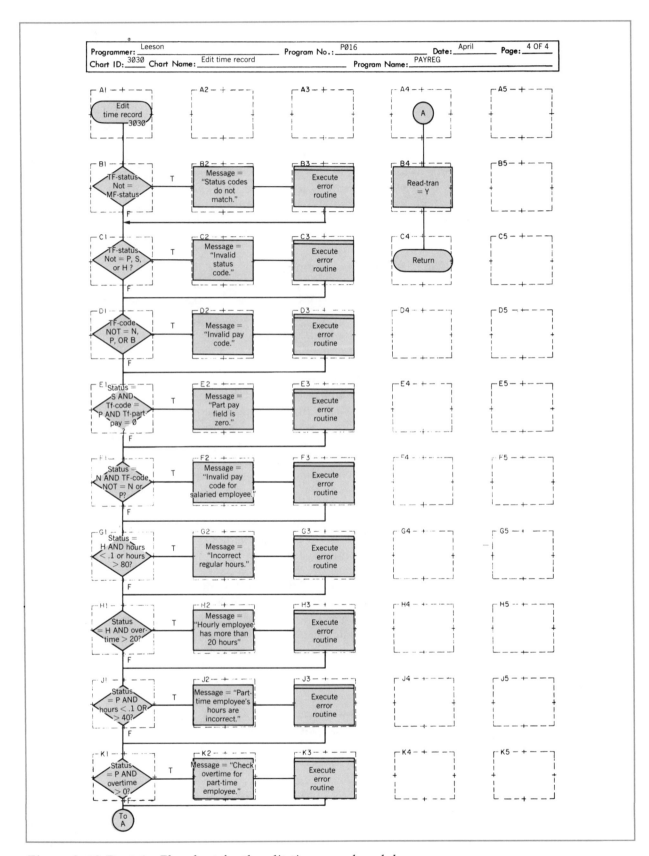

Figure 9–10 Part 4 *Flowchart for the edit-time-record module.*

READ TIME RECORD   In the read-time-record module, illustrated in Figure 9–10, Part 1, the read-transaction indicator is set to N. When there is a sequence error or a match on employee number, then read-transaction is set to Y and another time record will be read. In the sequence-error routine and in the edit-time-record module, the read-transaction indicator will be reset to Y. All hourly employees who are to be paid must have a time record; salaried employees who are not to be paid or who will receive only a portion of their pay must have a time record.

When the end-of-file is detected for the time-record file, there still may be records in the master file for salaried employees that must be processed. There-fore, rather than moving N to more-records, all bits are to set to ones (referred to as **high value**) in the TF-employee-number field. Since the high-value stored in the field will never be matched, another read-time-records command will not be executed.

SEQUENCE CHECKING   A sequence check is coded within the read-time-record module. If the record is out of sequence, a match will not occur and the edit-time-record module will not be invoked. Consider the following example:

EMPLOYEE NUMBERS

Master records	1	2	3	4	5
Time records	2	1	3	5	8

Since it is normal not to have a corresponding time record for each master file record, an error will not be detected when the 1 from the master file is compared with the 2 from the time file. A sequence error is not detected until the second time record is read. When coding a sequence-checking routine, a field such as save-employee-number is initially set to zero. Since 2 is higher than the 0 stored in the save-employee-number field, the sequence error is not detected until the second time record is read and the employee-number is less than save-employee-number. Each time a record is in sequence, the new em-ployee number is moved to save-employee-number.

When a new master file record is read, a match occurs on employee num-ber, the edit routine is invoked, processing occurs, the employee number (2) is stored in the save-employee-number field, and a new time record is read. When 1 is compared to the 2 stored in save-employee-number, the sequence error is detected. "SEQUENCE ERROR" is moved into the message field, and the execute-error-routine module is invoked.

If employee number 1 is an hourly employee, the employee will not be paid because the master file record was read prior to the time record. If em-ployee number 1 is a salaried employee, the employee was either paid an incorrect amount or was paid when he should not have been. When a match occurs for a salaried employee, either a no-pay or part-pay record will be processed.

Although provision should be made for a sequence error, it is highly un-likely that records will be out of sequence when disk files are sorted on a field such as employee number. If a sequence error is detected, the file will be re-sequenced before the payreg program is rerun.

EDIT-TIME RECORD   The edit routine is invoked when the TF-employee-number matches the MF-employee-number. As illustrated in Figure 9–10 Part 4, each time an error is detected, a unique message is stored in the field called mes-sage. Although the rest of the editing could be bypassed by using more com-

© SRA 1988, 1983

plex IF/THEN/ELSE statements, it seems wise to continue editing other fields stored in the record because more than one error may be detected. In most installations, it is considered standard operating procedure to edit the entire record and find all of the errors. In the edit-time-record module, read-transaction is set to Y which will cause another record to be read.

EXECUTE ERROR ROUTINE   If the execute-error-routine module is invoked, good-data is set to N which will cause most of the statements within process-payroll-records to be bypassed. The contents of the message field, as well as the data in the time record, are stored in the data structure established for the error file and the write-error-file module is invoked. One is also added to the error-counter field. If no errors are detected and error-counter is equal to 0 when the statements within the termination module are executed, the message "NO EDITING ERRORS DETECTED" will be printed.

CHECKING FOR AN EMPTY FILE   When there are no records in a file (the file is empty), the end-of-file condition will be detected on the initial read. Since more-records will be set to N, the commands within the process-payroll-records module will never be executed. Control passes to the termination module, the print-payreg-totals module will be invoked, and zeroes will be printed. As a control total the statement "TOTAL NUMBER OF RECORDS PROCESSED: 0" will be printed.

If the programmer does not wish to print zero totals or to execute other commands located within the termination module, a special indicator is set to Y when an empty file is detected. Assuming the indicator was called empty-file, the following pseudocode illustrates how the commands within the termination module can be bypassed:

```
*Initialization module
      . . .
 PERFORM 3010-Read-time-record
 IF more-records = N THEN
     Empty-file = Y

*Process-payroll-records module
 DO-WHILE (more-records = Y)
      . . .   none of the commands will be executed
 END DO

*Termination-module
 CLOSE files
 IF Empty-file = Y THEN
     PRINT  'Transaction file does not contain any records.
            All processing was suspended. '
 ELSE
     PERFORM 3090-print-payreg-totals
     PRINT control totals
 END IF
```

The decision to use an additional indicator in order to bypass some of the statements within the termination module should be made by determining what statements will be executed and the advantage or disadvantage of bypassing the statements.

Flowcharts for the payroll register program

As illustrated in Figure 9–10, the process-payroll-records module contains more logic than similar modules in other programs. It also controls more support modules. Both the process-payroll-records and edit-time-record modules contain a number of IF statements needed to execute the logic illustrated in the flowchart.

As indicated in Figure 9–10 Part 2, a salaried employee can be paid when there is not a match on TF-employee number and MF-employee number. However, *if* a salaried employee has a valid time record that passed the edit test (Good-data still equals Y) and the pay-code is not equal to N, the employee will receive part of his normal gross pay. The amount the employee will receive is recorded in the time record.

After the end of the time-record file is reached, the master file may still contain unprocessed records for salaried employees who are to be paid. When the end-of-file condition is detected for the payroll master file, more-records will be set to N.

The other modules controlled by process-payroll-records contain mostly statements that will be executed sequentially in a straightforward manner. Therefore, the only modules illustrated in Figure 9–10 are the read-time-record, process-payroll-records, edit-time-record, and the execute-error-routine modules. These modules illustrate how errors are detected, how an appropriate message is created, and how a file is created to produce an error report.

When the source code is developed, the calculate-net-pay module may seem to be excessively long and a decision may be made to divide the module into two modules: determine voluntary deductions; and determine net pay.

Stub testing is used in Interactive Exercise 9–1 in order to test the process-payroll-records, edit-time-record, execute-error-routine, and the read-time-record modules.

CHECKPOINT QUESTIONS

34. Why is it unnecessary to include records in the time file for salaried employees who will receive their full bi-weekly salary?

35. When will the error messages used to explain the errors detected while editing the time records be printed?

36. Why is it better to always use a TF-pay-code rather than leaving the field blank for hourly or part-time employees?

37. If two errors were detected when the payreg program was executed, what must be done so that all employees will be paid their correct bi-weekly wage?

38. If high-values is moved to a four-position numeric field, what will the field contain after the move is completed?

39. Why will the program be terminated after the end-of-file condition is detected for the master file rather than when it is detected for the time file?

40. The master file contains records 1,2,4,6,7 and so forth. The time file contains the records 1,4,2,7, and so forth. What procedure is used to detect the sequence error? When will the error be detected?

41. Is it always necessary to use an empty-file indicator?

42. Could the order in which the edit routines were coded be changed?

© SRA 1988, 1983

43. Why is the read-transaction indicator set to Y in the edit-time-record module?

44. Why is a unique message generated for each type of error?

45. Why is a separate module used for the statements included in the execute-error-routine module?

46. Why does moving high-values in the TF-employee-number field prevent any more records to be read from the time record file?

47. What indicator is used to control the execution of the majority of the statements within the process-payroll-records module?

48. When the source code is written, what changes might be made in the hierarchy chart shown in Figure 9–9 on page 341?

49. In what ways is the hierarchy chart in Figure 9–9 on page 341 different from those that were previously illustrated?

50. How will the error-counter which is normally incremented in the execute-error-routine module be used?

SUMMARY
- When data is entered into an interactive transaction-processing system, editing occurs as the data enters the system and before it becomes part of a file or report.

- In order to edit data entering a system, the programmer or analyst must work closely with the persons who understand the data and the relationships that exist between the fields in the transaction and the master file records.

- Source code may be developed to apply a reasonableness test, within range test, limit check, class test, or relationship check.

- When a limited number of codes, account numbers, or item numbers are used, a binary or sequential search may be made of the numbers or codes stored in a table in order to determine if the one being entered is valid. Binary searches are more efficient for large tables than are sequential searches.

- When a transaction file is created, a programmable terminal may be used offline and programmed to provide some of the routine editing. Although additional editing can be done when master files are available, the cost of entering the data in an online, interactive environment may be prohibitive.

- When a transaction file is created, control totals may be recorded in a trailer record. Totals are often maintained for the number of records entered, number of items sold, or for the regular and overtime hours entered.

- Reports listing errors detected when data is being processed should be analyzed to see if additional controls or validations techniques can be utilized to reduce the number of errors that occur.

- A control record, containing the date for a report and other required constants, may be recorded in a file rather than being keyed in while the program that needs the information is being executed. Delays in the execution of a program may be caused by requiring the operator to respond to too many requests for information.

- A separate edit module is often created to edit transaction records. Whenever an error is detected, a unique message and the contents of the transaction record will be stored in an error-file. Either by using a separate module or program, an error report will be printed after all of the transaction records are processed.

- When records from two files are processed sequentially, provision must be made for checking the sequence of the records and for determining which of the two end-of-file conditions will be used to terminate the program. In some cases, the job may be determined when the end-of-file condition is detected for either of the files.

- Often one file contains records for all items or accounts while the second file contains records for only those items or accounts that must be processed. When a match occurs on item or account number, an edit or processing routine may be invoked.

- An indicator can be turned on when an empty file is detected. The indicator can then be used to bypass some or all of the statements within the termination module.

DISCUSSION QUESTIONS

1. Contrast the editing techniques that can be used in an interactive transaction-processing system with those used when a programmable terminal is used offline to create a transaction file.

2. Describe the difference between a reasonableness test and a within-range test; describe a situation in which each might be used.

3. Why should an analyst consider how the data stored in a field will be used before its attributes are described to the computer?

4. Why is it sometimes necessary to redefine a numeric field?

5. Of what significance to a programmer is the binary collating sequence?

6. In regard to how it is executed, what is the difference between a sequential and a binary search? Determine when each type of search should be used.

7. Why are the relationships that exist between fields of data considered important in determining how data can be edited?

8. Why are many organizations replacing nonprogrammable terminals with programmable terminals?

9. Describe a situation in which one or more control totals might be used to determine the validity of the output.

10. Identify the differences between a trailer record and a control record; describe the data that each might contain.

11. Why should a confirmation report be printed when new items are added to the inventory master file? How should the report be used?

12. Why is each of the following fields of data pertaining to an invoice stored in a customer's master file record: invoice number, invoice date, shipping date, due date, and invoice total?

© SRA 1988, 1983

13. In the payroll register program, how was the data stored in the error file and when was the error report printed?

14. If errors are detected in the time file, why must the payroll register program be rerun?

15. Why might an analyst or programmer wish to use an empty-file indicator?

KEY WORDS

audit trail

bad debt

binary collating sequence

binary search

burst mode

class test

combination checking

connect time

control record

control total

EBCDIC

high value

limit check

nonprogrammable terminal

programmable terminal

offline

reasonableness test

redefine a field

sequential search

smart terminal

trailer record

within range test

PROJECTS

EXERCISE 9–1

Refer to the information pertaining to the payroll master file (pages 239–240), the time file (page 340), the hierarchy chart for the payroll register program (page 341), the program specifications, and the flowcharts for the payroll register program that are already developed (pages 342–345). Review all of this material and then complete the following assignments:

1. Develop a print layout chart for the payroll register.
2. Develop a detailed logic plan for the print-payroll-register and print-payroll-headings modules.
3. Identify the source of all of the data printed on the payroll register.

EXERCISE 9–2

Using the same information as listed for Exercise 9–1, complete the following assignments.

1. Develop detailed logic plans for the calculate-salaried-gross, calculate-hourly-gross, and calculate-net-pay modules. External subroutines are used to calculate FICA, federal income tax, and state income tax.
2. Identify the source of all of the data utilized in the required calculations.
3. If the initialization module is completed before designing the modules controlled by the process-payroll-records module, why might it be necessary to add additional statements to those already provided?

PROBLEM 9–1

The payroll transaction file created during the execution of the payroll register program is used to produce a variety of reports. Assume that the records are sorted by account number within the cost center. The specifications for the cost center report program are as follows:

	Description
Output	
Printed report	The report for each cost center will be on a separate page. The total cost for regular and overtime pay charged to each of the payroll account numbers will be listed. The total charge for the cost center will be printed at the bottom of the page.
	Final totals will be printed for the total gross, total regular, and total overtime pay.
Input	
Payroll transaction file	The following fields will be utilized: cost center number, account number, regular pay, overtime pay, and gross pay.
Table	The description of the 69 cost centers is stored in a table located within the memory of the computer. When the table is defined, it is automatically loaded with the cost center names.
Control record	A separate file contains a record that has the dates the pay period covers and the date of the report. This information will be printed on the heading for each cost center report.
Controls	The totals printed after all the records are processed must agree with the total gross pay, regular pay, and overtime pay printed for the payroll register.

© SRA 1988, 1983

1. Develop a print layout form for the individual cost center reports and one for the control totals that will be printed on a separate page.
2. List the tasks that must be performed and determine the modules that will be required.
3. Develop a hierarchy chart for the cost-center report program.
4. Develop a detailed logic plan for the cost-center report program.

INTERACTIVE EXERCISE 9–1

The payreg program is used to illustrate stub testing and editing. Study Figure 9–8, page 340, and determine the data that will be stored in each time file record. Also refer to the hierarchy chart, illustrated on page 341, and determine the modules that will be used. Listed are the modules shown on the hierarchy chart and the status of each module.

Module Number	Name	Status
1000	Execute payroll register	Completed
2000	Initialization	Partially completed
2010	Process payroll register	Completed
2020	Termination	Changed in order to print an error report
3000	Read control record	Completed—data not used
3010	Read time record	Completed
3020	Read master record	Completed
3030	Edit time record	Completed
4000	Execute error routine	Changed in order that error messages will be stored in a table and printed at end-of-job
3040	Calculate salaried gross	Stub
3050	Calculate hourly gross	Stub
3060	Calculate net pay	Stub
3070	Write transaction file	Stub
3080	Print payroll register	Modified to list the employees who will be paid
4010	Print payroll headings	Not included

Display commands have been included that will illustrate which records are being read and how control passes to the various stubs. The display statements would be removed after the program is completely tested. The following statements are displayed:

READ TIME RECORD 2	TF-employee-number is 2
READ MASTER 1	MF-employee-number is 1
2 1	Control is in Process-payroll-register module. Shows which records are available. First number is for the time record; second for the master record.
CONTROL PASSED TO—NAME AND NUMBER OF MODULE	
READ MASTER 2	
2 2	
CONTROL PASSED TO EDIT MODULE	Occurs when there is a match on time file and master file employee numbers.

When a response is required, the cursor flashes to indicate that a response is needed. Since a response is requested in order to give you time to read the messages and evaluate what is occurring, press **ENTER** after you have read the message.

The payroll master file contains the following records:

Employee Number	Status	Name
1	S	SMITH, JOAN
2	H	BROWN, BEN
3	S	BENSON, GEORGE
4	H	NEAL, TOBBY
5	S	LOCKHART, FRED
6	P	BRODY, LILA

Using good testing procedures, Test 1 contains valid records and all of the employees will be paid. Tests 2–5 are designed to test various error routines. Rather than being stored in a file and printed later, the error messages are printed as they occur. The name and number of each employee who will be paid is stored in a table and printed after all of the records are processed.

Directions

1. Boot the system, load **BASIC**, load **Menu,** select menu **4,** option **24.**

2. Before you run the program, **list 290.** The statement should read

OPEN "TIME1.DAT" FOR INPUT AS #3

   If a number other than a **1** follows TIME, change the number to a 1 and press the **ENTER** key. Press **F2.**

3. TIME1 is the name of the test file that will be used for Test 1 and it contains the following data.

File ID	Status	Number	Pay Code	Part-pay	Reg Hours	Overtime Hours
T	H	2	B	0	80	0
T	H	4	B	0	80	0
T	P	6	B	0	40	0

4. Enter **RUN.** In response to "If statement 190 is correct, press enter." press **ENTER.**

   a. In response to ENTER TEST NO, enter a **1.**

   b. Remember when there is a delay and you see the blinking cursor, press the **ENTER** key. Describe how you would determine that the correct employees were paid.

   _____

   _____

   _____

   Do not exit to the menu program.

5. **LIST statement 290** and change TIME1 to TIME2. The statement should read:

290 OPEN "TIME2.DAT" FOR INPUT AS #3

   After you make the change, **RUN** the program. In response to ENTER TEST NO, enter a **2.** Which employees had records in the time file?

   _____

© SRA 1988, 1983

Which editing routines were used to detect the errors listed?

_____

_____

Were the correct employees paid?

_____

If not, describe the problems that occurred. _____

_____

_____

Do NOT exit to the menu program.

6. **List statement 290** and change TIME2 to TIME3. Enter **RUN**. Enter **3** as the test number. Which editing routines were used to detect the errors listed?

_____

_____

The first record was for a salaried employee, **P** was entered as a pay code, and 500 was entered in the part-pay field. How was the record edited?

_____

Why were two messages printed for employee number 6? _____

_____

Do not exit to the Menu program.

7. **LIST statement 290** and change **TIME3** to **TIME4**. Enter **RUN**. Enter **4** as the test number. Which editing routines were used to detect the errors listed?

_____

_____

Since Joan Smith was not listed as being paid, what data must have been stored in the first time record? _____

Do NOT exit to the menu program.

8. **LIST statement 290** and change **TIME4** to **TIME5**. Enter **RUN**. Enter **5** as the test number. Which editing routines were used to detect the errors listed?

_____

_____

Do NOT exit to the menu program.

9. Either by studying the flowcharts provided on pages 342–345, or by listing statements using **LLIST 1430–1730,** determine how many of the editing routines were dependent on relationships that existed between two or more fields. Comments were added to the source code so that you could identify the various tests.

_____

_____

_____

10. The test data used was in correct sequence and contained records for employees 2, 3, and 6. However, control failed to pass to the edit-time-records module.

When should control pass to the edit module? _____

In what module would you look for a possible error? _____

What display was added during the test phase of the program that indicates when control should pass to the edit module? _____

---

11. Refer to the flowchart provided on page 345, or to the source code for the edit-time-records module, and the error listings generated during all five test runs and answer the following questions:

    Were all of the edit routines tested? Support your answer by identifying the test number and routine tested.

    _____

    _____

    _____

    _____

    _____

12. Why were multiple test files used rather than using one test file to test all of the error routines?

    _____

    _____

    Exit to the menu program and select option **6.**

Name _____

Section Number _____

I. Record the term being defined or the one needed to complete the statement in the space provided.

_____ 1. The Internal Revenue Service often uses a _____ test, based on the tax-payer's gross income, to determine if a deduction should be challenged.

_____ 2. If codes are stored in a small table with only 15–20 areas a code entered from the terminal or from a file can be checked by using a _____.

_____ 3. Programmable or _____ terminals can be programmed to do routine editing such as determine if non-numeric data is in a numeric field.

_____ 4. The last record in a file which contains control totals is referred to as a _____ record.

_____ 5. When regular hours must be greater than 0 and less than 80.1, a _____ test will be used.

_____ 6. When _____ checking occurs, a statement such as IF STATUS = "S" AND CODE NOT = "N" OR CODE NOT = P" THEN . . . is used.

_____ 7. When totals are printed for the regular hours and overtime hours entered from the time file, the totals are referred to as _____.

_____ 8. When the end of the time file was detected, _____ value was moved into the TF-employee-number field.

_____ 9. Comparisons of two values are made by the computer using the _____ sequence to determine which value is higher.

_____ 10. When EBCDIC code is used, the letter A has a _____ binary value than the digit 4.

_____ 11. If a programmer wishes to insert commas into a field which was originally defined as a numeric field, it will be necessary to _____ the field.

_____ 12. In COBOL a _____ test can be used to determine if a numeric field contains non-numeric characters.

_____ 13. The invoice number is usually included as part of the invoice record in order to provide a clearly defined _____.

_____ 14. When data is transmitted over a telecommunication network in a _____, the data is transmitted without interruption.

_____ 15. A _____ check may be used to determine if a customer's order can be processed.

II. Multiple choice. Record the letter of the *best* answer in the space provided.

_____ 1. When a customer number is entered, it can be verified or edited by
   a. displaying the name from the record retrieved and comparing it with the name listed on the source document.
   b. doing a binary search to see if the number is one stored within a table.
   c. using a class test to determine that only numeric data is stored within the field.
   d. any or all of the above methods.

_____ 2. The validity of an item number keyed in and used to randomly retrieve a record from a VSAM file can be verified by using
   a. a limit check.
   b. a reasonableness test.

       c. an invalid key.

       d. all of the above.

       e. none of the techniques listed.

_____ 3. When EBCDIC is used to store data,

       a. letters of the alphabet have a higher collating sequence than special characters.

       b. special characters have a higher collating sequence than digits.

       c. digits have the lowest collating sequence.

       d. letters of the alphabet have the highest collating sequence.

_____ 4. Invoices for January 3–7 are being processed and the date is entered as mmddyyyy (01031989). The most effective way to check the dates being entered is to use

       a. a limit test.

       b. a reasonableness test.

       c. a within range test.

       d. any one of the above tests.

       e. none of the above tests.

_____ 5. A binary search can be compared to

       a. an IF statement.

       b. a DO-WHILE statement.

       c. a game in which an individual is asked to guess a number.

       d. count-controlled loop.

_____ 6. When new records are added to an existing ISAM or VSAM master file,

       a. it is not necessary to edit the data entered as a confirmation report will be printed.

       b. an invalid-key routine cannot be used.

       c. the data listed on the confirmation report should be compared with the data recorded on the source document.

       d. a confirmation report is not needed if all of the data entered by the operator is visually verified or edited within the program.

_____ 7. In the payroll register example, the edit-time-record module was invoked,

       a. as soon as a time record was read.

       b. whenever a master file record was read.

       c. when the employee number in the time record matched the employee number recorded in the master file record.

       d. whenever a sequence error occurred.

_____ 8. The execute-error-routine module was invoked,

       a. each time the edit module was executed.

       b. whenever a sequence or editing error was detected.

       c. whenever a match on employee number occurred.

       d. so that the read-tran indicator could be set to Y.

_____ 9. When a sequence error was detected,

       a. the execute-error-routine module was invoked.

       b. read-tran was set to Y.

       c. read-master was set to N.

       d. all of the above occurred.

       e. none of the above occurred.

_____ 10. An empty-file indicator is used

       a. to by-pass commands executed within the process-payroll-records module.

       b. to eliminate the transfer of control to the termination module.

       c. rather than a more-records if end-of-file indicator.

       d. to by-pass many of the commands located within the termination module.

© SRA 1988, 1983

III. True or False. Record either a T or F in the space provided. If the answer is false, indicate how the statement should be changed to make it true.

_____ 1. When experienced data entry operators key in data, programmers should assume that it is correct.

_____ 2. Usually variable data entering the system is alphanumeric data.

_____ 3. In order to determine if there is enough of an item on hand to process an order, a within range test should be used.

_____ 4. A mathematical statement cannot be executed as part of an IF statement. Therefore, the following pseudocode is incorrect: IF A − B > 99 THEN . . .

_____ 5. If an operator keys in 10,000 rather than 10000, when BASIC is used the computer will detect the inclusion of a comma in a field defined as numeric.

_____ 6. A class test is used to determine if a field contains non-numeric data.

_____ 7. EBCDIC is used more extensively than any other code for storing data in the memory of a medium- or large-sized computer.

_____ 8. If the analyst understands the relationship of the data being entered to the record being processed, it is not necessary to determine the relationship of the data to other fields within the record or program.

_____ 9. Many organizations are replacing nonprogrammable terminals with smart terminals.

_____ 10. A trailer record often contains control totals that are printed and used to determine the validity of the output.

_____ 11. Since the total of all quantities ordered is meaningless, it cannot be used as a control total.

_____ 12. When sales data is entered from a remote location and transmittd over a telecommunication system, a confirmation report should be transmitted to the sender listing the orders that were received and processed.

_____ 13. When a control record is used for entering constants rather than having an operator key in the required information, it is usually considered less efficient. The file must be created by using a separate program and then opened and closed in the program in which the information is required.

_____ 14. Relationship checks, or editing, are also referred to as combination checking.

_____ 15. The error report was printed when the print-error-report module was invoked by statements included within the termination module.

_____ 16. When the second READ command is used to read records stored in a transaction file, an empty-file condition may be detected.

_____ 17. It would never be considered normal to open a file in which no records are stored.

_____ 18. When data stored in transaction records is being edited, once an error is detected in one of the fields stored within the record no further editing of the fields stored within the record should occur.

_____ 19. Stub testing could occur if the initialization, process-payroll records, and edit-time-record modules were coded.

_____ 20. The majority of the edit routines coded for the payreg program utilized combination-checking procedures.

© SRA 1988, 1983

MENUS AND VARIABLE LENGTH RECORDS

10

After reading the chapter and completing the learning activities, you will be able to:

- Construct a detailed logic plan for developing a menu program.

- Explain how CHAIN and CHAIN MERGE are used to create a menu program.

- Determine the similarities and differences between the modules controlled by the select-sub-menu module.

- Identify how and why tables are used in creating the menu program.

- When given a description of a program, determine the type of information that might be included in one or more help screens.

- Describe the difference in the data stored in format-1 and format-2 records.

- Explain why it is advantageous to use variable length records for storing transaction data rather than storing the data within a table contained within the master file record.

- Identify the difference between a primary key and an alternate key.

- Explain how format-1 and format-2 records are added to a master file.

- Explain why changes are required for format-1 records and why corrections may be needed for format-2 records.

- Identify when transaction records flagged for deletion can be deleted from the accounts receivable master file.

- Describe master files, other than the accounts receivable master file, that may require records of varying length and with alternate keys to be included.

As you have used the menu program and selected the screens and options available for the interactive exercises, have you wondered how the menu was created? When greater emphasis was placed on creating a user-friendly environment for nondata processing professionals, menus became widely used.

In the sales order entry program illustrated in Chapter 3, a help menu was displayed that permitted the operator to obtain information regarding how data was to be entered and verified. If you completed Interactive Exercise 3–1, you responded to messages and reviewed the available help screens. When you selected the option to execute, a branch occurred within the program that caused an internal subroutine or module to be executed. Control always returned to the module that invoked the help routine.

The menu program you have been using to run the Interactive Exercises **chains** back and forth between the application programs to be executed and the menu program. In this chapter, the hierarchy chart and detailed flowcharts for the menu program will be explained. In addition, varying length records created for the accounts receivable master file will be discussed.

CREATING A MENU PROGRAM

Most menu programs are developed using the same general format. When there are a large number of options from which to select, the main menu lists the available submenus. For example, the menu for the payroll system might list the options illustrated in Figure 10–1.

Each of the five menus lists the available programs. For each program listed, there may be one or more screens of information to provide a general description of the program and its input/output requirements. A portion of the report program menu is displayed to illustrate how one number is used to obtain RUN instructions and documentation. A second number causes the program to be executed.

Figure 10–1 Main menu for the payroll system.

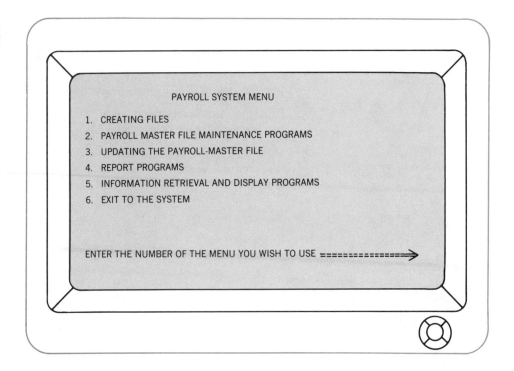

```
                      PAYROLL SYSTEM MENU

          1.  CREATING FILES
          2.  PAYROLL MASTER FILE MAINTENANCE PROGRAMS
          3.  UPDATING THE PAYROLL-MASTER FILE
          4.  REPORT PROGRAMS
          5.  INFORMATION RETRIEVAL AND DISPLAY PROGRAMS
          6.  EXIT TO THE SYSTEM



      ENTER THE NUMBER OF THE MENU YOU WISH TO USE ===============⟹
```

© SRA 1988, 1983

Report Programs

Payreg	Calculates payroll deductions and net pay.
1	Documentation and run instructions.
2	Run program.
Paycheck	Reads the transaction file and prints the paychecks.
3	Documentation and run instructions.
4	Run program.
Payroll Summary	Reads payroll master file and prints YTD summary.
5	Documentation and run instructions.
6	Run program.

If an operator selects option 4 from the main menu, the submenu for the report programs briefly describes the program and provides two options: one for obtaining documentation and a second option for executing the program. If the operator selects option 2, the payroll register program will be loaded into memory and executed.

Chaining commands

When an option is selected which loads and runs a program, the name of the program is used as part of the **CHAIN** command. When a statement such as CHAIN "PAYREG" is used, the library is searched for the PAYREG program. If the program is found, it will be loaded into memory. If a line number is not included as part of the CHAIN statement, the program loaded into memory will be executed in its entirety.

It is also possible to execute part of a program and then chain out to a second program. After the second program is executed, a statement within the second program chains back to the first program in order that the remainder of the program can be executed.

Although the statement may not be identified as CHAIN in some languages, statements similar to those illustrated are usually available.

CHAIN "PAYREG"	Loads in the complete payreg program which will replace the menu program.
CHAIN "MENU", 190	Menu is loaded into memory and control passes to line 190 of the menu program.
CHAIN MERGE "PAYMF"	PAYMF contains the file open and field statements that describe the payroll master file and its data structure. The statements are retrieved from the file called PAYMF and included in the program in which the CHAIN MERGE statement is used.

CHAIN MERGE is similar to the COPY statement used in COBOL and in other languages such as PL/I. In BASIC, COBOL, and PL/I, the statements to be included in the application program will replace the CHAIN or COPY statement. Using CHAIN MERGE or COPY saves coding and makes certain that in each program the data structures are identical. When using COBOL or PL/I the file is copied into the program containing the COPY statement each time the program is compiled. Therefore, program maintenance is much easier; the changes in the statements copied into several programs are made only in the original source code that is stored in the file being copied.

It is also possible to delete some of the lines containing statements from the chaining program before loading in the chained-to program. Since the CHAIN statement leaves files open, it is the responsibility of the programmer to close the files in the first program before chaining to the second program. A series of programs can be executed by chaining from program A to program B, from B to C, from C to D and so forth. If the chaining is made optional and based upon the response of an operator, each of the programs can also be executed as independent, stand alone programs.

Using tables

In the menu program you have been using, the descriptions and the names of the programs are loaded into two separate tables. When program descriptions are listed, a unique number is used to identify each program. When the number is keyed in, the menu program checks to see that it is within range for the menu being used. If the number is valid, it is used as a subscript and the name of the program is retrieved from the table. The statement used was coded as

CHAIN PROGRAMS$ (I)

In the illustration, the name of the table is PROGRAMS$ and field I contains the option entered. If I = 24, the 24th area of the table is accessed and the name payreg is retrieved and used to obtain the program, load it into memory, and cause the program to execute. Although single letters are used for subscripts, both the flowchart (pages 366–369) and the internal documentation provided in the initialization module of the source code describe the functions performed by the letters. For example the following statements are included in the menu program:

```
A$                     'USED TO ENTER RESPONSES
X                      'CONTROLS SELECT-SUB-MENU LOOP
```

When the termination module executes, you are asked RETURN TO MAIN MENU? Y OR N? If you replied with a Y or y, the following statement was executed:

IF A$ = 'Y' OR A$ = 'y' THEN CHAIN 'MENU', 190

If line 190 had not been specified, the entire menu program would have been executed and the SRA logo would have been displayed. Instead line 190 is specified which causes the initialization module to be invoked.

Hierarchy chart for the menu program

Module 3000, display submenus, lists the six options available. If the operator selects one of the first four options, control transfers to the submenu selected and the available options are displayed. The operator is asked to enter the number of the option desired. The number entered is used to retrieve the name of the program from the table. When tables are used:

1. Count-controlled loops are used to load the table. The flowchart on page 366 illustrates how the tables are loaded.

2. A count-controlled loop is used to display the available options which saves a great deal of coding.

3. Only one statement is needed in each loop to retrieve the name of the program to be executed.

© SRA 1988, 1983

Because tables are used, fewer statements are required to code the program. Using tables also reduces the number of complex IF/THEN/ELSE statements needed and makes it easier to understand the source code.

Flowchart for the menu program

SELECT-SUBMENU MODULE   The flowchart on page 367 indicates that a conditional WHILE loop is created for the select-submenu module. If the operator selects one of the first four options, commands within the selected module are executed and a new program is loaded into memory. However, if option 5 is selected, the display-help-options module is executed and control returns to module 2010. The operator can then elect to exit to one of the submenu modules or to select option 6 which causes 7 to be stored in the field called X. Since X is equal to 7, an exit will be made from the WHILE loop.

DISPLAY-SUBMENUS MODULE   Although the source statements could have been coded within the select-submenu module, a separate module is used to display the options available. A range test is used to determine if the digit entered is between 0–7. The value stored in I, the field in which the operator's choice is entered, is returned to module 2010.

DISPLAY MODULES   *Except* for the count–controlled loop created to display the descriptions of the programs and the numbers used to identify the available options, modules 3010-3040 are identical. Module 3010, display C1-4 options, has a count-controlled loop that is controlled as follows:

```
DO (count = 1 TO 7)
```

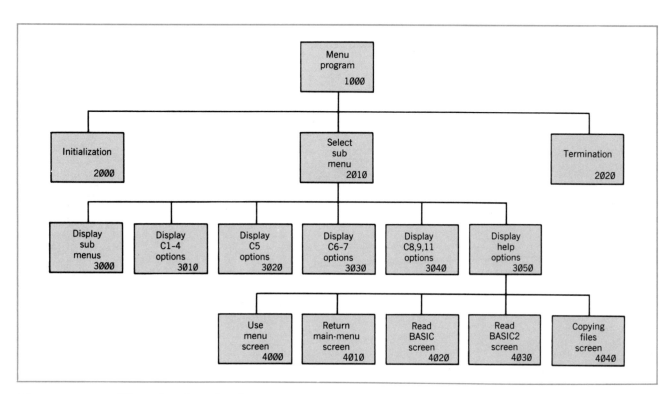

Figure 10–2   *Hierarchy chart for the menu program.*

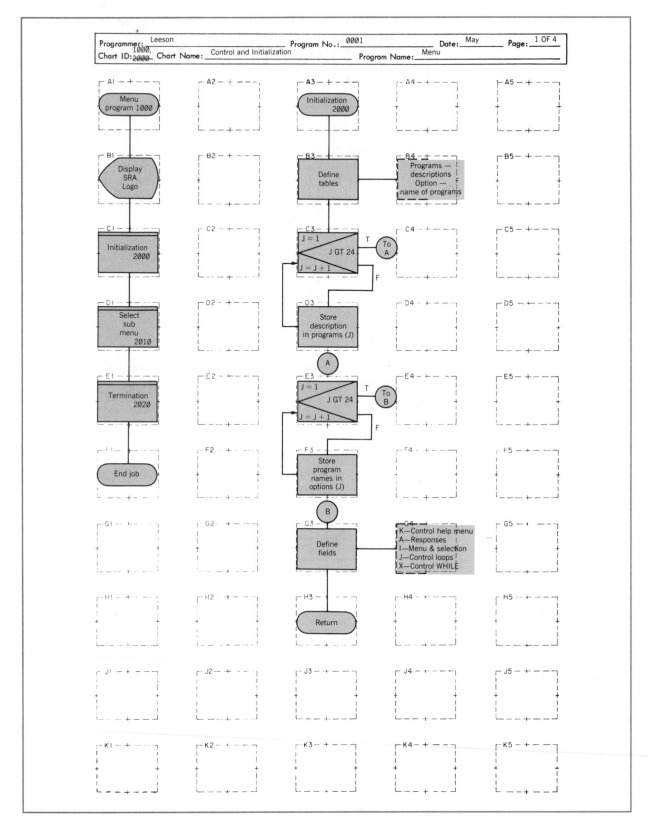

Figure 10–3 Part 1   Flowchart for the menu program.

© SRA 1988, 1983

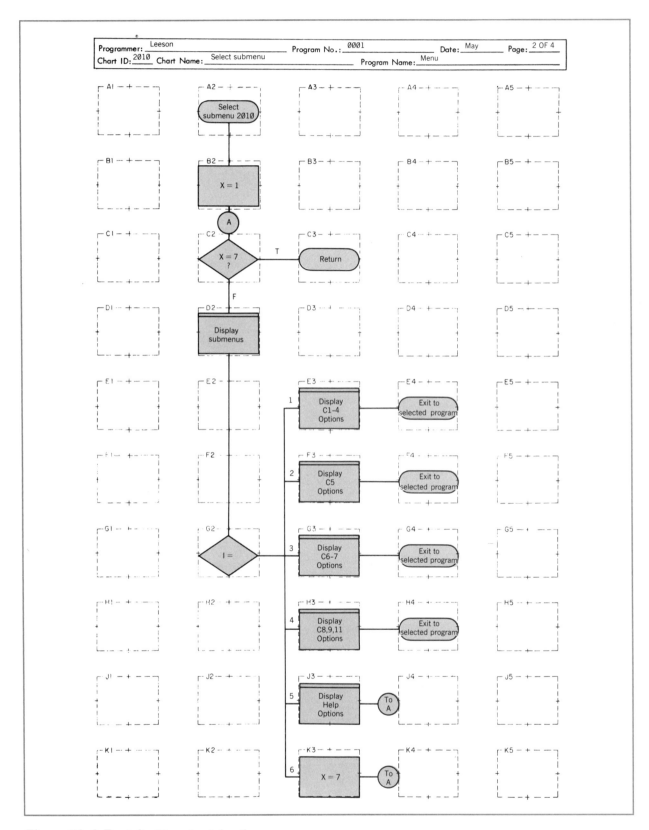

Figure 10–3 Part 2   *Flowchart for the menu program.*

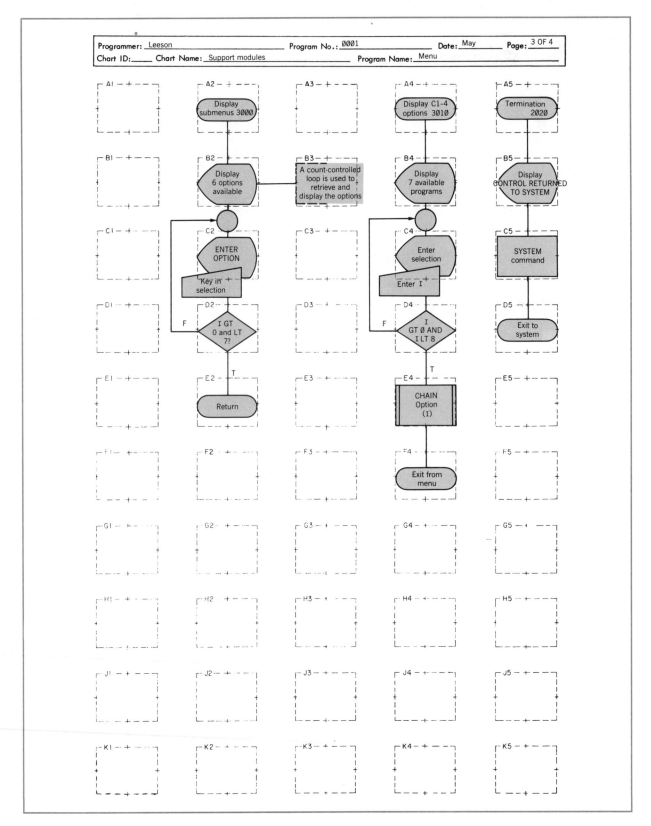

Figure 10–3 Part 3   *Flowchart for the menu program.*

© SRA 1988, 1983

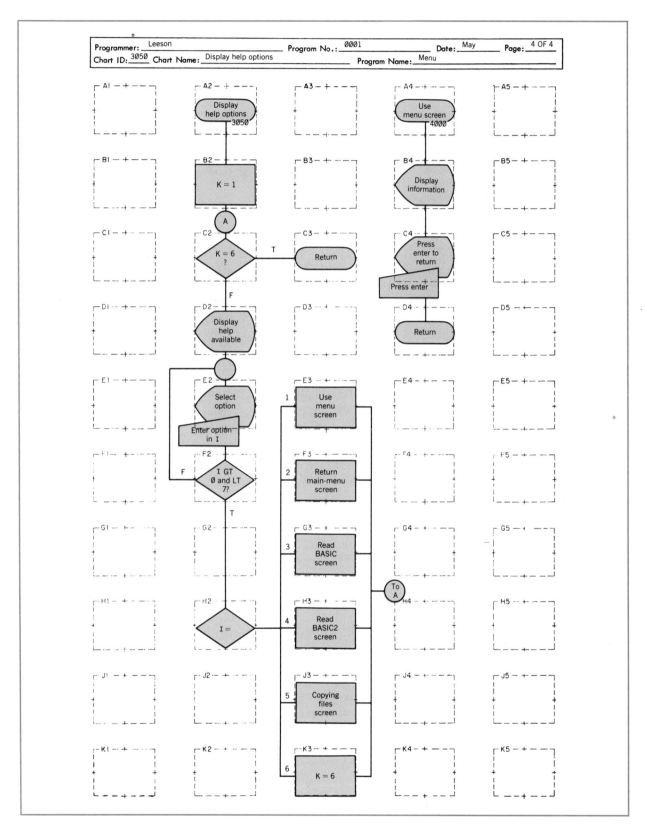

Figure 10–3 Part 4   Flowchart for the menu program.

Therefore, the first seven descriptions and program names can be accessed. In module 3020, the same code is used. However, the loop is controlled by a statement such as:

```
DO (count = 8 TO 13)
```

Also, the range test used to check the number entered by the operator checks to see that I is greater than 7 and less than 14. If the number entered is outside the allowable range, an error message is displayed and control returns to the point where the number was entered.

DISPLAY-HELP-OPTIONS MODULE   The display-help-options module, illustrated on page 369, also indicates that a conditional loop is needed. Control will remain within the module until the operator enters a 6. When a 6 is entered, K is set equal to 6 and an exit will be made from the loop.

Each of the five help modules is developed as indicated on page 368. The information is displayed on the screen by using a series of PRINT statements. After the information is displayed, the statement PRESS ENTER TO RETURN TO THE HELP MENU is displayed. A response is needed in order to give the operator time to read the messages.

In writing the help modules, the programmer should make certain the information displayed is easy to read and understand. When the ongoing evaluation of a program indicates that there are too many data-entry or execution errors, it may be an indication that more help screens are needed or that the ones displayed are poorly written.

TERMINATION MODULE   When the operator enters a 6 in response to ENTER NUMBER OF DESIRED OPTION, control returns to the main-control module and the termination module is invoked. As illustrated in the flowchart on page 368, the statement CONTROL RETURNED TO THE SYSTEM is displayed. The SYSTEM command is then executed and the computer is under the control of DOS. If the SYSTEM command is eliminated, a more normal termination routine would occur and the computer would wait for a new command to be entered, such as LOAD new-program.

When the menu program is terminated, the programmer can display whatever message seems appropriate and cause control to either return to DOS (the SYSTEM) or to a language such as BASIC which permits the operator to load a new program or menu.

Comments regarding menu programs

Although a great deal of source code may be required to write a menu program, most of the routines are very similar and a COPY statement can usually be used to copy routines that can be modified to meet the requirements of a specific module.

A menu program is unique since files are not used for entering data and no actual output is produced. Most of the source code either provides the data for loading the required tables or prints the help menus. In a well-organized CIS department, a menu format may be available that can be tailored to the requirements of the system being developed.

© SRA 1988, 1983

CHECKPOINT
QUESTIONS

1. Menu programs may be created for each system such as payroll, accounts receivable, inventory, and accounts payable. In what ways will the menus be similar?
2. Contrast what occurs when CHAIN "UPDATE" and CHAIN MERGE "ARFILE.DCL" are used.
3. Why should CHAIN MERGE or COPY statements be used?
4. When chaining to a program such as PTPAYCK (print paycheck), is it possible to execute only a portion of the program?
5. What two tables are created and used in the menu program?
6. If tables are used in creating a menu program, why will less source code be required than if tables are not used?
7. In what ways are modules 3010 through 3040 similar? How do they differ?
8. What factors should be considered when developing help menus? Why is it sometimes necessary to modify the help menus?
9. Why should files be closed before a statement such as CHAIN "MENU" is executed?

VARIABLE LENGTH
RECORDS

Refer back to pages 330–331 and review the information that is recorded in a typical sales-transaction file. Figure 9–2 identifies and explains the data recorded in each record of the sales-transaction file. On page 337 the information that should be retained in the accounts receivable master file regarding the sales invoices is identified.

The information regarding each invoice should be retained

1. until the customers are sent itemized statements that list all transactions within the billing period.
2. until the invoice is paid. Information pertaining to paid invoices can be deleted *after* the itemized statements are printed.

The information pertaining to the unpaid invoices must be available to determine each customer's ending balance and to prepare reports such as the **schedule of accounts receivable**, which lists of all customers and their balances, and the **aged trial balance**, which lists each customer and the age of each amount owed. The aged trial balance usually lists the information in the same manner as it appears at the bottom of each customer's statement. The amounts owed are often listed as current, over 30 days, over 60 days, and over 90 days. When statements are prepared, the computer program may calculate interest on all amounts which are listed as being 30 days or more over due.

Reports such as itemized statements and aged trial balances can only be prepared if the required information is included in the accounts receivable master file and can be accessed randomly. Review the information that must be retained for each invoice:

Field	Type of Data	Bytes Required
Invoice Number	AN	6
Date of Invoice	N	8
Shipping Date	N	8
Due Date	N	8
Invoice Total	N	8

Unless the numeric data is packed, or the 19 is dropped from the date and a date such as Dec. 10, 1988 is recorded as 121088, a minimum of 38 bytes of storage will be required for each invoice. A table could be established within the accounts receivable record to store the information. Or the information pertaining to invoices, payments from the customer, and credit granted for returns and damaged merchandise could be recorded in separate records that follow each customer's master file record. If a field is included for customer number, the data pertaining to unpaid invoices can be maintained in a separate file.

Using tables rather than variable length records

If tables are used, file space may be wasted. While one customer may have only one or two transactions in a billing period, another customer may have fifty or sixty transactions. Depending on the language used, it may be necessary to maintain the same size table for each customer. Also, more maintenance is required to keep the information pertaining to the unpaid invoices in a logical order.

If the programming language used supports variable length records, and either VSAM or a similar organizational method, a better solution for providing the required information is to create a detail record for each transaction. The detail records and the master record will be stored in the same file. However, the length and data structure of the two types of record will differ. Because variable length records usually proves a better solution, the logic required to create, utilize, and maintain variable length records will be discussed.

Creating variable length records

FORMAT-1 RECORDS   Figure 10–4 illustrates the records that will be stored within the accounts receivable file. The first byte of a **format-1 record** contains the delete code and the second byte an "M" for master file. The master record contains two keys:

1. Record number   An **alternate key** that is *unique to the set of transaction records*.
2. Customer number   A unique **primary key** used to retrieve randomly a customer's master record.

The alternate key is listed first so that the field will be in the same location as the record number field located in the transaction records. When variable-length records are used, it is usually easier to work with the data if fields that appear in both types of records are in the same location.

If the file is organized as a VSAM or a similar type of file, the customer master file record can be retrieved randomly by using the customer's number. Sequential access is then used to obtain the transaction records that contain

© SRA 1988, 1983

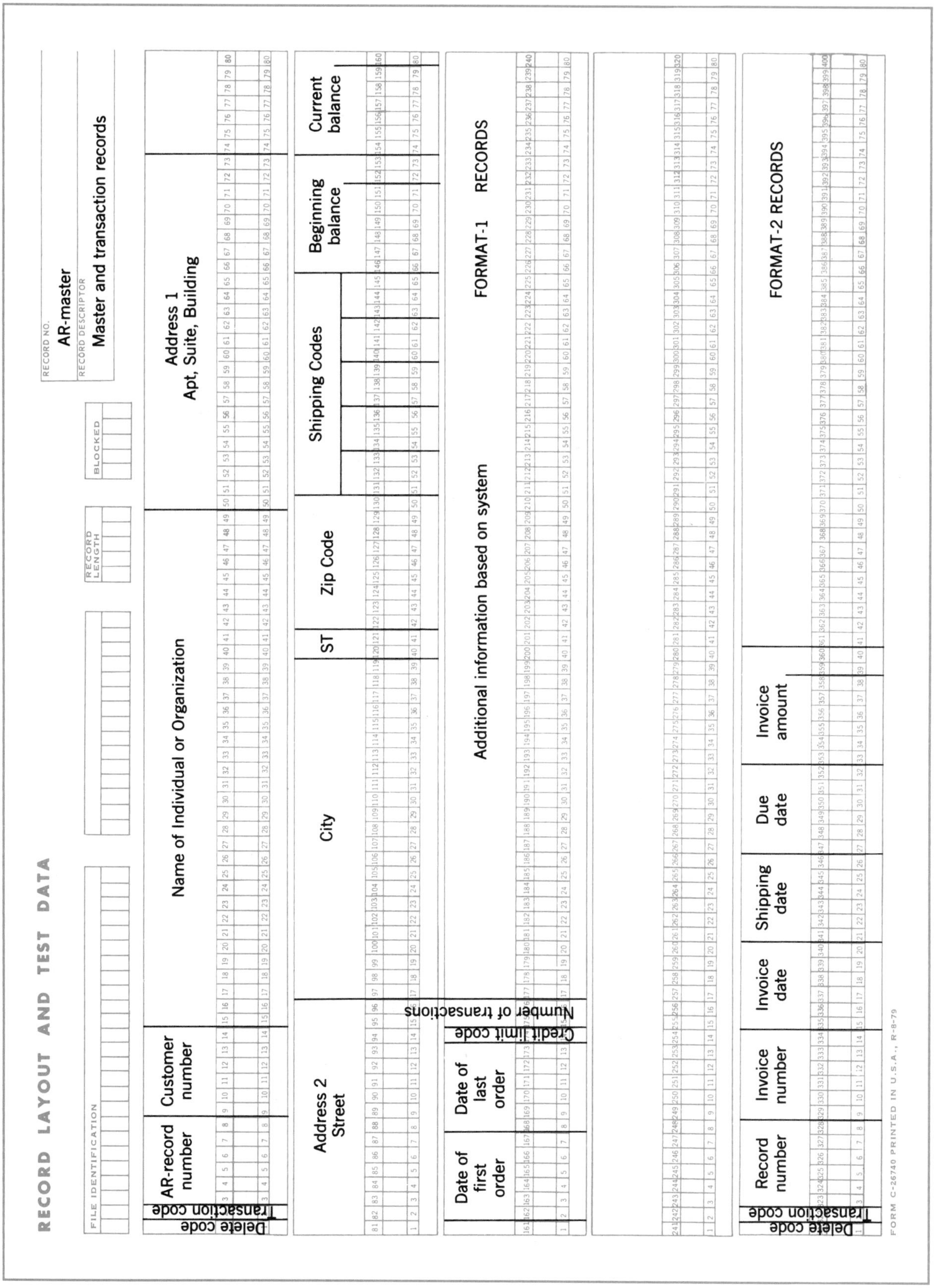

Figure 10–4 Variable length records for the accounts receivable file.

detailed information regarding the transactions that are "open"—such as unpaid invoices, returns relating to an unpaid invoice, or credit relating to an unpaid invoice. Records can be read sequentially until the record number changes.

The date recorded in the date-of-first-order field or date-of-last-order field is recorded in an unpacked format and treated as alphanumeric data. Since the fields contain space for only six bytes of data, the 19 will not be recorded in the field. However, when the date is printed, it will be split into its components—month, day, and year. The three fields are then concatonated with spaces, a comma, and the constant 19. Or, the field can be printed as mm/dd/yyyy. In the second example, slashes and 19 will be concatonated with the month, day, and last two digits of the year.

The field number-of-transactions will be incremented each time a new transaction record is added and decremented each time a transaction record is deleted. Since the field contains the current number of transaction records, it can be used to control count-controlled loops that sequentially read the transaction records and look for a "match" on invoice number.

FORMAT-2 RECORDS   When you refer to Figure 10–4 it is obvious that the transaction records require less storage space than the master records. Also, while each customer has only one master record, each customer may have an unlimited number of transaction records. Figure 10–5 explains how the fields used for the **format-2** records are used.

When the file is created, the programmer must describe both the format-1 and format-2 data structures. In addition, to describe the general characteristics of the file, both the primary key and the alternate key must be identified.

Figure 10–5   Fields located within the Format-2 records.

Field	Function
Delete code	A "D" indicates the record will be deleted after the statements are printed.
Transaction code	The codes used are: S = sales invoice P = payments received from customer C = credit granted to customer R = return of merchandise
Record number	Alternate key unique for the set of transaction records identified with each customer.
Invoice number	Depending on the type of transaction, the field is used for either the invoice number, the payment number, the credit memo number, or the return memo number.
Invoice date	The transaction date will be recorded in the field.
Shipping date/due date	The date of either the shipment, the payment, the return of merchandise, or the establishment of credit is recorded in the field.
Invoice amount	Contains the amount of the invoice, cash received, value of returned merchandise, or credit granted to the customer.

© SRA 1988, 1983

When the file is initially created, only the master records will be written into it. The ADDNEW program will also add only new master records to the accounts receivable master file.

Adding sales transaction records

When the sales-transaction file is processed and the sales invoices are printed, a new record will be recorded in the accounts receivable master file for each invoice. The hierarchy chart for the sales invoicing program is shown in Figure 10–7 and the program specifications are illustrated in Figure 10–6.

SALES INVOICING PROGRAM SPECIFICATIONS

Output

Sales invoices	An invoice may list one or several items and will include the information specified on the print layout chart.
Write error file	Errors detected due to invalid account or item numbers, insufficient quantity on hand to fill an order, or insufficient available credit will be recorded in the file.
AR-Format-2 records	The information specified for the Format-2 records illustrated on the record layout form will be recorded in the file.
Updated AR-master records	For each sales invoice, one is added to the number-of-transaction-records field. Also, if the customer's order is processed, the amount of the invoice is added to the current balance field. The date of the invoice is also recorded in the MF-date-of-late-order field.
Updated inventory master records	The quantity-on-hand field is reduced by the number of items ordered.
Control report	The report will print the control totals and the percent of records rejected due to each type of error that occurred. In a separate program the error file will be used to create a report listing all of the errors that were detected.

Input

Sales transaction file	The job will be terminated when the end-of-file mark is detected.
AR-master records	The customer number recorded in the sales transaction records is used to randomly retrieve the required records. The information needed to check the customer's credit and to print the top portion of the sales invoice is obtained from the file.
Inventory master records	The quantity-on-hand must be reduced by the quantity sold.
Control record	The invoice date and the number of the first invoice will be recorded in the control record.

Controls

Invalid-key routines will be used to detect invalid account or item numbers. A record count of the sales-transaction records read, processed, and rejected will be printed along with the total quantity read, rejected due to insufficient quantity on hand, and processed. The total value of all invoices printed and recorded in Format-2 records will also be printed. This figure will be used in determining the accuracy of the **accounts receivable control account.**

Figure 10–6   Program specifications for the sales invoicing program.

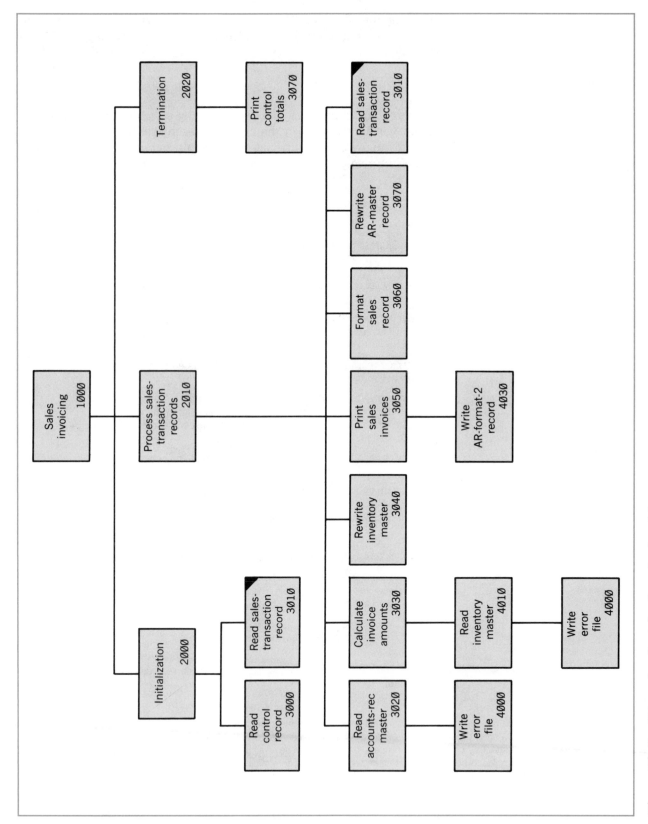

Figure 10–7 Hierarchy chart for the sales-invoicing program.

© SRA 1988, 1983

Although the master (format-1 records) and the transaction records (format-2 records) are in the same file, they are treated differently. The master record is retrieved randomly, updated, and then rewritten into its original location in the file.

The data to be moved into the format-2 data structure is obtained from the following sources:

Field	Source of Data
Delete code	The constant " " is recorded in the field.
Transaction code	The constant "S" is recorded in the field.
Record number	Obtained from the customer's master file record.
Invoice number	Calculated within the program. The beginning invoice number is entered and 1 is added after each invoice is printed.
Invoice date	Recorded in the control record.
Shipping date	Recorded in the sales-transaction file.
Due date	Calculated within the program by adding a fixed number of days to the shipping date.
Invoice amount	Calculated within the program.

After the required data is moved into the format-2 data structure, a write command is used to enter the new record in the file. The new entry will be inserted after the last record that has the same alternate key.

Adding cash received, credit memos, and return records

Following the "keep it simple" concept, three separate programs will be developed to write format-2 records that contain data pertaining to cash received on account, credit memos issued, and merchandise returned. Three separate programs should be used because

1. Each type of data is usually originated, or approved, by a different department or individual within the organization.
2. Different source documents are used to either create the transaction file or to enter the data in an interactive-mode.
3. Different confirmation and control reports are required.

In all three programs, the format-1 master record will be retrieved to determine the record number and to update the master record. Before rewriting the master record, 1 will be added to the number of transactions and the amount of the transaction will be subtracted from the current balance field.

In recording data pertaining to cash received on account or credit granted for returns or other adjustments, a search must be made to locate the format-2 record with the information pertaining to the invoice(s) being paid or adjusted. If cash receipts are recorded in an interactive mode, the customer number is entered and used to retrieve the customer's master record from the file. After retrieving the master record, the operator enters the number of the sales invoice being paid or adjusted. The invoice number is edited, then used to search for the required format-2 record. The following pseudocode illustrates how the search will be conducted.

```
*Find-invoice-record module.
 Good-invoice-number = Y
 Count = 0
 PERFORM Read-Format-2-record

 DO-WHILE (TF-invoice-number < > MF-invoice-number)
     IF Count = MF-number-of-transactions THEN
         DISPLAY 'NO MATCH ON INVOICE NUMBER. '
         DISPLAY 'DATA FOR DOCUMENT nnnn NOT PROCESSED. '
         Good-invoice-number = N
     ELSE
         PERFORM Read-format-2-record
         Count = Count + 1
     END IF
 END-DO
 IF Good-invoice-number = Y THEN
     IF  (MF-invoice-amount - TR-amount) = 0 THEN
         MF-delete-code = 'D'
     ELSE
         MF-delete-code = ' '
     END IF
 ELSE
     NULL
 END IF
 END DO
*end of module
```

In the illustration, TF-invoice-number is entered by the operator and MF-invoice-number is stored in the required format-2 record. When control returns to the enter-data module, if good-invoice-number = N the operator will be asked to check the invoice number. If the operator entered the one on the document, a notation will be made on the document and no further processing will occur. The operator will proceed to the next document.

If good-invoice-number = Y, the operator will key in the remainder of the required information. The data will be used to format a new format-2 record which will be added to the file. The master record will *not* be updated unless good-invoice-number = Y.

Correcting and changing data

A change program will be needed to provide the normal maintenance required for the master record. In reviewing Figure 10–4, it would be considered normal to change the name or address fields, the ship via codes, and the credit limit code. When a customer has established a good credit rating with the company, a new code to increase the line of credit may be stored in the credit-code field.

A CORRECT program will be needed to make changes in the format-2 records. It is unlikely that corrections will be needed in the records that have an S transaction code. If you refer to page 377 and see how each field of data was obtained, you will see why it is unlikely that there are errors in the sales records. However, if data for the cash and credit records is entered by an operator, there is a possibility that the wrong amount could have been entered and the error not detected until the control totals did not balance.

Printing accounts receivable statements

When the accounts receivable statements are printed, the records in the file are accessed sequentially. The information stored in the format-1 record supplies the data needed to print the top portion of the statement. The format-2 records contain the detailed information pertaining to each transaction. For each transaction, the date of the transaction, document number, description of the transaction, and the amount are listed. An IF/THEN/ELSE statement is used to convert the transaction-code into a description such as "sales transaction" or "cash received on account." Since the records are added to the file according to the date of the transaction, the transaction will be printed on the statement in chronological sequence.

As each sales transaction record is processed, the age of the invoice is determined so that the amount can be added to either the current, 30–60, 61–90, or over 90 total. When a cash or credit memo transaction is detected, the amounts will be subtracted from the appropriate total.

When an "M" is detected in the transaction-code field, the totals for the first statement are printed and added to the report totals, and the totals are set to 0. A new form will be advanced in the printer and the heading information will be printed for the new customer.

Deleting records

After the statements are printed and the validity of the control totals verified, the file will be recreated. Records with a "D" in the first byte of the record will be deleted from the file. What should be deleted are all paid-in-full invoices and the records of cash and credit transaction records related to invoices with a zero balance. Although the file is backed up whenever records in the accounts receivable master file are changed or added to, records cannot be deleted until after the customers' statements and reports such as the aged trial balance are printed.

Other applications that require variable length records

The master record of a newly created inventory file contains a primary and alternate key, general product information, cost, selling price, and names of vendors supplying the product. Format-2 records may record the shipments received, the unit-cost of items, the quantity received, and the date of the shipment. The information needed to compute the cost price of the items sold depends on the inventory method used.

When the accounts payable file is created, the master record contains the name and address of the vendor, a primary and alternate key, balance owed, and other information. The format-2 records contain detailed information about transactions such as the date of a bill or purchase invoice, the due date, and the amount owed.

© SRA 1988, 1983

CHECKPOINT QUESTIONS

10. Why will a file such as the accounts receivable master file contain variable length records?

11. Why is it necessary to retain detailed information regarding each sales invoice?

12. Why is using format-2 records to store the detailed information about transactions preferable to creating a table within the accounts receivable master file records?

13. Why, if the sales invoice program has been well-designed and tested, is it unlikely that errors will occur in the format-2 sales invoice records?

14. When the accounts receivable file was created, why were only format-1 records added to the file?

15. Why are three separate programs designed and developed for adding cash, credit, and return records to the accounts receivable file?

16. If all of the cash, credit, and return documents are processed in the organization's corporate center, why would it be advantageous to design the cash, credit, and returns applications as interactive jobs?

17. If customer 1278 submits payment for invoice 12569, how will it be determined if the invoice number is correct and if the full amount was remitted?

18. Would a typical CHANGE program update fields in the format-1 or format-2 records?

19. What term, in relation to processing time, would be used to describe when statement totals are to be printed?

20. Why are the format-2 records with a "D" in the delete code field physically deleted from the file only after the statements and aged trial balance are prepared?

SUMMARY

- Menu programs usually have a main menu which is used in selecting the various submenus available.

- When the program to be executed is selected from a menu, a CHAIN statement is executed. The CHAIN statement causes the program identified in the statement to be retrieved, loaded into memory, and executed.

- CHAIN MERGE is used to retrieve source code stored in an online library and incorporate it into the program in which the statement is used. The statements will be listed along with the rest of the source code and can be modified to meet the needs of the application program in which they are being used.

- In creating a menu program, the descriptions of the programs and the names under which they are stored are loaded into tables. A count-controlled loop is used to display the options on the screen. When an option is selected, the number of the option is used to retrieve the name of the program from the program table.

- In the termination module of the menu program, a command is often used that returns control to the operating system. The operator can then opt to conclude the session or load a different program or menu into memory.

- When a chained-to application program is executed, the operator is often given the option of returning to a menu program and selecting another option.

- In developing help screens, the needs of the operator should be analyzed to determine what information should be displayed. The information presented on the screens should be written and formatted so that it is easy to read and understand.

- When variable length records are used within a master file, the master record often has both a unique primary key and an alternate key. The alternate key is unique for the set of records which provide the transaction information needed.

- When the primary key is used, the master record can be retrieved randomly from the file. The records with the corresponding alternate key can be accessed sequentially. In order to utilize this concept in a program, the system software must support a type of file organization in which records within a single file can be accessed, within a single program, both randomly and sequentially.

- Often the secondary, or format-2 records, are created using one or more programs that process transaction data such as cash received on account or sales on account. New records are inserted after the last record in the file that has the same alternate key as the new record.

- While the records that contain transaction data may need to be corrected, many of the fields located within the master record may need to be updated in order that the accuracy and integrity of the data are maintained.

- In printing the accounts receivable statements, totals were printed when a level break occurred on the alternate key.

- Records flagged for deletion are physically deleted from the file after the detailed information contained within the records is no longer needed.

DISCUSSION QUESTIONS

1. Why are both a main menu and one or more sub-menus displayed in a typical menu program?
2. How does the use of tables decrease the amount of source code needed to develop a menu program?
3. What are the differences between using the CHAIN and CHAIN MERGE statements?
4. Why should files be closed in the first program before chaining to the second program?
5. If a menu program contained five screens that listed the options available, what statements would be common to the five modules that displayed options?

6. If a programming language supports both variable length records and primary and alternate keys, why is it advantageous to develop a file using variable length records rather than storing transaction data within a table which is part of the master file data structure?

7. What is the difference between a primary and an alternate key?

8. In developing a program to list each customer's balance and the age of the unpaid invoices, will the records in the file be accessed randomly or sequentially? What technique should be used so that only customers with a balance greater than zero are listed on the report?

9. Although the organization for which you work has always printed an aged trial balance, interest has not been charged to customers with past due accounts. What type of program might be developed to indicate to management how much interest would be generated if customers were charged 1% for each 30 days that an invoice is overdue? Is there sufficient information stored in the accounts receivable master file to produce the required report? What factors should management consider in addition to the amount of revenue that would be produced?

10. How does the data stored in a format-2 record differ from that in a format-1 record? How is each type of record added to the file? What type of programs are required to maintain the accuracy, integrity, and security of the records stored within the accounts receivable file?

KEY WORDS

accounts receivable control account	format-1 records
aged trial balance	format-2 records
alternate key	primary key
chain	schedule of accounts receivable
chain merge	

© SRA 1988, 1983

PROJECTS

Refer back to the information provided on pages 372–373 regarding the data stored within the accounts receivable master file.

1. Design an accounts receivable statement that can be sent to your customers. The date, transaction number, description of the transaction, and the amount should be listed for each transaction. Preprinted forms are used for printing the statements and the information in the format-1 records are used to print the customer's name and address. Totals are to be printed at the bottom of the statement. Although most customers have only 3 or 4 transactions per month, the preprinted statements provide space for 20 transactions.

2. Develop the program specifications for the program which will print the accounts receivable statements. The accounts receivable manager has indicated that only 60 percent of the customers have accounts with balances greater than zero. At the bottom of the statement, the total amount each customer owes is to be printed. In addition, the invoices must be analyzed to determine if the amount is current, or past due by 31–60 days, 61–90 days, or more than 90 days.

   Additional information to consider:

   A control record that has a C in position one contains the current and due dates.

   Interest is not charged for past due accounts.

   Customers with a zero beginning and current balance will not receive a statement.

   Final totals for each of the 4 categories are to be printed.

   The age of the invoice is determined mathematically using the current date and the due date.

   An external subroutine is called to determine the age of the invoice.

   Invoices less than 30 days past due are considered current.

3. List the tasks to be accomplished within the program.
4. Based on the tasks listed, develop a hierarchy chart.
5. Develop a detailed logic plan for the program which prints the statements.

PROBLEM 10–1

The inventory system is being revised and the inventory manager would like to have more of the programs developed as interactive programs that can be executed by selecting options listed on a menu.

The proposed programs for the inventory system are:

Create master file.

Add new master records to the existing file.

Add new items to the existing file. Each shipment is recorded in a separate transaction file.

Record items returned. A separate record will be used for each shipment of merchandise that is returned.

Change data stored in the master record.

Correct data stored in the transaction records.

Back up the file.

Recreate the master file and delete records flagged for deletion.

Exception report—list items below the reorder point.

Inventory report—list all inventory items.

Critical report—list out-of-stock items.

Location report—list items according to where the item is stored.

Inactive report—list all items that have not been ordered in the past two years.

Turnover report—based on total sales of an item and the amount in stock, the amount of times the item has "turned over" per year is calculated.

Display — information regarding an item can be retrieved randomly and displayed.

Although the inventory is decreased when sales orders are processed, the sales invoice program is not included in the menu.

1. Which of the above programs should be executed in an interactive mode rather than being run as a batch application? Divide the programs into two lists; one for interactive process and the second for batch processing applications.

2. Develop a menu program that will permit an operator to run a program by selecting one of the options identified in a menu. Do a screen layout for each menu and describe the type of information that you would display in the help screens. In developing the menu program
   a. List the tasks required to create the menus.
   b. Based on the tasks listed, develop a hierarchy chart.
   c. Develop a detailed logic plan for the menu program.

INTERACTIVE EXERCISE 10–1

LOAD menu and then perform the following tasks:

1. **LIST 740-830**
   a. Why is a GOTO used when the operator selects a number from 1 through 4 and a GOSUB when the operator selects option 5?

   _____

   _____

   b. When will the exit condition be met and control returned to module 1000?

   _____

   _____

   c. **LIST 860–1070 and 1100–1200.**
   Although both modules list the options available and ask the operator to enter a response, why does module 3000 require more statements than module 3010?

   _____

   _____

   _____

   d. **LIST 1210–1310.**
   How does the code for module 3020 differ from the code listed for module 3010?

   _____

   _____

   _____

   e. What routine is repeated in modules 3000, 3010, and 3020?

   _____

   _____

© SRA 1988, 1983

f. **LIST 640–720.** Read the source code and also review the flowchart on pages 366–369. The source code listed is part of what module?

_____

What are "ADDSTOCK", "CHANGE", and "PAYREG"?

_____

Explain when and how the names stored in table PROGRAMS$ are retrieved?

_____

_____

_____

g. **LIST 1600–1750**

When will the code located at line 2260 in the module be executed?

_____

Why is WHILE/WEND used to create a conditional loop for the module?

_____

_____

Refer to the flowchart on pages 366–369 and determine where control will return to when the exit test for the display-help-options module is met.

_____

_____

h. **LIST 182–260.**

Why are the remarks listed in statements 184–186 included in the program?

_____

_____

Why in chaining to menu is line 190 specified rather than returning to the beginning of the menu program?

_____

_____

© SRA 1988, 1983

SELF-EVALUATION TEST 10

Name _____

Section Number _____

I. Record the key term being defined in the space provided. A small blank in the statement indicates where the term is needed.

_____ 1. A unique number or combination of characters used to randomly retrieve a record from a file which permits multiple keys to be defined.

_____ 2. A statement, similar to the COPY statement, used to add source code stored in a file to the program being written.

_____ 3. The key used to identify the transaction records that provide detailed information for the master record with the same key.

_____ 4. A listing of customers and their current balances.

_____ 5. A general ledger account that contains the total amount that all customers owe.

_____ 6. The number of the _____ selected becomes the subscript used to retrieve the name of the program to be executed from the program-name table.

_____ 7. Format-2 records flagged for deletion can only be physically deleted from the accounts receivable file after _____.

_____ 8. The records that contain detailed information regarding sales or cash received on account are called _____ records.

II. Multiple Choice. Record the letter of the best answer in the space provided.

_____ 1. When executed, the chain statement
   a. transfers control to a module within the program being executed.
   b. loads a new program into memory and causes the program to execute.
   c. closes the files in the first program and then loads a new program into memory.
   d. rewrites the first program back into its file.

_____ 2. Program B is executed as the result of executing the CHAIN command located in program A. After B is executed,
   a. control automatically returns to program A.
   b. program C may be chained to and executed.
   c. control returns to the operating system.
   d. depending on the termination routine used in program B, any of the above could occur.

_____ 3. In the menu program,
   a. all modules were controlled by establishing a conditional loop.
   b. only the select-submenu module that controlled the execution of the 3000 level modules was controlled by a conditional loop.
   c. only the display-help-options module was controlled by a conditional loop.
   d. the select-submenu and display-help-options were controlled by establishing a conditional loop.

_____ 4. In the termination module of the menu program,
   a. files were closed.
   b. control totals were printed.
   c. the SYSTEM command was used to return control to the operating system.
   d. the operator was given an option of returning to the operating system.

_____ 5. In processing records stored in the accounts receivable file,
   a. all records can be accessed randomly.
   b. the records can only be accessed sequentially.
   c. only records with an alternate key can be accessed randomly.
   d. only records with a primary key can be accessed randomly.

———— 6. When processing the sales-transaction file and printing the sales invoices,
    a. it is unnecessary to provide invalid-key routines since the data stored in the file was edited.
    b. an invalid-key routine is only coded in an attempt to retrieve a record from the inventory master file.
    c. an invalid-key routine is only coded in an attempt to retrieve a record from the accounts receivable master file.
    d. an invalid-key routine should be provided whenever an attempt is made to randomly retrieve a master file record.

———— 7. In the sales invoicing program, the program will be terminated
    a. when all of the master file records are processed.
    b. when the operator responds Y to the question "MORE RECORDS? Y OR N?"
    c. when the end-of-file mark is detected for the sales transaction file.
    d. after the error report is printed.

———— 8. In the sales invoicing program, messages will be written in the error file if
    a. there is an insufficient amount of merchandise on hand to fill the order.
    b. the number used as a key is not one of the primary keys recorded in an accounts receivable record.
    c. the record for the item number entered has been deleted from the inventory file.
    d. any of the above conditions exist.

III.   True or False. Record a T or F in the blank provided. For each false statement, indicate why the statement is false or make the changes needed to correct the statement.

———— 1. A menu listing the programs available often provides an option for obtaining documentation and instructions as well as executing the program.

———— 2. The program chained to will always be executed in its entirety.

———— 3. CHAIN MERGE is very similar to the COPY statement used in COBOL.

———— 4. In the menu program, all of the count-controlled loops had their counters initially set to 1.

———— 5. In coding the data used to load the program name and description tables, the operator must take care to list both the program names and their descriptions in the same sequence.

———— 6. In the statement CHAIN PROGRAMS$ (I), the value of I is determined by the count-control loop.

———— 7. The statement CHAIN "MENU", 190 was used rather than CHAIN "MENU" in order to eliminate displaying the SRA logo.

———— 8. After executing the display modules identified as 3010–3040 control returned to the select-sub-menu module.

———— 9. Since fewer bytes are required for the format-2 records, using variable-length records in the accounts receivable file saves file space.

———— 10. In the sales invoicing program, records from the accounts receivable and inventory master files are read as input but not updated.

———— 11. When an accounts receivable format-1 record was added to the file, an "M" was stored in the transaction-code field.

———— 12. When a sales invoice is paid in full, a "D" is recorded in the delete-code field and the record is physically removed from the file.

———— 13. In the menu program, a range test was used to determine the validity of the operator's response.

———— 14. Variable length records can only be used when VSAM files are supported by the operating system.

———— 15. Storing transaction data within a table located within a master file requires less source code and maintenance than when format-2 records are used.

© SRA 1988, 1983

© SRA 1988, 1983

DOCUMENTATION FOR THE PAYROLL REGISTER PROGRAM

11

Upon completion of the chapter, you will identify why each of following items should be included as part of the documentation for the payroll register program.

- Design checklist
- Documentation cover sheet
- Program objectives and overview for the payroll register program
- Payroll register report specification form
- Print layouts for the payroll register and payroll summary reports
- Payroll master file specification and record layout form
- Payroll current file specification and record layout form
- Specification and record layout forms for the time-records and error-message records
- Hierarchy chart for the payroll register program
- Production run instructions for the payroll register program
- Detailed logic plan
- Source listings

The most satisfactory type of documentation for data processing programs and what such documentation should include are often debated. Documentation should provide historical information regarding the development of the project, information for management on how the data is processed, and how the validity of the output is determined. Also a detailed logic plan, source listings, and instructions for the operator should be included.

The historical documentation includes memos, design checklists, documents, and summaries of interviews and phone calls. In this chapter, not all the documentation for the payroll register program is included. However, the documentation included provides management with an overview of the project, operators with the information needed to execute the job, and maintenance programmers with the information needed to modify and retest the programs.

During the developmental stages of a program, all documentation should be considered as "working copy." Also, when a complete system is being developed, only rarely is the first draft of the file or report specifications the same as those submitted as part of the final documentation. Although programmers and analysts usually prefer to design and code programs rather than complete the required documentation, using word processing to create and update documentation has made the task much easier. When word processing is used, the information is recorded in a file. The file can be retrieved and its contents reviewed and modified. Words, sentences, or paragraphs can easily be inserted, deleted, or moved to a new location.

HOW DOCUMENTATION IS USED

While part of the documentation for PAR012 (the payroll register program) is historical in nature and is used to develop the detailed logic plans, much of it will be used by the maintenance programmer to modify the program. Management and auditors who wish to obtain an understanding of how the input is processed and how the validity of the output is determined will also refer to the documentation.

Design checklist

A design checklist serves as a reminder of the decisions to make and the type of specifications to develop before the hierarchy chart and detailed logic plan can be completed.

A design checklist similar to the one illustrated in Figure 11–1 guides the programmer through a series of questions that must be answered to identify the tasks needed to process the input and produce the required output. If you had studied Figure 11–1 before learning about files, editing data, creating reports, and printing error messages, many of the questions would be be meaningless. The checklist now serves as a reminder of the ingredients that go into the design and development of a well-written program.

Additional space could be provided on the checklist for notations that reference other materials or call attention to decisions that have not been made.

Documentation cover sheet

A documentation cover sheet similar to the one illustrated in Figure 11–2 is the first page of the documentation prepared for programmers or analysts who must modify the program and for the operations staff who are responsible for

© SRA 1988, 1983

the execution of the program. It is imperative that changes in a production program be requested, reviewed, and approved. Each time a program is modified, the changes are highlighted on the source listing and both the new and old source listings become part of the documentation. Before the modified program is put into production, a test plan should be developed for testing the changes. After the changes are tested, the documentation should be changed to incorporate the required additions, deletions, or modifications.

Program overview

The program overview should be written in a clear, concise manner using nontechnical terms that management, auditors, users, and operations personnel can understand. An overview similar to the one illustrated in Figure 11–3 should provide the program objectives and overview, the output, input, and processing requirements, a description of the error report, the control totals and how they are used, and directions for modifying the program.

Report specification form

The report specification form, illustrated in Figure 11–4, is completed during the early part of the design phase and is used in developing the print layout forms and will probably be included as part of the historical documentation. The report specification form briefly describes the headings, detail, and total lines that will be printed. Since error messages are not printed by PAR012, the error report that is printed by running PAR013 is also described. The distribution section of the specification form provides information that should be included on the production run instruction form.

Print layout forms

The print layout forms are developed using the report specification form and the file specification forms. The layout forms, illustrated in Figure 11–5 and 11–6, must be developed before the program can be written. In completing the forms the programmer must use established standards, for example, placing Xs where variable data will be printed and locating constants where they will be printed.

In order to complete the form, the programmer must know the type of data stored in each field, the size of the field, and the number of digits that must be provided for fields that are calculated.

The person who requested the report should approve the print layout form and the design of preprinted forms such as payroll checks or sales invoices. If a printed report must be modified, the maintenance programmer will need to refer to the print layout forms. For example, a request might be made to consolidate the data printed on the payroll register and deduction register into one report. In studying the two print layout forms, and reviewing the specifications for the printer being used, it might be determined that the request is not feasible because the online printer only prints a maximum of 132 characters on a line.

Record layout forms

Although the information recorded in the file specification form is duplicated on the record layout form, both are usually included in the final documentation. Record layouts like the ones in Figure 11–8 and 11–11 are usually less technical than the file specification form and the exact name of the field is seldom used. The forms give a good visual image of what is recorded in the file and where each field is located. Figure 11–11 shows the design of the payroll current file, employee time records, and error-message records.

File specification form

File specification forms, such as those illustrated in Figures 11–7, 11–9, and 11–10, should be included. The form should include the location of the field, the type of data stored within the field, the name of the field, and a brief description of the data. The information is useful for determining how the data can be verified for accuracy, edited for output, and used in performing comparisons or mathematical calculations.

New fields can be created and added to the record by decreasing the amount of FILLER. For example, if employees are required to contribute to their hospital insurance, two new fields would be added to the file specification form and to the record layout form. The first field would indicate the amount to be deducted per pay period and the second field used for the cumulative year-to-date deduction.

If only one or two fields are deleted, the file will probably not be completely reorganized. If the total amount of each employee's term insurance is to be paid by his or her employer, the field illustrated on Figure 11–7, Part 2, named MF-TERM-INS would no longer be needed. The field might be renamed SKIP1 or OMIT1 which would indicate it is no longer needed within the record. However, this seemingly simple change requires many of the programs that use the payroll master file to be modified; programs that add new employee records to the existing file, those that change the data stored within existing records, update the payroll master file, and print the payroll and deduction registers all must be modified.

Hierarchy chart

A hierarchy chart like the one illustrated in Figure 11–12 provides an overview of the relationships between the various modules. The chart is directly related to the source code by using comments or remarks that identify the name and number of the module.

When a program is being modified, the programmer can usually determine what modules will need to be changed by referring to the hierarchy chart. When major changes are required, it may be necessary to create one or two additional modules and add them to the existing chart.

Software that can be used to create a hierarchy chart is available. The source code is read as input and the hierarchy program determines the relationships that exist between the modules and prints an accurate, up-to-date chart.

Production run instructions

A production run sheet, similar to the one illustrated in Figure 11–13, should be available for each job that is initiated by computer operations personnel. Although the form is primarily designed for operations personnel, a copy should be included in the documentation provided for the maintenance programmers. When a program is modified, it may be necessary to change the run instructions. Unless the run instructions provided for operators are accurate, jobs may abort or may need to be rerun.

Detailed logic plans

After the program is tested and considered operational, the detailed logic plans should be reviewed to make absolutely certain that they truly reflect the way that input is processed to obtain the required output. Standards must be developed and enforced, regarding the type of logic plans that *must* be submitted before a job is considered operational. Otherwise the logic plan may not reflect the changes made during the design walkthrough, program walkthrough, and the final testing.

© SRA 1988, 1983

It is also imperative whenever a program is modified, that the logic plan be updated to show the changes. Each installation should develop standards for documentation describing the type of logic plans that must be submitted and procedure that must be followed in modifying production programs.

Since a wide variety of detailed logic plans have been illustrated, the complete logic plan for the payroll register program is not included in the example.

Source listing

Because a program such as the payroll register program is frequently altered due to changes in policies or in federal or state requirements, a policy is usually established concerning the number of versions that must be included as part of the documentation. Each version should be dated, the changes highlighted, and a copy of the change authorization form that describes the required modifications should be attached. If a program that has been in production for several months aborts or creates invalid output, the highlighted changes should be examined to determine if they are the source of the problem.

In order to modify a program, the programmer must obtain the most recent source listing. If the required changes are coded on the listing, a new copy should be obtained before the program is modified.

DISCUSSION QUESTIONS

1. Review the design checklist illustrated in Figure 11–1 to determine how it might be revised to make it a more effective design tool. What questions would you delete or add to the checklist?

2. What information is recorded on the documentation cover sheet?

3. Who would be most likely to utilize the information provided in the program overview illustrated in Figure 11–3? Should technical terms be used in writing the overview?

4. What other type of documentation is developed with the information recorded on the report specification form? What list might be developed with the information recorded on the form?

5. Why is the location of the field within the record considered important? What is the difference between NP, NZ, and AN data?

6. In reviewing Figures 11–7, 11–9, and 11–10, describe a convention that was used in developing the file specification forms. How would the maintenance programmer use the specification forms?

7. Why should the print layout forms be included as part of the final documentation?

8. If the production run instruction form is developed for operations personnel, why should a copy be included in the documentation used by maintenance programmers?

9. How is the hierarchy chart related to the source listing and how would it be used by a maintenance programmer? Give an example of when, and how, the hierarchy chart for the payroll register program might be changed.

10. Bill Henderson, a maintenance programmer in your organization, has indicated that he only keeps the most recent listing of the source code. If you were the manager why would you establish a policy that the last five versions should be retained?

Design Checklist for: _____   Program Number: _____

Analyst/Programmer: _____   Contact: _____

I. Is the job description complete?

   A. Is a system overview available?
   B. Are overviews of the jobs that make up the system available?
   C. Is a job description available?
   D. Are job objectives available?
   E. Are job specifications available?

II. What are the primary purposes of the program?

   A. Provide a report?
   B. Edit data?
   C. Update a file by adding, changing, or deleting records?
   D. Extract data, sort records, and provide a report?
   E. Create a transaction file?
   F. Create a master file?
   G. Process input and create additional output files?

III. Are the output requirements defined?

   A. Is a file being created?

      1. In what other programs will the file be utilized?
      2. How should the file be organized?
      3. Are file specifications and record layouts available?
      4. Will file maintenance programs be required?
      5. Should the file be backed up?

   B. Will a report be printed?

      1. Is the report an external or internal report?
      2. Will preprinted forms or stock paper be used?
      3. Is the report an exception, detail, or group printed report?
      4. What headings are required?
      5. What detail lines are required?
      6. What total lines are required?
      7. Is a report summary or control totals required?
      8. How is the validity of the report determined?

   C. What VDT displays are required?

      1. Is a menu required?
      2. Are help screens required?
      3. Will data be entered by an operator?
      4. How will the data entered by an operator be verified?

IV. Has the origin of the output been identified?

   A. What data originates from a master file?
   B. What data originates from a transaction file?
   C. What control information is required?
   D. What constants are required?
   E. What data is stored in a table?
   F. What data is calculated?

Figure 11–1 Part 1   Design checklist form.

© SRA 1988, 1983

Design Checklist for: _____ Program Number: _____

Analyst/Programmer: _____ Contact: _____

V. How will the validity of the output be determined?

    A. What control totals are required?

    B. What record counts should be maintained?

    C. What data is visually verified?

    D. Who is responsible for determining the validity of the output?

VI. Are the input requirements defined?

    A. What master files will be used?

        1. How is the file organized?

        2. What access method should be used?

        3. Are a file specification form and record layout available?

        4. Can the data structure be copied from the library?

    B. What current file should be used?

        1. What program was used to create the file?

        2. How is the file organized?

        3. What access method should be used?

        4. Are a file specification form and record layout available?

        5. Can the data structure be copied from the library?

    C. What transaction files are needed?

        1. Where does the data originate?

        2. How and where should the data enter the system?

    D. Is a control record needed?

        1. What data should be entered?

        2. How will the record be identified?

VII. What fields should be edited?

    A. What editing and verification methods should be used?

    B. What error routines are needed to handle invalid data?

    C. Will the error messages be displayed or recorded in a file and printed?

VIII. What calculations are required?

    A. What steps are needed to provide the required calculations?

    B. What constants are required?

    C. What special formulas are needed?

    D. Are functions or subroutines available?

IX. What programming aids can be used?

    A. Are there functions, subroutines, or utility programs that can be used?

    B. Can copy or chain merge statements be used?

X. What program in the system is most like the one being designed and can the same techniques be used?

XI. What is unusual about the program?

XII. What approach should be used in developing the logic?

Figure 11–1 Part 2   *Design checklist form.*

PROGRAM NAME: PAR012		FUNCTION: Calculate gross, deductions, and net pay.		LANGUAGE USED: COBOL	

JOB NUMBER: PAR012   PROGRAMMER: Leeson   DATE: April 1988

CONTACT FOR EXECUTION PROBLEMS: McNeal

REVISIONS: BY:	AUTHORIZED BY:	REASON	DATES COMPLETED:		
			PROGRAMMING	TESTING	DOCUMENTATION

Figure 11–2   Documentation cover sheet for the payroll register program.

© SRA 1988, 1983

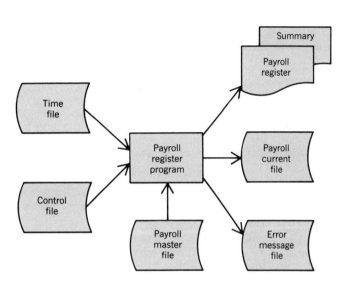

Program Objective

The program will calculate each employee's gross and net pay and print a payroll register which can be used as part of the payroll audit trail. A current file will also be created that can be used to update the payroll master file, print the bi-weekly paychecks, and print reports such as the stock deduction credit union, and payroll distribution report.

Program Overview

The program determines which employees are to be paid and calculates their gross pay, voluntary deductions, deductions for taxes, and net pay. Salaried employees need a time record if they are not to be paid or if they are to receive more or less than their regular bi-weekly salary. Hourly or part-time workers who are to be paid must have a time record.

Output Requirements

A payroll register will be printed that lists each employee's name, gross pay, taxes withheld, voluntary deductions withheld, net pay, and check number. Totals will be printed for each of the fields listed. In addition a summary report will be printed that indicates the total amount withheld for each voluntary and involuntary deduction.

Figure 11–3 Part 1   Program overview for the payroll register program.

When the data from the time file is edited, a file is created that contains the error messages. Each record will contain the employee's name and number, an error message, and the data recorded in the time record. The current file will contain the necessary information to update the master file, print the paychecks, a deduction report, and a payroll distribution report.

Processing

Information stored in the payroll master file is used to calculate deductions for taxes, FICA, and voluntary deductions. External subroutines are used to calculate the federal tax, state tax, and FICA. Unless a salaried employee has a nopay or part-pay record, his or her gross earnings are calculated by dividing the contracted salary by the number of installments over which it is to be paid. In order to be paid, hourly and part-time employees must have a time record. Totals are accumulated for regular earnings, overtime earnings, withheld taxes and voluntary deductions, and net pay.

Input Requirements

A control record provides the report date and the beginning check number. The time records contain the record identification code, employee's number, status code, pay code, amount salaried employees are to be paid, and regular and overtime hours for hourly employees.

The payroll master file contains the data required to compute each employee's regular and overtime earnings and voluntary deductions for stock, credit union, term insurance, and United Fund. The data required to calculate FICA, federal income tax, and state tax is also stored in the master file records.

Error Report

The error file will be used as input for PAR013 which prints an error report. Unless the message NO ERROR IN RUN is printed, the error report will be transmitted to the payroll department. The payroll department is responsible for determining the cause of each error message and for making the necessary corrections in the time-record file. The corrected time-record file will be used to rerun the program.

Control Totals

The total number of employees paid in each category must agree with the totals established by the payroll department. The total regular hours and overtime hours must agree with the total established when the time-record file was created and verified. The total net pay must equal total earnings less total deductions. When the payroll current file is used as input to print the deduction register, the deduction register totals will be compared with the totals printed on the payroll summary report.

Program Modifications

Modifications to the production program must be requested in writing by the manager of the payroll department. The proposed changes to the program will be reviewed by a project team and then approved by the manager of the payroll department. The payroll master file will be copied into the test library and used with a time-record test file designed to test the modifications. After the testing is completed, the documentation updated, and personnel affected by the changes notified, the revised program will be placed in the production library. The changes made in the program will be highlighted on the new source-code listing. The old source-code listing will be retained as well as the new listing.

Figure 11–3 Part 2   Program overview for the payroll register program.

© SRA 1988, 1983

REPORT SPECIFICATION FORM

System: Payroll   Program Name: PAR0012   Report Name: Payroll Register

Forms: 8 1/2″ × 11 stock paper   Spacing: Double   Lines per page: 25

Headings:

PAYROLL REGISTER, DATE, PAGE NUMBER

NAME, GROSS PAY, VOLUNTARY DEDUCTIONS, TAX DEDUCTIONS, NET PAY, CHECK NUMBER

Detail Lines:

Data	Source
Employee name	Payroll master file
Gross pay	Calculated using data in master file and time file.
Voluntary deductions	Calculated using stock deduction, term insurance, credit union, and United Fund master file fields.
Tax deductions	Calculated using the federal tax, state tax, and FICA subroutines.
Net pay	Calculated using the gross pay, voluntary deduction, and tax deduction fields.
Check number	Beginning number is in the date-control file.

Report Totals:

Gross pay, voluntary deductions, tax deductions, and net pay.

Summary Report and Control Totals:

Total number of part-time, hourly, and salaried employees paid.
Total regular and overtime hours.
Total earnings for part-time, hourly, and salaried employees.
Total amount withheld for federal income tax, state income tax,
  FICA, stock deduction, credit union, term insurance, and United Fund.

Error Report:

A separate program, PAR013, is used to print an error report which contains a description of the error and the contents of the time record being edited when the error was detected.

Distribution:

Transmit to data-control section for verification. If the message NO ERRORS IN RUN is printed, the date and check numbers are verified and the report is transmitted to the payroll department for further verification.

Figure 11–4   Report specification form for the payroll register.

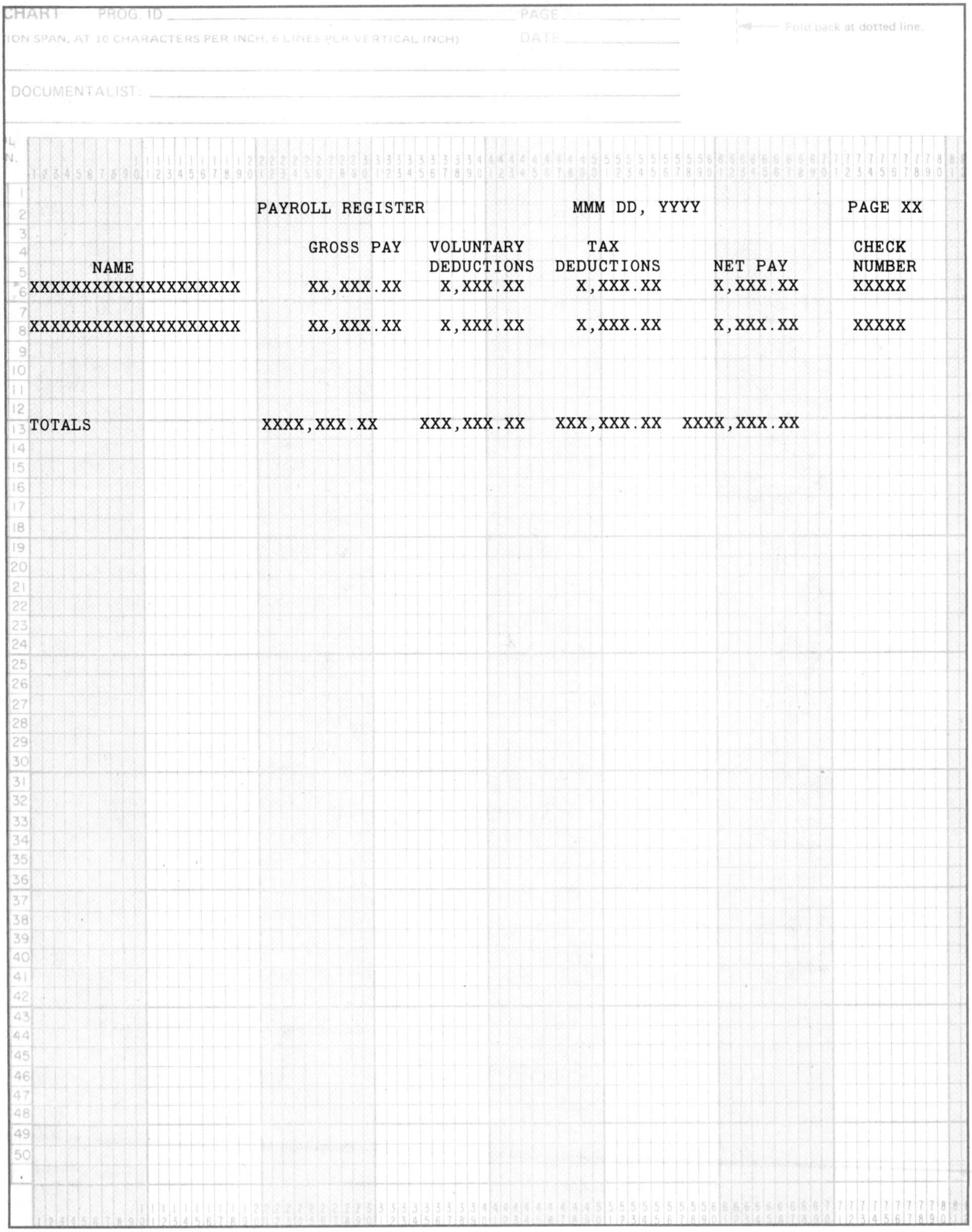

CHART   PROG. ID _____   PAGE _____

(ION SPAN, AT 10 CHARACTERS PER INCH, 6 LINES PER VERTICAL INCH)   DATE _____

◄— Fold back at dotted line.

DOCUMENTALIST: _____

```
                      PAYROLL REGISTER              MMM DD, YYYY            PAGE XX

                      GROSS PAY   VOLUNTARY     TAX                         CHECK
       NAME                       DEDUCTIONS    DEDUCTIONS    NET PAY       NUMBER
XXXXXXXXXXXXXXXXXXXX   XX,XXX.XX   X,XXX.XX      X,XXX.XX      X,XXX.XX      XXXXX

XXXXXXXXXXXXXXXXXXXX   XX,XXX.XX   X,XXX.XX      X,XXX.XX      X,XXX.XX      XXXXX




TOTALS               XXXX,XXX.XX  XXX,XXX.XX    XXX,XXX.XX   XXXX,XXX.XX
```

Figure 11–5   *Print layout chart for the payroll register.*

© SRA 1988, 1983

```
                    PAYROLL SUMMARY REPORT                      MMM DD, YYYY


                    HOURLY        SALARIED      PART-TIME


EMPLOYEES PAID      XXXX          XXXX          XXXX

TOTAL REGULAR HOURS XXXXXXX.X                   XXXXXXX.X
TOTAL OVERTIME HOURS XXXXXXX.X

TOTAL EARNINGS      XXX,XXX.XX  X,XXX,XXX.XX    XXX,XXX.XX    X,XXX,XXX.XX

                    DEDUCTIONS WITHHELD


FEDERAL INCOME TAX                             X,XXX,XXX.XX

STATE INCOME TAX                               X,XXX,XXX.XX

FICA                                           X,XXX,XXX.XX

STOCK DEDUCTION                                X,XXX,XXX.XX

CREDIT UNION                                   X,XXX,XXX.XX

TERM INSURANCE                                 X,XXX,XXX.XX

UNITED FUND                                    X,XXX,XXX.XX

    TOTAL DEDUCTIONS                                         X,XXX,XXX.XX

NET PAY TOTAL                                               X,XXX,XXX.XX
```

Figure 11–6   Print layout chart for the payroll register summary.

<table>
<tr><td colspan="4" align="center">File Specification Form</td></tr>
<tr><td>System: **Payroll**</td><td>File Name: **PAYMAST—Payroll master**</td><td colspan="2">Organization: **ISAM**</td></tr>
<tr><td>Key: **MF-NUMBER**</td><td>Record size: **352**</td><td>Blocking factor: **20**</td><td>Block size: **7040**   Page 1 OF 2</td></tr>
</table>

Location	Length	Type		Data
1	1	AN	MF-DELETE-CODE	Blank or D.
2–7	6	AN	MF-NUMBER	Employee number.
8–23	16	AN	MF-LAST	Last name.
24–35	12	AN	MF-FIRST	First name.
36	1	AN	MF-Middle	Middle initial.
37–60	24	AN	MF-ADDRESS1	First address line.
61–84	24	AN	MF-ADDRESS2	Second address line.
85–108	24	AN	MF-ADDRESS3	Third address line.
109–113	5	AN	MF-ZIP1	Five digit zip code.
114–117	4	AN	MF-ZIP2	Four digit zip code.
118–118	1	AN	MF-STATUS	S = salaried, H = hourly, P = part-time.
119–124	6	NZ	MF-HIRED	Date hired—MM/DD/YY
125–130	6	NZ	MF-TERMINATED	Date terminated—MM/DD/YY
131–135	5	NP	MF-SALARY	Salary as XXXXXX.XX for salaried employees only.
136–137	2	NP	MF-TIMES	Number of payments salary is distributed over.
138–140	3	NP	MF-HOURLY-RATE	Hourly rate for hourly and part-time employees—XX.XXX.
141–144	4	NP	MF-STOCK-DED	Stock deduction per pay period.
145–148	4	NP	MF-STOCK-BAL	Balance in stock deduction account.
149–151	3	NP	MF-STOCK-SHARES	Total number of shares purchased for the employee.
152–156	5	NP	MF-STOCK-TOTAL	Total amount contributed by the employee to the stock plan.
157–160	4	NP	MF-CREDIT-UN	Amount deducted for credit union each pay period.
161–164	4	NP	MF-TERM-INS	Term insurance deducted during the second pay period of each month.
165–168	4	NP	MF-UNITED-FUND	Total amount of United Fund pledge.
169–170	2	NP	MF-INSTALLMENTS	Number of installments United Fund pledge is to be paid over. The deduction is made the first pay period of each month.

Figure 11–7 Part 1   *Specifications for the payroll master file.*

© SRA 1988, 1983

File Specification Form

System: **Payroll**   File Name: **PAYMAST—Payroll master**   Organization: **ISAM**

Key: **MF-NUMBER**   Record Size: **352**   Blocking Factor: **20**   Block size: **7040**   Page **2** OF **2**

Location	Length	Type		Data
171–172	2	NP	MF-INSTALL-MADE	Number of installments made.
173–176	4	NP	MF-UNITED-DED	Total amount of pledge deducted.
177–179	3	NP	MF-UNION-DUES	Deducted the first pay of the month from the earning of hourly employees.
180–181	2	NP	MF-ACCOUNT-NO	Although there are 150 different account numbers, the payroll account numbers range from 41–65.
182–183	2	NP	MF-COST-CENTER	The cost centers are numbered from 1–69.
184–192	9	NZ	MF-SOCIAL-SEC-NO	Social Security number.
193–194	2	NP	MF-NO-EXEMPTS	Number of exemptions declared for federal tax.
195–195	1	NZ	MF-TAX-STATUS	1 = single status; 2 = married status.
			Quarterly Deductions and Earnings	
196–199	4	NP	MF-QTR-FICA	Social Security deducted.
200–203	4	NP	MF-QTR-FEDTAX	Deduction for federal income tax.
204–207	4	NP	MF-QTR-STATE-TAX	Deduction for state income tax.
208–211	4	NP	MF-QTR-GROSS	Gross paid earned.
			Year-to-date Earnings and Deductions	
212–216	5	NP	MF-YTD-GROSS	Gross earnings.
217–221	5	NP	MF-YTD-FEDTAX	Federal income tax.
229–226	5	NP	MF-YTD-STATETAX	State income tax.
227–231	5	NP	MF-YTD-FICA	Social Security deducted.
231–236	5	NP	MF-YTD-STOCK-DED	Total stock deduction for the year.
237–241	5	NP	MF-YTD-CREDIT-UN	Total credit union deduction.
242–246	5	NP	MF-YTD-TERM-INS	Total term insurance deduction.
246–251	5	NP	MF-YTD-UNITED-FD	Total United Fund deduction.
252–352	101	AN	MF-FILLER	When the file is created, this area will be filled with spaces. This area might be referred to as the "expansion area."

Figure 11–7 Part 2   Specifications for the payroll master file.

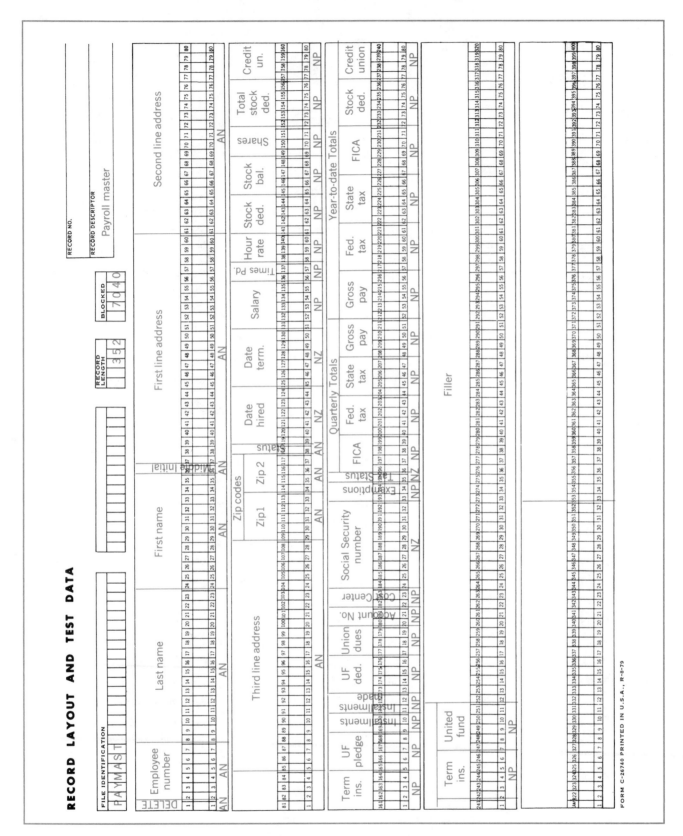

Figure 11–8   Record layout for the payroll master file.

© SRA 1988, 1983

FILE SPECIFICATION FORM

System: **Payroll**   File Name: **PCURRENT**   Organization: **Sequential**

Key: **none**   Record size: **240**   Blocking factor: **30**   Block size: **7200**   Page 1 OF 1

Location	Length	Type	Field name	Data
1–6	6	AN	CF-NUMBER	Employee number.
7–22	16	AN	CF-LAST	Last name.
23–34	12	AN	CF-FIRST	First name.
35	1	AN	CF-MIDDLE	Middle initial.
36–59	24	AN	CF-ADDRESS1	First line address.
60–83	24	AN	CF-ADDRESS2	Second line address.
84–107	24	AN	CF-ADDRESS3	Third line address.
108–112	5	AN	CF-ZIP1	First five digits of the zip code.
113–116	4	AN	CF-ZIP2	Last four digits of the zip code.
117–123	7	NZ	CF-GROSS-PAY	Employee gross pay.
124–129	6	NZ	CF-OVERTIME	Employee overtime earnings.
130–135	6	NZ	CF-FEDERAL-TAX	Federal tax withheld.
136–141	6	NZ	CF-STATE-TAX	State tax withheld.
142–147	6	NZ	CF-FICA	FICA withheld.
148–153	6	NZ	CF-STOCK-DED	Stock deduction withheld.
154–159	6	NZ	CF-TERM-INS	Term insurance withheld.
160–165	6	NZ	CF-CREDIT-UNION	Credit union deduction.
166–171	6	NZ	CF-UNITED-FUND	United Fund deduction.
172–173	2	NZ	CF-ACCOUNT-NO	Account number.
174–175	2	NZ	CF-COST-CENTER	Cost center.
			Year-to-Date Totals	
176–182	7	NZ	CF-YTD-GROSS	Gross earnings.
183–189	7	NZ	CF-YTD-FEDTAX	Federal tax.
190–196	7	NZ	CF-YTD-STTAX	State tax.
197–203	7	NZ	CF-YTD-FICA	Contribution for Social Security.
204–210	7	NZ	CF-YTD-STOCK-DED	Stock deduction.
			CF-YTD-CREDIT-UN	Credit union deduction.
211–216	6	NZ	CF-YTD-TERM-INS	Term insurance deduction.
			CF-YTD-UNITED-FUND	United Fund deduction.
217–223	7	NZ	FILLER	
224–230	7	NZ		
231–240	10	AN		

Figure 11–9   Current file specification form.

FILE SPECIFICATION FORM

System: **Payroll**   File Name: **TIME-RECORDS**   Organization: **Sequential**

Key: **None**   Record size: **32**   Blocking factor: **40**   Block size: **1280**   PAGE **1** OF **1**

Location	Length	Type	Field Name	Data
1	1	AN	TR-IDENTIFICATION	Identification code.
2–7	6	AN	TR-NUMBER	Employee number
8–8	1	AN	TR-STATUS	Employee status code.
9–9	1	AN	TR-PAY-CODE	Pay code.
10–16	7	NZ	TR-PART-PAY	Amount salaried employee with a time record will be paid.
17–19	3	NZ	TR-REG-HOURS	Regular hours XX.X.
20–22	3	NZ	TR-OT-HOURS	Overtime hours XX.X.
23–32	10	AN	TR-FILLER	
Date-control record:				
1	1	AN	DC-IDENTIFICATION	Record identification code.
2	1	NZ	DC-PAY-PERIOD	Used in determining which voluntary deductions should be included.
2–13	12	AN	DC-REPORT-DATE	MMM DD, YYYY
14–19	6	NZ	DC-CHECK-NUMBER	Beginning check number.
Error-message record:				
1–30	30	AN	EM-PRINT-MESSAGE	Message identifying the cause of the error.
31–31	1	AN	EM-IDENTIFICATION	The record identification and other fields recorded in the time-record are moved into the error-message structure.
32–37	6	AN	EM-NUMBER	
38–38	1	AN	EM-STATUS	
39–39	1	AN	EM-PAY-CODE	
40–46	7	NZ	EM-PART-PAY	
47–49	3	NZ	EM-REG-HOURS	
50–52	3	NZ	EM-OT-HOURS	
53–56	4	AN	EM-FILLER	

Figure 11–10   *Time record, date-control record, and error-message specification form.*

© SRA 1988, 1983

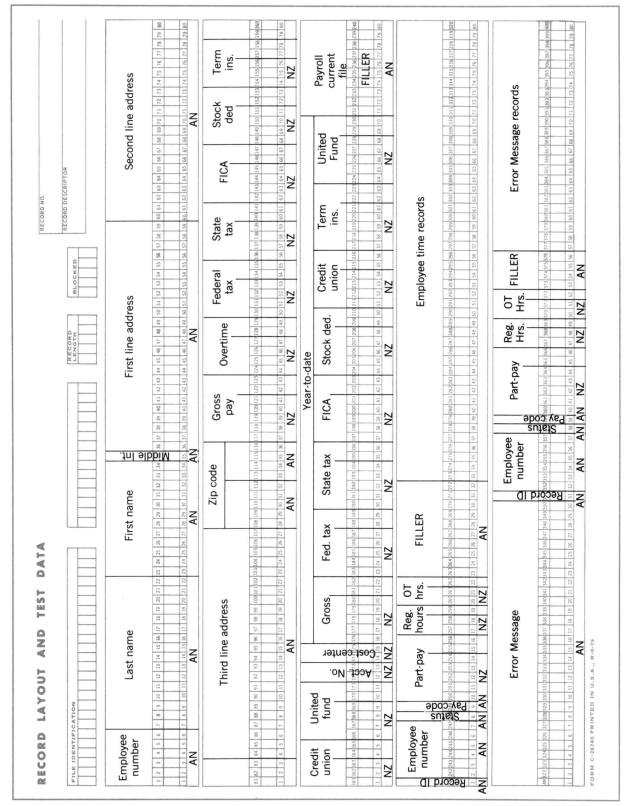

Figure 11–11   Record layouts for the payroll current, time-record, and error-message records.

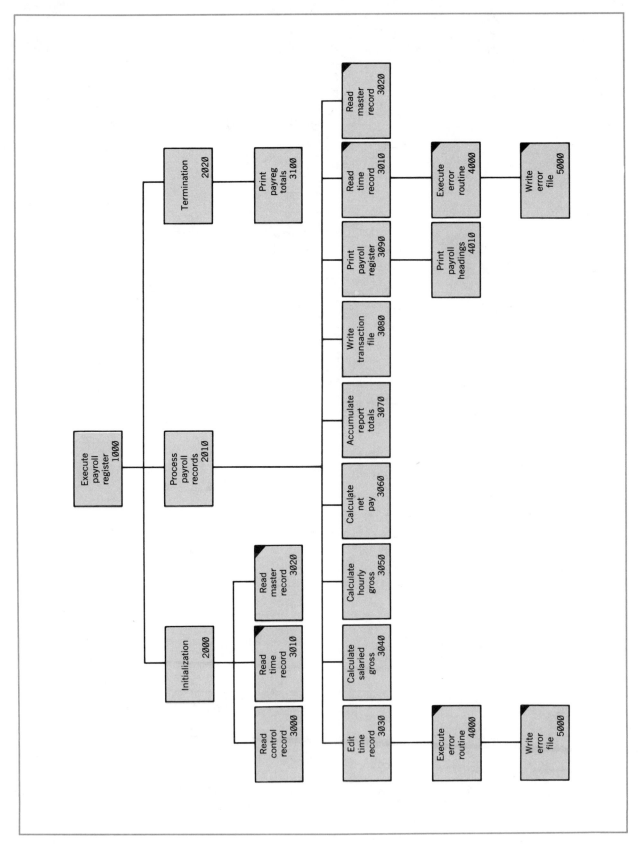

Figure 11–12 Hierarchy chart for the payroll master program.

© SRA 1988, 1983

PRODUCTION RUN INSTRUCTIONS		

PROGRAM NAME PAR012 Payroll Register	FREQUENCY Bi-weekly
JOB NUMBER PROGRAMMER DATE PAR012 Leeson April 1988	TYPE OF RUN: ○ MAINTENANCE ✗ REPORT

DATE-CONTROL RECORD:
 	
    File Name: DATE012
    Contents:
        Report date: mmm dd, yyy
        Check number: XXXXX
	Library: **SYSRES**

	Report Distribution:
	FORM TYPE
	SPACING: ○ 6LPI ✗ 8LPI
	CARRIAGE: ✗ STANDARD ○ OTHER _____

DISK OR TAPE FILE NAME	Input/output/ update	Organization	Access
PAYMAST	Input	VSAM	Sequential
TIMERECORDS	Input	Sequential	Sequential
PCURRENT	Output	Sequential	
PERROR	Output	Sequential	

SPECIAL INSTRUCTIONS:

1. Date-control file must be created before the job is scheduled for execution.

2. Two-part 8½″ × 11″ stock paper must be mounted in the printer.

3. The register and the error report produced by running PAR013 are transmitted to data control. Problems which cannot be resolved by data control will be referred to the payroll department.

4. Unless the message NO ERROR IN RUN is printed, the job must be scheduled for a rerun. Before rerunning the job, the necessary corrections must be made in the TIMERECORDS file.

PROGRAMMED MESSAGES

The error messages are placed in a file, PERROR, and printed by running PAR013.
Any messages displayed on the console should be recorded and transmitted to the maintenance programmer.

CONTROLS

1. Total number of employees paid in each category.
2. Total number of regular and overtime hours worked.
3. Control totals are established that will be used in verifying the accuracy of the deduction register.

Figure 11–13   Production run sheet for the payroll register program.

Appendix I
HIPO CHARTS

In some installations, HIPO (Hierarchy plus Input-Processing-Output) diagrams are used rather than flowcharts. A separate HIPO chart is constructed for each module to show the required input files and individual fields, the required output files and fields, and the processing required to achieve the objectives of the module.

Figure I–1 illustrates the three major sections of a typical HIPO chart. The name of the indicator, more-records, and the name of the record—student master file record—are listed under output. In order to obtain the output, the student master file and a field called more-records must be available; they are listed under the input section. The processing steps necessary to obtain the input and produce the required output are listed. Step 4 indicates that control will return to module 1000.

CONSTRUCTING A HIPO CHART

Until the programmer understands the problem fully and until the record and print layouts and display screens have been completed, work should not begin on the HIPO chart. After the problem is defined and the I/O requirements and formats determined, the programmer should list the tasks required, determine the modules that are needed, construct a hierarchy chart, and then begin work on the required HIPO charts. The following tasks will be performed in completing a HIPO chart for each module.

1. Fill in the heading. For the initialization module of the student record retrieval program illustrated in Figure I–1, the following data is included.

Type of Heading	Example
Author	Programmer's name
System/Program	Student record retrieval
Date	Date the HIPO is constructed
Page	Page 2 of 6
VTOC ID*	2000
Module name	Initialization
Function	Establish indicators, open files, and retrieve the initial record

2. Record the output and input requirements. In the high-level modules (initialization, process student record, and termination), usually it is necessary only to identify the files and records. In the detailed modules, the data elements or fields must also be defined.

*VTOC (Visual Table Of Contents) is the name IBM often uses for a hierarchy chart.

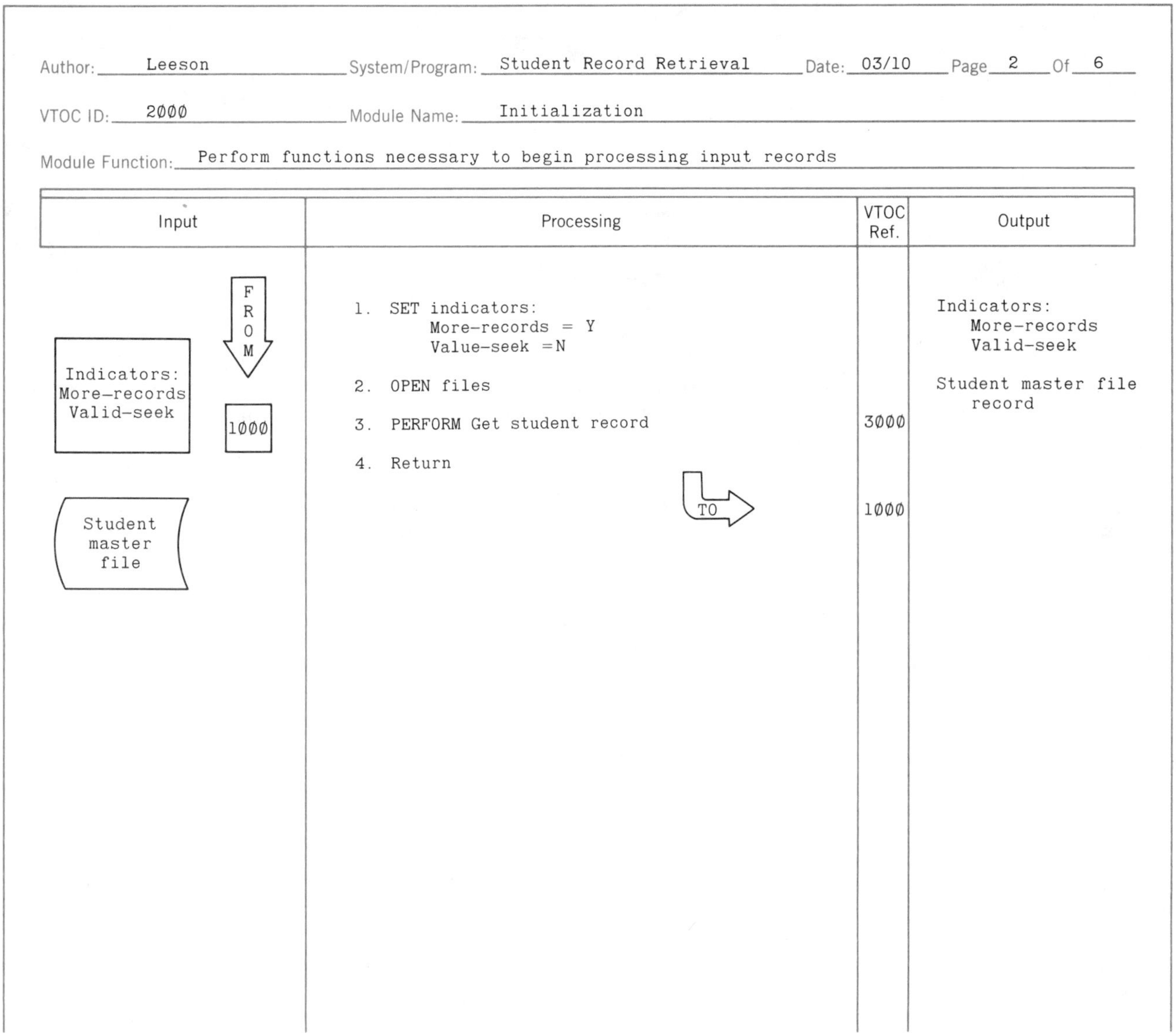

Author: __Leeson__ System/Program: __Student Record Retrieval__ Date: __03/10__ Page __2__ Of __6__

VTOC ID: __2000__ Module Name: __Initialization__

Module Function: __Perform functions necessary to begin processing input records__

Input	Processing	VTOC Ref.	Output
F R O M 1000 Indicators: More—records Valid—seek Student master file	1. SET indicators: More—records = Y Value—seek =N 2. OPEN files 3. PERFORM Get student record 4. Return TO	3000 1000	Indicators: More—records Valid—seek Student master file record

Figure I–1   HIPO for the initialization module.

Often forms such as the one illustrated in Figure I–2 are used to construct the HIPO. The programmer starts by listing the output, then the input, and then the processing steps.

3. Write the required pseudocode. Under the processing section of the chart a step-by-step description of the steps required to obtain the input and produce the output is provided. The key words described in the pseudocode section, found on pages 44–50, must be used to describe the required processing. The key words are recorded using capital letters. Other data and file names are written in lowercase letters.

4. Record in the VTOC reference column the VTOC ID number of the modules invoked. Figure I-1 indicates that control passes to module 3000 and that after the commands within the module are executed control returns to module 1000. Under the FROM symbol, it indicates that control

© SRA 1988, 1983

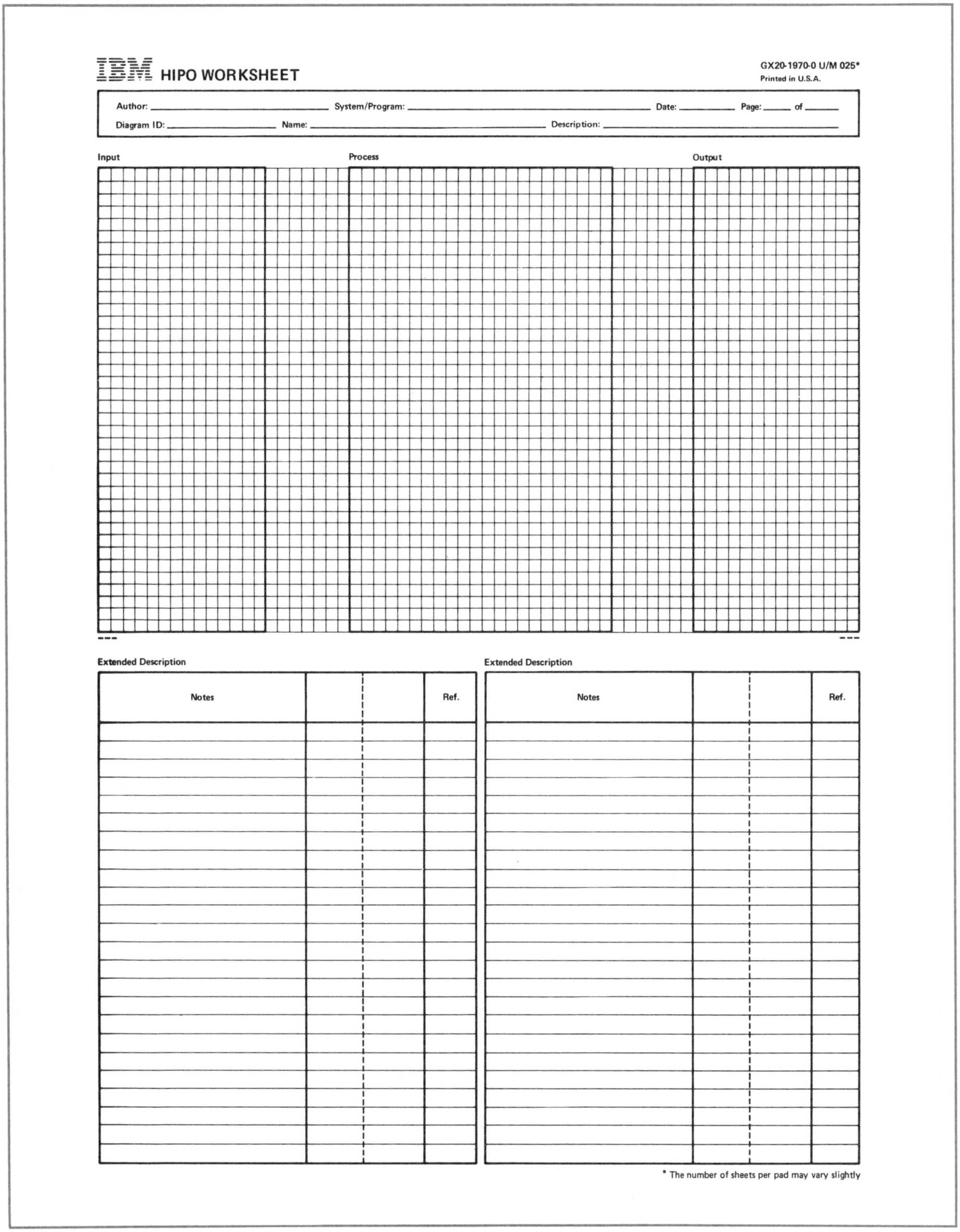

IBM HIPO WORKSHEET

GX20-1970-0 U/M 025*
Printed in U.S.A.

Author: ____ System/Program: ____ Date: ____ Page: ____ of ____
Diagram ID: ____ Name: ____ Description: ____

Input | Process | Output

Extended Description | Extended Description

Notes		Ref.	Notes		Ref.

* The number of sheets per pad may vary slightly

Figure I–2 *IBM HIPO worksheets. (Courtesy of International Business Machines Corporation)* passed from the main control module, 1000, to initialization, module 2000.

5. Provide a narrative description of the processing steps. The extended description form, illustrated in the bottom portion of Figure I–2, can be used to provide the narrative. A reference to external documentation, such as a federal income tax bulletin or to an internal form or memo, may also be included as part of the extended description.

6. Modify the HIPO. Just as the VTOC may need changing as the detailed logic plans are developed, when the source code is written and tested the data entered on the HIPO may need to be modified.

ADVANTAGES AND DISADVANTAGES OF USING HIPO CHARTS

Each module is independent of the other modules. If you must reference other modules in order to complete the module you are constructing, something is wrong. Only the tasks described in the module functions portion of the heading should be included in the pseudocode.

The major advantage of using HIPOs over detailed flowcharts is that the programmer must analyze the input and output requirements. As more detailed modules are constructed, the individual fields used for both output and input must be defined.

HIPOs are easy to construct and can be enhanced by using symbols for files and data items. The template used for drawing the symbols is illustrated in Figure I–3 and they are explained in Figure I–4. If additional documentation is required, the extended description portion of the HIPO form can be used.

One of the major disadvantages of using a HIPO rather than a flowchart is the lack of graphic representation of the problem. HIPOs *list* what must be done but do not show *how* the objectives will be achieved. Also, unless the pseudocode is well formatted and carefully written, it is difficult to read.

If the installation standards indicate that HIPOs are to be used to develop programming logic, then detailed instructions should be available regarding

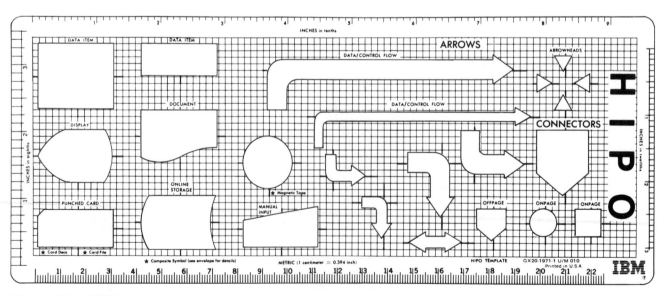

Figure I–3   HIPO template. (Courtesy of International Business Machines Corporation)

© SRA 1988, 1983

Figure I–4 Standardized symbols used to construct HIPO charts.

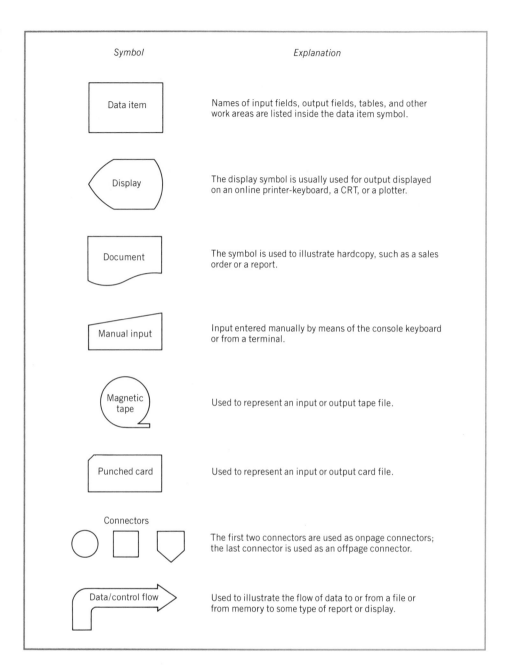

Symbol	Explanation
Data item	Names of input fields, output fields, tables, and other work areas are listed inside the data item symbol.
Display	The display symbol is usually used for output displayed on an online printer-keyboard, a CRT, or a plotter.
Document	The symbol is used to illustrate hardcopy, such as a sales order or a report.
Manual input	Input entered manually by means of the console keyboard or from a terminal.
Magnetic tape	Used to represent an input or output tape file.
Punched card	Used to represent an input or output card file.
Connectors	The first two connectors are used as onpage connectors; the last connector is used as an offpage connector.
Data/control flow	Used to illustrate the flow of data to or from a file or from memory to some type of report or display.

the conventions to be used to construct the processing, or pseudocode, section of the diagram. It is imperative that standardized key words and formatting be used in listing the required processing tasks.

USE OF FORMS AND SYMBOLS

Although the programmer should use a form that provides the required heading information and is divided into three major sections (input, processing, and output), some programmers object to the size of the IBM form illustrated in Figure I–3. The actual form is approximately 11″ × 17″. Some organizations have developed their own forms which are 8½″ × 11″ in size. Although the smaller forms have space for a heading, input, processing, reference, and output section, they do not provide an extended description section. This can be a problem when the logic is complex and needs to be documented and references must be made to other information.

Some programmers think that using the symbols illustrated in Figure I–4 enhances the chart and gives it a more polished look; others believe that using symbols does not add to the clarity of the chart. Perhaps the two most important symbols used in Figure I–1 are the ones used for FROM and TO. In constructing a logic plan, it is essential that the programmer always be aware of which module invoked the module being developed and where control will return after the statements are executed.

Appendix II
DECISION TABLES

In constructing a **decision table**, the programmer must consider all combinations that can exist. This is perhaps the major advantage of using a decision table. For example, assume that you are assigned to develop a new payroll program. One module that must be developed requires that FICA be computed. Although the law regarding Social Security deductions is constantly changing, in this example 8 percent will be deducted on the first $40,000 an employee earns. According to law, the employer can only deduct $3,200 (40,000 × .08). Any amount deducted over $3,200 must be returned to the employee. Therefore, when the employee's new year-to-date earnings are equal to or greater than $40,000 the amount to be deducted is calculated by subtracting year-to-date FICA deductions from $3,200. When deductions are computed for the next pay period, old year-to-date earnings will be equal to or greater than $40,000 and the amount deducted for FICA will be zero.

In considering the problem, two questions must be answered.

1. Are the employee's old year-to-date (YTD) gross earnings $40,000 or more? If this is the case, the FICA deduction will be zero.

2. Are the employee's new year-to-date gross earnings $40,000 or more? The new year-to-date earnings are calculated by using the old YTD earnings plus the employee's current gross pay. If new YTD is $40,000 or greater, the employee's contribution is calculated by subtracting what has already been deducted from the maximum required under the present law ($3,200).

The decision table in Figure II–1 illustrates the three components that make up decision tables. The questions are restated and listed in the **decision stub.** What will occur, based upon whether the questions are true or false, is stated in the **action stub.** The decision stub and action stub are combined to make up the **rule.**

CONSTRUCTING A
DECISION TABLE

As illustrated in Figure II–1, two decisions result in four possible combinations. Each decision increases the number of combinations by the power of 2. For example:

Number of Decisions	Possible Combinations
1	2
2	4
3	8
4	16
5	32
6	64

Figure II–1 Exploded decision table showing logic for FICA deductions.

	Rule	1	2	3	4
Decision Stub	OLD YTD ≥ 40,000	T	F	F	T
	NEW YTD ≥ 40,000	F	T	F	T
Action Stub	FICA = 0	X			X
	FICA = Gross * Rate			X	
	FICA = Maximum amount– Amount paid		X		

Because having more than sixteen possible combinations makes it difficult to work with a decision table, usually no more than four decisions are used in constructing a table. Decision tables can be used to develop and support other types of logic plans such as flowcharts or pseudocode. The following steps are used to develop a decision table:

1. Explode the table. The term **explode** indicates that *all* possibilities must be included. When the FICA decisions were exploded, the four possibilities that are illustrated in Figure II–1 are listed.

2. Determine if any of the decisions are irrelevant. In the illustration if OLD YTD is greater or equal to $40,000, NEW YTD must also be equal to or greater than $40,000. A dash, as illustrated in the revised FICA decision table, can be used rather than an F. The dash indicates that the second decision has no bearing on the rule that will be developed.

3. Determine what action should take place for each combination that occurs. An X is used to indicate what action will occur for each combination of T and/or F answers. In both Figure II–1 and II–2, FICA will equal zero whenever the OLD YTD is equal to or greater than $40,000.

4. Eliminate any redundancy. In looking at the original table there is redundancy between the first and fourth columns. Therefore, the fourth column is eliminated when Figure II–2 is created.

5. The rules, or columns, are placed in a more meaningful sequence. In Figure II–1 the sequence is the same that would be used in writing the source code so there is no need to reorder the columns.

ADVANTAGES AND DISADVANTAGES OF USING DECISION TABLES

Obviously a decision table with more than four decisions becomes difficult to handle. The advantage in using a decision table is that when it is exploded, as in Figure II–1, all combinations must be considered. Probably logical errors caused by not considered all possibilities that can exist will not occur. The programmer can eliminate any duplication and combinations that do not influence the logic of the program.

© SRA 1988, 1983

*Figure II–2 Revised
FICA decision table.*

Rule		1	2	3
Decision Stub	OLD YTD ≥ 40,000	T	F	F
	NEW YTD ≥ 40,000	—	T	F
Action Stub	FICA = 0	X		
	FICA = Gross * Rate			X
	FICA = Maximum amount— Amount paid		X	

Decision tables can be used in conjunction with other types of logic development. In the example, the FICA chart could have been used to support the internal subroutine called in by the compute-tax-deductions module illustrated in Figure II–3. Figure II–3 also illustrates how a flowchart would be used for expressing the same logic illustrated in the FICA decision table.

Figure II–3   Flowchart of the FICA module

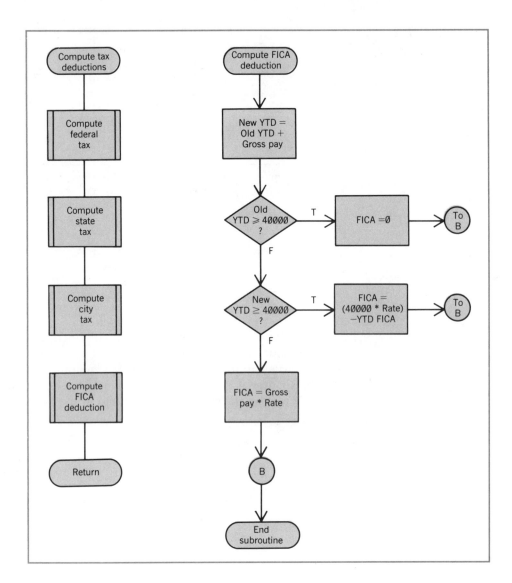

© SRA 1988, 1983

Appendix III
ANSWERS TO CHECKPOINT QUESTIONS

Chapter 1

1. Programmers are usually responsible for developing detailed logic plans, writing source code, testing programs, and documenting programs.

2. A detailed logic plan is a blueprint for a program. Programmers who write source code without developing a logic plan usually spend far more time debugging and testing their programs than programmers who develop a detailed plan.

3. Programmers should "resist the urge to code" and completely define the program, develop specifications, develop a detailed logic plan, and test the plan *before* attempting to write the source code.

4. If each programmer writes source code in a different language, it is more time consuming and costly to do the required maintenance. Also, if one programmer uses a language unfamiliar to other programmers within the organization, a problem is created if the programmer who developed the programs no longer maintains them.

5. Each routine within a program must be tested. The usual procedure is to test each routine using valid data and then invalid data. The last step may be to test the program using no data.

6. Internal documentation is intended for the programmers and analysts who must work with the programs and for users or operators who enter data. External documentation is intended to provide instruction and information about the programs; this includes items such as specification forms, record layouts, print layouts, and detailed logic plans.

7. The driving forces behind the development of design and coding standards were the high cost of developing programs, the lack of productivity, and the amount of time required to maintain poorly written and poorly documented programs.

8. Although software included in the operating system software reduced the amount of detail that programmers had to include in source code, the productivity of programmers increased less than might have been anticipated.

9. Management seemed to be concerned primarily with getting systems and programs developed in less time and within projected budgets. They seemed less concerned about program design and development.

10. In some installations, design and program standards do not exist, systems and programs are poorly designed, programmer productivity is low, programming costs are excessive, and projects are seldom completed according to schedule.

11. A hierarchy chart shows the modules that will be used in a program and their relationship to each other. By looking at the chart, a programmer can determine what support modules each major module can invoke.

12. An indicator is a field that contains data used to control the execution of the logic. The content of the field is controlled by the programmer; it is used to determine if a condition is true or false.

13. Structured programs are usually written using only the sequence, selection, and iteration control structures.

14. Well-written structured programs are modular, well designed, easy to follow, well-formatted, constructed by using meaningful names for files and data, well documented, and developed using sequence, selection, and iteration.

15. Users often have a better understanding of what is needed and of what problems must be solved by the new system or program. If users are directly involved in the design of the system or program, then objectives and specifications will more clearly reflect and meet their needs.

16. The output required determines what input must be used and how it must be processed to obtain the desired results.

17. First, the tasks that must be programmed are determined; then the programmer determines which modules will be needed. Usually each major function will have its own module.

18. The hierarchy chart shows which modules are used in much the same way that a book's table of contents lists its major topics. Therefore, the name VTOC (Vi-

sual Table Of Contents) accurately describes the hierarchy chart.

19. The name and number used for each module on the hierarchy chart are also used to identify each module's logic plan and source code.

20. The logic plan should show what occurs when data is entered as input, processed, and either displayed, printed, or written into a file. It is important that the logic plan be understandable to nondata processing personnel who may want to refer to the plan. Auditors and managers sometimes need to determine how data is being processed and what controls are built into a system to determine the validity of its input and output.

21. No. Designing and developing a program should be a team effort which involves users, analysts, operations personnel, and programmers. A programmer should take pride in his or her work but should not consider a program as his or her private endeavor.

22. Well-formatted code is easier to understand and less costly and time consuming to maintain.

23. The calculations required to compute the monthly interest, new balance, and total interest for the five-month period were calculated and then compared to the output created by running the program.

24. Internal documentation is intended primarily for the use of terminal operators and maintenance programmers. Also it would be difficult to include as internal documentation the record layouts, print layouts, hierarchy charts, and detailed logic plan.

25. Operations personnel are interested in documentation that describes how a program is loaded into memory for execution, what I/O devices must be readied, and what type of error messages might be generated during the execution of the program. Programmers are interested in the program specifications, record layout, print layout, hierarchy chart, and detailed logic plan.

Chapter 2

1. A separate HIPO chart is developed for each module and is divided into three sections. The first section is used to list the input needed to perform the required processing. The middle section contains the process required to produce the output for the module. The third section lists the output produced by processing the input.

2. Yes. IBM, which developed and supported the use of HIPO charts, designed worksheets and templates to use in developing the charts. The worksheets contain an identification section at the top, sections for input, process, and output, and additional space at the bottom of the form for an extended description of any of the information recorded on the top portion of the worksheet.

3. Both HIPO charts and pseudocode are developed using key words and by formatting pseudocode statements to make it easier to understand how the data will be processed.

4. The method used to illustrate the logic of a program must: be standardized so that others can understand what is occurring; be easy to construct; be easy to understand; be easy to maintain; provide documentation; and provide a means of cross referencing the logic plan to the hierarchy chart and to the source code.

5. Pseudocode is a user-defined noncompilable shorthand. It can be used independently to express the logic of a program or as part of a Warnier-Orr, a Nassi-Shneiderman, or a HIPO chart.

6. A logic plan can be developed faster using pseudocode than when any other method is used. Once the author understands the meaning of the key words and how pseudocode is to be formatted, pseudocode is easy to write. The major disadvantage in using pseudocode is the tendency to write it so fast that it is difficult for others to understand.

7. Key words are used to describe basic functions. For example, using "PERFORM read record 3000" is the same as stating "branch down to read record, module 3000, execute the statements in the module, and return to the statement following the one that caused control to transfer to the read record module."

8. a. ACCEPT indicates that data is to be entered from the operator's console, whereas READ indicates a record is to be read from a file.

   b. DO-WHILE is used to specify that the statements within a loop are to be executed as long as the expression is true. For example, when DO-WHILE EOF = NO is used, then as long as NO is stored in the EOF field, the statements in the loop will be executed. DO-UNTIL EOF = YES causes the statements within the loop to be executed until YES is stored in the EOF field.

   c. Both DO 3000-enter data and PERFORM 3000-enter data cause a branch to occur to the module referenced as 3000-Enter data. After the commands are executed, control of the program returns to the statement following the DO or PERFORM.

© SRA 1988, 1983

d. WRITE usually indicates that a record is to be added to a file whereas PRINT usually indicates a line is to be printed on a report.

9. NULL is used to indicate that no action is required. Consider the following pseudocode:

```
IF A = B THEN
    PERFORM Math-3020
ELSE
    NULL
END IF
```

If A and B are not equal, control goes immediately to the statement following the IF statement. NULL is used to show that no omission occurred.

10. A form should be used for writing pseudocode so that the proper identification information is recorded at the top of each form. Also, vertical lines can be included that remind the programmer to make the necessary indentations. If horizontal lines are included on the forms, the author's penmanship is usually better than when unruled paper is used. If forms are not provided for students, ruled notebook paper should be used rather than blank paper.

11. Flowcharts are probably the oldest method used to illustrate the logic of a program. Structured flowcharts, one flowchart for each module, are newer than the original unstructured flowcharts.

12. ANSI symbols should be used to develop flowcharts so that the reader knows what is occurring. Almost all computer information service employees, as well as auditors and other individuals who work with flowcharts, are familiar with the ANSI symbols.

13. Flowcharts are developed from top to bottom and from left to right.

14. Within a process symbol a statement, such as calculate gross, or a mathematical expression, such a gross = (Hours * Rate) + (Overtime * Rate * 2), can be used.

15. The annotation symbol is used to clarify what is recorded inside a preparation or process symbol.

16. To develop a structured flowchart, a programmer uses the program specification, the hierarchy chart, flowcharting worksheets, and a template.

17. An offpage connector is used to continue the flowchart for a module onto a new page.

18. Arrowheads need not be used to show the usual top to bottom or left to right flow. If there is any question regarding the direction of flow, arrowheads should be used.

19. If a connector with an A is used, there must be a second connector that also has an A. The first connector

may be at the top of the loop and the second one at the bottom that includes the statement "TO A."

20. An external subroutine has been coded, tested, and documented. Therefore, a logic plan has already been developed. If necessary, it can be referenced.

21. A Nassi-Shneiderman chart is constructed using symbols for process, decision, case entry, and for creating loops.

22. A decision is shown by creating a rectangle and dividing it into three triangles. The triangle at the top contains a question such as "salaried employee?" or "regular hours > 40?". The triangles on the left and right contain a T or an F. Usually the T for true is on your left and the F for false is on your right.

23. A loop is created by using an inverted L. At the top, the condition, such as WHILE EOF = NO, is provided. Within the L the statements to be executed are listed and may include the process, decision, or case entry structures. Within the main loop, there may also be one or more inner loops.

24. A case entry control structure can be used whenever there are two or more conditions. However, at any one time only one condition can be true. For example, employees have a status code that indicates if they are salaried, hourly, or part-time. The status code can be either a S, H, or P.

25. To ensure that the required identifying information is recorded on each chart, a standard form should be used.

26. Inside the process symbol can be a pseudocode statement, a mathematical expression, or documentation.

27. A universal is used to indicate the name of a module and is part of the internal documentation. An executable is a mathematical expression or a statement that will be written in source code, translated into machine language by a compiler or interpreter, and then executed by the computer.

28. A Warnier-Orr chart is described as a hierarchy chart that has been laid on its side and developed by using pseudocode to illustrate the logic of a program.

29. In constructing a decision point, the condition is stated twice. A symbol, constructed by placing a + mark within a circle, separates the two statements. A horizontal line is placed above the second statement to signify that the action specified occurs when the statement is false. A brace containing the required statements or NULL must be used for both the true and false portion of the decision. For example,

$$A = B \{$$
$$\oplus$$
$$\overline{A = B} \{$$

30. A loop is constructed by using WHILE or UNTIL. WHILE or UNTIL, along with the required expression, are placed within parentheses.

31. Warnier-Orr charts are faster to construct than either Nassi-Shneiderman diagrams or structured flowcharts. Also, when Warnier-Orr charts are developed, it is recommended that the supporting modules be included on the same chart as the major modules. However, as more complex programs are developed many of the modules will require the use of a separate sheet.

32. The form used to develop a Warnier-Orr chart should provide the name of the programmer, the name of the program, the date, page number, and module reference number, name, and function.

Chapter 3

1. In the previous chapters simple IF statements and case entry were discussed.

2. When a branching instruction occurs, the next command in sequence is not executed. Instead, control branches to a module or internal subroutine and the commands are executed. Control then returns to the statement following the branching instruction.

3. Before the branching instruction is executed, the address of the next instruction in sequence is stored in a special register.

4. No. Depending on the language being used, a field defined as alphanumeric must be compared to alphanumeric data; a numeric field must be compared to a numeric constant or a field containing numeric data. It should be noted that a field defined as alphanumeric can contain a number rather than alphanumeric data.

5. A simple IF statement can specify action to occur when the condition is true, when the condition is false, or when the condition is either true or false.

6. Relational operators are =, <>, <, >, <=, and >=.

7. When AND is used, all of the conditions specified must be true for the action specified for the true portion of the statement to be executed. When OR is used, only one of the conditions specified must be true for the action specified for the true portion of the statement to occur.

8. When NOT is used, the truth of a single argument is reversed. If the values stored in A and B are equal, comparing the two results in the condition being true.

However, when NOT is used, the truth is reversed and the statement becomes false.

9. Sometimes the use of NOT, AND, and OR makes a program more complex than is necessary and more difficult to maintain. If complexity can be avoided by including additional IF statements and avoiding the use of NOT, AND, and OR, it may be wise to do so.

10. Omitting parentheses may cause the execution of the arithmetic operations to occur in a different order than intended and the answer will be invalid. Using the parentheses in writing pseudocode will remind the programmer that they must be used when the source code is written.

11. The sequence in which the expression is executed is as follows:
    a. 1) Parentheses are cleared—45 − 40 = 5.
       2) Proceeding from left to right, 5 is multiplied times 12 to produce 60.
       3) 60 is then multiplied times 2 to obtain the final answer of 120.
    b. Without the parentheses, the following would occur:
       1) rate is multiplied times 40 (40 × 12 = 480).
       2) 480 is multiplied times 2 (480 × 2 = 960).
       3) 960 is subtracted from 45 (45 − 960 = −915).

12. a. If the parentheses were omitted, the error should have been detected during the code walk-through. If the error isn't detected then, it should be found when the program is tested. The programmer should have calculated the answer to be $120. When the computer produced an answer of −915, the error should have been detected.
    b. Without the parentheses, all overtime pay will be incorrect.

13. Each IF statement must have its own ELSE and ENDIF.

14. The ELSE for condition-2 would be matched with the IF for condition-3 and the ELSE for condition-1 would be matched with the IF for condition-2. The results obtained when the computer evaluates the statement will be invalid.

15. Correct matching of an IF with its ELSE is essential. Well formatted statements are easier to check for accuracy or for omissions.

16. No. A statement such as the following might be coded in BASIC.

           IF A = B THEN GOSUB 1000

An ELSE statement is not required. However, in developing most logic plans, a NULL ELSE will be included to indicate that there has not been an omission. Some programming languages also provide ways of coding a NULL ELSE.

© SRA 1988, 1983

17. If an attempt is made to divide by zero, a program will usually abort. Therefore, the programmer should include the following statements:

```
IF  X  =  0  THEN
     GOSUB nnnn
ELSE
     ANSWER  =  Y  /  X
```

18. If an employee is not to receive a bonus, the bonus-pay field must be set to zero. This could have been done at the beginning of the cycle used to calculate each employee's pay or can be done as part of the IF/THEN/ELSE statement.

19. Yes. Many programmers believe that all numeric fields recorded in current files or printed as part of a detail line should be restored to zero between execution of program cycles. A cycle includes inputting the data, making the required calculations, and creating the required output. However, some fields, such as the one used to accumulate the number of records processed, cannot be reset to zero.

20. IF/THEN/ELSE statements nested within an outer statement are indented. For example,

```
IF  A  =  B  THEN
     IF  C  =  D  THEN  X  =  Y
     ELSE  X  =  Z
ELSE  X  =  0
```

21. The word PERFORM followed by the name of the module to be executed was used to indicate that a predetermined process (or subroutine) was to be executed.

22. If five levels of nesting are required, there is little space for the innermost IF statements and it is difficult to show what will occur.

23. When a bar appears about a statement, it indicates the action specified will occur when the statement is false.

24. Nesting is shown on a Warnier-Orr diagram by using additional braces. There must be a brace for each IF/ELSE plus one for the action specified for both the IF and ELSE portion of the statement.

25. a. Since the pay period field contains a zero, the error routine specified as 3080 will be executed. Bonus pay will be $200.

    b. Since the rate for the hourly employee is 0, multiplying hours times 0 would produce 0 pay.

    c. The employee's regular pay would be calculated at $380—38 hours at $10 per hour. Overtime is calculated as $90 —(44-38) * 10 * 1.5.

26. The error should have been detected when the master file record was created. When a record for an hourly employee was created, a statement should have been used to see if the amount in the rate field was greater

than 0. Yes, a statement such as IF MF-RATE <= 0 THEN. . . . should have been included in the calculate-gross module as well as in the file-create program. When the record was created, an error message could have been displayed and ignored by the data entry operator.

27. a. ```
    IF MF-STATUS = S
    AND MF-SALARY < = 0 THEN
         DISPLAY 'ENTER SALARY'
         INPUT MF-SALARY
    ```

    ```
    IF  MF-STATUS  =  S  AND
    MF-PAY-PERIODS  <  =  0  THEN
         DISPLAY 'ENTER PAY PERIODS'
         INPUT MF-PAY-PERIODS
    ```

    b. ```
    IF MF-STATUS = H AND
    MF-PAY-PERIODS < = 0 THEN
         DISPLAY 'ENTER HOURLY RATE'
         INPUT MF-RATE
    ```

    c. ```
    IF MF-BONUS > 0 AND
    MF-BONUS-PAYMENTS < = 0 THEN
         DISPLAY 'ENTER NO. OF PAYMENTS'
         INPUT MF-BONUS-PAYMENTS
    ```

28. Usually, but not always, a case entry has a default routine. For example, if the STATUS field can contain an H, P, or S and different calculations are used for each payroll classification, a default routine should be provided if an invalid status code is in the STATUS field.

29. When case entry is used, as soon as a true evaluation is made and the statements specified are executed, the remainder of the conditions are not checked. If single IF statements were used rather than case entry, all of the conditions specified will need to be checked.

30. Case entry could have been used to determine if the STATUS field contains either an S or an H. If neither character is stored within the field, a default routine could have been invoked. If the status were equal to an S, nested IF statements could still be used. If the status were equal to an N, one additional IF statement would be required.

31. Yes. Prompts are required whenever data is keyed into an interactive program. The operator must know what is to be entered and the length of the field.

32. Most initialization modules provide the code for performing the following tasks:

    a. Work fields, total areas, and tables are established and set to their initial value.

    b. Constants that are to be hardcoded are established.

    c. Indicators are defined and set to their initial value.
    ```

d. An option is provided which permits the operator to display the help menu and specific directions for entering data.

e. Constants, such as the date, are entered by the operator. The operator must be able to verify the data entered visually and an opportunity must be provided to rekey data already entered.

f. Files are opened.

g. The initial record or records are read so that data is available when control passes to the process-records module.

h. A provision is made to allow the operator to cancel the job without executing the process-records and termination modules.

33. The operator could enter the code required to display directions for entering:

a. the date and invoice number.

b. the account number.

c. the item number.

d. quantity ordered.

34. Scrolling can be prevented by having the operator use the ENTER key or depressing any of the keys on the keyboard after reading the information displayed and before any new data is displayed on the screen.

35. The display symbol was used with the necessary information printed within the figure. Along with the symbol and information, another symbol was used for keyboard input. The two symbols were used together to illustrate that after information was displayed, some type of response was needed.

Chapter 4

1. The two major types of loops used in constructing programs are count-controlled and conditional.

2. In a WHILE loop, the exit-condition test is made prior to the execution of any of the commands. In an UNTIL loop, the commands are executed and then the exit-condition test occurs.

3. In the DO WHILE flowchart, the exit-condition test is at the top of the loop. The exit-condition test is at the bottom of the DO UNTIL loop.

4. The pseudocode for the statements within the two types of conditional loops is identical. Where the exit-condition test occurs is not shown in the pseudocode.

5. No. The WHILE or UNTIL statement provides the necessary exit-condition test.

6. The PERFORM/UNTIL statement that controls the execution of the 2000-process-sales-records module is located in the 1000 level main-control module.

7. When a PERFORM/UNTIL is used, the test is made prior to executing the commands within the loop.

8. Since end-of-file controls the execution of the commands within the loop, it is considered an indicator. Some programmers refer to indicators as switches or flags.

9. The statement that establishes the count-controlled loop establishes the initial value of the counter, sets up the exit-condition test, and provides the number used to increment the counter.

10. If the counter is to be incremented by a value other than 1, STEP must be used in the FOR statement.

11. a. UNTIL loop.

b. Count-controlled loop.

c. Nested count-controlled loop. The outer loop (year loop) will be executed 10 times; the inner loop (month) will be executed 12 times for each of the ten years.

d. WHILE loop.

e. Count-controlled loop.

f. UNTIL loop.

12. A counter is a field used to control the execution of a count-controlled loop. The counter is given an initial value, incremented by a pre-determined number, and tested to see if it is greater than the maximum established for the loop. In FOR J = 1 TO 100 STEP 2, the counter is set at 1, incremented by 2, and an exit from the loop will occur when J is greater than 100.

13. A count-controlled loop is shown by dividing a rectangle into three triangles. One triangle contains the initial value of the counter (J = 1), the second contains the exit test (J > 100), and the third contains the value used to increment the counter (J = J + 2).

14. The statements within the outer loop are indented. The inner loop is established and its statements are also indented. For example,

```
DO (year = 1 to 10)
   any statements
   DO (month = 1 to 12)
      any statements
      DO (day = 1 to 30)
         any statements
      END DAY
   END MONTH
END YEAR
```

© SRA 1988, 1983

15. When conducting a search, the match might be found before all of the items within the table are retrieved and compared to the number used in conducting the search.

16. The statements within the loop will be executed 3 times when the counter has a value of 1, 5, and 9.

17. A loop is shown on a Nassi-Shneiderman chart by using an inverted L. When nested loops are required, the inner loops are located within the outer loops.

18. A separate brace is used for each loop and the inner loops must be completely enclosed within the brace used for the outermost loop.

19. When a PERFORM/VARYING is used to establish a count-controlled loop, the commands to be executed are located in the module specified in the PERFORM/VARYING statement. When a FOR/NEXT is used, the FOR/NEXT and the commands to be executed within the loop may be in the same module. However, a GOSUB could be used to create a branch to and back from a second module.

20. Both a PERFORM/VARYING and a FOR/NEXT

    a. Give the initial value to a counter.

    b. Test to determine if the exit-condition specified is met.

    c. Increments the counter by the number specified.

    d. May be nested.

Chapter 5

1. When data is accessed randomly, an address is generated to allow the required item to be retrieved without accessing the preceding items. In sequential access, the first item stored in the table is accessed, then the second, and so forth.

2. When tables are used,

    a. Less space is needed in the master or transaction file to record the code used as the subscript than to record the data in the file.

    b. Fewer keystrokes are needed to record the subscript in the file.

    c. Less file maintenance is required.

    d. Less coding is required to process the data.

3. The value stored in the field used as a subscript must be a whole, positive number and within range of the table. In addition, subscripts are enclosed in parentheses and separated by commas.

4. The values stored in the subscript field may have been: read from a file; keyed in by an operator; generated by a count-controlled loop; or determined by a mathematical expression or by using IF/THEN/ELSE statements.

5. No. When sales invoices are being prepared, records from the inventory master file must be retrieved that contain the product description, price of the product, and quantity on hand. Since the product description is included in the master file records, there would be no reason to store product descriptions in a table.

6. a. DECLARE table (20, 11)

   b. DO (row = 1 to 20)
          DO (col = 1 to 11)
              table (row, col) = 0
          END COL
      END ROW

   c. The row subscript would be determined by using case entry:
      IF grosspay < 150.01 THEN
          ROW = 1
      ELSE IF grosspay < 200.01 THEN
              ROW = 2   and so forth.
      The col subscript would also be determined by using case entry:
      IF exempno = 0 THEN
          col = 1
      ELSE IF exempno = 1 THEN
              col = 2 and so forth.

   d. If the percentages are stored in a table, far less file maintenance is required. Also, a separate field does not need to be used for the percentage. Both fields needed to determine the subscripts are available. The number of exemptions (exempno) is stored in the employee's master file record and grosspay is computed for each employee.

7. When TABLE (J,K,L) is used: J is the table number; K is the row number; and L is the column number.

8. The main control module of the survey program differs from the ones used in previous examples because in this type of program all data must be read and stored in a table *before* processing can occur. The others used as examples were the more typical input-processing-output programs.

9. A three-dimension table was needed because the results were to be analyzed on the basis of how females and males responded to the questions. The other two dimensions were needed for question number and answer.

10. The tables are only cleared once. Therefore, the statements cannot be part of a major processing loop.

11. If read-record is invoked by the first statement within

a WHILE loop, when the end-of-file is detected *after all records are processed,* the statements within the loop have already started to execute. Either an IF statement must be used to prevent this from occurring or the principle of "single entry, single exit" must be violated and an exit made from the processing loop. If one of the two actions specified is not taken, either the last record will be processed twice or the program may abort. What occurs depends on the language being used.

12. If one table is used to store the survey results and a second the percentages, table-to-table processing can occur. Only one statement is needed rather than 25 different calculation statements for both men and women. Since the report is to list the way each question was answered and the precentages of responses, both sets of data must be available when the report is printed. The table-to-table approach is easier to understand (keep it simple) and easier to maintain than other approaches that could have been used.

Chapter 6

1. The four major classifications of application programs are maintenance, report, information retrieval, and transaction processing.

2. Records stored in master files are always changing. New records are added, obsolete records deleted, and information stored within existing records is corrected, changed due to normal occurrences, or updated by adding new data to existing totals.

3. When an application is designed, the programmer must consult the user regarding what information is needed, when it is needed, and how it should be displayed or printed.

4. The volume of printed information may be reduced by printing reports on demand rather than on a scheduled basis, by displaying data on a VDT rather than printing a report, or by writing reports on a magnetic medium such as tape.

5. He or she would request an exception report.

6. An internal report is usually printed on stock paper and the information is used within the organization. An external report is printed on preprinted forms and sent to other organizations, stockholders, or to some branch of the government.

7. Some reports printed on a scheduled basis were "filed" but never used. Requiring individuals to submit a written request for a report decreases the number of reports printed but seldom used.

8. Where variable information is to be printed is indicated by using Xs. When COBOL is used, 9s may be used to represent variable numeric data.

9. Asking the person who requested the report for prior approval avoids controversy regarding what should be on the report. The analyst feels confident in developing the detailed logic plan that will provide the required information.

10. A standard list tape has a punch in the top-of-form position and another in the overflow position. The programmer controls the vertical spacing of the report being printed. Standard list tapes are usually used when internal reports are printed.

11. When printing checks, invoices, mailing labels and other types of reports that require special forms, special carriage tapes with punches that coordinate with the required locations of the print lines are used.

12. Depending on the length of the paper being used, the programmer knows how many single-spaced lines can be printed. From the total (such as 66 when 11-inch paper is used) the number of lines used for the top margin, headings, and bottom margin must be subtracted. The resulting figure determines the number of lines that can be used for printing detail lines.

13. How the report will be used determines if the information will be single or double spaced. For example, student grade reports are read once by the student and then filed. Therefore, ease of reading is not an issue and to save space, the detail lines listing courses and grades will be single spaced.

14. The print layout form illustrates heading, detail, and total lines.

15. The statement is false. How print lines are formatted is language-dependent.

16. Each of the fields used from the inventory master file records were edited and verified as the data was entered into the records or changed. Also, it would be difficult to determine if the fields used in the inventory exception report contained valid data.

17. The hierarchy chart in Figure 6–3 illustrates a print-detail module that invokes the print-heading module.

18. In the initialization module, the line counter is set to the maximum number of lines that will be printed on a page. As a result, the first time the test condition is evaluated, headings will be printed. Using this approach, the printing of all detail lines is treated in the same way.

19. The line counter is set to zero each time a heading is printed.

© SRA 1988, 1983

20. Because the date subroutine has already been tested and documented, it is not necessary to include a logic plan for the module each time it is called.

21. No. The data stored in a field described as numeric only includes the digits 0–9 plus a sign to indicate if the data is positive or negative.

22. An edit mask is defined and the numeric data is transferred into the edit mask.

23. The inventory exception report program is typical of many report programs because only a limited number of records are printed and the program that determines which records are to be printed has very few IF/THEN/ELSE or calculation statements.

24. The multilevel sales analysis program requires 7 different print lines: 2 heading lines, 1 detail line, 1 total line for each sales representative, 1 department total line, 1 store total line, and 1 report total line.

25. The report illustrated in Figure 6–2 is a detail report. One line is printed for each item sold.

26. When a level break occurs and a record containing an order from a new sales representative is read, a total for the previous sales representative is printed.

27. The statement is true. The department total must be added to the store total and the total for the department printed *before* the data entered in the first record for the new department can be processed or printed.

28. If department numbers are compared first, the department change routines will be executed but the store change routines will not be executed.

29. The sales-representative-change, department-change, and store-change modules must be executed before the end-of-job routine can be executed.

30. Special print fields are used in order that the sales representative's name and number will only be printed once. After they are printed for the first time, spaces are moved into the print fields.

31. If the department names are stored in a table, only 3 bytes are required in each master file record to record the number of the department. If the department names are recorded in the file, as many as 20–30 bytes will be required. This increases the cost of entering data into transaction files.

32. In the sales invoice program, either 1 or 2 is added to the line-counter each time a line is printed. Frequently the line-counter will not equal 47. The counter may have advanced from 46 to 48 because a department line, followed by a blank line, was printed.

33. In order to print multilevel reports, the control number (such as sales representative) must be saved, the new number entered must be compared to the saved number. If a level break occurs, the total must be added to the next higher level of total, the total field reset to zero, and the new number saved.

34. When special forms are used, it is important that the information is printed in the exact location specified on the print layout form. Often the preprinted form illustrates exactly where both the dollars and cents amounts must be printed.

35. A transparency of the paycheck can be prepared and overlayed on the check printed on stock paper.

36. A typical report specification form lists the fields to be printed, where (or how) the data originated, the size of the field, and the type of data stored within the field.

37. The customer's name and address are printed *after* the previous total lines are printed and *before* any detail lines are printed for the new invoice.

38. When a new invoice number is detected, the calculation and print-total modules are invoked before the data from the new transaction record is processed. The tasks that will be executed are calculating the totals needed, printing the totals, and printing the heading information on the new form.

39. The outer loop will be executed as long as there are records to be processed and the end-of-file condition has not been detected. The inner loop will be executed as long as the new invoice number is equal to the stored invoice number.

40. A systems flowchart indicates only data flow, input, processing, and output. However, the way the input is processed in order to produce the required output is not depicted.

41. If only a few fields are required for a limited number of records, it is more efficient to extract, sort, and print than to sort all the records and select only those to be processed.

42. If the credit-union field was greater than zero, the required data was extracted and stored in a new record.

43. The credit-union report is a listing that will be used internally as well as being submitted to the credit union as an external report.

44. A report is to be sent to each of the area newspapers listing the students who have more than a 3.7 grade point average. Only 10 percent of the students have more than a 3.7 and only 50 bytes of information is required for each student listed on the report. Each student's master file record has over 600 bytes of information.

45. In a transaction-processing system data is entered and immediately processed. Since a transaction-processing system is defined as "one in which data is processed in time to influence the transaction," errors must be detected as soon as the information enters the system.

46. When an error-message is printed or displayed, it may be necessary for the operator to consult several resources before the cause of the problem can be de-

tected. Each error causes a delay in processing. If errors are accumulated and processed in a "batch," the processing of the valid data is not delayed.

47. When the first report is being printed, the data required for the second report is extracted and stored in a file. After the first report is printed, the transaction file is closed, then reopened, and the program that prints the second report is executed. If SPOOLing is supported, it may be possible to redesign the program so that both reports are printed by one program.

48. Top-management wants only condensed information. For example, top management is interested only in department totals and not in the listing of the various account totals.

Chapter 7

1. The four major sources are data that is recorded in files, keyed in by operators, calculated, or retrieved from tables.

2. Data is stored more densely on hard disk and retrieval of data is much faster than when diskettes are used.

3. Magnetic tape is used to back up files, to store historical information, and to store infrequently used files.

4. When reports are submitted on magnetic tape rather than in a printed format, standardized tape should be used. Magnetic tape can also be used to provide communication between two different computer systems.

5. The medium or device used impacts the design less than the type of organization and access methods available.

6. Sequential files should usually be used for recording transaction files that do not require maintenance. Transaction files are used in a limited number of applications and are usually replaced, within a short period of time, with a newer version.

7. VSAM files can have multiple keys, are automatically reorganized, and obsolete records are physically deleted from the file. In a single program, records in a file can be accessed sequentially and randomly.

8. The logic of most programs that utilize ISAM files would not be changed if VSAM files were used. Some of the maintenance programs would be changed and a few programs that require both random and sequential access to records would be redesigned.

9. When a system is being designed, the required programs will be determined. The output required for each program will be analyzed in terms of the most effective way to obtain the information. In most business applications, a large percent of the information required for information retrieval and reports comes from master files or databases.

10. The file specification form contains identifying information regarding the file, such as its name, record size, blocking factor, and how it is organized. In addition, the form supplies the name, size, location, and type of data stored in each field.

11. The file specification form is used to determine what data is available, how the records are accessed, and how each data item must be handled. For example, if the Social Security number is one continuous alphanumeric field, a function might be needed to break it into its three components before it is printed as output.

12. A logical record contains data about one individual or item. A physical record usually contains one or more logical records. Logical records are processed by the program; physical records are read into memory and written onto the storage medium. Operating system software takes care of the blocking and unblocking of physical records.

13. The programmer is concerned only with logical records.

14. A byte is one storage location within memory which consists of 8 bits for storing data and a parity bit.

15. Usually few, if any, editing commands are available for alphanumeric data. Alphanumeric data cannot be used in arithmetic commands and must be compared with other alphanumeric data.

16. When file structures are copied into memory, less time is needed to write the source code and there is less chance of making an error. Also, whenever the structure is used, the same field names must be used. When the data structure is changed, only the source code that is copied needs to be modified.

17. The data dictionary should be consulted to see which programs use the fields associated with state income tax. The programs in which the fields are used should be reviewed to determine if any changes are needed.

18. If the individual quarterly and year-to-date fields are adjacent to one another, one statement may be used to clear the entire quarterly or year-to-date substructure. Also, program maintenance is easier if like items are grouped together.

19. Keying in data is time consuming, costly, and subject to human error.

20. If a new system is being designed, data may not be available in a form that can be read into the system and used to create the required master files.

© SRA 1988, 1983

21. The programs in the old system have been tested and used over a period of time. Therefore, it seems wise to use those programs to update the data before creating the new file.

22. The listing of employees added to the master file was transmitted to the payroll department for confirmation. When a master file is created, or additional data added to it, every precaution should be taken to make sure it contains complete and accurate information.

23. During the creation of an ISAM file, the invalid-key condition will occur if an attempt is made to write a record which is out of sequence or one that has a duplicate key.

24. Sometimes, in order to obtain the print attributes that are desired, the printer must be declared a file. For example, in some versions of BASIC, the default is to an 80-character wide print line. If it is necessary to print more than 80 characters on a line, the printer must be declared as a file and the width of the line specified.

25. When fields are concatenated they are put together to form a continuous string of data that can be treated as one field.

26. The end-of-file mark is recorded at the end of a file so that it can be detected when the file is processed sequentially. When this occurs, the programmer can specify what action is to occur.

27. Each time an error was detected, one was added to counter. In order to store each error message in a separate area of the error table, the counter was used as a subscript.

28. For employees who request direct deposit in one of twenty local banks, the organization has agreed to supply the banks with a magnetic tape to permit the information to be processed electronically. The bank number in which the deposit is to be made must be stored in the employee master file records.

29. When a new field such as YDT-city-tax is added, it will be used in an arithmetic statement such as YDT-city-tax = YDT-city-tax + current-city-tax. Unless the field is first cleared to zeroes, the first time the command generated by the statement is executed the job may abort due to a data exception.

30. When data is keyed in by an operator, it is stored in a buffer until the **ENTER** key is pressed. When the **ENTER** key is pressed, the data is transferred into the data structure located within the memory of the computer.

31. No. The size of the blocking factor does not impact the design of the program.

32. In a sequential update, a transaction and a master record are read. If there is a match (the employee number is the same in both records), the master record will be updated and both a transaction and master record will be read. If there is not a match, only a master file is read. In a random update program, only the records to be updated are retrieved.

33. Within an installation, there may be general guidelines, such as when thirty percent or more of the records are to be updated by using data stored in a transaction file, the master file should be accessed sequentially. However, regardless of the percent of records to be updated or used in a report, if a search is made by the computer to determine which records are to be used, the master file must be accessed sequentially.

34. If an invalid-condition occurs during the rewriting of an updated record, it is the result of a logical error in the design of the program. The program should be aborted and the error corrected.

35. The "single entry, single exit" guideline is violated. Since immediate action is required, the simplest solution is to display a message, close the files, and abort the job.

Chapter 8

1. The programs needed to maintain a typical file are those designed to add new records, make normal changes, correct errors, add new fields and data, update records, back up the file, and to recreate the file.

2. Programs requiring a limited amount of data and those that must be executed frequently are often designed to be executed in an interactive mode. In the payroll example, the program to add new records and to change or correct existing records is run in an interactive mode.

3. The CHANGE program needs to be executed more frequently and will require more maintenance than the CORRECT program. In accord with the aim to "keep it simple and avoid undue complexity," it seems wise to develop two programs.

4. For each change the operator enters the employee's number, the change code, and the new value to be recorded in the field being changed.

5. The CHANGE program is a random update program and is executed in an interactive mode. An operator keys in and visually confirms the data, the data is used to update the record, and the updated record is rewritten.

6. The descriptions of the changes are constants. By using the code entered by the operator as the subscript, the description can be displayed and the operator can determine if the correct code was entered.

7. When an employee's United Fund contribution is recorded, it is also necessary to record the number of pay periods over which the contribution will be spread.

8. When an invalid response is entered, the cursor is returned to the point where the entry was made, an error message is displayed, and the prompt asking MORE RECORDS? Y OR N? is displayed.

9. A pause or delay can be created by using a command such as **SLEEP,** by requiring the operator to respond to a statement such as **PRESS ENTER TO CONTINUE,** or by creating a loop that takes a few seconds to execute.

10. Because code is equal to **2,** control will go to the second module listed, the stock-change.

11. The statement could have been coded:

```
IF change-code = 1 THEN
    PERFORM salary-change
ELSE IF change-code = 2 THEN
        PERFORM stock-change
    ELSE IF change-code = 3 THEN
            PERFORM name-change
END IF
```

12. Alphanumeric fields are justified to the left; numeric fields are justified to the right.

13. The information was obtained from the following sources:

number	keyed in by the operator
name	retrieved from the MF
description	retrieved from the table
old data	value stored in the MF
new data	keyed in by the operator

14. The report is sent with the source documents to the person who authorized the changes. The changes listed on the report should be compared with those recorded on the source document. A note should be made on the source document and the document returned to the individual reponsible for entering the changes.

15. Since each module executes only one major task and closely related minor tasks, there is no need to create additional modules.

16. Visual confirmation is made to determine if the right record is accessed, if the right field is being changed, and of the value entered by the operator. Whenever possible the data entered by the operator is also edited. For example, the pay-period field is checked to determine if the number is greater than 26; the status code must be an S, H, or P. The number of records updated must also agree with the number of documents submitted.

17. Since a typical screen has 25 horizontal display lines, displaying 12 prompts on one screen would make the information harder to read than if it is split between two screens.

18. When a negative number is added to a positive value, the smaller is subtracted from the larger and the answer carries the sign of the larger field.

19. When the key entered by the operator cannot be found in the file's index, an invalid-key condition will occur.

20. Usually one path is followed if the operator responds with a **Y** and a second path followed for an **N** response. If the response isn't checked a **U** might have been entered rather than a **Y** and the programmer might have coded the program so that it is treated as an **N** response.

21. If an error is not detected until it becomes part of a report or information database, it is far more costly and time consuming to correct than if the error is detected before the data enters the system.

22. Before rewriting the record, the new data is stored in the appropriate field and the old data is destroyed. Therefore, it is more logical to store the data in print fields, print the detail line, and then replace the old data with the new data and rewrite the record.

23. When the correct program is executed, a number of fields are changed for each record. The easiest way to format the report is to print a separate page for each record changed. Since it is seldom necessary to correct data stored in the payroll master file records, it would be very unusual to correct more than one record at a time.

24. No. All new employees will have zeroes in all of the year-to-date and quarterly fields as well as some of the other fields, such as stock shares purchased and total value of their contribution. These fields within the data structure can be set to zero rather than requiring the operator to key in a zero.

25. The values from the transaction file for a pay period can only be added once to the records stored in the master file. Therefore, to make certain the program isn't executed twice, a lock is placed on the file. It is removed when the file is backed up and re-created.

26. Each time a transaction record is read, the read-transaction indicator is set to **N.** The read-transaction-records module is only executed when read-transaction is equal to **Y.** When a match occurs, read-transaction is reset to **Y** and another transaction record will be read.

© SRA 1988, 1983

27. When the end-of-file condition is detected for the transaction file, no more master file records should be read and the job should be terminated. In order to do this, more-records and read-master are both set to **N**.

28. The UPDATE program is a sequential update program that is executed in a batch mode.

29. The job is aborted by displaying a message and then setting the more-records and read-master indicators to **N**. Control will return to the main-control module and then pass to the termination module where the files will be closed and the number of records updated will be printed.

30. Very often when the master file is recreated, such changes as deleting records or resetting fields to zero are made. Most utility programs only provide for changing the size of the records and the size of the blocking factor.

31. In the payroll example, the MF-delete-code field must contain a D and the employee's year-to-date gross earnings must be zero before a record can be deleted.

32. At the end of the fourth quarter, both the year-to-date and quarterly totals will be set to zero.

33. A batch job is usually initiated by operations personnel and is often executed on a regular schedule; a remote batch job is initiated on a demand basis by using a terminal located outside of the computer center.

Chapter 9

1. There are usually more ways to verify or edit numeric data than are available for verifying alphanumeric data.

2. Usually it is more serious when a numeric field is incorrect than when an alphanumeric field is incorrect. If an employee's name is misspelled, his or her check will still be cashed and a correcting entry will not be needed. However, if an employee's hours are incorrect, his or her gross pay and his tax deductions will also be incorrect.

3. In an interactive transaction-processing system, data is usually edited as it enters the system and before it is processed.

4. No. Although the chances of retrieving an incorrect record for a customer with the identical name is remote, it can occur.

5. A limit check is made to see if your balance is less than your predetermined credit limit.

6. A customer's balance may be very close to the credit limit recorded in his or her master file record. When the value of the order being processed is added to the existing balance, the credit limit may be exceeded.

7. Since the new balance is only 5 percent more than the customer's existing credit limit, the credit history should be reviewed before the decision to process the order is made. Also, the impact of refusing to process the order will have on future dealings with the customer must be considered.

8. A class test is used to determine if data stored within a field is numeric, alphabetic, or non-numeric. The test can be used to detect the presence of non-numeric data in a numeric field.

9. The programmer may be able to redefine the field as a numeric field. The redefined field will be treated as containing numeric data.

10. In EBCDIC, a digit has a higher collating sequence (or binary value) than a letter of the alphabet.

11. The master file must contain the maximum quantity that will be ordered. The maximum quantity for each item is determined by studying the quantities ordered in the past.

12. The Internal Revenue Service determines, based on each taxpayer's income, what amounts are reasonable for deductions such as interest, contributions, and other types of expenses. If the amount exceeds what is considered reasonable, the person may be subject to a detailed audit.

13. Unless the minimum and maximum amounts used in a reasonableness test are reviewed, the quantities used become obsolete and too many records are flagged as containing data that should be checked for accuracy and reentered.

14. A limit test is used to determine if there is sufficient quantity on hand to process an order.

15. A range test might be used to determine if an individual's hourly rate is within the range determined for the department.

16. A sequential search can be made to see if the vendor's number, or code, is stored within the table.

17. The shipping date must be greater than the date used as the order or invoice date.

18. In order to edit data effectively, an analyst must work with the users who have expertise regarding the characteristics of the data to be processed; know how each field was originally defined; determine the minimum and maximum values that can be recorded for each field; understand the relationship of the data to the record being processed; and understand the relationship of the data being entered to other data items.

19. The cost associated with editing in an interactive environment must be weighed against the cost of not

20. A nonprogrammable terminal does not have a central processing unit and cannot be programmed to edit data. Its intelligence is derived from the host computer which provides the commands to edit or verify the data being entered by an operator. A programmable terminal has its own central processing unit and memory and can be used offline to enter and edit data.

21. The first and last sales order numbers can be entered and a range test can be used to see if each order number is within the allowable range.

22. When a large table must be searched, a binary search takes less time because fewer comparisons need to be made than when a sequential search is made.

23. All allowable codes are stored within a table. A search is made for the code entered by an operator. When a match is found, control leaves the count-controlled loop which controls the sequential search. If a match is not found, an error routine is invoked.

24. When the inventory and customer master files are online, the name of the customer and the description of the item ordered can be displayed and visually checked. A limit test can be used to determine if there is sufficient quantity on hand of the item ordered to fill the order. A limit test can also be used to determine if the customer has exceeded his credit limit.

25. Each time a transaction record is read, a check must be made to see if the record identification code is the one used to identify a trailer record. When the trailer record is identified, more records must be set to N.

26. It is considered normal to have a small percentage (perhaps less than one) of the customers exceed their credit limit and a limited number of orders request items not in stock.

27. If the message "invalid account number" is displayed too often, either the person placing the order was careless in recording the number or the table was not updated to include the account number.

28. When errors occur, an analysis should be made to determine why the error was made and what precautions might be made to prevent the error from recurring.

29. A control total is one that is accumulated as data is entered into the system or processed and used to determine if the output is accurate.

30. A confirmation report can be sent to individuals located in remote locations who entered data into the telecommunication network. Also, confirmation reports can be sent to the individuals who authorized the data recorded on source documents. The confirmation reports should be used in determining if correct data was entered into the system for processing.

31. Depending on how the data was entered and what data is included on the confirmation report, it may be possible to identify and correct invalid data before it is processed and becomes part of a file or report.

32. The data required for the control record can be entered, and verified, before the program begins to execute. Delays caused by the computer being required to wait for the operator to enter or verify the required information can be avoided.

33. Once the data is entered, verified, and becomes part of the accounts receivable master file records, it is used in many different reports. If invalid data enters the system and is processed, it will be more costly to make the necessary corrections than if the errors were detected *before* the data was processed.

34. If salaried employees do not have a no-pay or part-pay record, they will automatically be paid their normal bi-weekly salary.

35. The error file will be used as input for a separate program that prints the error messages. The program is considered as task 2 for a two-task job that prints the payroll register and the error messages.

36. If a field is blank, it could be due to an omission rather than by design.

37. The incorrect time records must be identified and corrected before the payroll register program can be rerun.

38. When high-values is used in COBOL after the move is completed, binary ones will be stored within the field. Storing all ones creates the highest number that can be stored within the field.

39. In the payroll register program, it is considered normal to have unmatched master file records. After all the time records are processed, it might be necessary to read and process data stored in several master file records.

40. Initially zero is stored in a field called save-number. When the first record is read, 1 is compared to 0. Since the condition stated in the source code as IF save-number < TF-employee-number THEN . . . is not true, a sequence error does not occur and 1 is stored in save number. Eventually the 2 stored in the time record is compared with the 4 stored in the save-number field and the sequence error is detected.

41. No. Sometimes the analyst or programmer is not concerned that all of the statements coded in the termination module will be executed when the transaction file is empty.

42. Yes. As long as all the edit tests are made, the sequence in which the tests are executed is not important. However, if complex IF/THEN/ELSE statements were used, for efficiency the sequence in which the statements are coded should be the same as the frequency with which an error might occur.

© SRA 1988, 1983

43. The edit-time-record module is only invoked when there is a match on employee number. Each time the data recorded in a time record is processed, a new record should be read.

44. A unique message is generated for each type of error in order that the person authorized to make the required corrections can determine what type of error occurred and which record contained the error.

45. The same statements must be executed each time an error is detected. Therefore, since several statements are required, it is more efficient to place the statements in a module that can be invoked when it is needed than to repeat the same source code several times.

46. When high-values are moved into TF-employee-number, it will always be larger than the value stored in MF-employee-number and a "match" on number will never occur and the READ-TRANSACTION indicator will always be equal to N.

47. The good-data indicator is used to control the execution of most of the statements that are coded within the process-payroll-records module. If the indicator is set to N, the statements are bypassed.

48. The calculate-net-pay module might contain a great deal of code and a decision might be made to split it into two smaller and more manageable modules.

49. The process-payroll-records module has a wider span of control and there are modules invoked by 4000-level modules that are referenced by using a 5000-level number.

50. In the termination module the error-counter will be compared to 0. If the value stored in the error-counter is equal to 0, a statement such as NO EDITING ERROR DETECTED may be printed and the second program which prints the error message will not be executed.

Chapter 10

1. A menu program typically has a main menu that lists the available submenus, a help option, and an option to exit from the program and return to the system.

2. When CHAIN "UPDATE" is used, the program named UPDATE is located, loaded into memory and executed. When CHAIN MERGE is used, the source code stored in the file specified is located and included in the program being developed.

3. Copying the source code reduces the amount of coding. Since the source code has already been debugged, it is more efficient than rekeying the statements and encountering the possibility of incorrectly keying the statements.

4. Yes. If CHAIN "PRPAYCK", 2020 is coded, the print paycheck program will transfer control to line 2020 before executing the program.

5. In the menu program one table is used to store the descriptions of the programs and a second table the names of the programs.

6. When the descriptions are stored in a table, a count-controlled loop which contains one print statement can be used to print the information rather than writing a series of print statements. Also rather than using an IF/THEN/ELSE statement to determine which program name should be retrieved, the option number entered by the operator is used to determine which name will be retrieved from the table.

7. All four modules display descriptions of the programs available, ask the operator to select the desired option, check the reply, and then chain to the desired program. The actual count-controlled loop used in each module is different.

8. Before a help menu is developed, a study should be made to determine what type of questions is most often asked pertaining to the task and in what areas will the operator need assistance. When a problem continues to occur, it may be necessary to add additional instructions to the help menu.

9. If a file is not closed, the last record entered may not have been written into the file. Since the execution of a CHAIN statement does not close files, the programmer should close the files before the CHAIN command is executed.

10. Variable length records should be used in order to conserve file space. The master record may require 300–400 bytes of storage while the transaction records are normally only 30–50 bytes in length.

11. Unless detailed information regarding sales and cash transactions is retained, itemized statements and aged trial balance cannot be prepared.

12. If a table located within each customer's master file record is used to store the data, it is usually necessary to provide enough space for the maximum number of transactions that might occur for a customer. While one customer has only 3 or 4 transactions per billing period, another customer may have 50 or more transactions.

13. The information stored in the sales-transaction records was either entered as control information, entered from the input file, or calculated within the sales-invoice program. All of the data read from the input file was edited and/or visually verified before it was recorded in the file.

14. New master records must be added to the file before transaction records can be added. The credit manager must approve the request for credit and a master record must be created before a sales order can be processed.

15. The source of the information and the type of report required is different in each of the three situations. Also, it is easier to maintain programs that each provide only one major function.

16. If the cash receipts, credits, and returns are entered in an interactive mode, additional methods can be used to verify the accuracy of the data entering the system. For example, when cash is received in payment of an invoice, a search can be made to determine if the invoice number is entered correctly.

17. The master record for customer 1278 is retrieved randomly from the accounts receivable file. A loop is then created that will read the format-2 records and search for invoice 12569. If a transaction record that contains that number is not found, an error message will be printed. The operator will either reenter the number or proceed to the next document.

18. A typical CHANGE program would be used to update data stored in the format-1 records.

19. When a level break occurs, the statement totals for the first customer are printed before the heading information is printed on the statement for the second customer.

20. Since the information must be available to print itemized statements, the records must be retained until the statements are printed and the control totals have been verified.

© SRA 1988, 1983

GLOSSARY/INDEX

Abort To end a program abnormally, due to operator error, computer malfunction, or error in the operating system or application software. *4*

Accounts receivable control account An account that contains the total of all amounts owed by all customers. All sales on account are added to the balance and cash receipts, returns, and credits are subtracted from the balance. *375*

Action stub Used on a decision table to describe the steps performed when certain conditions, listed on the decision stub, are either true or false. *419–420*

ADDNEW program A program designed to add new records to an existing file. *300–308*
    hierarchy chart *301*
    specifications *301*

Add-stock-amounts program *258–261*
    hierarchy chart *259*
    specifications *258*

Address An identification such as a label, number, or name used to designate a storage location on disk, tape, or within the memory of the computer. Labels, numbers, and names are translated by the compiler into the absolute address where the data or command is stored. *84, 86*

Aged trail balance A listing of accounts receivables and the amount of each balance that is current, from 31–60 days past due, from 61–90 days past due, or over 90 days past due. *371*

Alphanumeric data Data containing digits, alphabetic characters, and any special characters recognized by the computer or language being used. Alphanumeric data is sometimes called *string data*. *85*

Alternate key A key stored within a master record which is unique to the set of records belonging to the master record. *372*

American National Standards Institute (ANSI) An organization that coordinates the establishment of standards for products as well as programming languages and flowcharting symbols. *43*

Analyst A data processing professional who investigates a problem and then designs a solution. *2*

Append The incorporation of source code stored in an online file into an application program. *243*

Application program A program used to process data. Examples are payroll, accounts receivable, and inventory programs. *6*

Arithmetic operator *89*

Array An arrangement of elements in one or more dimensions that may be individually addressed. An array may also be called a table or matrix. An array can be located within memory or within a record stored on hard disk, magnetic tape, or on a diskette. *138, 158–174*
    advantages in using *162*
    examples of *159, 163, 166, 287, 364, 372*
    pseudocode used *161, 164*
    types of *160–166*
    survey example *165–174*

Audit trail A means of tracing transactions through the entire processing system. An invoice number may be included in the sales record in order to provide an audit trail which links the record with the source document. *331*

Backing up files *306*

Bad debt An amount considered to be uncollectable by the organization to which the money is owed. *322*

BASICA A version of the BASIC (Beginner's All-purpose Symbolic Instruction Code) language that was developed by Microsoft for use on personal computers. *11, 21, 130, 136, 323*

Batch application A system or procedure that requires data to be accumulated and then processed on a scheduled basis. For example, payroll data is accumulated and then processed once a week in a batch. *15, 279, 330*

Binary A numbering system based on two possibilities. In binary, a bit (the smallest storage unit within a computer) can be either ON or OFF. Various combinations of ON and OFF bits are used to represent numbers, letters, and special symbols. *242*

Binary collating sequence The binary value, from low to high, associated with special characters, letters of the alphabet, and digits. *324–325*

Binary search A technique used to reduce the time needed to find an item stored within a table. The search argument is compared with the midpoint value. Based on the results of the comparison, either the top or bottom half of the table is again divided and a new comparison is made. Dividing the table and comparing the search argument with the new midpoint value occur until either the search argument is found or it is determined the value is not stored within the table. *331–332*

Blocking factor *241*

Branching command A branching command causes a command other than the next one in sequence to be executed. *84*

Buffer A temporary storage area used for data or instructions. *188, 193, 241–242*

Burst mode Continuous, uninterrupted transmission of data. *330*

Byte An addressable location consisting of 8 bits. Sometimes a 9th bit is used to provide a parity check. *241*

Calculations required *397*

Carriage control tape A paper tape used on some printers to help control the vertical movement of the forms. While an instruction written by a programmer starts the form skipping, the sensing of the hole in the proper channel of the tape stops the skipping of the forms. *190, 192*

Carriage control tape channel A location in the tape used for a particular function. Channel 1 is reserved for the top-of-form; Channel 12 is reserved for forms overflow. The other 10 channels can be used by the programmer to stop the skipping of the form at a location where data such as the page footings or the shipping address is to be printed. *192*

Case entry A convenient way to use logic structure that describes multitest (more than two) conditional branching. Only one of two or more conditions can be true. *102, 104*

Cash sales program *44–49*
   hierarchy chart *45*
   pseudocode *47–49*
   specifications *44*

CHAIN A command used in Program A, the chained program, which results in Program B overlaying Program A. After the commands in Program B are executed, it is possible to *chain* back to Program A. In a menu program, the menu displays the descriptions of the programs that can be executed by using the chain command. When chain merge is used, the source code stored in the file identified in the command is merged in with the new program being created. *59, 243, 362–363*

CHAIN MERGE A statement used in BASIC to copy source code from a designated file where it is stored into the program being developed. *363*

CHANGE program A program designed to retrieve records randomly, to change one or more fields within a record, and to rewrite the updated record back into the existing file. *279–292*
   codes used *280–81*
   flowchart *282–84*

   printed report *290*
   pseudocode *288–89, 292*
   specifications *280–81*

Class test A test to determine if the content of a field contains numeric, alphabetic, or alphanumeric data. A class test can be used to detect non-numeric data in a numeric field. *323*

COBOL COmmon **B**usiness **O**riented **L**anguage A popular computer language used for business applications. *4, 134, 138, 323, 331*

Code Characters or digits used to condense data. For example, an account number or employee number used instead of a person's name. *279–281*

Column The areas located vertically within a table. They are identified by the use of a second subscript. In the statement X = TABLE(J,K), K refers to the column. *158, 162–163*

Combination checking The consideration of two or more data elements in relation to one another. *339*

Compiler A program that translates a high-level language, such as COBOL or Pascal, into the machine language of the computer. If errors are found, messages are displayed or printed. *22*

Computer information services (CIS) *2, 19, 42*

Concatonated The process of joining two or more alphanumeric constants or variables to form a new field. *253*

Condensed reports *218–19*

Conditional loop A series of instructions executed repeatedly either until some specified condition is met or as long as a condition remains true. UNTIL A = B will cause the statements within the loop to be executed *until* A is equal to B. WHILE A = B causes the statements to be executed as long as the condition specified is true. *128–134*

Confirmation report *335*

Connect time The time that a terminal is online to a host computer and a communication medium is being used to transfer data to and from the host. *330*

Continuous form paper Connected paper forms that eliminate the need to position each form in a printer or typewriter. After a report is printed, a burster separates the pages. Some bursters also remove the portion of the form that has the pin-feed holes used to position the form in the printer. *192*

Control interval A storage area within a VSAM file that contains records. If a control interval is filled, a split occurs and part of the records are transferred to a new interval. New records can be inserted into their proper location within an interval. *236–237*

© SRA 1988, 1983

Control record A record containing one or more data items that must be available in order to execute the program. The information is read once and retained within the memory of the computer for the duration of the program that requires the information. *337, 397*

Control structure *10*

Control total A total used to determine the validity of the output. Examples are total records processed and the total number of employees in each category that will be paid. *335–336*

Controls Methods used to make certain data is entered and processed accurately in order to produce valid output. *15, 279, 292–293, 294, 301, 375*

Convention A generally accepted way of accomplishing a task. Conventions exist to develop detailed logic plans, write source code, test programs, and develop documentation. *9*

Copy statements *243, 363*

CORRECT program A program designed to randomly retrieve records and use input keyed in by an operator to correct data stored in a file. A record may need to be corrected because the data initially recorded in the record was wrong or because new data was incorrectly added to the record. *294–300*
   hierarchy chart *295–96*
   printed report *299*
   pseudocode *297–98*
   specifications *294*

Count-controlled loop *134, 143, 145, 169, 206, 288*

Counter A field which contains a value used to control the execution of the commands stored within a loop. Each time the commands are executed, one or more is added to the counter. When the counter is greater than a prestated maximum, an exit is made from the loop. *134, 136–38*

Create-stock-file program *256–259*

Data dictionary A file maintained by software or a chart kept manually that contains information relating to the data items within a file or database. The size of the field, type of data stored within the field, name of the field, programs in which the data item is used, and other information are provided. *244–245, 255*

Data exception Nonnumeric data is found in a field defined as numeric. When this occurs, software provided as part of the operating system may cause an error message to be displayed and the job to be canceled. *199*

Data names *243–244*

Data processing cycle The typical way data is processed by the computer. Data is inputted, processed, and the results are outputted. A continuous cycle of input-process-output occurs until all data is processed. *168*

Data types *241–242*

Database language A high-level language often used by nondata processing professionals to extract information from online databases. English-like expressions are used which are translated into machine-language commands and executed. *84*

Debugged A program free of errors. When a program is being debugged, errors are located and corrected. *6*

Decision stub The portion of the decision table listing the decisions that must be made. A decision combined with the required action makes up a rule. *419–420*

Decision symbol *65*

Decision table A table depicting the action to be taken when multiple decisions are made. A rule consists of the results of the decisions (stated as either true or false) and the action required. *419–421*
   advantages and disadvantages *420–421*
   construction of *419–420*
   examples *420–421*

Declarative statements Source code that defines and establishes addresses for fields, tables, and files. The number of declarative statements required in a program depends on the language being used. Providing these statements is considered part of the "housekeeping" function associated with developing programs. *110, 193*

Design checklist *392, 396–97*

Detail lines *192–93*

Direct access Individual records or data may be retrieved from a file, database, or table without referencing the preceding records or data items. Also called random access. *232–233*

Diskettes *232*

DO UNTIL Pseudocode used to establish a loop that will be executed until the condition specified is met. The commands within the loop established by using DO UNTIL X = 10 will be executed as long as X is not equal to 10. *128, 131–133*

DO WHILE Pseudocode used to establish a loop that will be executed as long as the condition specified is true. The commands within the loop established by using DO WHILE A = B AND C = D will be executed as long as both conditions are true. *128–131*

Documentation *4,22, 391–411*
   cover sheet *392, 398*
   documenting a program *4–5*
   file specifications *404–05, 407–08*
   hierarchy chart *394, 410*
   historical *392–93*
   program overview *393, 399–400*
   record layout *406, 409*
   report specifications *393, 401*
   run sheet *394, 411*
   use of *392*

EBCDIC An 8-bit code used to represent 256 unique letters, symbols, or numbers. EBCDIC is used to store data in real memory and on magnetic media such as tape and disk. *325*

ENIAC An early computer completed in 1946 by John Mauchly and J. Presper Eckert. ENIAC is sometimes cited as being the first electronic computer. *5*

Edit mask A field containing edit codes used to suppress zeroes and to insert nonnumeric characters such as minus signs, dollar signs, or commas into the numeric information to be printed. Usually a field containing edit characters cannot be used in a calculation. *199–200*

Editing data
formatting numeric data *199–200*
detecting errors *320–348, 397*

End-of-file mark *253*

Error reports *189, 218, 249, 333*

Error routine Source code designed to identify the source of an error and to provide a means of recovering from the error so that the program will not abort. *4*

Error traps Code to prevent a job from aborting when an error occurs. When an error such as the use of an invalid key is recognized, an error message is displayed or written into a file. The programmer writing the code determines where control will return to after the error routine is executed. *96*

Exception report A report that lists the deviations from normal. An exception report might list all customers who exceeded their credit limit or all items that are below the reorder point and must be ordered. *15, 190–191*

Executables Terms used to represent statements that will be coded and converted to machine-language commands by an interpreter or compiler. Executables written in pseudocode can be in the form of a mathematical expression or in a statement such as "calculate gross pay" or "read a master file record." *65*

Exit decision One or more comparisons made by the computer to see if the conditions specified for exiting from the loop are met. *129*

Explode a table Explore all possible combinations that can occur. *420*

External documentation *5*

External reports *189, 192, 211–15*

Extraction programs *216–17*

Field size *243*

File maintenance Programs used to add, delete, or change records stored in a file. Records can be changed to correct previous errors or to update information. *277–310*

File organization *234–38*
direct *235*
ISAM *235–36*
sequential *234–35*
VSAM *236–37*

File specification form *238–40, 394, 404–05, 407–08*

Flowchart Standardized symbols are used to construct a graphic representation of the logic of a program. *3, 51, 53, 88*
advantages and disadvantages *52*
count-controlled loops *135*
examples *20, 56–58, 107–109, 250–251*
guidelines for constructing *52*
PERFORM/UNTIL *133*
symbols used *19, 55*
templates *51*
UNTIL loops *132*
WHILE loops *130*
worksheets *54*

Flowcharting worksheet A standard form, developed by International Business Machines Corporation, used to develop structured flowcharts. The heading provides information regarding the identification and function of the module. Fewer symbols need to be drawn since the form consists of a series of numbered rectangles. Each rectangle is identified by a letter indicating the row and a number indicating the column. *51, 54*

Format-1 records The master record stored in a file containing variable length records that contain information such as the customer's name and address, credit limit, beginning balance, and current balance. Master records can be retrieved randomly by using the primary key. *372*

Format-2 records Transaction records which contain detailed information regarding transactions that occurred. Each record within the set has the same alternate key and is accessed sequentially. *374, 377*

FOR/NEXT statement *136–37*

Forms overflow position A location one space beyond the last print line. When an attempt is made to print a line at, or past, the overflow position a new form is advanced in the printer. When printers without carriage tapes are used, the printer can be adjusted to accommodate different page lengths. *192*

FORTRAN An acronym for FORmula TRANslation. FORTRAN was developed in the mid-1950s and is still used for writing mathematically oriented programs. Newer versions of FORTRAN permit the programmer to write structured programs. *86*

Function A series of commands that perform a given task. To use a function, the programmer must use its name and supply the necessary parameters. *199*

Functional modules *214*

GO TO statements *11*

GOSUB A branching statement used to transfer the control of a program to an internal subroutine. After the com-

© SRA 1988, 1983

mands in the subroutine are executed, control returns to the statement following the GOSUB. *84*

Hard-card system Files which are stored in RAM (random access memory) chips. The systems are designed to simulate direct-access storage on hard disk. *232*

Hardware Computers and peripheral equipment such as tape drives, disk drives, and terminals. *6*

Headings *193–94, 196, 213*

Help modules *108–11*

Hierarchy chart A chart which shows the modules included in a program and their relationship to each other. For example, a typical chart shows that the main control module controls the execution of the initialization, process-records, and termination modules. *9, 45*
    conventions *9*
    developing charts *17*
    examples *17, 28, 29, 106, 168, 249, 259, 410*

Hierarchy plus Input-Processing-Output (HIPO) A chart used to identify the input needed, the processing required, and the resulting output for each module. Pseudocode is used to list the steps required to process the data. Symbols may be used to enhance the chart. *42, 413–415*
    advantages and disadvantages *416*
    construction of *413*
    form used *415*
    illustration *414*
    symbols used *417*
    template *416*

High value Based upon the collating sequence, the highest value is moved into a field. When EBCDIC is used, high value results in a field being filled with binary ones. *346*

IF statements *86–101*
    arithmetic operators *89*
    early versions *86*
    logical operators *90*
    nested *86, 94–96*
    relational operators *88*
    simple versions *87*

Imperative statement A source code statement that will be translated into one or more machine-language commands. *110*

Indexed Sequential Access Method (ISAM) A method that maintains one or more indexes so that records can be retrieved randomly or sequentially. Since the records are stored in sequence, new records can be inserted into the correct location in an existing file. *235–236*

Indicator A field used to control the execution of a program. The programmer controls the contents of the field. For example, a field called END-OF-FILE might initially contain N. As long as the field contains N, the commands within the process-records module will be executed. When the value stored within the field changes to Y (or anything but N), control of the program returns to the main control module. *9, 11, 128, 131, 287*

Infinite loop A loop is created from which control of the program cannot exit without the intervention of an operator. For example, if a DO WHILE X = 0 loop is established, an infinite loop will be created if X is initially set to 0 and the value of X does not change. *11*

Information retrieval The methods and procedures for recovering specific information from a storage medium. *188*

Initialization module *18, 107, 110, 169–70, 253, 281–82*

Input *15*
    origin of *397*
    requirements *397*

Interactive programs *103, 279, 320*

Interfield relationships The correlations that exist between fields. For example, when an employee's status changes from hourly to salaried, a salary must be entered for the employee and the hourly rate changed to zero. Also, when a United Fund deduction is entered, a number ranging from 1–26 must also be entered to indicate the number of installments over which the contribution will be spread. *291, 339–340*

Interest program *139–43*
    flowchart *141–42*
    hierarchy chart *139*
    specifications *139*

Internal documentation *5*

Internal reports *189*

Interpreter A program that checks each line of source code for errors. If the code is valid, it is translated into machine-language. Error messages are printed or displayed when invalid source statements are detected. *2*

Invalid-key routine *253, 255, 259–61, 288, 321*

Inventory exception report *194–99*
    flowchart *196–199*
    hierarchy chart *195*
    print layout *191*
    specifications *195*

Iteration *10–11*

Key A field, such as student number or item number, used to randomly retrieve a record from a direct access storage medium. The keys may be stored in an index which is searched to determine the location of the required record. *235*

Key words Words that identify the basic functions that must be performed to input, process, or output data. Key words have the same meaning to all programmers and are used to write pseudocode and to develop HIPO, Nassi-Shneiderman, and Warnier-Orr charts. *45*

Laser-optical disk subsystem Also called video or optical disks. Low-intensive laser beams are used to record images on plastic disks. Early disks could be used only to record data and to read the data stored on the disks. Later developments permit the data recorded on disks to be read as input, updated, and then rewritten on the disks. The subsystem consists of the drives, channels, and software needed to interface the system with the computer. *232–233*

Letter-quality printer A slower printer that has both upper- and lowercase letters. Although slower than near-letter-quality or data processing printers, the quality of the output is similar to that produced by an electronic typewriter. Most letter-quality printers print a single character at a time. *188*

Level break When the first of a new series of records is retrieved, a level break occurs. During this period of time, totals may be printed and added to the next higher level of totals. After the processing for the first series of records is completed, the first record for the new series is processed. *206*

Limit check A test is made comparing the contents of a numeric field against maximum and/or minimum values. *321–322, 326*

Line counter *196, 199*

Line printer A heavy duty, high-speed printer usually located within the computer center and used to print reports and documents. Since its buffer contains a line of data, the entire line of information is printed at one time. *188*

Listing *189*

Lock A field within a record which can be used to determine if a record can be updated or if access to the record will be allowed. *302*

Logic plans *3, 19, 43, 394*

Logical operators The logical operators are AND, OR, and NOT. When logical operators are used, compound conditions such as IF A = B OR A = 10 OR C = 100 may be used in creating IF statements. *90–93, 129*

Logical record A single record as defined by the programmer. Logical records are processed by the computer; physical records are read into and out of memory. *241*

Magnetic tape *232, 234*

Mass storage system (MSS) A subsystem that utilizes magnetic tape, stored in cartridges, for storing files. When a file is needed, the cartridge is automatically obtained and the records are transferred to disk for processing. The system software takes care of finding the cartridge and transferring the disk. The application programmer is only concerned with processing the logical records stored on disk. *232*

Master file A file made up of records that contain constant and updated information. Each record contains information about one person or object. Master files are usually stored online and are often organized as ISAM or VSAM files. *188, 238, 247*
adding new fields *255*
reading records *259, 287–88*
rewriting records *260–61, 300*

Master file create program *247–54*
flowchart *250–52*
hierarchy chart *249*
procedure *247*
specifications *248–49*
system flowchart *248*

Menu program *362–70*
comments *370*
flowchart *366–69*
hierarchy chart *364–65*
main menu *362*

Module A section of code or part of a program dedicated to one function. Usually a module has 50 or fewer lines of code. One module might contain the code required to print detail lines and another module might contain the code needed to read a record from a file. *8*
constructing names *18*
determining modules needed *16*

Multilevel report *189, 201–10*

Nassi-Shneiderman charts Diagrams used graphically to represent a structured solution to a problem. Symbols are used for process, decision, looping, and case entry. *59*
advantages and disadvantages as others *60*
basic symbols *59, 61–62*
examples *61–63, 98, 104, 144*

Nested count-controlled loops *139–40, 169*

Nested IF statements An inner IF/THEN/ELSE statement is completely enclosed within an outer IF/THEN/ELSE statement. The depth of nesting permitted depends on the language and compiler being used. If the nesting is too deep, the logic may become difficult to follow and errors may result. *86*

Nonprogrammable terminal A terminal that cannot be programmed to function independent of the host computer. The commands are stored within the host computer and executed by the host. *330*

Offline An operation or a devise not under the direct control of a computer. *330*

Offpage connector A symbol used in developing a structured flowchart that shows the transfer of the logic or control to a new page. *53, 55*

O/I needs and formats *15*

On demand A method of printing reports as requested rather than on a scheduled basis. *188*

© SRA 1988, 1983

ON statement A coding statement used to determine which of the modules listed will be executed. If the parameter used with the ON statement is equal to four, the fourth module listed will be executed. *280, 289–290*

Online systems A computerized system in which terminals are used to enter or retrieve data from files or databases that are under the direct control of a centralized computer. *15*

Operating system Software that controls the execution of computer programs. An operating system may provide for timesharing, scheduling of jobs, input/output control, library management, error routines, and many other services. *6, 42*
    file organization *234*
    impact of *6*

Operational A system or program that has been designed, coded, tested, documented, and accepted by the operations department or users. Usually an operational program will be run on a regular basis and is considered part of a computerized data processing system. *5*

Order entry program *103–112*
    hierarchy chart *106*
    specifications *105*
    flowchart *107–109*

Output *15, 396–397*
    origin of *396*
    requirements for *396*

Overflow area An area reserved for records displaced by new records added to an ISAM file. When the file is reorganized, records stored in the overflow area are stored in their proper location in the prime area. *235*

Packed data *241, 243, 404–405*

Page footings Totals printed at the bottom of a page. Usually the individual page totals are added to the data stored in the final totals fields. *190*

Page printer An online printer that has a buffer large enough to accommodate a page of printing. Once the buffer is full, its entire contents are printed at one time. Many page printers print, in one operation, the form and the information. *188*

Password A unique combination of characters used to identify a user, program, or file. Passwords help to protect files and programs from being utilized by unauthorized users. *234*

PAUSE statement A statement used that provides a temporary halt in the execution of the program. *288*

Payroll register program *338–45*
    flowchart *345, 347*
    hierarchy chart *340*
    system flowchart *229*
    time files *340*

Payroll system
    adding new records *300–308*
    adding stock deductions *256–262*
    correcting records *294–300*
    file create program *247–54*
    maintenance programs *278–279*
    master record *239–40*
    payroll register program *338–348*
    recreating the master file *306–07*
    update program *302–307*

PERFORM/UNTIL A COBOL statement used to initiate a conditional loop. The commands within the loop will be executed until the condition specified is met. *133–134*

PERFORM/VARYING A COBOL statement used to create a count-controlled loop. The statements within the module invoked will be exucuted until the condition specified is met. For example PERFORM module-named VARYING COUNT FROM 1 BY 1 UNTIL COUNT > 50 will cause the commands within the module to be executed until count is greater than 50. *137–138*

Personal computer keyboard *30*

Physical records One or more logical records read from an input medium or written to an output medium. Before being processed, a physical record is unblocked by operating system software into logical records. *241*

Primary key A unique number or combination of characters used to retrieve a master record from a file containing variable-length records. *372*

Prime area The area reserved for storing records in a file that is organized as an indexed sequential access method file. *235*

Print layout A form showing what information is to be printed on a report and where each line will be printed. The layout shows the headings, detail, and total lines that must be printed. *5, 190–191, 211, 393, 402–403*

Procedure A formalized method for accomplishing one or more tasks. Procedures should be documented and the documentation used in on-the-job training and as a reference. *6, 247*

Program
    aids *397*
    evaluation of *23*
    overview *399–400*
    problems that may exist *8*
    purpose of *396*
    specifications *15*
    steps in designing *14–23*
    structured design *7*
    walkthrough *22*
    well-written programs *12–13*

Programmable terminal An input/output device that has its own central processing unit and memory. A programmable terminal can edit and store data while on line.

After all the data is entered, the terminal is put in an on-line mode and the information is transmitted to the host computer. *330, 332*

Programmers *2, 6*
lack of productivity *6–7*
tasks assigned *3*

Programming standards *5*
construction of names *13, 18*
development of *5*
problems that may exist *8*

Pseudocode A user-defined noncompilable shorthand used to describe the steps required to input, process, and output data. Keywords, such as PERFORM, READ, and INPUT, are used to describe the functions performed in entering, processing, and outputting data. *3, 44, 50*
advantages and disadvantages *50*
guidelines for developing *44*
examples *47–49, 130, 136, 143, 161, 259, 288–89, 292, 297–98, 307*
key words *45–47*

Random access A method of retrieving individual records from a file or data from a table without referencing the preceding records or data items. *158*

Reasonableness test A routine used to identify abnormal data values. Because abnormal values are sometimes valid, provision must be made for reentering the values into the system. *325*

Record layout A form used to show where within a record each field is located, the size of the field, and the type of data stored within the field. *5, 245–246, 373, 393, 409*

Redefine a field A field orginally defined as containing either numeric or alphanumeric data can be redefined so that the contents can be edited, checked for blanks, or compared to a constant or variable. *290, 324*

Relational operators Symbols (<, >, and =) used to compare two values to see if the second is greater than, less than, or equal to the first value. Relational operators can be used adjacent to each other to represent not equal (< >), greater or equal (>=), and less than or equal (<=). *88–89*

Relationship check *328–329*

Reports *188–194*
designing *190*
editing data *199–200*
print layout forms *190–91*
types of *189*
types of print lines *193–94*
questions regarding *396*

Roll totals When multiple levels of totals are required, such as totals for each month, each year, and a ten-year total as well, the month total (minor total) is added to the year total (intermediate total), and the year total to the ten-year total (major total). Each time a total is rolled, the field containing the amount added to the total being accumulated must be cleared to zero. *140*

Row The areas located horizontally within a table. The row is identified by the first subscript. In the statement TABLE (J,K), J specifies the row and K the column. *158, 162–163*

Rule A combination of the decision(s) and related actions used to construct a decision table. *419–420*

Sales analysis program *201–210*
flowchart *206–9*
hierarchy chart *203–204*
print layout *202*
specifications *201–3*
test data *204*

Sales invoice A form printed by the vendor which contains detailed information regarding the sale. *106, 111, 334*

Sales invoice program *211–15*
error report *333*
print layout *211*
specifications *213, 375*
system flowchart *333*

Sales transaction program *321–29*

Schedule of accounts receivable A listing of all accounts receivables with an unpaid or a credit balance. *371*

Screens
designing *196–97*
displays required *396*
providing delays *287–88*

Scrolling Information is displayed on a VDT without interruption. Lines may scroll off the top of the screen as new lines of data are displayed on the bottom of the screen. *111*

Selection *10–11, 84*

Sequence checking *346*

Sequential access A method of retrieving records in a file or data items in a table in the order they are stored. *158*

Sequential search A search made by comparing the search argument with each content area of a table. The search usually starts with the first area and progresses sequentially through the table until the argument is found. *327–328*

SLEEP A statement within a BASIC program which causes a delay before execution of the next statement in sequence. Usually the terminal is "put to sleep" in order that the operator can read instructions. When an attempt is made to read a record already in use, a SLEEP statement may be used to cause a delay before a second attempt is made to read the record. *288*

Smart terminal See **programmable terminal.**

Sorting files *217*

Source code Instructions written in a programming language that a computer cannot execute. Source code is converted by a compiler or interpreter into the machine language of the computer being used. *2, 395*
>   formatting *13, 21*
>   listing *395*
>   writing and entering *4*

Specifications Detailed information regarding the input, processing, and output needed to produce the desired results. *15*

SPOOLing *219*

Standard A uniform method of accomplishing a task. Standards are available for designing, coding, testing, and documenting systems and programs. *5*

Standard list tape A carriage tape that has a punch in channel 1 for the top-of-form location and a punch in channel 12 for the overflow location. The rest of the spacing is controlled by the programmer. Since mounting special carriage tapes is time consuming, the documentation for most internal reports printed on stock paper indicate that the standard list tape is to be used. *192*

Standard system action (SSA) The course of action pursued by default by the operating system when an error-recovery routine is not provided by the application programmer. *253*

String data See **alphanumeric data.**

Stock paper Paper without preprinted headings or rules which is used to print internal reports. Most installations stock several widths and lengths of stock paper. *190, 192–193*

Structured design A top-down approach used to develop a system or program. The objectives are determined before the specifications are developed. The design of the system or program will begin after the objectives and specifications are developed and approved. *7*
>   single entry, single exit *9*
>   stub testing *111–112*

Structured programming *7–8, 25*
>   control structures used *10*
>   evaluation of *12–13*
>   guidelines for developing *45, 291–292*

Stub testing Testing the main logic of a program before the supporting modules are developed. Stubs, or dummy modules, are used to illustrate the control passing to and from the main control modules to the supporting modules. *43*

Subroutine Prewritten routines usually stored in an on-line library. The routines are executed by a call statement located within an application program. Subroutines may be provided by the computer vendor or written by the installation's programmers. *46, 196*

Subscript An integer used with the name of a table to generate the address of an individual item a table. A subscript must be a whole, positive number that does not exceed the number of elements within the table. *138, 160–161*

Subscript out of range The value of the subscript is less than or more than the range specified for the table. The subscript used for a table defined as having space for 100 items must be a value from 1 through 100. The one exception is that when some versions of BASIC are used, there is a zero row and column. A one-dimension table defined as having 100 elements actually can store 101 items in locations 0–100. *160*

Survey program *165–174*
>   flowchart *168–172*
>   hierarchy chart *168*
>   input records *166–167*
>   specifications *166–167*

Syntactical error An error that is in violation of the rules of the programming language being used. *2*

System flowchart A graphic representation that shows the movement of data throughout the system. Both manual and computerized procedures are shown. Although symbols are used for input, processing, and output, the logic of the way that the input is processed is not shown. *216–217, 243, 306, 333, 339*

Table See **array.**

Template A device, usually made of plastic, which contains symbols. A flowcharting template contains the standard ANSI symbols used to develop a structured flowchart. *51, 416*

Termination module *18*

Testing
>   design of programs *21*
>   programs *4, 22, 204, 398*
>   test plan *392*

Top-down programming The program is divided into major modules which in turn may be divided into functional modules. Each module accomplishes one functional task and items closely related to that task. In developing the program, the programmer may design, code, and test the major modules before the supporting modules are developed. *8, 43*

Trailer record The last record in a file in which control totals are stored. For example, when the time records are created, totals may be established for the record count, regular hours, and overtime hours. After all the transaction records are written into the file, the totals are recorded in the trailer record. *332*

Transaction file The records stored within the transaction file contain current data. Usually a transaction file is used for a limited number of applications during the current fiscal period.   *15*

Transaction processing Data generated while transactions occur is immediately entered into the system for processing. In contrast, in a batch-processing system, the data is accumulated in files and then processed at one time.   *2, 188*

Truth table   *91–93*

Universals The names of procedures or modules that do not represent executable instructions. Universals are used for documentation and also in PERFORM statements to indicate that a branch will occur to the module specified.   *65*

Update a record A method of keeping files current in which a record is retrieved from its storage area in a file; then one or more fields within the record are changed; finally record is written back into its original storage location within the file.   *257–258, 336–337*

UPDATE program A program designed to read records stored in a master file either sequentially or randomly and to add the values stored in a transaction file to the value stored within the records being updated.   *162, 257, 302–307*

   flowchart   *304–05*
   hierarchy chart   *303*
   specifications   *302*

Utility program A frequently used program that performs a task such as copying a file, displaying data stored in a file on the printer, or sorting records stored in a file. Some utility programs are supplied by the computer manufacturer and others are developed in-house.   *201, 255*

Variable data Data that changes each time a program is executed.   *16*

Variable length records Within a file, records of varying lengths may be stored. In an inventory file, the main record, accessed by item number, contains most of the information regarding the item. The secondary records, which are much shorter, for the group contain the detailed information concerning individual shipments.   *236, 372–374, 379*

Virtual Storage Access Method (VSAM) A method of retrieving records stored within a file which can be accessed randomly by using one of several available keys. Within a single program, records can be accessed randomly and sequentially.   *236–237*

Visual Display Terminal (VDT) An output device, similar to a TV screen, used to display directions, prompts, and data. The term **CRT** (cathode-ray tube) is also used in referring to the output screen included as part of most terminals and microcomputers.   *2*

VTOC Visual Table Of Contents. See **hierarchy chart.**

Walkthrough A technique used to review either the design or coding of a program. In a design walkthrough, the purpose is to detect errors and to test the logic. In a code walkthrough, the purpose is to determine if there are errors or omissions in the source code.   *21–22*
   payroll example   *96–97*

Warnier-Orr diagrams A graphic representation of the logic of a program that is often described as structured pseudocode. The diagrams are constructed using braces containing the required pseudocode.   *60–67*
   advantages and disadvantages   *66*
   elements   *65*
   examples   *66–67, 99, 103, 144*
   rules for constructing   *66*

Weinberg, Gerald   *3*

Within range test A way to check whether the value stored within a field is higher than the low value and lower than the high value established for the range specified.   *326, 365*

Word processing Text, rather than numeric data, is stored and can be utilized in the preparation of documentation, letters, memos, and other types of printed materials.   *392*

Zoned data   *241, 404–405*